New Directions
in
Cognitive Science

EDITORS
Theodore M. Shlechter
U.S. Army Research Institute
for the Behavioral and Social Sciences, Ft. Knox, KY

Michael P. Toglia
State University of New York at Cortland

ABLEX PUBLISHING CORPORATION
NORWOOD, NEW JERSEY

Library of Congress Cataloging in Publication Data
Main entry under title:

New directions in cognitive science.

Includes indexes.
1. Cognition. 2. Cognition—Research.
I. Shlechter, Theodore M. II. Toglia, Michael P.
BF311.N495 1985   153   85-13442
ISBN 0-89391-230-1

Ablex Publishing Corporation
355 Chestnut Street
Norwood, New Jersey 07648

Contents

Preface   *vii*

1. Ecological Directions in the Study of Cognition   *1*
   Theodore M. Shlechter and Michael P. Toglia

2. Toward an Ecologically Oriented Cognitive Science   *17*
   Ulric Neisser

3. Psychobiological and Cognitive Studies Relevant to the Issues of a Unitary
   Memory System   *33*
   Norman E. Spear

4. Planning-in-Action Across the Life Span   *47*
   Jerome S. Meyer and George W. Rebok

5. Aging and the Development of Expert Cognition   *69*
   William J. Hoyer

6. Ecological Validity and Ideography in Developmental Cognitive
   Science   *88*
   Jurgis Karuza, Jr., and Michael A. Zevon

7. Reminiscence in Adulthood: A Social-Cognitive Analysis   *105*
   David J. Sperbeck and Susan Krauss Whitbourne

8. Social Cognition: A Life Span Perspective   *116*
   Paul Roodin and John Rybash

9. Personality, Affect, and Cognition: Reflections on Social-Cognitive
   Development   *135*
   Royal Grueneich

10. Examining Reading Problems as a Means to Uncovering Sex Differences in
    Cognition   *147*
    Myra Okazaki Smith

11. Sex Related Differences and Cognitive Skills   *158*
    Jane M. Connor

12. Sex Differences in Cognition: The Nature–Nurture Controversy
    Revisited   *173*
    Carolyne M. Weil

13. Ape Language: Communication Problems Among Researchers   *181*
    Carol A. Vázquez

14. Cross-Linguistic Perspective on Cognitive Development   *191*
    Richard M. Weist

15. Current Issues in Psycholinguistics   *217*
    Margaret W. Matlin

16. Can Involuntary Slips Reveal One's State of Mind?—With an Addendum on
    the Problem of Conscious Control of Action   *242*
    Bernard J. Baars

17. Remembering Past Experiences: Theoretical Perspectives Past and
    Present   *262*
    Douglas J. Herrmann

18. The Interface between Laboratory and Naturalistic Cognition   *276*
    Harold Gelfand

    Author Index   *295*

    Subject Index   *305*

This book is dedicated to our wives, Rae and Cathy, for their continued support, love, understanding, and encouragement throughout the many long hours devoted to this endeavor.

Preface

This book is the outgrowth of a State University of New York (SUNY) Conversation-in-the-Disciplines Program held at State University of New York at Cortland. This conference brought together many distinguished cognitive professionals to discuss and examine the current trends in the burgeoning field of cognitive science. Speakers at this conference—most of whom became contributors to this book—were chosen because they held unique perspectives on particular psychological aspects of this discipline.

Based on the conference presentations and discussions, the contributors then wrote their respective chapters. All authors were asked to write chapters which focused upon both the theoretical and methodological changes occurring in this field. They were also urged to write chapters which would be applicable to and readable for students and professionals in cognitively oriented disciplines as well as closely related disciplines. We thus believe that this book will be useful for all professionals and students interested in the cognitive related sciences, regardless of their particular orientation and speciality area.

There are several unifying themes found throughout the book. As discussed in the first chapter, a main theme is the expanding nature of cognitive science. This includes studying the broader aspects of human intellectual functioning (e.g.., linguistics and social cognition) and the individual variations and influences in such functioning. Other themes found throughout this volume include a focus on examining "real-life" cognitive behaviors/issues and the macro-environmental influences upon cognition. As also discussed in Chapter 1, the various themes each relate to the ecological movement in cognitive research.

This book is not intended to delineate all or even a majority of the new themes found in this field; such a task is impossible. Rather, this volume describes some of the more interesting and hopefully long-lasting of these trends. The editors hope that this volume has succeeded in capturing the excitement currently in this field—an excitement which relates to the changes brewing in the study and understanding of human cognitive functioning.

This book's chapters are grouped into the following units: (a) an overview of some of the primary psychological, ecological, and biological directions in this field; (b) developmental aspects of cognition; (c) social cognition; (d) sex-differences; (e) psycholinguistics; and (f) naturalistic studies of cognition. These areas represent some of the currently most important topics in cognitive science and (some) are relatively new research areas for cognitive professionals.

Two additional points must be noted about these chapters. First, many of them deal with issues found in other unit areas. For example, Karuza and Zevon's chapter, which is on the developmental aspects of cognition, also concerns social cognition and naturalistic memory issues. Some chapters are mainly discussant papers of other chapters in the previously mentioned topic areas. It is hoped that the book's format captures the rich diversity in the field, and reflects the dialogue which occurred at the SUNY Conversation-in-the-Disciplines Program.

We would like to thank the SUNY Research Foundation for funding the Conversation-in-the-Disciplines Program. We are also very thankful for the support and guidance given to us by Ms. Barbara Bernstein of Ablex Publishing Corporation. We are also extremely appreciative of all the individuals who helped with the completion of each chapter and the staff at SUNY, Cortland—Jennifer King, Joseph Ludewig, Kim Young, Nancy Sickmon, Donna Curtin, and Rae Shepherd-Shlechter, who helped with the production of this entire project from the initial SUNY Conversation-in-the-Disciplines grant proposal to this completed book. The first author must thank Dr. Paul Gump of the University of Kansas for all he taught him about psychology and psychological writing. The second editor expresses his gratitude to Gregory A. Kimble, William F. Battig, and Terry C. Daniel for preparing him for a career in psychology.

Cortland, New York
October, 1984

Chapter I

Ecological Directions in the Study of Cognition

Theodore M. Shlechter*
Michael P. Toglia
State University of New York at Cortland

Within the last few decades, the study of human behavior has undergone a revolutionary shift as documented by Baars (in press). This revolution, which began in psychology between 1955 and 1965, involves a radical change in the way behavioral scientists are doing research, from mainly examining the observable aspects of human behavior to concentrating on studying the unobservable constructs within the human mind. It has been a most pervasive revolution which has influenced nearly every area within the discipline, from basic experimental psychology to clinical, comparative, developmental, and social psychology. In a recent invited address to the Eastern Psychological Association, B. F. Skinner acknowledged the success of the cognitive movement's influence upon the thinking of contemporary psychologists (Skinner, 1984). Baars (in press) further delineates the influences that the cognitive perspective has upon the different areas and theoretical positions within psychology.

This cognitive revolution has most recently spread to disciplines outside of psychology. Professionals from such diverse fields as anthropology, biology, computer science, education, linguistics, philosophy, and sociology have become increasingly interested in studying cognitive processing. Consequently, a new discipline—the field of cognitive science—has been formed which includes professionals from a variety of disciplines and interests with the shared pursuit of studying and understanding the mysteries of the human brain.

One can trace the beginnings of this new discipline to the late 1970s and early 1980s, with the formation of the Cognitive Science Society and the journals *Cognition* and *Cognitive Science*. Another landmark in the formation of this field is Donald A. Norman's (1981) book, *Perspectives on Cognitive Science*. Norman and the other contributors to his book laid the foundations for this science by

---

* Theodore M. Shlechter is now at the United States Army Research Institute for the Behavioral & Social Sciences Field Station at Ft Knox, Ky 40121-5620

discussing the needs for such a science, and its basic perspectives. Foremost among these perspectives is the diversity which existed in this common search in the understanding of knowledge about cognitive processes. As Norman notes, "Cognitive Science is a new discipline created from a merger of interests among those pursuing the study of cognition from different points of view" (p. 11).

Tremendous diversity still exists in this field in that the scientists from the various subdisciplines are still exploring similar issues from a variety of viewpoints, interests, and methodologies. For example, speakers at the annual Cognitive Science Society meeting traditionally present different views on information processing, contextual effects, and linguistics, with the cognitive psychologists barely understanding the cognitive neuropsychologists, and vice-versa. Certainly, such diversity can be beneficial in helping scientists to discover further insights into the human brain. However, such diversity can have a detrimental effect upon the development of this science, as each subdiscipline goes in its own direction. As discussed in Vázquez's chapter on the ape-language literature, this lack of communication among cognitive researchers presents a major obstacle in the development of a coherent body of knowledge regarding human cognitive functioning.

The purpose of this book then is to present a coherent picture of the different directions within psychology that the field of cognitive science is taking. Even though the papers presented in this volume are primarily psychologically oriented, we believe that they are still relevant to the many other subdisciplines within this field. For example, the papers on psycholinguistics and sex-differences are certainly relevant to cognitive professionals in the areas of anthropology, biology, and sociology. This point about the applicability of these papers to other subdisciplines will be further discussed throughout this chapter. It is also expected that the trends delineated in this volume will be the focal point of interest to cognitive scientists for the next few years.

The most prominent new directions discussed in this volume's chapters are the recent focus by cognitive scientists on exploring cognitive behaviors for real-life situations/events and the organismic influences upon cognitive behaviors. Associated with these two new directions are additional trends concerning new cognitive science methodologies and new insights into cognitive processing. Thus, the four main new directions discussed in this book are: (a) real-life aspects of cognitive behaviors; (b) organismic influences; (c) new insights into cognitive processes; and (d) new methodologies. It must be noted that the distinctions among trends are at times artificial, and, although readers may suggest additional trends, we have chosen to focus on what we see as the most prominent and promising directions.

A common theme running throughout this chapter is that these four new directions relate to a movement by cognitive scientists toward an ecological approach to studying human cognitive functioning. As indicated by Neisser, and Karuza and Zevon, the term "ecological validity" means studying the contextual relationships which exist among the organism, its cognitive behaviors, and the environment. The ecological approach as stressed in this chapter has its roots in Brunswik's (1955) classic work delineating the Environmental-Organism-Environmental (E-O-E) arc involved in psychological functioning. The first E of this arc entails the distal objects (macro-environmental situations found in one's daily life) and the proximal stimuli aspects of one's environment. The O deals with the organism's cognitive processing and (a modification by this chapter's authors from Brunswik's basic position) the organismic factors, e.g., personality and developmental differences, affecting cognitive behaviors. The final E deals with the organism's proximal behavior to the proximal stimuli and distal behaviors (e.g., reading) to distal objects. As will be further discussed, this ecological approach marks a radical departure from the traditional beliefs and practices of cognitive psychologists in a number of ways. First of all, cognitive scientists have been mainly interested in studying only the relationships which exist between cognitive processing for proximal stimuli and behaviors, and have thus tended to neglect the study of cognition as it relates to the individual and the macro-environment. Therefore, this ecological approach expands the domains of cognitive science to include the entire arc which is involved in the human being's psychological functioning, and to the study of the interdependencies which exist among the different elements of this E-O-E arc.

REAL-LIFE COGNITION

As previously mentioned, a major trend found in this book is the focus on exploring issues related to the "real-life" aspects of cognition. Almost every chapter deals in one way or another with this trend.

The interest found in this book for exploring "everyday cognition" parallels the rapidly accelerating interest found in the cognitive science community for this research area. Only a decade ago, most cognitive researchers would have scoffed at conducting such nonlaboratory research. However, as indicated in Gelfand's chapter, if you scan the recent cognitive science literature you will find numerous reports which chart naturalistic cognition. Furthermore, there are new journals (e.g., *Human Learning: Journal of Practical Research and Applications*) and several recent books, such as those by Gruneberg, Morris, and Sykes (1978), Harris and Morris (1984), Neisser (1976, 1982), and Rubin (in press), which have discussed cognitive functioning as it exists in natural contexts and/or for everyday events.

The need for studying cognitive behavior as it occurs in naturalistic contexts is most eloquently articulated in Neisser's and Karuza and Zevon's chapters. Neisser argues that the traditional information-processing approach remains an unsatisfying account of human cognition because its basic paradigm takes cognition completely out of context. He further argues that typical information-processing and cognitive experiments take place in settings that strive for convenience rather than for "truth." Neisser then proceeds to call for an ecologically oriented cognitive science in which the context in which the cognitive behavior occurs, as well as the behavior and processes associated with the context, is studied.

These sentiments of Neisser are echoed in several other chapters. Spear, for one, discusses studies performed in his laboratory which revealed that the most mature rats for certain learning tasks were those trained and tested in contexts analogous to their home nest. He also notes that similar findings have been shown for the influences of environmental contexts upon human infants learning abilities. Baars and Weist in their chapters also present experimental findings which further substantiate the influences that situational contexts have upon human cognitive functioning.

Several other chapters—Connor's, Grueneich's, Hoyer's, Matlin's, Roodin and Rybash's and Vázquez's—further discuss the importance of studying cognitive behaviors vis-à-vis macro-environmental situations. Grueneich claims that cognitive scientists can gain a great deal of knowledge about people's social cognition by studying it vis-à-vis everyday action and social intercourse. For example, he notes that valuable insights into social cognition can be obtained by studying the kinds of knowledge and skills which must be possessed by a salesperson to convince a customer to buy a product. Furthermore, Connor strongly argues that macro-environmental conditions, i.e., socialization practices, are the cause of any sex-related differences found in human cognitive functioning.

Nearly every chapter in this volume examines cognitive behaviors associated with macro-environmental situations. These behaviors include people's: (a) speech and communication behaviors (see Baars', Matlin's, Weist's, and Vázquez's chapters); (b) memory behaviors for earlier life-experiences (see Gelfand's, Herrmann's, Neisser's, and Sperbeck & Whitbourne's chapters); (c) daily planning and social behaviors (see Meyer and Rebok's and Roodin and Rybash's chapters); and (d) daily task behaviors, e.g., behaviors for reading, arithmetic, and job-related tasks (see Connor's, Hoyer's, Smith's, and Weil's chapters). As already noted, this emphasis on investigating distal-type behaviors marks an important change in the cognitive scientist's focus, from mainly examining proximal cognitive behaviors as they related to proximal stimuli to exploring the many varieties of cognitive behaviors found in the real-world. In fact, both Gelfand and Neisser suggest that cognitive scientists should spend more time in observing real-life conditions so that they can develop a taxonomy of the cognitive behaviors which are likely to occur in such conditions.

"Real-life" cognitive investigations also deal with practical applied issues. Smith's and Spear's chapters are good examples of such works as they respectively cover the practical issues of reading problems and influences of alchohol on memory. At one time, cognitive researchers mainly concentrated on doing basic research while leaving the applied aspects to the practitioners. However, in recent years, cognitive research which concerns applied practical issues, such as reading problems, eyewitness memory, and memory improvement, has become a dominant trend in the cognitive science literature.

Everyday cognitive research also interfaces with a variety of disciplines within cognitive science. As discussed in several of the chapters, cognitive scientists in such diverse disciplines as anthropology, biology, education, linguistics, and sociology are interested in the findings on human cognition provided by everyday memory research. For instance, educators are especially interested in the recommendations derived from the findings of studies on reading such as Smith's studies (see Chapter 10).

As mentioned previously in this chapter, and more thoroughly discussed in Karuza and Zevon's chapter, these "real-life" aspects are only a part of the ecological paradigm. Another crucial element of this paradigm—individual-specific factors and influences—is discussed in the next section.

COGNITION AND THE INDIVIDUAL

The study of the individual and cognition has only recently been given serious consideration by cognitive psychologists. This is unfortunate because psychology is fundamentally a science of understanding the individual.

This lack of investigating the individual characteristics and constraints (mediating factors within the individual and environment) involved in human cognition is also tragic because it has led cognitive researchers to accept artificial models of cognitive functioning. Norman (1981), and Hoyer in this volume, note that traditional information-processing views of cognitive functioning are artificial because they do not take into consideration the mediating factors which affect the cognitive system.

Thus, cognitive scientists have in recent years given considerable attention to studying cognitive constraints. An early example of this attention in mediating factors is the classic study of Bransford and Franks (1971), which showed that when processing linguistic information, subjects derived semantic inferences based on their previous knowledge of that information. Both Jenkins (1979) and Bransford, Franks, Morris, and Stein (1979) have more fully discussed the importance of constraints upon cognitive functioning.

The issue of cognitive constraints is further explained in several chapters. Hoyer proposes a model of expert cognition which deals with the organismic (and situational) constraints affecting adults' cognitive development. His model—unlike computational models—takes into account the influences that personal goal selection and situational assessments have upon one's everyday cognitive behaviors.

Meyer and Rebok also discuss the influences that personal constraints, goals and situational assessments have upon cognitive behavior. They claim that individuals of various ages formulate and use plans on a pragmatic, plan-as-you-go basis (termed "Planning-in-Action") in which the immediate goals involved in any task affect one'e plans for completing that task. Thus, Meyer and Rebok are claiming that people's problem-solving behaviors follow the ecological paradigm, because these behaviors are determined by a complex interaction between task demands and people's internal constraints.

As discussed in Roodin and Rybash's, Spear's and Sperbeck and Whitbourne's chapters, there are other organismic constraints which influence one's cognitive behaviors and processing. Roodin and Rybash discuss the influences that affect has upon one's social cognitive processing. They argue that affect provides the glue for intense and deep social cognitive processing. To continue the theme of organismic constraints, Spear describes the effects that neurobiological changes associated with disease and drugs have upon cognitive performance.

Another internal constraint discussed in this book is language. Weist and Matlin both describe the mediating effects which language has upon people's intellectual functioning. Weist shows that language can influence children's cognitive development by making them more knowledgeable about concepts. Also, Matlin demonstrates a relationship between the usage of generic masculine terms and people's conceptualization of masculinity. It must be noted that Weist and Matlin are not taking a Whorfian position on language and thought, but rather are suggesting that cognitive scientists should further study and understand the influences that language has upon cognition.

There are other types of possible internal constraints which should also be further studied by cognitive researchers. For one thing, there is still much to be known about the influences of personal interests upon cognition. Practical experiences and research (for example by Chiesi, Spilich, and Voss (1979) and Spilich, Vesonder, Chiesi, and Voss (1979) concerning domain-related knowledge) indicate that such interests do affect people's memory abilities. For instance, a friend of these authors, who is very interested in food, can remember all of the courses of an insignificant dinner which she had with friends years ago. Research on such constraints would help shed additional light upon the relationship between "real-life" issues and cognitive behavior.

Individual differences in cognition

Traditionally, cognitive scientists have also unfortunately neglected to examine the individual variations which exist in human cognition, and, indeed, there are many reasons for this neglect. For one thing, cognitive scientists have believed that people, especially adults, fundamentally process information in a similar manner regardless of their individual make-up and history. Secondly, cognitive researchers have typically ignored developmental differences, partly because they assumed that the development of cognitive processes was completed by adulthood and these researchers primarily use adults as their subjects.

This neglect to study individual variations has also left cognitive scientists with an artifical view of human cognition, because the evidence from this book strongly suggests that there are important individual differences in human cognition. Both Sperbeck and Whitbourne's and Baars' chapters note the importance of personality factors in one's cognitive functioning. Sperbeck and Whitbourne found that there were individual differences in people's reminiscing behaviors associated with the personality dimension of environmental openness/closeness. They also claim that this personality variable was a more robust predictor variable of the differences in people's reminiscing behaviors than were the developmental characteristics also studied by them.

Contrasting views about the robustness of developmental characteristics as the predictor variable of the individual variations in cognition are found throughout this volume. Hoyer notes that there are both interindividual (between people for any given age-periods) as well as intraindividual (developmental) differences which may exist in human cognition. He also claims that certain domains of cognition may remain consistent regardless of age and disease correlates, and other domains may, depending on their function, either show improvement or deterioration with aging.

Meyer and Robok, Roodin and Rybash, and Weist, however, claim that there are important and consistent developmental differences found in one's cognitive performance. Weist found developmental differences in children's understanding of language which parallel developmental stages as postulated by Piaget. Meyer and Rebok also take a neo-Piagetian position on the developmental patterns found in people's planning-behaviors. Unlike Piaget, however, they found life-span and individual differences to exist in people's cognition.

Spear's chapter presents evidence which again challenges the view that developmental characteristics are the important indicators of the individual variations found in human cognition. Spear argues that developmental changes in animal and human cognitive capacities are not as great as previously speculated by developmental psychologists. He presents data obtained by Rovee-Collier and her associates at Rutgers (Rovee-Collier, Sullivan, Enright, Lucas, & Fagan, 1980) which showed that human infants by 2–3 months of age possess a greater capacity for long-term retention and learning than was previously thought. Spear is not saying that differences in cognitive performances between infants and older children do not exist, but rather that these differences are due to task demands and learning conditions.

Contrasting views are also found on the robustness of sex differences as an individual difference variable. Smith strongly argues that there are significant variations in human cognitive functioning associated with differences between the sexes in brain development. Smith's research indicates that differences in boys' and girls' perceptual-linguistic abilities associated with reading are—partially, at least—at the level of hemispheric differences associated with visual-auditory integration. Specifically, she suggests that visual-auditory connections are made in the left hemisphere for girls, while for boys it may be that only auditory processing occurs in the left hemisphere, with visual processing accomplished in the right hemisphere. She also strongly warns cognitive scientists that they are making a major educational and scientific mistake to deny for political reasons the possibility of viable sex differences in cognitive behavior.

Connor and Weil, on the other hand, play down the viability of sex differences in cognitive functioning. Connor, for instance, argues that the sex-role literature indicates that there are few if any noticeable differences in the cognitive behaviors of males and females. She also claims that those cognitive behaviors, e.g., math and visual-spatial abilities, for which there are reported significant differences between males and females, are the result of socialization practices rather than a function of deep-rooted biological differences. Connor furthermore strongly argues that "sexist" political reasons are the main motivator for continuing research on sex differences in cognition, because she cannot find any scientific and/or educational justifications to continue this area of investigation. This chapter's authors believe, however, that cognitive professionals should continue to study this issue of sex-differences to determine the viability of this area of investigation. Furthermore, the study of sex-differences would provide additional insights into the relative effects that genetic and environmental determinants have upon human cognition and development.

Perhaps these contrasting views found in this volume regarding sex and developmental differences can be explained vis-a-vis the ecological validity model. That is, depending upon the task being measured, each position can be considered to contain some "truth." For example, regarding sex differences, biological factors, as indicated by Smith, may be the determining influence in one's *reading abilities,* while *math proficiency* may be more a result of educational practices. It thus behooves cognitive scientists interested in understanding the individual variations in human cognition to study this issue vis-a-vis an ecological approach.

COGNITIVE PROCESSING

As previously mentioned, the ecological approach involves studying one's system of cognitive processing as it relates to "real-life" conditions and an individual's make-up.

Seemingly conflicting conclusions are found in this book about the different cognitive processes involved in everyday memory situations. Neisser presents his concept of "repisodic memory" (Neisser, 1981) to explain the type of recollection(s) which occur for daily situations. "Repisodic memories" consist of recalling an impression, usually accurate, that one has for the significant elements of daily situations. Furthermore, people's memories for the specific content of *any particular episode* are problematic, because these impressions are built on repeated experiences. For example, John Dean's memory was faulty for particular events and episodes occurring within the White House, but was extemely accurate for the overall situation and the continuously occurring events (e.g., President Nixon's million-dollar remark). In other words, people remember their impressions of essential and reoccurring elements of daily existence, while constructing from these memories the specific attributes found for any given episode. (See Neisser, 1981, for a more detailed discussion of "repisodic memory" and John Dean's testimony.)

Herrmann, however, presents data which indicate that people have very precise memories for specific attributes of particular episodes occurring in their lives. Herrmann shows that people claim to directly recall specific attributes, e.g., location, nature, and time, for personal episodes that occurred years ago. These findings seem to contradict Neisser's position about the constructive processes involved in real-life cognition.

Roodin and Rybash's notions about the importance of affective commitment or active involvement in social cognition may offer an explanation to reconcile the positions of Herrmann and Neisser. Perhaps Dean was only committed to dealing with the global picture of this social situation? After all, his role in the White House was to report on and handle the overall situation. It may thus be that people are able to directly recall specific attributes of daily situations which are salient to their specific social involvement, and construct the nonsalient occurences in such situations. Shlechter and Toglia (1984) have found evidence for this position on people's memory abilities for real-life episodes. In three different daily situations, e.g., the first day of class, their subjects were able to produce vivid memories about features they found salient about these situations, e.g., class expectations, while not being able to recall with any degree of consistency the nonsalient aspects, e.g., teacher's clothing. It does seem, then, that affect does influence the type and level of one's daily cognitive processing.

The issue of effortful vs. automatic processing is another area of disagreement found in this book about the underlying processes associated with daily cognitive performance. Herrmann implies that direct recalls—the most common and efficient processing strategy found by him for autobiographical memories—involve an immediate retrieval process, while inferred recalls require a collection of effortful processes. Hoyer also suggests that automatic processing may be more commonly used in routine daily situations in which one can employ an expert cognition mode. Sperbeck and Whitbourne, however, claim that effortful processing is the most efficient strategy for retrieving autobiographical events. They argue that recalling autobiographical memories involves an elaborative retrieval process.

Karuza and Zevon cite Taylor and Fiske's (1978) hypothesis regarding automatic processing, which can also be used to reconcile these different positions on automatic/effortful processing and daily cognitive behaviors. Taylor and Fiske (1978) claim that automatic processing is most likely to occur in, and be the most appropriate strategy for, situations that are familiar, frequent, redundant, and boring. It must be noted that Herrmann and Hoyer were discussing automatic processing for highly familiar and routinized tasks, e.g., experienced doctors examining routine x-rays, and that Sperbeck and Whitbourne claim that they were eliciting remote memories from their subjects. Automatic processing, then, may be the appropriate mode for recalling highly familiar life situations, while effortful processing may be needed to produce memories of the more remote and less frequently occurring life events and situations.

Another area of conflict concerns the role of cognitive scripts in people's daily cognitive functioning. Roodin and Rybash discuss Abelson's (1981) notion of "action scripts," which, when activated, organize comprehension of event-based situations, e.g., a birthday party. In a nutshell, action scripts are cognitive schemata in which information about daily events is organized in a sequential manner. Several contributors—Hoyer, Karuza and Zevon, Sperbeck and Whitbourne, and Weist—also mention the usefulness of scripts for some aspects of daily cognitive functioning. For example, scripts may help people to organize incoming information about daily situations. Neisser and Herrmann, however, downplay the role of scripts as an underlying mechanism in people's memory functioning for daily events. Neisser feels that a weakness with the concept of action scripts is that it fails to capture the significant enduring aspects of memories about life experiences.

The ecological model may offer a resolution to this conflict about the role of scripts in everyday cognitive activities. That is, cognitive scripts may only be useful for processing information for certain daily tasks and situations which occur in script-like fashion. Neisser, for example, does acknowledge the importance of scripts in people's comprehension of stories. And Abelson (1981) has discussed the importance of scripted behavior relating to certain social situations (e.g., complying with a request). It remains, thus, for researchers to further determine the extent to which script-like tasks and situations occur in people's daily lives.

Several chapters further expand on the importance and development of underlying cognitive schemata in people's mental functioning. As discussed in this book, schemata appear to guide people's cognitive functioning in the areas of: social behaviors (see Roodin and Rybash's chapter), linguistic behaviors (see Weist's chapter), daily planning behaviors (see Meyer and Rebok's chapter), and expert cognition (see Hoyer's chapter). It also appears that schemata are developed and modified through a dynamic interaction between environmental conditions and internal constraints. Certainly, as new knowledge is gained, it is either assimilated into existing cognitive structures, or accomodated by updating of schemata. These points about schemata are exemplified in Meyer and Rebok's notions about planning-in-action. They discuss the role that schemata have in internalized rule systems in organizing and guiding problem-solving behaviors, and that these internalized systems must sometimes change in response to the task demands and/or the person's assessment of the goals. It must be noted, however, that the ease of such malleability may depend on the type of schema.

For example, Roodin and Rybash suggest that social schemata are most likely to be altered under emotionally intense conditions.

The ecological approach also relates to the chapters dealing with the psychobiological aspects of cognitive processing. For one thing, it has traditionally been believed that a single unitary memory-system exists within the human mind. Spear, however, illustrates that there may be several distinct memory systems, each operating for a particular set of tasks and/or situations. For instance, amnesic patients can show astute memory for learned mental operations but have problems in indicating the particular information operated on. Similar notions regarding multiple memory systems are becoming more prevalent in the cognitive neuropsychology literature. Cohen and Squire have, for example, published recent articles supporting this view (Cohen, 1984; Cohen and Squire, 1980; Squire, 1982).

Several other chapters—Baars', Roodin and Rybash's, and Smith's—further discuss this relationship between specific cognitive domains and distinct internal capacities within the brain. Smith further documents the view that the linguistic abilities necessary for reading in American Society are a left brain-hemispheric function, while spatial abilities are a right brain-hemispheric function. Baars, in his model of consciousness, also describes the specialized aspects of the human brain's functioning. He points out that there is much evidence for the position that many areas of the cortex are specialized for certain cognitive domains. He argues, however, that, if the brain is going to adapt to new environmental demands, then it must work in an organized and coherent fashion. A global workspace mechanism (consciousness) is thus proposed to exist in the nervous system which allows the specialized processors of the different cortex regions to communicate with each other.

It thus appears that the traditional views of cognitive processing are being modified vis-a-vis the ecological approach. As with the case for most major changes in science, there seems to be some dispute among this book's contributors about the nature of human cognition. Such disputes are beneficial to this field, because they will lead cognitive scientists to further study and find new insights into the human being's mental mechanisms.

NEW METHODOLOGICAL PROCEDURES

One of the main problems inherent in examining the ecological aspects of cognition is devising the proper methodology. After all, students of memory have traditionally been trained to examine cognitive issues under laboratory conditions. They are thus unprepared to deal with the questions and issues involved in examining memory behaviors in their natural context and/or the individual aspects of cognition.

Several chapters provide insights into the proper procedures for conducting such ecological research. Karuza and Zevon, for instance, suggest that this research consists of an approach which uses both idiographic and nomethetic procedures. They cite Meyer and Rebok's study as a good illustration of such an approach, in that this study contained the controls found in traditional nomethetic procedures, while it used idiographic techniques to capture the richness associated with discovering each subject's particular planning strategy.

Karuza and Zevon also claim that studying environmental and individual influences upon cognition demands that cognitive scientists use case-studies and traditional learning theory research designs in their investigations. Cognitive researchers have traditionally scoffed at using such techniques. However, several of this volume's authors, e.g., Connor, Neisser, and Spear, report using similar techniques in their cognitive investigations. As previously reported, Neisser devised the notion of "repisodic memory" from his case-study investigation of John Dean's Watergate testimony, and Spear consistently reports data obtained from learning theory paridigms, e.g., discrimination and aversion learning tasks. For example, he discusses Rovee-Collier's revolutionary new methodology for testing infant's cognitive behavior, which is basically a modification of traditional conditioning tasks.

Several chapters furthermore suggest that ecological investigators look to other disciplines for appropriate methodologies. As Weist details his use of cross-cultural techniques to obtain naturalistic data on children's language development, so does Matlin elaborate on the use of sociological research methods in cognitive research. For example, Matlin maintains that psycholinguistic insights have been discovered by exploring the type of communication patterns and messages found in advertisements. As previously indicated, both Gelfand and Neisser also suggest that cognitive researchers who are interested in ecological information should follow the traditions of the ethologists by observing cognitive behaviors as they occur in real-life situations.

Another aspect of cognitive research—the appropriate tasks to be used for exploring "real-life" cognition—is also discussed in this volume. Herrmann responds that self-report memory questionnaires are the most efficient tasks to use for collecting naturalistic data on memory behaviors. He has argued previously that the beauty of these tasks is that they allow cognitive researchers to effectively obtain such data while circumventing the difficulties inherent in field research (Herrmann, 1982). For example, memory questionnaires can provide data about subjects' memory behaviors for directions, without having an observer wait indefinitely in the field for occasions when subjects need to remember directions. And in this volume, Herrmann describes a new questionnaire—Trace Attribute Inventory—which he created for obtaining information about the processes involved in autobiographical memories. He concludes that this instrument does have the necessary properties for obtaining viable data. However, Gelfand, skeptical about people's ability to recall their memory processes, questions the validity of this instrument.

Gelfand, moreover, argues that real-life cognitive investigations should consist of both naturalistic and laboratory tasks, with laboratory tasks being used to further and more "scientifically" study the discoveries made about "real-life" cognition vis-a-vis naturalistic-type tasks. It is interesting to note that examples of laboratory tasks to ascertain information about everyday cognition are found throughout this volume. Baars writes about the tasks used by his associates and himself (e.g., Motley, Camden, & Baars, 1979) to examine people's verbal slips in laboratory conditions which were analgous to everyday situations. One of their more interesting laboratory procedures involved male subjects in responding to sexually provocative stimuli while sitting next to a sensuously dressed female. Meyer and Rebok used a task commonly engaged in by people—card-sorting— to examine in a laboratory setting the "real-life" cognitive issue of planning-behaviors. And Sperbeck and Whitbourne investigated the naturalistic memory issue of reminiscing behavior by using a laboratory prompting task. From this body of work, it thus seems that "real-life" cognition can also be studied in the laboratory with the advantages inherent in such a setting, and, correspondingly, such research can be experimental as well as correlational.

It must be pointed out, however, that cognitive scientists should be extremely careful in their selection of such laboratory tasks. Karuza and Zevon, Gelfand, and Neisser all argue that selecting an appropriate task is a crucial element in conducting ecological research. Neisser claims that the failure of traditional cognitive science experiments and the information-processing approach is that these investigators used artificial tasks to explore cognitive issues. He then cites Rosch's work on natural categories (Rosch, 1975; Rosch, Mervis, Gray, Johnson, & Boyer-Braem, 1976) as examples of laboratory investigations which used ecologically oriented tasks to provide meaningful information about people's cognitive behaviors. According to Neisser, the tasks used by Rosch and her associates are ecologically valid because they related to tasks found in people's daily existence. He (and Gelfand) then suggest that another purpose for observing cognitive behaviors in the "wild" is to find appropriate cognitive tasks for further laboratory study.

Karuza and Zevon also indicate other crucial elements needed to insure a laboratory study's ecological validity. First of all, they point out that such laboratory tasks should be like those from social-psychological research with a high degree of mundane realism, e.g., Meyer and Rebok's study. Secondly, they state that the experimenter must create a mis-en-scène which does not interfere with the subjects' performance. Karuza and Zevon also note that the experimental task(s) must be a relevant measure of a given age group's (and person's) cognitive performance.

As emphasized in this section, the ecological approach requires that cognitive scientists can no longer be satisfied with just using traditional experimental procedures to make inferences about human cognitive processing, but rather they must employ a variety of techniques for this endeavor. Consequently, cognitive psychologists should also become more familiar with the scientific techniques devised and used by other disciplines and subdisciplines within psychology.

FINAL POINTS

As emphasized throughout this chapter,the ecological approach expands the domains of the cognitive scientist to include the entire E-O-E arc involved in human functioning. Cognitive scientists, hence, can no longer only be concerned with just studying proximal responses to proximal stimuli, but also must study cognitive behaviors as they relate to real-life situations. It has also been emphasized that the cognitive scientist should become more aware of and study the individual characteristics involved in human cognition, because such characteristics do influence cognitive functioning.

Underlying the ecological position is the view that people's psychological functioning is basically an adaptation process. People thus must be equipped with malleable cognitive processes which allow for maximum adaptation to different environmental conditions and demands. This point about cognition and adaptation has been repeatedly emphasized throughout this chapter, and correspondingly in this volume. An illustration of this emphasis is our discussion of how an individual's cognitive schemata change to meet environmental/task demands. Hence, the ecological approach requires that cognitive scientists understand and study human cognition as it relates to human adaptation.

The ecological approach also incorporates the methods and ideas of behavioral scientists from other traditions, disciplines, and perspectives. For example, B. F. Skinner has been considered by some psychologists to be the father of the idiographic movement. (J. Karuza, personal communication, August 20, 1984). This is because many of the ideas inherent in such research, e.g., single-subject designs, were initially formulated by B. F. Skinner and his followers. The learning theory approach is also evident in most of the chapters concerning macro-environmental influences on cognitive behaviors. Baars, furthermore, notes that psychodynamic theory has provided viable insights into the workings of the human mind. For instance, his theory of consciousness is rooted in psychodynamic theory. Thus, the noncognitive psychological traditions have not been, as suggested by Neisser (1982, and in this volume), swept away by cognitive science, but rather they have been somewhat engulfed by this discipline.

Correspondingly, it must also be noted that some of the new directions discussed in this volume relate to concerns and practices of psychologists since the beginning of psychology. Herrmann's self-report memory questionnaires represent a new and more efficient method of collecting introspection data, and Baars's notions of consciousness relate to the functionalism approach of William James. The cognitive revolution, then, must be seen as another evolutionary phase in the study of human intellectual functioning which is deeply rooted in past traditions and beliefs.

Finally, the study of cognition must now involve behavioral scientists from diverse perspectives and disciplines in working together so that a coherent and complete picture of human cognition can be developed. We look forward with interest to additional volumes of *New Directions in Cognitive Science* from other disciplines.

REFERENCES

Abelson, R. P. (1981). Psychological status of the script concept. *American Psychologist, 36*, 715–729.

Baars, B. J. (in press). *The cognitive revolution in psychology*. New York: Guilford Press.

Bransford, J. D., & Franks, J. J. (1971) The abstraction of linguistic ideas. *Cognitive Psychology, 2*, 331–350.

Bransford, J. D., Franks, J. J., Morris, C. D., & Stein, B. S. (1979). Some general constraints on learning and memory research. In L. S. Cermak & F. I. M. Craik (Eds.), *Levels of processing in human memory* (pp. 331–354). Hillsdale, NJ: Erlbaum.

Brunswik, E. (1955). *The conceptual framework of psychology. International encyclopedia of unified science* (Vol. 1, pp. 656–750). Chicago: University of Chicago Press.

Chiesi, H. L., Spilich, G. J., & Voss, J. F. (1979). Acquisition of domain-related information in relation to high and low domain knowledge. *Journal of Verbal Learning and Verbal Behavior, 18*, 257–273.

Cohen, N. J. (1984). Preserved learning capacity in amnesia: Evidence for multiple memory systems. In N. Butters & L. R. Squire (Eds.), *The neuropsychology of memory* (pp. 83–103). New York: Guilford Press.

Cohen, N. J., & Squire, L. R. (1980). Preserved learning and retention of pattern-analyzing skills in amnesia: Dissociation of knowing how and knowing that. *Science, 210*, 207–210.

Gruneberg, M. M., Morris, P. E., & Sykes, R. N. (1978). *Practical aspects of memory*. London: Academic Press.

Harris, J., & Morris, P. (1984), *Everyday memory, actions, and absentmindedness*. New York: Academic Press.

Herrmann, D. J. (1982). Know thy memory: The use of questionnaires to assess and study memory. *Psychological Bulletin, 92*, 434–452.

Jenkins, J. J. (1979). Four points to remember: A tetrahedral model of memory experiments. In L. S. Cermak & F. I. M. Craik (Eds.) *Levels of processing in human memory* (pp. 429–446). Hillsdale, NJ: Erlbaum.

Motley, M. T., Camden, C. T., & Baars, B. J. (1979). Personality and situational influences upon verbal slips: A laboratory test of Freudian and prearticulatory editing hypotheses. *Human Communication Research, 5*(3), 195–202.

Neisser, U. (1976). *Cognition and reality: Principles and implications of cognitive psychology*. San Francisco: W. H. Freeman & Company.

Neisser, U. (1981). John Dean's memory: A case study. *Cognition, 9*, 1–22.

Neisser, U. (1982). *Memory observed: Remembering in natural contexts*. San Francisco: W. H. Freeman & Company.

Norman, D. A. (1981). What is cognitive science. In D. A. Norman (Ed.), *Perspectives on cognitive science* (pp. 1–12). Norwood and Hillsdale, NJ: Ablex Publishing Corporation and Lawrence Erlbaum and Associates.

Rosch, E. (1975). Cognitive representations of semantic categories. *Journal of Experimental Psychology: General, 104*, 192–233.

Rosch, E., Mervis, C. B., Gray, W. D., Johnson, D. M., & Boyer-Braem, P. (1976). Basic objects in natural categories. *Cognitive Psychology, 8,* 387–439.

Rovee-Collier, C. K., Sullivan, M. W., Enright, M. K., Lucas, D., & Fagan, J. (1980). Reactivation of infant memory. *Science, 208,* 1159–1161.

Rubin, D. (Ed.) (in press). *Autobiographical memory.* Cambridge: Cambridge University Press.

Shlechter, T. M., & Toglia, M. P. (1984, April). *An investigation of people's biographical memories for typical everyday situations.* Paper presented at the meeting of the Eastern Psychological Association, Baltimore, MD.

Skinner, B. F. (1984, April). *Behaviorism and cognitive science.* Paper presented at the meeting of the Eastern Psychological Association, Baltimore, MD.

Spilich, G. S., Vesonder, G. T., Chiesi, H. L., & Voss, J. F. (1979). Text processing of domain-related information for individuals with high and low domain knowledge. *Journal of Verbal Learning and Verbal Behavior, 18,* 275–290.

Squire, L. R. (1982). The neuropsychology of human memory. *Annual Review of Neuroscience, 2,* 241–273.

Taylor, S. E., & Fiske, S. T. (1978). Salience, attention, and attribution: Top of the head phenomena. In L. Berkowitz (Ed.), *Advances in experimental social psychology* (Vol. 11, pp. 250–288). New York: Academic Press.

Chapter 2

Toward an Ecologically Oriented Cognitive Science

Ulric Neisser
Emory University

Although it is never possible to establish the precise moment when an intellectual movement begins, cognitive psychology is certainly over 21. Whether we start counting in 1958 with Broadbent's *Perception and Communication* or in 1960 with Miller, Galanter, and Pribram's seminal essay on *Plans* and Sperling's discovery of the icon, our field must be old enough to buy a drink in any state in the Union. As it comes of age, it is still undergoing a remarkable growth spurt. As early as 1967, when I reviewed the state of the art in a book called *Cognitive Psychology,* there was already a coherent paradigm and a good deal of research to support it. Since then, the rate of growth has been exponential. There are more cognitive psychologists publishing more papers in more cognitive journals today than anyone could have anticipated a few years ago. It would be unrealistic now to think of reviewing the field in a single book: multi-volume handbooks have become the rule, and even they are usually restricted to subtopics.

One consequence of this luxuriant growth is a certain amount of discontent with the term "cognitive psychology" itself. Some have suggested that our field is not so much a branch of psychology as a science in its own right: "Cognitive Science." That phrase occurs not only in the title of the present volume but in many other contexts: it is the name of a scientific society, the title of a journal, the focus of funding by foundations, the subject of excited articles in popular magazines. It is an appealing phrase, with a scope appropriate to the wide range of disciplines now involved in the study of cognition. But a new name creates a new responsibility; it raises certain legitimate expectations. To change one's name at the age of 21 or so is a significant act in our society. It always signals some important personal or political decision; it means that one has married, or joined a revolution, or adopted a new religious faith. In short, it announces an identity. Calling our field "Cognitive Science" should announce something too, but what?

There are two candidates for that identity, alternative directions in which cognitive science may go. They are not altogether different, of course. The future always builds on the past, and 21-year-olds are never as free to choose their identities as they would like to believe. Nevertheless there really are two alternatives, sketching out different scenarios for the future study of cognition. I will call one of them the "information processing approach" and the other the "ecological approach" to cognitive science. Both aim at understanding human cognition, but they define understanding differently and pursue it in somewhat different ways. I will begin by describing those differences, and then illustrate the ecological approach with work in three different areas: concept formation, perception, and memory.

All analyses of cognition begin with the information available to the perceiving and thinking individual. In the processing approach that information is called the "input," and it is treated as a display of single and separate bits that stimulate separate receptors. The input is meaningless; human beings bring a sophisticated processing system to bear on it to create the meaningful structures which appear in consciousness and in behavior. The aim of cognitive science is the understanding of that entirely hypothetical processing system, which is also called the "mind." The mind cannot be observed directly, even by introspection, but it can be modelled. Once a cognitive model has been formulated, its adequacy can be tested by appropriate experiments. The typical information processing study begins with a hypothesis about an internal mechanism, proceeds to an experiment specially designed to test that hypothesis, and concludes with an evaluation of the hypothesis against its competitors.

This approach to cognition has important achievements to its credit—the discovery of iconic memory and short-term memory and semantic memory and other "stages of processing"; the identification of various heuristics and strategies used in problem solving. The fact that the structure of the memories and stages is still controversial does not detract from the impressiveness of this research tradition. Its accomplishments have attracted the attention of scholars in many fields. Some of those scholars have even joined in the enterprise; cognitive science now includes linguists and neuroscientists and philosophers and students of artificial intelligence as well as psychologists. The linguists are needed to help formulate models of the processes by which language is produced and understood; the neuroscientists, because one would like to model the processes of the physical brain as well as those of the hypothetical mind; the philosophers, because the logical status of all the processes is still a bit shaky. The new discipline of artificial intelligence (AI) plays an especially central role, because models that actually run on real computers are more convincing than models that exist only as hypotheses on paper. The influence of AI on information processing psychology seems to have increased in the last few years, and computer models may soon dominate it entirely.

Despite these achievements, the information-processing approach remains somehow unsatisfying as an account of human nature. Its basic paradigms take cognition completely out of context. Because its experiments are designed to test hypotheses about the mind rather than about the environment, they are typically conducted in settings that strive for convenience rather than ecological validity. Instead of engaging in natural activities, subjects are confronted with arbitrary and stripped-down tasks designed to test particular theoretical models. This simplification reaches a logical conclusion in studies of artificial intelligence, where the environment is just a teletyped message (or a "blocks world") and there are no people at all. The situation in most cognitive experiments is less extreme, but often still unnatural: subjects are asked to memorize irrelevant materials, solve artificially constructed puzzles, or perform stereotyped tasks repeatedly and rapidly so that their response times may be measured. Such tasks do not seem to catch people at their best; they offer few opportunities for the exercise of ordinary cognitive skills.

The formulation of models has become so central to cognitive science that it may seem difficult to imagine any other paradigm. Nevertheless there is one: a different approach to the study of cognition that already has its own history and its own substantial achievements. It even has its own name, familiar in several scientific contexts and specifically adopted by J. J. Gibson (1979) for his theory of perception: the "ecological approach." In calling the ecological approach an alternative to information processing, I do not mean that they have nothing in common. There are many similarities between them, if only because both paradigms take human cognition as their central problem. I think that cognitive scientists of every persuasion get their ideas by considering some real experience—their own or someone else's—and trying to refine it into scientific understanding. But where the information processing theorist moves as quickly as possible to the formulation and testing of a mental model, the ecological cognitive psychologist is more likely to begin with a careful description of the environment and people's ordinary activities within it. At a minimum, such a description will determine the form that a cognitive model should take; at best, it may make modeling altogether superfluous.

EARLIER ECOLOGICAL APPROACHES

The approach under consideration here is not the first ecological movement to have appeared in psychology. There have been several others, including Brunswik's (1956) call for "ecological validity", Barker's (1965) ecological approach to the description of behavioral settings, and Bronfenbrenner's (1979) recent emphasis on contextual factors in child development. By far the most important such movement was the approach to animal behavior first associated with the names of Tinbergen and Lorenz, which became prominent in the 1950s under the name of "ethology." It was not altogether new then, of course (just as the ecological approach to cognition is not altogether new now), but its assumptions were strikingly different from those that generally prevailed. A brief review of those differences may be useful.

From the twenties to the fifties, American experimental psychology was dominated by a particular way of thinking about animal behavior. This approach was often called "behaviorism" and sometimes "stimulus-response theory," but the basic terms of the problem were accepted even by those who were hostile to behaviorism and critical of S-R assumptions. The goal of the enterprise was to establish the correct "theory of learning." It was an ambitious undertaking: books on learning theory had titles like *The Behavior of Organisms* (Skinner, 1938) and *Principles of Behavior* (Hull, 1943). Disputes among the giants of learning theory gave rise to innumerable experiments and were the staples of graduate instruction: whether one's allegiance was given to Hull or Guthrie or Skinner or Tolman, one had to master them all. With the advantage of hindsight, we can see that these theories all shared a key methodological assumption: it was taken for granted that theoretical issues about the nature of learning could be resolved in entirely artificial settings. The mazes and "Skinner boxes" that became the symbols of experimental psychology were designed to fit the convenience of the experimenter rather than of the animal. The subjects of the experiments did not engage in natural activities; they carried out specially contrived, theoretically relevant tasks instead. It didn't even seem to matter what animal was used. Some studies were done with rats and others used pigeons; a few even tested human beings. The logical climax was reached in the 1950s with the invention of mathematical models that made it unnecessary to test any real animals at all. "Stat rats" were used instead. The researcher simply varied certain probability parameters in the model, and simulated enough cases to establish the dominant outcome in each one. In a certain sense, these mathematical models of learning may be regarded as the precursors of modern "artificial intelligence."

Suddenly, in a matter of a decade or so, this once unchallengeable approach has almost melted away. Its paradigms seem exhausted, and its control of American psychology is over. Hardly anyone still wonders whether Hull, Guthrie, or Tolman was right. Skinner's influence continues, but his theoretical analyses now seem less important than his practical suggestions. Stimulus-response psychology has fallen on hard times. How did this change come about? It was not the result of theoretical argument or crucial experiment, although many good arguments had been presented and many good experiments performed. I believe that the most important factor was the presentation of an alternative paradigm by the small group of European scientists who called themselves "ethologists" (Lorenz, 1981). The ethologists were less interested in theories than in the animals themselves—in wolves and geese and wasps and sticklebacks and jackdaws. To understand those animals, it was necessary to conduct field studies, observing them in their natural habitats. The details of each environment were important. Each species is attuned to those details in its own way, fitting neatly into what we now call its "ecological niche." It is impossible to understand any piece of animal behavior without considering its context and its adaptive significance.

The general principles of learning that had been derived from so many laboratory studies were of little use in this work. It began to appear that different species had different learning abilities. Indeed, the very same animal may learn differently in different settings or at different stages of maturation. Many types of learning that occur in the field do not appear in the laboratory at all, unless the laboratory has been designed with the field in mind. A new view of animal behavior appeared, less model-oriented than the old one but just as scientific. It seems to have more ties to neurobiology and genetics and other aspects of biology than the old learning theory ever did, and may even have more applications to human life. Although the new "behavioral biology" may eventually be reconciled with the concepts and methods of "learning theory," the two approaches seem to be almost entirely separate at present.

Just as there were once two possible identities for the study of animal behavior, so there are now two paradigms for the study of cognition. The ecological approach is the one that begins by taking the environment seriously, focusing on cognition in ordinary settings. To study concept formation, one begins with an analysis of everyday concepts; to study perception, one begins with visual control of action in cluttered environments; to study memory, one begins with the kinds of things people ordinarily remember. Such an approach usually forces the researcher to look at temporally extended stimulus variables and behavior that occurs over time, rather than at the brief flashes and momentary responses popular in information processing research. It also implies a concern with cognitive development and cognitive change, including both the changes due to age and those that come with the acquisition of skill—i.e., with learning itself. Most important, perhaps, is that ecological psychologists are generally reluctant to construct models or to postulate hypothetical mental events. Too often, they believe, those hypotheses have substituted for careful analysis of the real environment and the real events that occur in it.

CONCEPTS

Stated in general terms, these principles do not seem very controversial. The ecological approach is distinguished less by a clear definition than by certain existing bodies of work; prototypical instances, as it were. That degree of ambiguity is what might be expected, given what has recently been discovered about the structure of concepts in general. Most nouns in English resist specific definition in the same way. Studies of natural concepts have shown that people do not usually apply words to things on the basis of explicit criteria, but by assessing their similarity to familiar instances or prototypes. If my definition of "ecological cognitive psychology" is vague, so are everyone's definitions of "tool" and "chair." Eleanor Rosch and her associates documented this state of affairs in the mid-1970s, and thereby revolutionized the psychological study of concepts. I will treat their work as a first example of the ecological approach to cognition. Although the similarities between the assumptions of Rosch and Gibson have not often been discussed (so far as I know, Rosch has never described her own work as ecological), I find them striking and important.

Rosch began by examining the meanings of ordinary words: "chair," "bird," "furniture," "tool." Philosophers had been interested in word meanings for years, but experimental psychologists had usually studied concepts from an entirely different point of view. In traditional experiments on concept formation, subjects were presented with arrays of cards on which figures had been drawn: large red circles, small blue circles, and perhaps squares and triangles of various sizes and colors. Some of the cards would be instances of a concept selected arbitrarily by the experimenter—"any small blue figure," for example, defined by the conjunction of the attributes "small" and "blue"—and others would not be. Such experiments were designed to test particular models of how concepts are formed. As it turned out, they were largely irrelevant to conceptual thinking outside the laboratory. Real progress in understanding concepts had to wait until Rosch began to study their *structure,* independently of any processing model. She began with an analysis of color terminology (Heider, 1972; Rosch, 1975a) and geometrical shapes (Rosch, 1973), but soon turned her attention to categories of everyday objects (Rosch, 1975b; Rosch, Mervis, Gray, Johnson, & Boyes-Braem, 1976).

Rosch's principal findings are now well-known. A category like "chair" is not defined by any precise set of features. One can list many typical attributes of chairhood, for example—having four legs, a back, a seat, about so high, built to be sat on—but none of them is decisive. An object possessing most or all of the most important attributes is a "prototype" of its category. Such objects can be categorized quickly and with certainty. We are sure about the chairs in the dining room, but there are other objects (barstools with low backs, bean bags, auto seats) about which we are much less certain. The borders of natural categories are fuzzy. In addition to demonstrating the existence of this prototype-to-fuzzy-edge structure, Rosch suggested a possible reason for it. Her hypothesis was that the attributes of real objects tend to occur together in patterns of correlation that justify the categories. (Most things of that size with four legs *do* have a back and *were* built to be sat on.) She also made some suggestions about the process of categorization as it occurs on particular occasions. In deciding whether to call something a "chair" or not, for example, we just evaluate its resemblance to prototypical chairs with which we are already familiar. It is the image of the prototype that comes to mind when we are asked to imagine a chair, and it is the prototype that we prepare for when we expect to be shown a chair. It is easier to learn the category names of prototypes than of marginal instances in the same category, and easier to remember them too.

Another of Rosch's discoveries also merits our attention. Many everyday concepts are arranged in categorical hierarchies, with the higher categories including the lower ones. One level of these hierarchies has a privileged status: she called it the basic level of categorization. "Chair" is a basic level category, for example; so are "table" and "rug." All three of them belong to the superordinate category called "furniture." "Armchair" and "kitchen chair," on the other hand, are subordinates of "chair." Rosch's principal contribution was not the identification of these hierarchies, which are obvious enough, but her demonstration that the basic level has a special status: it conveys more information than the other levels do. On being told that something is a chair, one can be reasonably sure of many things about it (at least if it is prototypical): how to use it, what its attributes are, even roughly what it looks like (Rosch et al., 1976). On the other hand, one learns very little by being told that something is an article of furniture. (Indeed, it is curiously difficult to list any distinctive attributes of "furniture" at all!) Learning that something is a "kitchen chair" adds only slightly to what one can conclude from "chair" alone. It is because basic-level concepts transmit the most information that they are so widely used. Children learn them long before they learn superordinate and subordinate terms (Rosch et al., 1976).

It seems to me that Rosch's work is firmly in the ecological tradition. She turned away from a laboratory paradigm based on artificial tasks and hypothetical models to examine an ordinary human cognitive activity—categorizing objects. She did not begin with hypotheses about the process of categorization, but the structure of the categories themselves. She even proposed an explanation of that structure based on ecological assumptions, suggesting that the graded structure of natural categories may be driven by observed correlations among real attributes in the environment. That explanation may be wrong: categories seem to have the same prototype-to-fuzzy-edge structure even when there has been little opportunity to sample environmental correlations. Young children's categories exhibit graded structure (Keil & Batterman, 1984), and so do ad hoc categories (Barsalou, 1983). It is reassuring to discover that ecological hypotheses are testable.

More recent developments in the study of concepts have continued to move in an ecological direction. The new interest in the cognitive analysis of concepts used by scientists provides a convenient example. While it is obvious that scientific concepts do not usually have a prototype-to-fuzzy boundary structure, it is equally obvious that they are not the feature-defined categories of the old laboratory paradigm. What are they really like? To find out, cognitive scientists are now beginning to focus on the conceptual processes of scientists as they solve actual technical problems (e.g., Chi, Feltovich, & Glaser, 1981), and educators are beginning to study the prescientific concepts that children bring with them to school (Resnick, 1983). These are encouraging developments. There is still much to learn about the natural use of concepts, but we have made a start (see Note 1).

PERCEPTION

Although I have presented Rosch's research as an example of the ecological approach, it is by no means the prototype. That honor belongs to James J. Gibson's theory of perception. Gibson's work is not new: *The Senses Considered as Perceptual Systems* appeared in 1966 when cognitive psychology itself was only beginning to develop. It is an astonishing book, as different from other works on perception as whales are from fishes. It does not begin with the eye and the ear but with the environment: its chief concern is not with sensory mechanisms but with an analysis of the stimulus information on which perception depends. Gibson later elaborated his views for the special case of vision in another book, *The Ecological Approach to Visual Perception,* published shortly before his death in 1979. By now, the "Gibsonian" approach has many enthusiastic supporters. They hold meetings, conduct research, and form the core of a new *Society for Ecological Psychology.* It is a vigorous movement, and a growing one.

The ecological approach to perception begins by distinguishing three levels of analysis. First, there is the environment itself. What kinds of things are perceivable? *The Senses Considered as Perceptual Systems* offered a kind of taxonomy of the perceptible world, based on considerations of evolution and behavior. There are surfaces, edges, objects, and holes; the ground, the horizon, oneself, other organisms; motions, transformations, disappearances, and events of all kinds. There are also opportunities for specific kinds of actions, which Gibson called *affordances.* These are what animals must perceive if they are to survive. (There are also marks, signs, and pictures, but I will not consider them here.) Things can be perceived when they are specified by objectively existing information: the second level of analysis concerns that information itself. If we are considering visual perception, the information consists of various kinds of optical structure. Gibson's most important single contribution was probably the detailed analysis of those structures and their relation to the environment, an analysis that he called *ecological optics.* Finally there is the perceiving animal, its visual system, and its activity. Perceivers come last in this very ecological approach, because we must understand the information available to them before we can begin to understand how they use it.

The information in the light exists objectively, whether or not anyone is there to pick it up. The stable information structure in an illuminated place—the optic array—can be "sampled" by any perceiver who is there with his or her eyes open. Even a single stationary sample of the array may specify a good deal about the layout of the environment: that the floor is level, for example; that there is a chair on the floor at a certain distance from the sampling station point; that there is a larger chair farther away, partly occluded by the first. Normally, however, perceivers are not restricted to stationary samples. Movement makes additional information available, of a kind that cannot appear at a single station point. The fixated displays used in many perceptual experiments eliminate much of the information on which vision normally depends. In a normally cluttered environment, every movement of the observer results in occlusion and disocclusion, as objects hide parts of other objects that lie behind them or are hidden in their turn. At every edge where occlusion is taking place, the microtexture and surface detail on one side progressively disappears while that on the other side remains unaffected. The object with the vanishing texture is always the more distant of the two. Experiments have shown that occlusion/disocclusion alone can create a compelling perception of one object going behind another (Gibson, Kaplan, Reynolds, & Wheeler, 1969).

Occlusion information actually specifies the positions of objects *relative to the observer* as well as to each other. All changes of optical structure have this double reference—they are informative about the environment and about the perceiver too. Movements of the observer produce smoothly organized changes in the entire array—optical flow fields. When one moves directly toward a vertical wall, for example, every bit of microtexture on the wall flows outward from a center of expansion which specifies the direction of the observer's movement. (The matter is more complicated for gaze directions off to one side.) To demonstrate the perceptual effectiveness of optical flow, Lee and Aronson (1974) built a small "room" with walls that could be silently moved back and forth. A toddler standing in this room falls down immediately when the walls move, and even adults have difficulty remaining upright unless they are squarely balanced. This effect occurs because any backward movement of the walls (for example) simulates the optical flow field that would normally be produced by a forward movement of the observer. The subject compensates for the misperceived movement with a muscular impulse in the opposite direction, and falls backward. Normally, of course, "visual kinesthesis" of this sort helps us to keep our balance rather than to lose it. In many situations the optical flow field is the most important determinant of posture, outweighing every form of feedback from muscles, joints, and labyrinthine receptors.

David Lee's many studies of visual kinesthesis (Lee & Thomson, 1982) are typical of the ecological approach in several ways. They focus on motion-produced stimulation, they deal with the relation between perception and action (a related paper is on "The regulation of gait in the long jump": Lee, Lishman, & Thomson, 1982), and they are based on a careful analysis of the information available in ordinary perceptual situations. It is worth noting that almost all this work (like Rosch's experiments on categories) was conducted under controlled laboratory conditions. The most typical characteristic of the ecological approach is not an aversion to the laboratory but an attempt to maintain the integrity of variables that matter in natural settings.

It is not entirely accurate to describe the information in the optic array as "optical structure." A deeper form of information is involved, one that is not purely optical. These are structures that appear identically in both the optic and the acoustic arrays, and perhaps even in the structure of action: the "amodal invariants'' (E. J. Gibson, 1982). Surprisingly, the human perceptual apparatus seems to be tuned to just this level of abstraction. A now-classic experiment by Elizabeth Spelke (1976) established this principle for 3-month-old infants. In her study, the subjects were presented with two movies projected simultaneously, side by side on the same screen. (Of course, the films were selected to be of interest to babies. In our own experiments we have used xylophones being struck, ''slinky'' toys moving, people playing pat-a-cake.) While the movies were being shown, one of corresponding soundtracks (but only one) was played through a centrally-located loudspeaker. On some trials it was the soundtrack for the film on the right; on others, for the film on the left. The results were clear: the babies looked toward the ''sound film'' most of the time. How could they have known which one it was? It seems quite unlikely that 3-month-olds have already formed associations between the sights and sounds of these toys. Indeed, a series of additional experiments (including one with analogous tactile-visual correspondences in 1-month-olds: Gibson & Walker, 1984) virtually rule out any explanation in terms of prior learning. Something in the soundtrack and the corresponding film must be the *same*. Further research has actually demonstrated the existence of several different kinds of ''sameness'' (amodal invariants) in this situation, including rhythm, tempo, synchrony, and abruptness. Infants' ability to perceive the world around them is much greater than might have been expected a few years ago. From the beginning, they see much the same world that we do, because they also pick up objectively existing information that specifies its properties.

These few examples are not intended as a general survey of the ecological approach to perception. That would be impossible within the scope of this chapter. More detailed accounts are available elsewhere, e.g., in a recent review of perceptual development by Gibson and Spelke (1983). I have only tried to convey something of the flavor of the research and its results. Its consistent commitment to the careful analysis of stimulus information (as opposed to the modeling of hypothetical mental processes) has revealed that we are far from a full understanding of the information structures on which perception and action depend (see Note 2). Some of those structures, as revealed in the studies of amodal perception, are surprisingly abstract. The real nature of objects and events in our environment is specified by information that appears invariantly in different forms of energy (optic, acoustic, mechanical) and can be picked up by several different sense modalities. Introspection does not reveal these structures, but the human perceptual systems seem to be innately prepared for them.

MEMORY

If the study of perception is the most theoretically sophisticated area of naturalistic cognitive science, the study of memory can claim to be the oldest. Research on the accuracy of witnesses' recall goes back to the turn of the century: William Stern founded a journal called *Contributions to the Psychology of Testimony* in Leipzig in 1904. Innumerable studies have now shown that witnesses can be wrong even when they are very confident (Clifford & Bull, 1978; Loftus, 1979; Neisser, 1982a). Their errors are of more than academic interest: many innocent people have been convicted and imprisoned as a result of mistaken testimony. Stern believed that the legal system should draw on psychological expertise to help prevent these miscarriages of justice, and many later psychologists from Munsterburg (1909) to Loftus (1979, 1983) have agreed. Nevertheless, the issue is not closed. According to McCloskey and Egeth (1983), expert testimony about memory is at least as likely to harm the cause of justice as to serve it. Jurors already know that memory can be mistaken on some occasions; what they must decide is whether *this* witness is mistaken on *this* occasion. Psychological experts usually have little to contribute to that critical question. While testimony that strongly emphasizes the fallibility of memory might reduce the overall frequency of convictions, we cannot be sure that such a shift is desirable.

The psychology of testimony is only one form of naturalistic research in memory, and not the most fundamental. It is focused on social problems rather than scientific ones; modern studies of witness memory are often published in the *Journal of Applied Psychology*. Basic and applied psychology can and should support one another, but they are distinct enterprises. The ecological approach to cognitive science is a scientific undertaking; it is the attempt to understand cognition while doing justice to the complexity of ordinary activities in ordinary environments. Practical applications may result from it, but they are not its principal goal.

Viewed in this light, the ecological study of memory is brand new rather than traditional or well-established. Nevertheless a number of interesting lines of research have already made their appearance. One particularly important domain is the study of "very long term memory," defined by the recall or recognition of material encountered years earlier. Remote memory is most easily studied by taking advantage of learning that has occurred outside the laboratory. It is only necessary to locate subjects who became familiar with particular bodies of material at known times in the past, and devise ways of finding out what they still remember. There have now been a number of such studies, with intriguing results. Several investigators have studied memory for people with whom their subjects had been acquainted in high school, using yearbooks to check the accuracy of the responses. When measured by recognition methods, memory for the names and faces of high-school classmates shows no decrement over periods of more than 30 years (Bahrick, Bahrick & Wittlinger, 1975). A modest decrement does appear in recall, but it may be due to changes in response rate rather than to genuine forgetting. Williams and Hollan (1981) have shown that the success of this kind of recall depends on the use of particular retrieval strategies, and that people preserve much more high-school-classmate information than they can recover in any short interval of time. Bahrick (1984a) has also studied very long term memory for an academic subject: Spanish language instruction in high school or college. Retention curves for this material show a decline only over the first 4 years or so; there is no additional forgetting for 20 years or more thereafter. Squire and Slater (1975) found a similar leveling off of the retention curve in a study of recognition memory for the names of television programs from previous years. An initial decline of 2 or 3 years seems to be followed by a long period in which no more forgetting takes place. The theoretical interpretation of these findings is still in dispute (Neisser, in press), but there is no doubt of their importance.

The ecological study of memory is not restricted to the retention of well-learned material, or of people with whom one was well acquainted. There has also been a great deal of interest in the recall of individual moments of experience, especially moments that were particularly meaningful. Brown and Kulik (1977) asked adult subjects to recall how they first heard that President Kennedy had been assassinated, and several other investigators have pursued the same line of inquiry (Rubin & Kozin, 1984; Winograd & Killinger, 1983: Yarmey & Bull, 1978). People often preserve very vivid memories of these moments, though it is not easy to check their accuracy. The existence of such "flashbulb memories" raises interesting theoretical questions. Why are they so vivid? What conditions bring them into existence? Many investigators have explained them in terms of the force of the original experience. Brown and Kulik (1977), for example, postulate a special mechanism call "Now Print!" which creates indelible records of important or especially emotional moments. My own view (Neisser, 1982b) is quite different. I believe that the moment when one heard the news of Kennedy's assassination is recalled primarily because it has symbolic value. We describe such moments to other people, rehearse them often, and remember them well because they serve as benchmarks that allow us to align our own lives with the course of history. The accuracy of a "flashbulb" memory is almost irrelevant to its symbolic function. Indeed, other studies of apparently vivid memories—incidents from childhood, recall instigated under hypnosis, moments recalled during psychotherapy—have often found serious errors and confabulations; "flashbulb" memories may be equally vulnerable despite their seeming vividness.

Ecological considerations suggest that the very concepts of "accuracy" and "inaccuracy" may require re-examination. In traditional laboratory paradigms, memory is defined with reference to the material that was presented on a specific occasion. Subjects are shown lists of words, or asked to read brief stories; their subsequent recalls can then be checked for fidelity to the original. To be sure, this "fidelity" need not be literal. Modern studies of memory for stories often begin by analyzing the text in terms of an underlying "schema" or "script," which is then used to score recall of meaningful propositions rather than literal words (Bower, Black, & Turner, 1979; Mandler & Johnson, 1977). Although this use of story schemata is a significant improvement over more literal ways of scoring recall, I think it still fails to capture the significance of many memories.

It seems to me that we do not usually recollect events to reproduce their actual features or even their schematic characteristics, but as a way of capturing significant aspects of our lives. The most important things in life are enduring rather than momentary: people, relationships, commitments, enterprises. Those are the things that we constantly try to understand, and the main function of autobiographical memory may be to symbolize them. I suggest that we recall individual episodes of life primarily as a way of thinking about repeated patterns that are hard to grasp in any other way. This function does not require accuracy in the ordinary sense. It is possible for a given memory to represent a repeated series of events—or the underlying structure of that series—even if it is inaccurate about the particular episode being remembered. I call such memories "repisodic" (Neisser, 1981), because they represent a repeated series of episodes.

The symbolic function of memory is particularly obvious in psychotherapy. It was from Freud that psychology first learned not to take memories at face value, but to seek deeper reasons for their appearance and disappearance. Why does just this memory come up in just this context? Why was it recalled first from one point of view and later from another? Literature, too, has much to tell us about the role of symbols in the reconstruction of the past. Unfortunately for research, however, the materials of psychoanalysis and literature are rarely verifiable. It is hard to be sure of the real significance of a given memory when the original facts are no longer available. Psychoanalytic interpretations are notoriously underdetermined by the evidence, as are most other forms of retrospection. In one recent case, however, an unusual series of events made it possible to circumvent this difficulty. A witness who became famous for the accuracy of his recall testified at length about certain conversations; later, it turned out that those conversations had been secretly recorded. The witness was John Dean, and the conversations took place in the Oval Office of the White House. In an attempt to take advantage of this opportunity, I have analyzed his testimony rather closely (Neisser, 1981).

There can be no doubt that John Dean was basically right in what he told the Senate Watergate Committee. None of the many investigations and trials that grew out of Watergate have cast any substantial doubt on his testimony. The impression Dean made when he testified—that he had a good memory and was determined to tell the truth, even if only because truth-telling would best serve his own interests—was essentially correct. Nevertheless, careful comparison of Dean's testimony with the White House tapes shows that his account was often seriously in error, not only about literal wording of statements but about the kinds of things that were said and who said them. He was telling the truth, but it was not so much the truth about a single conversation as about the situation in the White House that it reflected. Dean's memory conveyed the essential character of that situation faithfully, even when it misrepresented the event being recalled. Such recollections are "repisodic": faithful to the *significance* of a series of episodes even while mistaken about their content.

The ecological approach to memory is still very young, at least as a theoretical enterprise. Its future is open. I do not know what form a satisfactory theory of autobiographical memory will finally take, for example, or whether my hypothesis about the symbolic function of memory will turn out to be right. Another point of uncertainty concerns the relation between this approach and more traditional studies of memory. Potter (1983) has argued that the study of memory in natural contexts requires little or no conceptual equipment that is not already available in the laboratory. In a similar vein, Bahrick (1984a,b) uses very traditional concepts from learning theory to interpret his findings concerning memory for school-learned Spanish. As I have suggested elsewhere (Neisser, 1985), these interpretations may be too hasty. The history of ecological analysis in perception and in the study of concepts suggests that a simple commitment to take the environment seriously often has radical consequences. The same thing may yet turn out to be true of the study of memory (see Note 3). The ecological approach is a genuinely *New Direction in Cognitive Science,* and one can never be sure where new directions will lead.

NOTES

1. A recent and more systematic ecological analysis of concepts and categories appears in Neisser (in press a).
2. A more detailed discussion of amodal information structures appears in Neisser (in press b).
3. A new theoretical approach to autobiographical memory, based on ecological considerations, appears in Neisser (in press c).

REFERENCES

Bahrick, H. P. (1984a). Semantic memory content in permastore: 50 years of memory for Spanish learned in school. *Journal of Experimental Psychology: General, 113,* 1–29.
Bahrick, H. P. (1984b). Associations and organization in cognitive psychology: A reply to Neisser. *Journal of Experimental Psychology: General, 113,* 36–37.
Bahrick, H. P., Bahrick, P. O., & Wittlinger, R. P. (1975). Fifty years of memory for names and faces: A cross-sectional approach. *Journal of Experimental Psychology: General, 104,* 54–75.
Barker, R. G. (1965). Explorations in ecological psychology. *American Psychologist, 20,* 1–14.
Barsalou, L. W. (1983). Ad hoc categories. *Memory and Cognition, 11,* 211–227.
Bower, G. H., Black, J. B., & Turner, T. J. (1979). Scripts in memory for text. *Cognitive Psychology, 11,* 177–220.
Broadbent, D. E. (1958). *Perception and communication.* London: Pergamon.
Bronfenbrenner, U. (1979). *The ecology of human development: Experiments by nature and design.* Cambridge, MA: Harvard University Press.
Brown, R., & Kulik, J. (1977). Flashbulb memories. *Cognition, 5,* 73–99.
Brunswik, E. (1956). *Perception and the representative design of psychological experiments.* Berkeley: University of California Press.
Chi, M. T. H., Feltovich, P. J., & Glaser, R. (1981). Categorization and representation of physics problems by experts and novices. *Cognitive Science, 5,* 121–152.

Clifford, B. R., & Bull, R. (1978). *The psychology of person identification.* London: Routledge & Kegan Paul.

Gibson, E. J. (1982). The concept of affordances in development: The renascence of functionalism. In W. A. Collins (Ed.), *The concept of developement (Minnesota Symposium on Child Psychology, Vol. 15).* Hillsdale, NJ: Erlbaum.

Gibson, E. J., & Spelke, E. (1983). The development of perception. In P. H. Mussen (Ed.), *Handbook of child psychology.* New York: Wiley.

Gibson, E. J., & Walker, A. S. (1984). Development of knowledge of visual-tactual affordances of substance. *Child Development, 55,* 453–460.

Gibson, J. J. (1966). *The senses considered as perceptual systems.* Boston: Houghton Mifflin.

Gibson, J. J. (1979). *The ecological approach to visual perception.* Boston: Houghton Mifflin.

Gibson, J. J., Kaplan, G. A., Reynolds, H. N., Jr., & Wheeler, K. (1969). The change from visible to invisible: A study of optical transitions. *Perception and Psychophysics, 5,* 113–116.

Heider, E. R. (1972). Universals in color naming and memory. *Journal of Experimental Psychology, 93,* 10–20.

Hull, C. L. (1943). *Principles of behavior.* New York: Appleton-Century-Crofts.

Keil, F. C., & Batterman, N. (1984). A characteristic-to-defining shift in the development of word meanings. *Journal of Verbal Learning and Verbal Behavior, 23,* 221–236.

Lee, D. N., & Aronson, E. (1974). Visual proprioceptive control of standing in human infants. *Perception and Psychophysics, 15,* 529–532.

Lee, D. N., & Thomson, J. A. (1982). Vision in action: The control of locomotion. In D. J. Ingle, M. A. Goodale, & R. J. W. Mansfield (Eds.), *Analysis of visual behavior.* Cambridge, MA: M.I.T. Press.

Lee, D. N., Lishman, J. R., & Thomson, J. A. (1982). Regulation of gait in long jumping. *Journal of Experimental Psychology: Human Perception and Performance, 8,* 448–459.

Loftus, E. F. (1979). *Eyewitness testimony.* Cambridge, MA: Harvard University Press.

Loftus, E. F. (1983). Silence is not golden. *American Psychologist, 38,* 564–572.

Lorenz, K. Z. (1981). *The foundations of ethology.* New York: Springer Verlag.

Mandler, J. M., & Johnson, N. S. (1977). Remembrance of things parsed: Story structure and recall. *Cognitive Psychology, 9,* 111–151.

McCloskey, M., & Egeth, H. E. (1983). Eyewitness identification: What can a psychologist tell a jury? *American Psychologist, 38,* 550–563.

Miller, G. A., Galanter, E., & Pribram, K. H. (1960). *Plans and the structure of behavior.* New York: Holt.

Munsterburg, H. (1909). *On the witness stand.* New York: Doubleday Page.

Neisser, U. (1967). *Cognitive psychology.* New York: Appleton-Century-Crofts.

Neisser, U. (1981). John Dean's memory: A case study. *Cognition, 9,* 1–22.

Neisser, U. (Ed.). (1982a). *Memory observed: Remembering in natural contexts.* San Francisco: Freeman.

Neisser, U. (1982b). Snapshots or benchmarks? In U. Neisser (Ed.), *Memory observed: Remembering in natural contexts.* San Francisco: Freeman.

Neisser, U. (1984). Interpreting Harry Bahrick's discovery: What confers immunity against forgetting? *Journal of Experimental Psychology: General, 113,* 32–35.

Neisser, U. (1985). The role of theory in the ecological study of memory. *Journal of Experimental Psychology: General, 114,* 272–276.

Neisser, U. (in press a). From direct perception to conceptual structure. In U. Neisser (Ed.), *Concepts reconsidered: The ecological and intellectual bases of categorization.* New York: Cambridge University Press.

Neisser, U. (in press b). The role of invariant structures in the control of movement. In M. Frese & J. Sabini (Eds.), *Goal-directed behavior: The concept of action in psychology.* Hillsdale, NJ: Erlbaum.

Neisser, U. (in press c). Nested structure in autobiographical memory. In D. Rubin (Ed.), *Autobiographical memory.* New York: Cambridge University Press.

Potter, M. C. (1983). Neisser's challenge (Review of "Memory Observed"). *Contemporary Psychology, 28,* 272–274.

Resnick, L. B. (1983). Mathematics and science learning: A new conception. *Science, 220,* 477–480.

Rosch, E. H. (1973). Natural categories. *Cognitive Psychology, 4,* 328–350.

Rosch, E. (1975a). The nature of mental codes for color categories. *Journal of Experimental Psychology: Human Perception and Performance, 1,* 303–322.

Rosch, E. (1975b). Cognitive representations of semantic categories. *Journal of Experimental Psychology: General, 104,* 192–233.

Rosch, E., Mervis, C. B., Gray, W. D., Johnson, D. M., & Boyes-Braem, P. (1976). Basic objects in natural categories. *Cognitive Psychology, 8,* 382–439.

Rubin, D. C., & Kozin, M. (1984). Vivid memories. *Cognition, 16,* 81–95.

Skinner, B. F. (1938). *The behavior of organisms: An experimental analysis.* New York: Appleton-Century-Crofts.

Spelke, E. (1976). Infants' intermodal perception of events. *Cognitive Psychology, 8,* 553–560.

Sperling, G. (1960). The information available in brief visual presentations. *Psychological Monographs, 74,* No. 11.

Squire, L. R., & Slater, P. C. (1975). Forgetting in very long-term memory as assessed by an improved questionnaire technique. *Journal of Experimental Psychology: Human Learning and Memory, 104,* 50–54.

Williams, M. D., & Hollan, J. D. (1981). The process of retrieval from very long-term memory. *Cognitive Science, 5,* 87–119.

Winograd, E., & Killinger, W. A., Jr. (1983). Relating age at encoding in early childhood to adult recall: Development of flashbulb memories. *Journal of Experimental Psychology: General, 112,* 413–422.

Yarmey, A. D., & Bull, M. P. (1978). Where were you when President Kennedy was assassinated? *Bulletin of the Psychonomic Society, 11,* 133–135.

Chapter 3

Psychobiological and Cognitive Studies Relevant to the Issue of a Unitary Memory System*

Norman E. Spear

State University of New York at Binghamton

I mentioned to a colleague that my discussion of biological aspects of cognitive functioning is somewhat ironic because I know so little about either biology or cognition. He said that was an advantage, because I could then be completely unbiased. I took that as only a little insulting and a reasonably funny remark. But the term "unbiased" did seem appropriate. Why? I think it is because we frequently think of biological and cognitive approaches to psychology as in conflict, or at least not mutually helpful. I will try to illustrate that, for some questions about behavior, these two extremes of experimental psychology have in fact interacted in important ways.

What do I mean by important? I think any development that causes scientists to question established working assumptions, or more, to change those assumptions, is important.

I begin with an example involving a mild interaction between biology and cognition. This example is concerned with effects of alcohol on human memory. Next, I discuss two other topics that have benefited from interaction between the research areas of biology and cognition—the ontogeny of learning and memory, and memory in brain-damaged persons. An underlying theme is that this interaction may lead us to conceptualize the "memory system" as in fact partitioned into relatively independent subsystems.

As a process, "memory" has been viewed commonly as a unitary entity, especially with reference to clinical practice in medicine or psychology, but also in the research discipline labeled "neuroscience." It is common in the latter to refer to neural structures such as the hippocampus as central to memory, or to a

*This research was supported by grants from the National Institute of Mental Health (1 R01 MH35219) to N. E. Spear, and the National Institute of Alcohol Abuse and Alcoholism (NIAAA 5-RO1-AA03141) to S. A. Lisman and N. E. Spear. I am grateful for the secretarial assistance of Teri Tanenhaus and the technical expertise of Norman Richter.

special set of neurotransmitters such as the cholinergic system as critical to memory. Only one "memory" is assumed. The implicit notion is that, regardless of what is to be remembered, or when, where, or how it was learned, the maintenance and expression of acquired knowledge is controlled by a common memory process that is more or less singular.

The notion is not unique to biologically oriented psychology. It is implicit in much of the thinking and the empirical products in psychology, whatever the philosophical basis of the work. Even while cautiously limiting the extent of generalizability about memory from a single set of experiments, psychologists rarely suggest that what they have discovered empirically applies only to memory for locations when the rat is foraging for food, or only to memories of a tone that predicts pain when the rat is afraid, or only to memories for verbal expressions when a human has one of his or her few experiences in a laboratory. Perhaps because so many of our memories seem (probably mistakenly) to be funneled through a common linguistic process, we have been biased toward an analogous view for other animals, too: the view of a common memory process through which the residue of all experience passes, whether a particular experience involves acquiring food, escaping danger, or reproduction, and whether it occurs in early infancy or adulthood.

The idea that all information we take in is processed for remembering by a common system has been a frequent assumption by most psychologists. This is a parsimonious view; and it is a very old one, seen in the notions of the Greeks, even before Plato. In the sixth century B.C., Parmenides guessed that memory required a special relationship among four elements of the body, Light, Heat, Dark, and Cold. And memory was memory; there was only one system. There are, of course, many other examples of such unitary systems, including most or all metaphoric "models" of memory (Roediger, 1980).

There have also been important exceptions to the view of memory as a unitary system. Some versions of the distinction between "short-term memory" and "long-term memory" have been sufficiently extreme as to actually suggest the operation of two different, quite separate processes. This distinction did not remain viable for long, and is no longer useful. But there are differences in memory processes other than temporal.

My intentions are not to provide a full picture of what it means for a memory system to be unitary or not. This would require a great deal of space, as well as speculation that would be dull. I hope only to have provided the gist of the concept. I now try to illustrate that relatively broad consideration of psychobiological and cognitive studies can provide a useful combination for deciding about the unitary nature of memory.

IMPLICATIONS OF THE EFFECT OF ALCOHOL ON MEMORY

Alcohol is a drug that affects cognition. Most of us know this from personal experience. Alcohol is not a particularly analytical tool for understanding the relationship between brain and cognition, because its biochemical effects on the brain and elsewhere are so diffuse. Tests with this drug do provide, however, a convenient place to start studying extreme deficits in memory among the general population. In addition, the work has some practical implications.

Steve Lisman, Christian Mueller, and I were especially interested in alcohol as a means for studying state-dependent retention in humans. While it would seem simple enough to have a subject drink and study, then drink and take a test, the fact is that the control and protection procedures—e.g., the need to entertain subjects until they sober up—requires a good deal of time and effort. This makes progress slow and also augurs for limited empirical aspirations, focusing on basic phenomena.

After these several years' work on this project, we have become convinced of two general facts. First, and of no particular importance to the rest of this chapter, state-dependent retention in humans is a less robust phenomenon than we had expected. The second, and more pertinent, fact for this chapter is that alcohol has seemed inevitably to disrupt learning and its expression, and with surprising, almost boring, uniformity. I am thinking now of when blood alcohols are about .08 or .10% (.10% or above typically defines intoxication if driving; to give you an idea of the alcohol dose, it's a very large martini for a 150-pound person). At this level, learning always seems to be impaired significantly, whatever the response measure and whatever the nature of the processing required by the subject. The generality of this effect is illustrated by the following examples from our experiments.

(1) When persons are given a list of words to remember, it is well known that the more "semantic" the processing of an item, the better it will be recalled. Subjects asked to use a word in a sentence remember it better than if asked instead whether it rhymes with another word, or if it is presented in capital or lower case letters (e.g., Craik & Tulving, 1975). It has been suspected that semantic processing in particular is less likely to occur spontaneously when intoxicated. If so, intoxicated subjects induced to encode words semantically might learn and remember as well as sober subjects, or at least show less of a deficit. We conducted two extensive studies to test this idea and found that, uniformly, among a wide variety of conditions, the alcohol deficit was stable regardless of the type of encoding engaged in by the subject (Mueller, Lisman, & Spear, 1982; two similar studies from other laboratories have verified this).

(2) We conducted a second set of experiments within this same rationale, but focusing on processing after, rather than during, presentation of words to be remembered. The hypothesis was that persons intoxicated with alcohol would be deficient in rehearsing in a conducive, semantic fashion. We conducted four substantial experiments to determine whether the alcohol deficit could be reduced when intoxicated subjects are made to rehearse in an explicitly semantic manner. In other words, we instructed them to rehearse semantically; in one sense we forced them to do so in order to answer the orienting questions we

asked about each item (e.g., "Use _____ in a sentence"). While these experiments yielded interesting results in some ways, the memory deficit among the subjects given alcohol was remarkably constant throughout, regardless of how they rehearsed (Mueller, Lisman, & Spear, 1981).

(3,4,5) Three cases can be mentioned without explaining the hypotheses for the studies. These, too, reflect relative invariance in the alcohol deficit. (3) When subjects who have studied a set of words are given part of that set to cue recall of the remainder—"part-set cueing"—net recall is impaired whether intoxicated or not, and impairment by intoxication is the same, with as without cueing. (4) Subjects tested for recall ordinarily show a consequential increment in their subsequent recall—"learning on test trials." In comparison to sober subjects, learning on test trials is impaired among intoxicated subjects to the same degree as occurs for learning on regular study trials. (5) In spite of the variety of functional differences in memory assessed by recall compared with recognition, we have found that the alcohol deficit in terms of recognition memory has a magnitude roughly comparable to that when recall is measured.

(6) Finally, although studied less thoroughly than the previous factors, our data suggest that neither amount of retroactive interference, presence of proactive interference, nor the forgetting that occurs during a retention interval have any special relationship with alcohol intoxication. The alcohol-induced deficit in memory occurs to about the same extent regardless of retroactive interference, proactive interference, or retention interval.

I don't mean to imply that we have found no new interesting positive effects of alcohol (cf. Mueller, Lisman, & Spear, 1983). Rather, I mean to emphasize that the alcohol-induced deficit in memory has been quite ubiquitous in our experiments, regardless of the nature of the cognitions we have tried to impose on our subjects.

One possible explanation is that alcohol somehow "dampens" a unitary memory system. This idea is reasonable. To explain a general dampening or deficiency in such a system might require only something like a deficit in the production or turnover of one or more neurotransmitters or a general reduction in rate of protein synthesis. I am not suggesting that these factors have been found to clearly yield general effects on memory—they have not—but only that this is the form such an explanation might take, if we are in fact dealing with a memory system that is unitary.

PSYCHOBIOLOGICAL EVIDENCE INCONSISTENT WITH A UNITARY MEMORY SYSTEM

I turn now to two general phenomena that have often been taken as indicating a pervasive deficit in a memory system that acts in a unitary fashion on all information processed by an organism. I will suggest that these phenomena now illustrate, instead, that there may be no unitary memory or learning system, or, perhaps more accurately, that this is not the best way to think of it. Perhaps more significant for this book, the evidence providing the illustration is psychobiological in nature, involving analysis of behavior in conjunction with organismic variables to help us understand cognitive effects, and vice versa. By adding the "vice versa," I am suggesting a genuine interaction between these areas, that understanding the cognitive effects is also helping us understand the functions of their neurophysiological substrates.

The first phenomenon I want to mention is the poorer learning and remembering by infant animals or people than by adults. The second is the "global amnesia" observed in humans with certain types of brain damage or in the advanced stages of the Korsakoff Syndrome.

Ontogenetic Differences in Learning and Memory

A good deal of the work in our animal laboratory has been directed toward understanding infantile amnesia. I have a longstanding interest in why adult humans remember little or nothing of their activities before the age of about 3 years (Campbell & Spear, 1972). Nearly all experimental work on this problem has been done, by necessity, with animal models, usually the rat. But I want to focus more on the learning of the developing rat and human than on their forgetting. I view this as a topic of relevence for cognition.

To review briefly, the rat is an altricial animal with a central nervous system and corresponding behaviors that are strikingly immature at birth, very much like the human. Until the past 6 or 8 years, there was little indication that the neonatal rat is capable of learning or remembering, not until after the first week of life, about 8–9 days of age. It was as if learning is unimportant to the infant rat during its first postnatal week.

Two developments led to a change in this view. One was theoretical, influenced by a biological orientation inspired by Peter Anohkin (e.g., 1964) of the Soviet Union. For Anohkin and his followers, the major unit for developmental psychobiological analysis is the "functional system," by which is meant a functional combination of different organizations and processes on the basis of the achievement of the final effect. The best examples of such systems are alternative types of feeding or sexual behavior, systems that most obviously emerge in mature fashion at different ages. The important point is that when a functional system becomes effective will depend on its adaptive value at that particular age. This begins to make some contact with Professor Neisser's (this volume) astute observations on the value of ecological considerations for understanding some laboratory phenomena of learning and forgetting.

American psychologists supplemented the approach of Anohkin with careful observations, experimental and otherwise, of how the developing animal responds to its particular biological challenges. This permitted tests that carefully accommodate the organism's age, specific ecological niche, and age-related stimulus and response dispositions. Recent methods for analyzing the associative processes of the physiologically immature rat have taken into account that, during the first few weeks of life, the rat is dominated by tastes and odors, temperature differences, and low frequency sounds, with head movement and crawling its only notable instrumental behaviors. Thereafter, visual stimuli and noises or different frequencies than before appear to gain in importance, increased mobility requires new mechanisms for the pup's safe return to the nest, and items of a familiar taste but somewhat new texture begin to be consumed.

Within this ecological orientation, the results of many laboratories began to suggest that, perhaps especially during the infancy of rats, different sets of event contingencies are not remembered and learned with uniform effectiveness. Certain tasks readily acquired by adults lead to less learning or none at all in infants, while with other tasks, learning seems equally effective for infants and older animals. This might be to some extent a matter of task complexity or of differences in the number or type of elements to be processed for learning; this has not yet been fully determined. Or perhaps the particular kind or combination of events to be learned is critical. But along with identification of these limitations has come the realization that we have severely underestimated the associative capacity of developing animals, and humans too, from birth to adolescence.

In the last few years, it has been shown that rats 3 or 4 days of age can acquire an aversion to an odor paired either with an illness or a cold temperature; the aversion can be expressed either in the rat's decreased preference for that odor or in terms of the animal's heart rate when exposed to it. It has been reported that rats only a week old can learn a spatial discrimination about as rapidly as adult rats, if their reward is a reunion with mother. Rats several days younger than 1 week can show higher order conditioning, and rats only slightly older can learn and remember an active avoidance response. These examples all deal with an age range where it had previously seemed there was little associative capacity, and none for instrumental learning. Yet it has since been shown that, when rats are only 36 hours old, they can learn to discriminate between two miniature switches in order to receive milk, and learn also to move the correct switch but not the incorrect one; and even earlier, prenatally in fact, an aversion to a particular flavor/odor may be conditioned by injecting it into the amniotic fluid surrounding pups, followed by a second injection to make them ill. Further evidence suggests that the newborn rat uses its capacity for classical or instrumental learning for such challenges as finding a nipple for its first postnatal meal a few minutes after birth (for review and elaboration of these developments, see Spear & Campbell, 1979; Kail & Spear, 1984).

It is relatively uninteresting to observe that the reason previous experiments failed to see learning during the first week of life was because they used the wrong techniques. These discoveries tell us more than that. The more interesting message for present purposes is this: early associative capacity seems not to be evident for all kinds of events at a particular age. Apparently, the capacity to learn and remember depends on what is to be learned and remembered. And this is not just because of simple sensory or perceptual deficiencies. For instance, there is no doubt that infant rats can detect a footshock during the first week of life. They are in fact somewhat more sensitive to it than are older rats. Yet, during this period, infants have great difficulty learning an aversion to an odor that is paired with a footshock, even though under the same circumstance an aversion to that odor is readily conditioned if paired instead with an illness or with a shock in the vicinity of the stomach and gut. Also, such infants can acquire a preference for that odor if it is paired with an injection of milk. As another example, 7-day-old rats that cannot learn a position discrimination to escape a footshock, can do so if reward is access to an adult rat.

The point is that infants are not simply deficient in terms of a unitary memory capacity. We have found still other evidence to verify this point. For instance, tests of infant learning and remembering with animals have conventionally exposed the infant to a special kind of context characterized by isolation from its home and siblings. The infant is removed from its home, and then, in a strange, often cold and uncomfortable place, is presented the episode to be learned and later remembered—hardly, in Professor Neisser's terms, "ecologically representative." A conventional experimental apparatus and procedure is no doubt a strikingly unique experience for any rat, but we know that, in addition, the mere act of removing an infant from its home and mother can have profound psychological and physiological consequences that alter the infant's internal context. Let me give you a quick example: if a 15-day-old rat is isolated from its parents and siblings, within a minute or so general activity triples, the number of vocalizations increase more than fivefold over 5 minutes, and over the same 5-minute period heart rate increases 25% or so, from about 400 beats per minute to nearly 500. If it remains in isolation, the nature of the syndrome changes somewhat. After a while, for instance, its heart rate begins to drop and the posture of the infant makes it look as though it were depressed, and throughout there occurs a regular sequence of neurophysiological and behavioral events much more complex and interesting than can be described in a few lines (see Hofer, 1981, for further information).

The question I am leading up to is this: How does the infant's learning and memory differ for episodes presented when it is or "feels" at home, in comparison to when it is isolated? We thought they might learn different things in these two circumstances. Some strikingly good learning reported for infant rats had suggested that they might also learn more at home, or in the presence of home-like things, than elsewhere (see Spear & Campbell, 1979, for a review).

We have found that infants trained and tested in the context of odors from their home nest seem more mature than otherwise for some learning tasks. In this sort of environment, for example, 16-day-old rats behave as though they were several days older in their learning of an aversion to a particular location, or in learning to withhold a punished response. I might note that analogous effects have begun to appear for human infants tested in the home rather than the laboratory (e.g., Acredolo, 1979). There seem, however, to be some things that the infant learns more slowly in the home than when isolated from it, such as a conditioned aversion to a flavor that is paired with an illness. It has been hard to compare these contrasting effects, because the conditions surrounding them are so different. But recently, with more comparable conditions, Dave Kucharski and Tim Wigal in our lab found that, in comparison with isolated animals, preweanlings in the home learned more about the relationship between two flavors and less about the relationship between the flavors and an illness.

In further contrast to the notion of a generally "deficient memory" among young organisms, we have found that the infant sometimes learns more than the adult about redundant aspects of a particular task. More precisely, animals appear to be less selective than adults about what they learn. We have been surprised to find that, even when processing multiple elements of compound stimuli, infant rats can be almost as effective in learning as adults, and could be said to be more effective in the sense of using more of the information that is available. We have found that, relative to adults, for instance, preweanlings show more potentiation in classical conditioning of one element when it is given in the presence of another element to form a stimulus compound (Spear & Kucharski, 1984).

To summarize so far, recent progress in ontogenetic research on learning and memory has required a rejection of the view that the infant rat learns and remembers less well than the adult because it has a fundamentally deficient memory capacity. I can amplify this briefly with an example of a study with infant humans that has begun to parallel our experiences with the infant rat. During the early portion of the 20th century, it was concluded by some psychologists that the human infant has little or no capacity for learning or memory before the age of 6 months. Even within the past 5 years, theories in this area have been built with the assumption that a human's capacity for remembering is limited to a few minutes or at most a few hours,   until the age of 6–8 months (Kagan, Kearsley, & Zelazo, 1978). It is now clear, however, that the newborn infant can show substantial learning, and, by 2–3 months of age , can show a reliable capacity for remembering after much longer intervals than previously supposed.

Much of this information, especially with the long-term retention, is the consequence of research by Professor Carolyn Rovee-Collier of Rutgers. For this project, an ingeniously simple instrumental learning task has been used. From a mobile suspended above a 3-month-old infant, a ribbon is tied to the ankle. The infant is now in a position to experience "conjugate reinforcement," which means that, the harder the infant kicks, the more the mobile moves; infants apparently like to see the mobiles move and will work to achieve it. Rovee-Collier and her colleagues have shown that this task has many of the fundamental characteristics of instrumental learning in general, as we have known it. But, more pertinent here, she has also found that, in studies modeled after work on the alleviation of forgetting in infant rats, 3-month-old humans can show substantial remembering as long as a month after instrumental learning, if a reactivation ("reminder") treatment precedes the retention test (Rovee-Collier, Sullivan, Enright, Lucas, & Fagan, 1980). It is problematic whether learning for all types of events is subject to such good retention at this age.

Equally important for the interaction between biological and cognitive approaches is other evidence of similar ontogenetic effects in memory among young animals and children. An example is the apparent development of selective learning in rats that is paralleled by analogous effects with children. For instance, the tendency for preschool children to treat compound stimuli as integrals, while older children treat them as separable compounds, seems to have appeared by analogy in our experiments with the developing rat (Spear, 1984).

Collectively, the evidence above illustrates how joint consideration of biological and cognitive factors has required rejection of a view that the relatively poor learning and retention of the immature rat is due to a fundamentally deficient capacity in its global, unitary memory system. This questions the latter concept of how memory works.

Global Amnesia

Persons classified as "global amnesics" were once characterized as having complete absence of permanent memory for any new information. We now know that this characterization is wrong. I refer here to individuals with relatively discrete lesions in the temporal area of the brain, persons in the advanced stages of the Korsakoff Syndrome (where the lesions are fairly well known but not usually as discrete) and to some cases of Alzheimer's Disease (where the neural etiology is even more diffuse). The most analyzable of these are cases in which the memory deficit is accompanied by neither substantial perceptual difficulties nor decrease in general IQ.

The point I want to emphasize is that such amnesics have been found to have quite significant retention for some aspects of an episode, but they also deny verbally that they remember anything about it. This dissociation is illustrated by the following examples: (a) Weiskrantz and Warrington (1979) conducted a systematic study of eyelid conditioning with amnesic patients. These patients exhibited substantial conditioning and good remembering of the conditioned eyeblink 24 hours later, but, when questioned about it, they not only denied that any learning had occurred, they also gave no indication of remembering anything about the rather obtuse apparatus that had been used to deliver airpuffs to their eye. The amnesics said they did not remember having been exposed to such a machine. (b) Among the amnesics tested over the years have been two musicians who remained capable performers. They even were able to learn new tunes, but, afterward, they would give no indication that they had learned a new tune nor that they had performed at all. (c) Finally, the well-studied amnesic, H. M., who had bilateral temporal lesions surgically induced to control epileptic seizures when in his mid-twenties, frequently displayed this lack of memory. Although he has been able to learn and remember several things—visual form discrimination remembered after several minutes, reverse-mirror drawings after a period of 24 hours, a tactual maze over a period of 2 years, and a task with a substantial component of perceptual learning (Gollin figures) over a period of 13 years—he has in each case stated that he could not recall ever having participated in any such tasks before.

In all, the list of tasks for which amnesics show effective memory includes the pursuit rotar, mirror drawing, memory for simple paired associates, the identification of Gollin figures (figures that look like they had been drawn with pencil and then partially erased), words treated the same way as Gollin figures, classical eyelid conditioning, rapid reassembly of jigsaw puzzles, the solution of previously solved, jumbled sentences, reading inverted print, the McGill picture tests, solution to a small tactual maze, and re-application of a mathematical rule previously learned and applied. The important point is that in none of these cases did any of the amnesics give any indication they were aware that they had remembered, or could remember, this learning (for further review, see Moskovitch, 1982; Schacter & Tulving, 1982; Spear & Isaacson, 1982).

It is pertinent that an analogous dissociation in what is remembered can be seen in a variety of cases not involving brain damage. This had led to a synergistic effect on research in this area. The dramatic effects seen in brain-damaged persons have stimulated more investigation of the similar effects in normals, and vice versa (cf. Jacoby & Witherspoon, 1982). One common example of such effects with normals is "source amnesia"—when persons placed under hypnosis, given new information and later asked questions about this information, reply as if they have learned it but claim that they have no idea *where* they learned it (Hilgard, 1977).

More generally, it is hardly news to experimental psychologists that what the experimenter chooses to measure might not be the "best" index of learning. It is similarly no surprise to these scientists that persons dissociate verbal and nonverbal behavior—say one thing and do another. Their research frequently has established that humans can learn a general rule for solving anagrams without being able to verbalize the rule, can have their verbal behavior conditioned by subtle remarks such as "good" and yet be unable to say why their verbal behavior changed, and can employ verbal mediators as aids in learning without being able to verbalize any particular mediators they used.

It is significant that the extreme cases of dissociation seem more than merely a matter of sensitivity of measurement or a difference in the efficacy of verbal and nonverbal learning. The phenomenon is more general than that. For instance, unilateral circumscribed damage to the occipital region of the brain can be associated with a similar affliction in spite of no real memory load. Weiskrantz has termed one such effect "blindsight." For certain patients who claim they cannot see, Weiskrantz holds a stick up at varying heights above the ground and says, "If you *could* see, where would the stick be?"—the patients point to the stick. The scope of these phenomena of dissociation in amnesics can be seen also in a distinction that Squire and his colleagues have termed "procedural" vs. "declarative" forms of remembering (Squire & Cohen, 1982). Several years ago, Kolers (1976) asked whether humans who had learned to read inverted print would differ in how well they remembered the content of the print relative to the general skill of reading inverted print. He found that the latter, more general skill was remembered relatively well a year later. Cohen and Squire (1980) applied this sort of test to compare the learning and forgetting of patients suffering amnesia from one of three sources: a discrete lesion of the diencephalon from a fencing accident, Korsakoff Syndrome, or a recent series of electroconvulsive shocks. They found that, whereas these amnesics could learn to read inverted print quite well and could remember this skill ("procedures") about as well as normals, they forgot much more of the content, the "declarative form" of information.

It has been known for some time within the study of human memory that there can be a striking dissociation in what is remembered about a multi-event episode. An example common to our personal experience is the "selector mechanism." All of us who claim to be normal can remember very much more accurately what was *not* on a list to be learned than what was actually on it. An example I particularly like is an experiment with paired-associate learning by Underwood (1966), in which the subjects made 1424 errors, only one of which was a word that did not appear somewhere on the list; someone said "yellow" when the correct response was CANARY.

A related case of normal dissociation in memory is in, it seems to me, the distinction between controlled and automatic processing. I am thinking in particular of the striking data of Hasher (1981) illustrating the dissociation between recall of words and judgments regarding how frequently the words were presented for study. Specifically, for a variety of variables, there is a substantial effect on recall: (a) Between the ages of 5 and 80, from preschool children to the elderly, recall first increases then decreases; (b) There is poorer recall by depressed college students than by nondepressed; (c) Persons not informed or misinformed about the presence of a subsequent recall test show poorer recall than those who are fully informed about it; (d) College students with relatively low scores on the SAT exams recall less effectively than those with higher scores; and (e) Recall of lists of words improves regularly the more the recall of such lists is practiced. None of these results is especially surprising. The striking result is this: In all of these experiments, which involved multiple presentations of the words to be remembered, other subjects were asked how frequently each word had appeared in the list; none of the above variables made a difference in how accurately the frequencies were estimated.

Finally, Jacoby and Witherspoon (1982) recently conducted experiments that illustrate nicely how innovative assessment of cognition can help us understand the nature of memory dysfunction. I find these experiments particularly interesting because the dissociation in memory they illustrate for Korsakoff patients is between recognition of previously studied lexical material and semantic aspects of that material, but in an unexpected direction. You may recall that one explanation of Korsakoff amnesia emphasizes these patients' semantic deficiencies (Cermak, 1982). Jacoby found, however, that, after hearing some sentences, the amnesics' behavior indicated memory for the semantic but not the lexical aspects (nor did they remember that any sentences had been presented at all).

The way Jacoby and Witherspoon did this is so clever as to warrant brief explanation. The general strategy was to test memory, not by asking "Tell me all you remember," but by asking how what they had learned affects contemporary behavior—a sort of transfer test, which in this case involved the biasing of a homophone. They presented Korsakoff patients and normal controls with a set of questions intended to bias the meaning of a homophone toward that of its less frequent usage. An example: If the Korsakoff patient was asked to "name a musical instrument that employs a reed," the critical word was the homophone "reed" (read). The issue was whether amnesics exposed to such questions would later tend to spell the homophone in accord with the biased meaning presented in the questions (e.g., reed) rather than the more common meaning ("read"). If the former, memory would be indicated. Of course, Jacoby and Witherspoon also included a variety of control items. On later tests for recognition of the words previously presented, the amnesics were only about one-third as accurate as the normals; they were, however, equally or more likely than normals to spell the homophone in accord with the meaning that was biased by the previous materials. At the same time, the amnesics spelled *other* homophones normally, in accord with their most frequent meaning (exactly as did the normals). In this test, false recognitions were low and equal for Korsakoff and normals. And of special significance, Jacoby and Witherspoon's data indicated that this dissociation is not simply a matter of different thresholds for different memories, because performance on each test was independent. Recognition memory was not a prerequisite for the effect on semantic interpretations, and vice-versa.

SUMMARY

What I have been trying to illustrate are instances in which an aspect of a stored memory seems dissociated from that of another aspect. The expression of knowledge of a particular episode in memory is not all-or-none. Extreme cases of memory dysfunction are in fact characterized by a sparing of certain "kinds" of memories despite the apparently complete obliteration of others. Persons classified clinically as amnesic can show astute memory for mental operations they have learned, but indicate little or none for the information they operated on. The same persons may have their perception altered by an experience, but report no memory for that experience. This pattern suggests that truly global impairment of a general memory capacity is unlkely. From research on the ontogeny of learning and memory in animals or children, we have learned that, once "communication" is established in terms consistent with the special dispositions of infancy, the apparently general deficit in memory disappears—newborn rats learn and remember well an odor that makes them ill or leads ot food, and 3-month-old children remember an instrumental behavior a month after learning it. These characteristics of amnesia and memory development argue against a unitary memory system. Yet, these indications of separable capacities for memory of certain things or in certain circumstances are unlike those seen in studying how alcohol affects memory. The memory impairment observed with even light-to-moderate doses of alcohol is so ubiquitous as to suggest that some singular memory process might actually be affected. More generally, these areas of research demonstrate a few cases in which a profitable interaction has taken place between biological and cognitive approaches for understanding a basic issue of memory.

REFERENCES

Acredolo, L. P. (1979). Laboratory vs. home: The effect of environment on the 9-month old infant's choice of spatial reference system. *Developmental Psychology, 15,* 666–667.

Anohkin, P. K. (1964). Systemogensis as a general regulator of brain development. In W. A. Himwich & H. E. Himwich (Eds.), *The developing brain: Progress in brain research* (pp. 54–86). Amsterdam: Elsevier Publishing Co.

Campbell, B. A., & Spear, N. E. (1972). Ontogeny of memory. *Psychological Review, 79,* 215–236.

Cermak, L. S. (1982). *Human memory and amnesia.* Hillsdale, NJ: Lawrence Erlbaum Associates.

Cohen, N. J., & Squire, L. R. (1980). Preserved learning and retention of pattern-analyzing skill in amnesia: Dissociation of knowing how and knowing that. *Science, 210,* 207–210.

Craik, F. I. M., & Tulving, E. (1975). Depth of processing in the retention of words in episodic memory. *Journal of Experimental Psychology: General, 104,* 268–294.

Hasher, L. A. (1981, November). *The automatic encoding of information into memory.* Invited address at meetings of the Eastern Psychological Association, New York.

Hilgard, E. R. (1977). *Divided consciousness: Multiple controls in human thought and action.* New York: Wiley.

Hofer, M. A. (1981). Toward a developmental basis for disease predisposition: The effects of early maternal separation on brain, behavior, and cardiovascular system. In H. Weiner, M. A. Hofer, & A. J. Stunkard (Eds.), *Brain, behavior and bodily disease* (pp. 209–228). New York: Raven Press.

Jacoby, L. L. (1982). Knowing and remembering: Some parallels in the behavior of Korsakoff patients and normals. In L. S. Cermak (Ed.), *Human memory and amnesia* (pp. 97–122). Hillsdale, NJ: Erlbaum.

Jacoby, L. L., & Witherspoon, D. (1982). Remembering without awareness. *Canadian Journal of Psychology, 36,* 300–324.

Kagan, J., Kearsley, R. B., & Zelazo, R. R. (1978). *Infancy: Its place in human development,* Cambridge, MA: Harvard University Press.

Kail, R., & Spear, N. E. (Eds.). (1984). *Memory development: Comparative perspectives.* Hillsdale, NJ: Erlbaum.

Kolers, P. A. (1976). Reading a year later. *Journal of Experimental Psychology Human Learning & Memory, 2,* 554–565.

Moscovitch, M. (1982). Multiple dissociations of function in amnesia. In L. S. Cermak (Ed.), *Human memory and amnesia.* (pp. 337–370). Hillsdale, NJ: Erlbaum.

Mueller, C. W., Lisman, S. A., & Spear, N. E. (1981, November). *Alcohol, rehearsal and decrements in recognition memory.* Paper presented at meetings of The Psychonomic Society, Philadelphia.

Mueller, C. S., Lisman, S. A., & Spear, N. E. (1982, April). *Additional evidence that alcohol increases confusion among memories.* Paper presented at meetings of Western Psychological Association, Sacramento, CA.

Mueller, C. W., Lisman, S. A., & Spear, N. E. (1983). Alcohol enhancement of human memory: Tests of consolidation and interference hypotheses. *Psychopharmacology, 80,* 226–230.

Roediger, H. L. (1980). Memory metaphors in cognitive psychology. *Memory & Cognition, 80,* 231–246.

Rovee-Collier, C. K., Sullivan, M. W., Enright, M. K., Lucas, D., & Fagan, J. (1980). Reactivation of infant memory. *Science, 208,* 1159–1161.

Schacter, D. L., & Tulving, E. (1982). Memory, amnesia and the episodic/semantic distinction. In R. L. Isaacson & N. E. Spear (Eds.), *The expression of knowledge: Neurobehavioral transformations of information into action* (pp. 33–66). New York: Plenum Press.

Spear, N. E. (1984). Ecologically determined dispositions control the ontogeny of learning and memory. In R. Kail & N. E. Spear (Eds.), *Comparative Perspectives on the Development of Memory.* Hillsdale, NJ: Erlbaum.

Spear, N. E., & Campbell, B. A. (Eds.). (1979). *Ontogeny of learning and memory.* Hillsdale, NJ: Erlbaum.

Spear, N. E., & Isaacson, R. L. (1982). The problem of expression. In R. L. Isaacson & N. E. Spear (Eds.), *The expression of knowledge: Neurobehavioral transformations of information into action* (pp. 1–32). New York: Plenum Press.

Spear, N. E., & Kucharski, D. (1984). Ontogentic differences in the processing of multielement stimuli: Potentiation and overshadowing. In H. Roitblat, T. Bever, & H. Terrace (Eds.). *Animal Cognition* (pp. 545–568). Hillsdale, NJ: Erlbaum.

Squire, L. R., & Cohen, N. J. (1982). Remote memory, retrograde amnesia, and the neuropsychology of memory. In L. Cermak (Ed.), *Memory and amnesia* (pp. 275–304). Hillsdale, NJ: Erlbaum.

Underwood, B. J. (1966). Motor skills learning and verbal learning: Some observations. In E. A. Bilodeau (Ed.), *Aquisition of skill* (pp. 489–516). New York: Academic Press.

Weiskrantz, L., & Warrington, E. K. (1979). Conditioning in amnesic patients. *Neuropsychologia, 17,* 187–194.

Chapter 4

Planning-in-Action Across the Life Span*

Jerome S. Meyer

Craig Developmental Center
Geneseo, New York

George W. Rebok

State University of New York at Geneseo

The purpose of this chapter is threefold: (a) to examine various theoretical positions in the psychological study of the construct of planning, (b) to present a transactional opportunistic approach to planning-action sequences, and (c) to report data from a life-span study of planning and problem solving bearing on the proposed approach. In recent years, there has been a steadily growing interest in studying the topic of planning, "planning" being generally defined here as "the predetermination of a course of action aimed at achieving some goal" (Hayes-Roth & Hayes-Roth, 1979). One of the major reasons for this interest is the increased recognition of the importance of planning in everyday activities and problem-solving. Successful planning involves a wide variety of cognitive skills, including mentally representing future actions and their results, keeping track of goals and subgoals in memory, evaluating alternative solutions, and consciously monitoring planning processes.

Currently, the two most popular theoretical approaches to the investigation of planning are the information-processing and transactional perspectives. In information-processing, attention has been primarily focused on the examination of initial plan formulation and its effect on problem solving. The transactional approach draws heavily from the work of Piaget, Flavell, and the action theories of Soviet psychologists such as Vygotsky and Leont'ev; it is concerned with the changing relationships between plans and actions, and especially the effects of actions on subsequent planning.

INFORMATION-PROCESSING APPROACHES TO PLANNING

The study of planning from an information-processing perspective can be traced to Miller, Galanter, and Pribram's (1960) influential book *Plans and the Struc-*

* The authors wish to thank the administration, faculty, and students of the Avon and Cortland, New York, school systems, and the Mt. Morris Senior Citizens, for their gracious participation in this study. We also wish to thank Kristine Consiglio, Ted Brewer, and Angela Kessler for their assistance in the collection and transcription of data, and Pauline Johnson for typing the manuscript.

ture of Behavior. In their book, Miller et al. underscored the importance of plans as higher-order units for understanding all human behavior. Specifically, plans consist of a hierarchically organized sequence of goals and subgoals, and a set of behaviors (*operations*) for reaching them. In order to determine if a given behavior is relevant, the organism conducts a series of *tests,* which provide feedback for performing subsequent behaviors. This entire test-operate-test-exit, or TOTE, sequence is presumed to operate in a systematic "top-down" fashion, with high-level (more abstract) plans being *successively refined* at progressively lower levels of abstraction. In Miller et al.'s formulation, plans are not limited to overt behaviors, but can also be applied to the acquisition, storage, and processing of information.

In the 1960s and 1970s, Miller et al.'s successive refinement view of planning was incorporated into the problem-solving literature by a number of information-processing researchers, most notably Allen Newell and Herbert Simon (Newell & Simon, 1972). The concept of a planning hierarchy sorted well with emerging theoretical developments in the field of computer science, with plans being conceptualized as "structurally identical" to computer programs. Formally, plans were represented as "symbolic structures" that "guide action through a problem-solving space" (Newell & Simon, 1972, p. 822). According to Newell and Simon's model, the major feature of planning is to *simplify* the search for a problem solution. This planning-by-simplification process involves omitting the details of a problem, forming a more general, abstract problem, and using the solution to provide a plan for solving the original problem.

The computer analogy of planning has been pushed even further by researchers working in a subbranch of computer science called "artificial intelligence" (Sacerdoti, 1977; Stefik, 1981; Wilensky, 1981). For the most part, this work has dealt with simplified problem domains involving sequences of discrete physical actions such as arranging blocks on a table. Recently, however, computerized planning models have been extended into a variety of more complex, "real-life" problem domains, including processing language (Hobbs & Evans, 1980; Schank & Abelson, 1977), designing behavior genetics experiments (Stefik, 1981), and programming electronic circuitry (McDermott, 1977).

As planning models are developed and applied to increasingly more complex problems, earlier assumptions about planning as a strictly "top-down," hierarchical process have been gradually replaced by more dynamic conceptions. One such conception is the *opportunistic* model of planning proposed by Barbara and Frederick Hayes-Roth (Hayes-Roth & Hayes-Roth, 1979). The Hayes-Roths suggest that, as the planner works down the hierarchy of abstraction toward the goal state, lower-level decisions may suggest revision or abandonment of higher-order plans, which in turn suggest different subplans, etc. Thus, the Hayes-Roths conceptualize planning as a multidirectional, opportunistic process instead of a unidirectional, hierarchical process. Planning is also seen as opportunistic in the sense that initial plans are rarely fully formulated or integrated at the highest level of abstraction. Rather, plans can be built upon "real world" details from the "bottom up," as well as being hierarchically refined (concretized) from "top-down" abstractions (e.g., see Byrne's 1977 study of menu planning).

The Hayes-Roths's opportunistic model evolved from detailed protocol analysis of adult subjects' performance on an errand-planning problem. The subjects' job is to plan which errands to run after being given a list of errands and a map of a hypothetical town. Based on their protocol analysis, the Hayes-Roths further characterized the planning process along five different levels or planes of abstraction: plan, plan-abstraction, knowledge-base, executive, and meta-plan. Planning decisions at each level of the hierarchy may refine each of the levels above. For example, on the errand problem recognition that one errand is easier to run than another (knowledge-base) may force revision of how the planner approaches the entire planning problem itself (meta-plan).

Although the Hayes-Roths's model is largely speculative at this time, it does provide a conceptually powerful framework for studying planning processes. In particular, it builds on other recent advances in information-processing such as Simon's notion of "learning by doing" and the work on adaptive computer program (production) systems (see Anzai & Simon, 1979). By making the assumption that people learn simpler low-level plans before more complex, abstract ones, the model can predict specific learning sequences (Hayes-Roth & Hayes-Roth, 1979). The model also implies a general developmental sequence in the acquisition and formulation of planning skills. Children, for example, would presumably need to formulate low-level plans (plan level) before being able to plan abstractly (meta-plan level). In a recent study examining this notion, Pea (1982) found, that, as expected, fewer younger children than older children incorporated meta-planning principles into their plans.

Unfortunately, the developmental implications of the opportunistic model have not been fully exploited. The Hayes-Roths's model, like most information-processing models of planning (e.g., Newell & Simon, 1972), is adult-centered and nondevelopmental. It describes how young adults think out loud when they have been specifically instructed to plan. Although individual and task differences are considered (e.g., Goldin & Hayes-Roth, 1980), there is no guarantee that the same differences will be found at other developmental levels and on different tasks.

There have been attempts by Neo-Piagetian researchers such as Klahr (1978) and Siegler (1978) to formulate a developmental model of planning and problem-solving skills. Their work represents the newer information-processing perspective, since it emphasizes developmental changes in cognitive processing skills on age-appropriate logical reasoning tasks. Using the familiar Tower of Hanoi problem, Klahr (1978) found that few children could verbalize a plan beyond a few moves, and those who could tended to be older (5-year-olds) than those who could not (3- and 4-year olds). Siegler's (1978) work, sometimes referred to as the rule-assessment approach, looks at the decision rules children use in solving problems such as the balance beam scale. On the balance beam problem, children must predict which side of the scale will go down, given a certain number and configuration of weights. Siegler reports that children around 5 years of age only consider one dimension (weight) in solving the problem. Nine-year-olds take distance of the weights from the center of the scale into account if the number of weights is equal. Only 13- and 17-year-old subjects consider both weight and distance all the time.

While Klahr and Siegler's work represents an important new direction in information-processing research, it has only begun to identify the factors (e.g., encoding ability, memory strategies, plan knowledge) that can *explain* observed developmental differences in planning and problem solving. Moreover, it does not address the question of what produces adult developmental variations in planning processes. But perhaps most importantly, it focuses almost exclusively on the first phase of problem solving, plan *generation,* and fails to seriously consider how the individual *monitors* plan execution by using feedback from planned actions.

TRANSACTIONAL APPROACHES TO PLANNING

In contrast to the information-processing approach, which most often defines planning as a preliminary organizing stage in problem solving, the transactional approach views plans as internalized actions which both direct and are derived from problem-solving activities.

In the United States, interest in transactional approaches to cognition expanded rapidly following Flavell's initial work on production deficiencies (e.g., Flavell, 1970) in the use of memory strategies. In this research, it was found that preschool children did not spontaneously utilize mnemonic strategies, whereas older children did. Furthermore, although the younger children showed improved memory when they were explicitly provided with appropriate mnemonic strategies, they did not use these strategies spontaneously in subsequent trials. Preschool children could not be said, therefore, to have a "mediation deficiency" because they were capable of benefiting from the imposed mediators, but they could be said to have a "production deficiency" in that they did not planfully produce these beneficial mediating strategies. In a more general sense, the finding of production deficiencies encompasses the notion that the ability to engage in an operation serving to facilitate a cognitive activity precedes the ability to use this operation in an intentional and *planful* fashion. The study of such developmental transitions has become a major factor in contemporary cognitive developmental psychology.

The roots of this research program extend back in two directions. Flavell, of course, was steeped in the Piagetian tradition, and the notion that reflective thought lags behind action is quite consistent with Piaget's theory. The second antecedent was one that did not originally influence Flavell, although he came quickly to an understanding of its significance. This was Soviet psychology as elaborated in the Marxist-based theories of Vygotsky, Leont'ev, Zinchenko, Smirnov, and others. Flavell's work (e.g., Flavell, 1977), along with the increased availability of translations of Soviet work (e.g., Cole, 1978; Cole & Maltzman, 1969) have sparked a surprisingly strong interest among American cognitive psychologists in the work of the Soviets.

The Piagetian approach

Piaget's theory of cognitive development bears on the issue of planning in two different ways. His earlier work, starting with *The Origins of Intelligence in Children* (1952) through *The Growth of Logical Thinking from Childhood to Adolescence* (Inhelder & Piaget, 1958), bears on the relationship between the quality of planful behaviors at different age levels and the cognitive structures that underlie them. Piaget's more recent efforts, as represented by *The Grasp of Consciousness* (1976) and *Success and Understanding* (1978), focus more on the process by which the ability to plan develops.

In his earlier, structurally-oriented work, Piaget traced the development of planning skills through several stages: (a) the "fortuitous activity" of early infancy; (b) the "intentional," albeit purely practical, coordination of means and ends of later infancy; (c) the intuitive one-way anticipations of early childhood; (d) the more logical though rigid reasoning of middle childhood; and finally (e) the combinatorial, hypothetico-deductive logic of adolescence and adulthood. Perhaps Piaget's most dramatic demonstration of the development of planning skills is found in his "colorless liquids task" (Inhelder & Piaget, 1958). In this study, individuals of different ages are asked to determine which of four colorless liquids, when combined with a fifth, will produce a yellow color.

The youngest subjects approach this task in a nonplanful manner. They tend to combine flasks randomly, rarely more than two at a time, and often produce duplicate combinations. At the level of middle childhood, subjects tend to develop systematic plans often based on the experimenter's demonstration, but when the strategy fails they are lost. At the level of early adolescence (12–14), initial plans are limited and typically unsuccessful, but here, in contrast to the concrete operational child, the individual, after applying initial inadequate plans, comes to a realization that all possible combinations should be tried and often that some record should be kept of exhausted combinations. Finally, by later adolescence, subjects begin with a comprehensive and sufficient plan with an eye toward proving or disproving hypotheses.

The all-encompassing plan of approach, as demonstrated by the adolescents in the colorless liquids task, is termed by Piaget a "reflected abstraction" indicating that the individual has attained an understanding of the coordinations of his or her actions which, when applied, will result in success. The process by which such understanding develops is termed "reflexive abstraction" and is a focus of Piaget's later work (1976, 1978).

In *Grasp of Consciousness,* Piaget looks at the development of children's ability to understand their early developing and successful actions. For example, in one study he investigates the ability to accurately describe the actions of crawling. Piaget concludes from his studies that (a) action is an early form of knowledge which is subsequently conceptualized by conscious reflections on the actions, and (b) understanding is initially derived from reflection on the external consequences of actions, gradually proceeds to an "analysis of means employed and finally to bear on . . . the central, but at first unconscious, mechanisms of the action" (Piaget, 1976, p. 214).

In *Success and Understanding,* Piaget investigates the interactive roles of action and conceptualization through development. One study traces this interaction using a task requiring that a lump of sugar, placed at the end of a lever, be moved either up or down. The difficulty of the task is varied based on the number and arrangement of interconnected levers and the ability to move pivots. Initially the child is able to perform the task using a single lever, but does not even understand that his or her finger needs to move one side of the bar in a direction opposite from the direction in which he or she wants the other side to move; understanding lags behind action. Gradually there develops an understanding of the actions of the lever and an anticipation of the effects of one's actions on the lever based on reflexive abstractions; at this stage, there is a reciprocal relationship "between active trials and errors and conceptual inferences" (Piaget, 1978, p. 217). Finally, at the age of about 11–12 years, subjects discover the laws by which the levers interact and are able to plan their actions successfully prior to acting even in the most complex cases; reflexive abstraction thus yields to reflected abstraction and conception guides action.

The Soviet approach

Clearly, there is no one theory of Soviet psychology, any more than there is a single theory of American psychology. However, much of the Soviet work is unified by adherence to a general Marxist or dialectical materialistic model. The first Soviet psychologist to develop a theory of higher psychological process based on the tenets of Marxism was Vygotsky. It is his theory which is most closely identified with the Soviet position, despite the fact that he died over 50 years ago in 1934.

In Vygotsky's theory, one of the essential aspects of development is the increasing ability of children to control and direct their own behavior, a mastery made possible by the development of new psychological forms and functions and by the use of signs and tools in this process (John-Steiner & Souberman, 1978). The most important of these sign-related behaviors is speech, and it is the use of speech in the form of "sign operations" which Vygotsky sees as instrumental in developing control over one's behavior and allowing for projection of actions into the future.

In Vygotsky's theory, the developmental course of the ability to plan is similar to that of other higher-order psychological processes. Initially, children's actions are largely biologically conditioned and immediate. From birth, however, children are immersed in a social and cultural environment which controls and directs their activity. Gradually, the means imposed by social influences on children are adopted by the children themselves and are used as external supports for individual activity. Eventually, many of these external processes are incorporated into "systems of functioning" and internalized.

When presented with problems, very young children approach them in a groping, trial-and-error fashion. Early in development, however, parents begin to direct children's problem-solving activity, providing them with verbal and nonverbal prompts, heuristics, and algorithms. Children thus come to learn that others, especially parents, can serve the function of complementing their own problem-solving efforts. This notion that one needs to consider childrens' ability to make use of socially available information in assessing their level of functioning is inherent in the currently popular notion of "zone of proximal development" (e.g., Brown & French, 1979). As children learn the (mostly) verbal rules for solving problems, they often produce them as external accompaniments to the activity. As their repertoire increases, these "sign operations" are incorporated into organized problem-solving systems and become internalized. "Now speech guides, determines, and dominates the course of action" (Vygotsky, 1978, p. 28).

Perhaps the most well-known Soviet research on the regulating function of speech is Luria's (1961) study of the effects of other-produced and self-produced verbalization on a simple discrimination task. The task involves having children respond to one color light by squeezing a rubber bulb, and to a differently colored light by not squeezing the bulb. At the youngest age level, ongoing verbal direction by the experimenter is somewhat helpful, but self-produced verbalization hinders performance. At the next level, some regulation can be effected by the child's own verbalization, but control is of an "impulsive" type. That is, verbalization tends to produce action in an indiscriminant fashion (e.g., a self-direction to "don't squeeze" is likely to result in a squeeze). At the third level, self-produced verbalization is effective in producing controlled *and* differentiated behavior, and gradually overt speech becomes unnecessary as it is replaced by the covert signal system.

Although there has been difficulty in reproducing Luria's specific results (e.g., Miller, Shelton, & Flavell, 1970), Vygotsky's theory of verbal regulation of behavior is still influential. For example, the cognitive behavior modification approaches of Meichenbaum and others depend heavily on the verbal control of behavior (e.g., Meichenbaum & Goodman, 1979).

Current trends

Research on the development of planning skills from a transactional perspective has taken three major directions since Flavell's initial work on production deficiencies. Flavell himself has been concerned primarily with the individual's awareness of his or her own cognitive processes and how this awareness affects behavior. This area of investigation, which is similar in some ways to Piaget's work on reflective abstraction, is now known as "metacognition". A second line of work, which is derived from the efforts of Vygotsky and Luria, is concerned with the use of speech for purposes of self-regulation. A third stream, which is also consistent with the Soviet work, especially Leont'ev's theory of activity (e.g., Wertsch, 1979), has to do with the ability to coordinate means and ends (operations and goals) in intentional activities.

Metacognition. An important facet of planning is the ability to conceptualize a problem and to select and evaluate operations which will be effective in attaining desired results. The Hayes-Roths (1979), for example, posit a "meta-plan phase" of their planning model at which level such information is registered. The study of the knowledge of one's own cognitive processes is now a major field of investigation termed "metacognition." While research in metacognition was initially focused on the area of memory (e.g., Flavell & Wellman, 1977), more recent efforts have been expanded to meta-attention (e.g., Miller & Bigi, 1979), metalinguistic skills (e.g., deVilliers & deVilliers, 1973) and comprehension monitoring (e.g., Markman, 1977). As applied to the development of planning skills, metacognition encompasses the awareness that certain tasks require planful use of cognitive functions, as well as the specific knowledge of those factors influencing cognitive processes and how they are related to task performance.

Speech-for-self. Much of the earliest American research on speech-for-self was concerned with untangling theoretical issues surrounding the relationship between language and thought, and particularly on differentiating between Piagetian and Vygotskyan positions on egocentric speech. The data of primary interest were therefore frequencies of speech-for-self and social speech in different settings (e.g., Kohlberg, Yaeger, & Hjertholm, 1968). More recent efforts have focused on issues more closely related to planning skills, notably the relationship between spontaneous self-regulating speech and problem-solving performance (e.g., Beaudichon, 1973) and the efficacy of private speech in producing more planful behavior (e.g., Meichenbaum & Goodman, 1979).

Coordination of means and ends. The third line of planning research from a transactional perspective is consistent with Leont'ev's theory of activity (see Wertsch, 1979). Leont'ev, a student of Vygotsky, proposes a distinction among three levels of activity. In order of increasing level of abstraction these are: (a) activities and associated motives, (b) actions and associated goals, and (c) operations and associated conditions. The level of activities pertains to unconscious responses often to social or biological motives (e.g., hunger) and is only indirectly implicated in the development of planning. In contrast, the second level, that of actions, refers to behaviors aimed at conscious goals, and is thus quite germane to the planning process. The third level, operations, refers to those means, relevant to specific conditions, by which actions can be effected. According to Leont'ev, operations typically originate as goal-related actions and eventually become sufficiently well-learned and routinized so that they can be utilized as means in the planning process.

Two recent research programs related to the theory of activity are Meacham's (e.g., 1982) work on remembering planned actions, and Paris's efforts on the development of the coordination between means and goals in cognitive activity (e.g., Paris, 1978; Paris, Newman, & McVey, 1982). Meacham (1982) utilizes Leont'ev's model to elaborate four levels of operation/action sequences at which remembering planned actions may be discussed. He stresses that remembering to execute planned actions is an ecologically prevalent activity motivated by the social context (e.g., remembering to carry out designated responsibilities is an integral part of socialization from the earliest years on).

Paris's work is directed toward an understanding of the process by which children develop the ability to coordinate means and goals in cognitive activities such as remembering (Paris, 1978). His focus is on the transition from the use of cognitive skills in ordinary daily activities to the intentional utilization of those skills for specific cognitive goals (e.g., memory) to the automatic execution of well-practiced skills. He suggests that cognitive strategies are originally developed "as an automatic consequence of interaction with a meaningful environment" (Paris, 1978, pp. 267–268), but are used in a planful goal-related fashion only after practice, instruction, and feedback help the child to understand the functional significance of the skill.

TRANSACTIONAL OPPORTUNISM IN PLANNING

In their information-processing model, the Hayes-Roths (1979) view planning as the first stage of a two-stage sequence of problem solving. The second, or control stage, involves monitoring and guiding the execution of the plan to successful conclusion. Although their opportunistic model seems to accurately reflect what most adults do in the "planning phase" of problem solving, transactional models would suggest that planning frequently does not stop once the control or execution phase begins. Rather, actions are used as a guide for future planning.

Our position, which we have termed *transactional opportunism,* is that problem solving is a process involving a dynamic interrelationship between plans and actions. Thus, the individual is viewed as entering the execution phase of problem solving after having made plans which vary in their completeness but which often require feedback from performance for further elaboration and successful execution. Further, subsequent plans are very much dependent on prior executions.

Unlike most previous approaches to planning which have been either adult-oriented and nondevelopmental or focused solely on preadult changes in planning, the transactional opportunistic approach suggests a specific life-span developmental sequence. In the young child, initial plans are lacking in specificity and sufficiency (and sometimes are lacking entirely). Problem solving is carried out largely on a pragmatic, plan-as-you-go basis which we have called "planning-in-action." Planning ability is initially constrained by a number of interrelated limitations on the child's cognitive system, among them plan representation, working memory, knowledge about appropriate strategies, and self-monitoring.

As the child develops, he or she becomes increasingly able both to project actions into the future and to abstract from past actions. At this second level, initial plans are becoming increasingly adequate to the demands of the task but still require a great deal of "planning-in-action." The major developmental advance here is that individuals seem to be able to abstract from actions in previous problems to formulate more adequate plans for subsequent ones.

Even at the adult level, plans are frequently less fully elaborated than one might expect and thus require some "planning-in-action." In some cases, this may be due to the individual having incomplete knowledge regarding the nature of the task or the appropriateness of specific strategies. Or it may derive from an inability or lack of motivation to mentally simulate future actions and their outcomes. In any event, adults are better able than younger individuals to abstract from both previous actions *and* mental operations in elaborating subsequent plans.

The transactional opportunistic approach is somewhat less explicit about the developmental progression of planning skills in later life. While recent research suggests older adults can formulate adequate plans if instructed (Adams & Rebok, 1982–1983), the interaction between their plans and actions has not been studied. Based on the work of Labouvie-Vief (1982), we might expect older adults to show greater pragmatism in planning. Further, their abstractions would likely be based on the personal and social meaningfulness of planning vis-a-vis the task at hand rather than the formal, abstract aspects of problem solving. Thus, we would expect to find considerable "planning-in-action" at the older adult level.

In the present life-span developmental study of planning based on the "transactional opportunistic" approach, we were particularly concerned with: (a) the degree to which initial plans are elaborated, (b) the number and type of changes individuals make in their plans during actual problem solving, and (c) the way in which task-derived information is used to formulate and modify subsequent plans.

DEVELOPMENTAL STUDY OF PLANNING-IN-ACTION

Subjects

The subjects were 25 third-graders ($\bar{X} = 8.48$ years), 18 eighth-graders ($\bar{X} = 13.1$ years), 20 young adult college students ($\bar{X} = 19.9$ years), and 20 community-residing old adults ($\bar{X}$ = 70.3 years). The school-age subjects were recruited from public schools in central and western New York State. The young adults were recruited from the psychology subject pool at S.U.N.Y. at Geneseo, as part of a course requirement. The older adults were volunteers from a senior citizens' organization in Mt. Morris, New York.

Method

The task involved sorting identical standard decks of playing cards, which had been shuffled together, into separate piles. This particular task was selected because it was: (a) a problem with a well-defined structure and specific goal state; (b) a task which utilized stimuli familiar to most, if not all, of our subjects, but which had been previously attempted by very few; (c) a problem which has many possible solutions varying considerably in their efficiency; and (d) a problem which was meaningful and could be successfully solved by individuals from elementary school-age through adulthood. Sorting instructions were as follows:

Sort 1—There are 2 complete decks of cards in this pile that have been shuffled together. Please sort the pile into 2 separate complete decks as quickly and with as few errors as possible.

Sort 2—In this pile there is 1 complete deck of cards plus a bunch of extra cards that do not make a full deck. Please sort the cards so that the complete deck is separated from the pack, etc.

Prior to sorting the cards, subjects were asked to plan aloud how they would perform the task. After each sort, subjects were asked to describe: (a) whether they were happy with their plan, and (b) how they would change their plan and why. Experimenters taped the plans and recorded the actual sorting procedures to facilitate comparison with the plan. Sorts were timed with a stop watch and total number of errors per sort was recorded.

Half of the subjects in each age group received one of two sequences of three sorting tasks. Group A received Sort 1 first, followed by Sort 2, then Sort 1 again. Group B received the Sort 1 instructions three consecutive times. With Group A, we were interested in seeing how the 1+ deck sort would affect planning on the subsequent 2 deck sort. We felt that changes in strategy precipitated by the 1+ deck sort might generalize, at least among our eighth grade and adult subjects, to planning strategies on the subsequent sort. In reality, this did not happen in most cases, but there was an unexpected effect of the A condition which will be discussed later. With Group B, we were interested in seeing how individuals would self-regulate planning activities over three identical trials. Because, for most of the qualitative data, there were no apparent differences between conditions A and B, results in Tables 1 and 2 are presented collapsed across sort condition.

Results

Individual plans and sorts were categorized by two independent judges according to a scheme presented in Table 1. Additional subcategories were used to classify plans and sorts according to whether or not the subject used ordering strategies, splayed versus collapsed arrangements, or discard piles. Interjudge agreement was near perfect, except for categories 3 and 7, where minor discrepancies were noted: these were subsequently resolved prior to analyzing the data. Table 1 also presents the percentage of subjects in each age group who used a particular sorting strategy. There were two findings of interest here: (a) the percentage of subjects sorting by suit and number simultaneously (i.e., #3, 4, & 7) as opposed to successively (i.e., #1 & 2) increased with increasing age; (b) the percentage of subjects producing sorts which were redundant (i.e., #5 & 6) decreased with increasing age. Both of these findings suggest that, with increasing age, individuals are increasingly able to use strategies in which their attention is simultaneously focused on multiple as opposed to single dimensions, and to disregard redundant or unnecessary dimensions.

In order to determine if initial plans were sufficiently elaborated for subsequent sorts, we first examined the number of subjects at each age level who mentioned either *no* task constraints or only *partial* task constraints in their initial plans, versus those who included all *necessary* task constraints. Plans with partial task constraints made mention of one dimension of the card sorting task (e.g., color or suit or number), but not a combination of necessary dimensions. Plans with necessary task constraints additionally included the recognition that the cards had to be divided both by suit and number to create two separate decks. A chi-square analysis on the number of partial (or no) task constraints versus necessary task constraints by age group yielded a significant effect, χ^2 (3) =

Table I. Percentage of Subjects by Age Group Using a Particular Sorting Strategy

	Third Grade	Eighth Grade	Young Adult	Old Adult	Total
1. Sort by Suit then Face Value	19.51	30.77	14.71	10.71	18.60
2. Sort by Face Value then Suit	29.27	23.08	26.47	25.00	26.36
3. Sort by Suit with Face Value Attempted Concurrently	2.44	7.69	14.71	32.14	13.18
4. Sort by Face Value with Suit Attempted Concurrently	14.63	26.92	26.47	21.43	21.71
5. Sort by Color then Suit then Face Value	2.44	0.00	0.00	0.00	.78
6. Sort by Face Value 1 at a time (Aces through 2's . . .)	7.32	7.69	0.00	0.00	3.88
7. 13 × 4 Matrix Sort	7.32	0.00	17.65	7.14	8.53
8. Mixed	0.00	3.85	0.00	0.00	.78
Other	17.07	0.00	0.00	3.57	6.20

16.43, $p < .001$. Inspection of the frequencies shows that the number of subjects who included ony partial or no constraints in their initial plan decreased with age through young adulthood, and then increased in old age (16, 6, 2, and 12 for the third grade, eighth grade, young adult, and old adult, respectively), while the number of subjects including the necessary task constraints increased and then decreased (9, 12, 18, and 8, respectively). Thus, as expected, the initial plans of the third graders and the old adults were less completely elaborated at the beginning of the sorting task than those of the eighth graders or young adults.

To assess the relationship between plans and actual strategies used during sorting, we devised the five categories shown in Table 2. In Category 1, "Follow Plan Completely," the individual showed no deviation from his or her stated plan. In Category 2, "Follow Plan with Additions," changes were made in order to make the plan sufficient for task solution. Category 3, "Follow Plan with Elaborations," included such items as adding a discard pile, while Category 4, "Change Plan in Process," involved either minor alterations (e.g., ordering the cards numerically) or major changes in organization (e.g., sorting by face value instead of suit). In Category 5, "No Plan or Follow Insufficient Plan," the individual either failed to use a plan or used a plan that failed to solve the task (e.g., sorting the cards into a red pile and a black pile). The percentages of subjects at each age level and in each sort trial falling into these five categories are also shown in Table 2. There are several important points to note about these data. First, the percentage of subjects following their plan completely increased across the three sort trials, suggesting that with increasing task experience, individuals are less likely to alter their plan, especially if successful. Further, the percentage of subjects following their plan with aditions or elaborations, or having an insufficient plan, declined not only with increasing age but also with greater task experience. This finding lends added support to the earlier findings regading the lack of sufficient elaboration in the youngest children's and oldest adults' plans.

The number of times individuals changed their planned strategies from one trial to the next was assessed by assigning each subject a score of 0 (used a different plan on all three sort trials), 1 (used the same plan on two of the three sort trials), or 2 (used the same plan on all three sort trials). A two-way (age by sort condition) analysis of variance was then performed, using an unweighted means solution for unequal cell frequencies. A significant main effect for age, $F (3, 75) = 7.62, p < .01$, on the number of times plans were changed from trial to trial was found. Third graders and old adults were more likely to use the same plan across the sort trials than were eighth graders or young adults, but, contrary to expectations, Group A subjects were equally likely to use the same plan on different sort trials as Group B subjects. Perhaps the latter result indicates that subjects were unsure of how to handle the 1½ deck sort, and chose to use the same plan rather than change to a novel one. The interaction between age and sort condition was not significant.

Table 2. Relationship of Plans to Sort Strategies by Age and Sort Trial

Sort Trial	Third Grade			Eighth Grade			Young Adult			Old Adult		
	1	2	3	1	2	3	1	2	3	1	2	3
Follow Plan Completely	4.0	32.0	40.0	5.6	33.3	55.6	15.0	55.0	65.0	30.0	40.0	55.0
Follow Plan with Additions	16.0	12.0	0.0	16.7	5.6	0.0	0.0	0.0	0.0	0.0	0.0	0.0
Follow Plan with Elaborations	32.0	12.0	16.0	22.2	38.9	11.1	5.0	10.0	10.0	35.0	15.0	0.0
Change Plan in Progress	16.0	40.0	40.0	55.6	22.2	33.3	80.0	35.0	25.0	35.0	45.0	45.0
No Plan or Follow Insufficient Plan	32.0	4.0	4.0	0.0	0.0	0.0	0.0	0.0	0.0	0.0	0.0	0.0

Note: Entries are percentages of subjects showing a particular type of change.

To assess the way in which task-derived information is used to formulate and modify subsequent plans, we examined the number of times strategy was altered from sort to subsequent plan. Each subject was given a score of 0 (used a different plan from the immediately preceding sort on both trials 1 and 2), 1 (used the same plan from either the immediately preceding sort trial 1 or 2), and 2 (used the same plan from both the immediately preceding sort trials 1 and 2). A two-way analysis of variance for unequal cell frequencies with age and sort condition as factors was then performed. A significant main effect for age, $F(3, 75) = 3.67$, $p < .05$, was found on the number of changes from sort to subsequent plan, but neither sort condition nor the age by sort condition interaction effects reached significance. The age effect indicated that third-graders were more likely to adopt the strategy of their previous sort as their subsequent plan than eighth-graders or old adults, and eighth-graders and old adults were in turn more likely than young adults to use the strategy developed in the sort as the strategy for their subsequent plan.

After subjects had completed each sort, we asked them how satisfied they were with their plans and if they could think of ways to make their plans more efficient. This provided us with an indicator of subjects' explicit awareness of the efficiency of their planning strategies. For each of the three plans, we recorded the number of subjects at each age level who indicated an explicit awareness of their plans, and of how they could be changed, versus those who did not indicate such an awareness. Using a chi-square statistic, significant effects at the .001 level were found for Plan 1, $X^2 (3) = 39.92$, Plan 2, $x^2 (3) = 35.28$, and Plan 3, $X^2 (3) = 30.71$. Inspection of the mean scores indicated that awareness of plan efficiency vis-a-vis the task increased through young adulthood, but showed a decline in later adulthood, and also that greater experience with the task is accompanied by more explicit task awareness.

Two direct measures of task efficiency were used in the present study: (a) mean sort times, and (b) mean number of errors. The mean sort time scores across the three sort trials are reported in Table 3. As shown by the table, the sort times of the young and old adults, but not the third or eighth-graders, improved across the sorting trials in Condition B. Some improvements in time for third and

Table 3. Mean Sort Times for Each Sort Condition and Trial by Age Group

	Condition A			Condition B		
	1	2	3	1	2	3
Third Grade	11'33.84"	8'26.70"	11'21.12"	7'23.88"	9'14.76"	8'25.68"
Eighth Grade	6'08.80"	3'20.00"	4'59.10"	4'58.30"	4'51.10"	5'06.00"
Young Adult	4'30.78"	2'58.92"	3'44.52"	4'13.8"	3'33.00"	3'09.78"
Old Adult	9'00.30"	5'08.34"	6'33.84"	7'02.58"	6'11.28"	5'04.04"

eighth-graders are seen in Condition A. Overall, the eighth-graders and the young adults had the fastest sort times, and the third graders and the old adults had the slowest. With regard to error scores, few subjects in any age group made errors in sorting the cards, given that they were able to successfully separate the decks, and errors that were made were usually corrected. Third graders, however, were more likely to fail to separate the decks properly than the other three age groups.

Discussion of sample protocols

In order to illustrate the planning process as was observed in the present study, we will discuss a sample protocol from each age level. While these examples are not necessarily typical in the specific strategies used, they are characteristic of the planning processes which characterize the different age levels.

The third grader we have selected is a 9-year-old girl in the B condition. Her initial plan was to divide by color and then color into suits. This failure to recognize that such a plan will not achieve the required goal state was fairly common among third graders. (Other subjects at this age level were able to specify the dimensions required to attain the goal state, but were frequently not able to describe the procedures they planned to use.) In the actual sort, the subject divided into red and black and then apparently realized the necessity of sorting into face value. She sorted first the reds then the blacks into 13 piles of four cards each. She then went through each pile, creating two piles with one of each suit, and finally combined the pairs into 2 decks (time, 8'23"). After the sort, she claimed that she had not changed her plan at all and would sort the same way in the next trial. Both the failure to recognize that her plan *had* changed, and the claim that the previous sort would be the next plan, are characteristic of many third graders and are indicative of a failure to differentiate plans from actions. In the next sort, the strategy was changed in that cards were sorted by color and face value simultaneously (time, 6'54"). Again there was no recognition that the plan had been altered in process, and the plan for the next trial was to be "the same as I just did it." The third sort, in fact, was identical to the first sort and not the second. When asked specifically about this change, she was able to say that it was easier to sort by color first rather than sorting by color and number at the same time (time, 6'5"). This is a type of metacognitive awareness, but it reflects a very subjective awareness of task efficiency.

The eighth grader we would like to discuss is a 13-year-old male in the A condition. His first plan was to "sort into 13 piles by face value." In the sort, he went through the deck, pulling out all the aces, then separating them into two piles with one ace from each of the four suits in each, then going through the deck, pulling out the twos, separating them into piles, and laying them on top of the ace piles. This procedure was followed through to tens, at which point he separated the picture cards by value, separated each value into piles of one of each suit, and placed them on existing piles (time, 9'30"). It is important to note here that, toward the end of the sort, this subject started using a strategy that did not require going through the whole deck once for each card value, but he did not discuss this as a deviation from his plan and, more importantly, it was not carried over to his next plan. In fact, when asked how he would change his plan if he were to repeat the sort, he said he didn't know, but would have to wait until he started sorting. This approach, which is common to the eighth-graders, characterizes what we have called "planning-in-action." The second plan, which was for the 1½ deck sort, involved laying out piles for each value, as in the first plan, until four of each suit were represented, then discarding the rest. He started his sort, as in the first, by looking through the deck for aces and placing them into a pile. He then took the extra aces and placed them into a single reject pile. At this point he departed from his plan, looking through the deck for values from 2 to 6 and placing them in separate piles, then placing duplicates in a reject pile. This was followed by the same procedure for cards 7–10 and then picture cards. He seemed to be rediscovering in this sort that it was unnecessary to go through the entire deck once for each value, but rather than applying this to all 13 values, he acted as if it would overtax his cognitive capacity in some way (e.g., that he might have to keep all 13 values in memory as he was sorting). However, in his next plan he finally made the leap and stated that he was going to sort by placing cards in piles according to face value in numerical sequence and then separate by suit. He actually did not place them in numerical sequence, but was satisfied with his performance anyway (time, 3'5").

The college subject we will discuss is a 20-year-old female in the B condition. She developed a plan in which she would sort in rows according to suit while simultaneously sorting by face value. This plan is relatively efficient, since only one sort is required. In her sort, she placed the cards in unordered lines by suit, with discard piles for each suit at the bottom of each line. Although she carried this through to completion, she was dissatisfied with the tedious scanning process necessitated by the disordered arrays. In order to deal with this, she developed a second plan which included an initial sort into 13 piles each containing eight cards of the same numerical value and arranged in numerical sequences, followed by a second sort according to suit. The strategy, when executed, effectively bypassed the troublesome scanning problem and cut her sorting time by 25% in spite of the addition of the second sort. In her third plan, this subject stated that she liked her second plan except she would spread each pile so that she could see which suits were already there and set up duplicate piles under each value pile. Thus, she chose to employ a strategy which requires a limited amount of scanning and yet involves only a single sort. During the sort, however, her plan was improved upon by: (a) putting all duplicates in a single discard pile, and (b) collapsing piles when all suits were present for a value. The former alteration reflects a realization that having two piles for each value was redundant; the later reflects recognition that even the small amount of scanning can be reduced. (This last strategy, by the way, is the most efficient we have been able to discern. It is noteworthy that this subject was one of very few to use this strategy, and this was only on the third trial.)

The planning processes most characteristic of old adults can be seen in the protocol of a 65-year-old female in the A condition. She initially planned to line up four aces of one deck with four duplicate aces beneath the first piles, and then said she couldn't think of what else to do but would see "once I get to it." This "planning-in-action" approach also characterized several other older adult subjects in our sample. After this particular subject had rank ordered ace through king of each suit with four duplicate rows of cards as planned, she collapsed each pile, which shows metacognitive insight, i.e., less visual scanning is required when completed sorts are set aside (time, 5'11"). Interestingly, however, this knowledge did not generalize to the point of eliminating the splayed duplicate rows. For her second 1½ deck sort, she decided to start the same way, but planned to use a single discard pile. Once again, she sorted by the two dimensions of face value and suit, but did not collapse the piles when completed (time 2'51"). In the final 2-deck sort, she departed from the plan of both previous sorts by not ordering the cards and by not using a discard pile. The reason behind this seemingly less planful sorting behavior (which took almost a minute longer than her first sort, time, 6'09") perhaps can be found in her comment that she wanted to do it a different way "for curiosity," a remark made by several other older (and younger) adult participants.

GENERAL DISCUSSION

In general, the present findings support our contention that planning is a "transactional opportunistic" process. First, plans were often found to be only partially elaborated prior to the execution phase of the task. Even among the young adult subjects, only 15% followed their plans completely on the first sort. Second, plans changed significantly as a function of opportunity to engage in the task. For example, 55% of young adults used either a different plan or a plan with a major change (addition or deletion of a component) on each of the three planning trials. Third, changes made in plans were based either on opportunistic actions taken during previous sorts (more frequent among the younger subjects) or reflection upon the relative efficiency of actions taken during previous sorts (more frequent among the older subjects).

The developmental predictions of the "transactional opportunistic" model were also generally supported despite considerable individual variation at each age level. First, young children and older adults produced initial plans which were less fully elaborated and more frequently insufficient than those of younger adults. This is reflected in the fact that a higher percentage of third graders, eighth-graders, and old adults introduced additions and elaborations to their plans during the execution phase of the task than did young adults (48%, 38.9%, 5%, and 35%, respectively, for trial 1).

Second, the tendency to differentiate plans from actions increased with increasing age through young adulthood. What this means is that young children had a greater tendency than older children and adults to see their actions as consistent with their plans, even when dramatic changes in strategy were made, and also that they had a greater tendency to adopt their previous actions as a strategy for subsequent plans. The former trend may be seen in data on satisfaction of subject with their plans. Although only 4% of third graders actually followed their initial plans completely, and 12% had no plan at all, 95.83% of them expressed basic satisfaction with their plans. In comparison 83.33% of eighth-graders, 65% of young adults, and 90% of old adults expressed basic satisfaction with their initial plans. The latter trend is reflected in the fact that there was a decreasing likelihood with increasing age up to young adulthood of adopting the strategy of the previous sort as the subsequent plan. In fact, when asked to describe subsequent plans, many third graders made statements like "the same as I just did it," and required prompting for further elaboration.

Third, younger children were less likely than older children, who were less likely than adults, to base changes in plans on explicit awareness of the relationship between their actions and task efficiency. Only 32% of third graders, as opposed to 83% of eighth-graders, 100% of college students, and 85% of old adults, demonstrated this type of metacognition, even on the third trial. In addition, the nature of these metacognitions seemed to differ across age. The third grade subjects expressed awareness that actions they were taking were "easier" or "harder" than previous actions, and on that basis either stayed with the same strategy on subsequent plans or went back to earlier strategies, respectively. The eighth-grade subjects showed an increased ability to reflect upon specific actions taken in previous sorts, to identify them as making the task faster or slower, and to use them selectively in subsequent plans. Other eighth-graders, like our sample subject, tended to eschew reflection, relying instead on the execution phase of the tasks for opportunistic inspiration. Many young adult subjects, in contrast, showed an ability not only to reflect on the relative efficiency or inefficiency of specific actions but also to use knowledge of their cognitive processes vis-a-vis the task to generate new strategies. Older adults recognized that there are different ways of solving the card problem, but they tested that recognition by trial and error, not by fully elaborating plans of action based on metacognitive knowledge. In general, they seemed to be unable to state explicitly what effect their changes in planning task strategy would produce.

SUMMARY AND CONCLUSIONS

In this chapter, we have discussed information-processing and transactional approaches to planning, as well as some new research directions suggested by those perspectives. From the information-processing perspective, the objective is to describe what individuals do on a moment-to-moment basis during the initial planning phases of problem solving. The transactional approach, as derived from Piaget's theory and Soviet activity theory, focuses on internalized actions and verbal rule systems that organize and guide problem-solving efforts. Current trends in planning research, seen most clearly in the work on metacognition, self-regulating speech, and coordination of means and goals in problem solving, represent a confluence of various transactional approaches. Introduction of information-processing methods into transactionally oriented research has begun to allow for a more fine-grained analysis of ongoing processes involved in planning.

In discussing these various research directions, we have emphasized the importance of studying planning research within a life-span developmental framework. From previous developmental literature on planning, there appears to be considerable evidence that individuals of various ages formulate and use plans on a pragmatic, plan-as-you-go basis, which we termed "planning-in-action," rather than by exclusively elaborating and executing plans based on prior knowledge. This notion has been used to develop and test a preliminary model of planning called "the transactional opportunistic model." Evidence in support of this model was found in our developmental study of planning involving third graders, eighth-graders, young adults, and old adults. Based on our results, we conclude that there is considerable planning-in-action, even on relatively simple problems and even among experienced planners. Further research on planning employing the transactional opportunistic model should permit a more precise specification of the nature, couse, and extent of planning processes across the life span.

REFERENCES

Adams, C. C., & Rebok, G. W. (1982–83). Planfulness and problem solving in older adults. *International Journal of Aging and Human Development, 16*, 271–282.

Anzai, Y., & Simon, H. A. (1979). The theory of learning by doing. *Psychological Review, 86*, 124–140.

Beaudichon, J. (1973). Nature and instrumental function of private speech in problem solving situations. *Merrill-Palmer Quarterly, 19*, 117–135.

Brown, A. L., & French, L. A. (1979). The zone of potential development: Implications for intelligence testing in the year 2000. In R. J. Sternberg & D. K. Detterman (Eds.), *Human intelligence: Perspectives on its theory and measurement*. Norwood, NJ: Ablex.

Byrne, R. (1977). Planning meals: Problem-solving as a real data-base. *Cognition, 5*, 287–332.

Cole, M. (Ed.). (1978). *Soviet developmental psychology: An anthology*. White Plains, NY: Sharpe.

Cole, M., & Maltzman, I. (Eds.). (1969). *A handbook of contemporary Soviet psychology*. New York: Basic Books.

deVilliers, J. G., & deVilliers, P. A. (1973). A cross-sectional study of the acquisition of grammatical morphemes in child speech. *Journal of Psycholinguistic Research, 2*, 267–278.

Flavell, J. H. (1970). Developmental studies of mediated memory. In H. W. Reese & J. P. Lipsitt (Eds.), *Advances in child development and behavior* (Vol. 5). New York: Academic Press.

Flavell, J. H. (1977). *Cognitive development.* Englewood Cliffs, NJ: Prentice-Hall.

Flavell, J. H., & Wellman, H. M. (1977). Metamemory. In R. V. Kail, Jr., & J. W. Hagen (Eds.), *Perspectives on the development of memory and cognition.* Hillsdale, NJ: Erlbaum.

Goldin, S. E., & Hayes-Roth, B. (1980, September). Individual differences in planning processes. A Rand Note. (N-1488-ONR).

Hayes-Roth, B., & Hayes-Roth, F. (1979). A cognitive model of planning. *Cognitive Science, 3,* 275–310.

Hobbs, J. R., & Evans, D. A. (1980). Conversation as planned behavior. *Cognitive Science, 4,* 349–377.

Inhelder, B., & Piaget, J. (1958). *The growth of logical thinking from childhood to adolescence.* New York: Basic Books.

John-Steiner, V., & Souberman, E. (1978). Afterword. In M. Cole, V. John-Steiner, S. Scribner, & E. Souberman (Eds.), *Mind in society.* Cambridge, MA: Harvard University Press.

Klahr, D. (1978). Goal formation, planning, and learning by pre-school problem solvers, or: 'My socks are in the dryer.' In R. S. Siegler (Ed.), *Children's thinking: What develops?* Hillsdale, NJ: Erlbaum.

Kohlberg, L., Yaeger, J., & Hjertholm, E. (1968). Private speech: Four studies and a review of theories. *Child Development, 39,* 691–736.

Labouvie-Vief, G. (1982). Dynamic development and mature autonomy: A theoretical prologue. *Human Development, 25,* 161–191.

Luria, A. R. (1961). The genesis of voluntary behavior. In N. O'Connor (Ed.), *Recent Soviet psychology.* New York: Liveright.

Markman, E. (1977). Realizing that you don't understand: A preliminary investigation. *Child Development, 48,* 986–992.

McDermott, D. (1977). *Flexibility and efficiency in a computer program for designing circuits.* Cambridge, MA: MIT AI Laboratory Technical Report 402.

Meacham, J. A. (1982). A note on remembering to execute planned action. *Journal of applied Developmental Psychology, 3,* 121–133.

Meichenbaum, D., & Goodman, S. (1979). Clinical use of private speech and critical questions about its study in natural settings. In G. Zivin (Ed.), *The development of self-regulation through private speech.* New York: Wiley.

Miller, G. A., Galanter, E., & Pribram, K. H. (1960). *Plans and the structure of behavior.* New York: Holt, Rinehart and Winston.

Miller, P. H., & Bigi, L. (1979). The development of children's understanding of attention. *Merrill-Palmer Quarterly, 25,* 235–263.

Miller, S. A., Shelton, J., & Flavell, J. H. (1970). A test of Luria's hypotheses concerning the development of verbal self-regulation. *Child Development, 41,* 651–665.

Newell, A., & Simon, H. A. (1972). *Human problem solving.* Englewood Cliffs, NJ: Prentice-Hall.

Paris, S. G. (1978). Coordination of means and goals in the development of mnemonic skills. In P. A. Ornstein (Ed.), *Memory development in children.* Hillsdale, NJ: Erlbaum.

Paris, S. G., Newman, R. S., & McVey, K. A. (1982). Learning the functional significance of mnemonic actions: A microgenetic study of strategy acquisition. *Journal of Experimental Child Psychology, 34,* 490–509.

Pea, R. D. (1982). What is planning development the development of? In D. L. Forbes & M. T. Greenberg (Eds.), *Children's planning strategies.* San Francisco, CA: Jossey-Bass.

Piaget, J. (1952). *The origins of intelligence in children.* New York: International Universities Press.

Piaget, J. (1976). *The grasp of consciousness: Action and concept in the young child.* Cambridge, MA: Harvard University Press.

Piaget, J. (1978). *Success and understanding*. Cambridge, MA: Harvard University Press.

Sacerdoti, E. D. (1977). *A structure for plans and behavior*. New York: Elsevier.

Schank, R. C., & Abelson, R. P. (1977). *Scripts, plans, goals, and understanding*. Hillsdale, NJ: Erlbaum.

Siegler, R. S. (1978). The origins of scientific reasoning. In R. S. Siegler (Ed.), *Children's thinking: What develops?* Hillsdale, NJ: Erlbaum.

Stefik, M. (1981). Planning and metaplanning. *Artificial Intelligence, 16,* 141–170.

Vygotsky, L. S. (1978). *Mind in society*. Cambridge, MA: Harvard University Press.

Wertsch, J. V. (1979). The regulation of human action and the given-new organization of private speech. In G. Zivin (Ed.), *The development of self-regulation through private speech*. New York: Wiley.

Wilensky, R. (1981). Meta-planning: Representing and using knowledge about planning in problem solving and natural language understanding. *Cognitive Science, 5,* 197–233.

Chapter 5

Aging and the Development of Expert Cognition*

William J. Hoyer

Syracuse University

The central purpose of this chapter is to examine cognitive change during the adult years. Three main sources of age-related cognitive differentiation are identified as follows: (a) intra-individual change and inter-individual differences in the elementary or component processes of complex cognition; (b) change in the control processes affecting activation, selection, and integration of requisite elementary processes or knowledge stores; and (c) intra-individual change and inter-individual differences in acquired, rule-based ''production systems'' or knowledge stores. Research and theory in each of these areas of mental performance is reviewed, and a model of expert cognition which incorporates at least these functions is proposed.

INTRODUCTION AND OVERVIEW

Developmental change (and regularity) in cognition arises from transformations of tacit knowledge, as well as from age-related change in fundamental or elementary information processing structures and processes, and in the operations that control these elementary processes. Three broad classes of factors which account for individual differences in cognitive performance can be identified. These are (a) elementary or component information processes; (b) cognitive control processes involving the activation, selection, and integration of requisite elementary processes and knowledge stores, and (c) acquired knowledge in the form of rules and scripts. The values of the variables represented by these three general factors exhibit change with age during the adult years. That is, cognitive efficiency in different aged adults has been found to vary as a function of characteristics of the information being processed (e.g., its familiarity, salience, affective value, and

* Preparation of this chapter was supported by NIA research grant 02713.

Author address: Department of Psychology, 430 Huntington Hall, Syracuse University, Syracuse, New York 13210 complexity), the kinds of elementary information processing skills required for efficient performance, the coordination of these elementary operations, and the task-relevant acquired knowledge structures and competencies of the performing individual.

The study of cognitive aging, like most if not all areas of scientific inquiry, takes place in a fragmented, diversified fashion, with investigations designed to test singular hypotheses or mini-theories rather than whole systems or models. In this chapter, I propose a relatively comprehensive model of cognitive change during adulthood, based on cognitive aging research and on current theory in the areas of computational modeling and expert systems.

Points of departure

In 1958, Welford reported that there were three well-established findings in the cognitive aging research literature. First, age-related deficits in cognitive performance increase as task difficulty increases. Second, performance becomes slower with advancing age. Third, there is increased inter-individual variability as we move along the adult age continuum. Many studies conducted in the past 25 years have provided support for Welford's three conclusions. Task difficulty is typically treated as an information load or complexity factor in studies of cognitive aging (e.g., Cerella, Poon, & Williams, 1980), and researchers continue to call attention to the "problem" of age-related increases in inter-individual and intra-individual variability in various aspects of cognitive functioning (e.g., Hoyer, 1974; Krauss, 1980; Rabbitt, 1982a).

Age-related deficits have been reported for many aspects of cognitive processing, including visual sensory memory (Kline & Scheiber, 1981), perceptual and psychomotor speed (Birren, Woods, & Williams, 1980; Cerella, Poon, & Williams, 1980), simple and choice reaction time (Talland & Cairnie, 1964), rate of information processing (DiLollo, Arnett, & Kruk, 1982; Salthouse, 1985), and memory search and retrieval processes (Anders & Fozard, 1973). Explanations of such findings are typically based on the position that there is less of some construct like cognitive capacity, and thus the elementary mechanisms presumed responsible for carrying out various mental operations are slower or in some unspecified way less efficient. That age differences generally increase under conditions of increased task complexity or information load is taken as general support for capacity deficit explanations of age-related cognitive change. Such explanations of cognitive change are qualified by recent evidence suggesting minimal or reduced age-related differences when older adults are given extensive practice in the task (Plude & Hoyer, 1981; Plude, Kaye, Hoyer, Post, Saynisch, & Hahn, 1983; Salthouse & Somberg, 1982b). Further, age-related gains in cognitive performance are common on tasks which are dependent on experience-based accumulated knowledge (Demming & Pressey, 1957; Kramer, 1983; McFarland & O'Doherty, 1959), or which are personally meaningful or ecologically useful (e.g., Dittman-Kohli & Baltes, 1985; Mergler & Goldstein, 1983; Scheidt & Schaie, 1978).

Cognitive functions do not show an orderly pattern of decline with advancing age. Within- and across-individuals, different mental abilities improve, stay at roughly the same level, or decline at different rates (e.g., see Cunningham, 1981; Schaie, 1979). I begin this review of the research and theory on cognitive aging by attempting to identify the major sources of age-related individual differences in cognitive function.

SOURCES OF COGNITIVE AGING

As previously stated, it is assumed that the status of an individual's cognitive performance is determined by (a) the efficiency of the relevant component or elementary processes involved in carrying out complex cognitive functioning, (b) the efficiency of the control processes responsible for activating and integrating appropriate component processes and knowledge stores, and (c) the applicability of acquired knowledge structures (in the form of rules, scripts, or schemas) for specifying what information is relevant to the particular task or problem at hand. Investigations of adult age differences in cognitive performance are organized and examined in terms of each of these three functions.

Developmental differences in elementary mental operations

It is generally assumed that the elementary operations of pre-attentive processes, recognition time, feature extraction, rate of information processing, memory search, and so on are involved in more complex cognitive processes as measured by tests of intelligence and problem solving, and that the efficiency and speed of elementary operations should in part account for individual differences in complex information processing. Posner and McLeod (1982) noted that much of the research on cognitive psychology based on laboratory paradigms would be rather pointless without this general assumption.

The work of Earl Hunt and his colleagues (Berg, Hertzog, & Hunt, 1982; Hunt, 1978) exemplifies recent progress in identifying the elementary operations used in such complex cognitive tasks as reasoning and reading comprehension. With regard to adult age differences, Berg, Hertzog, and Hunt (1982) found that speed of mental rotation slowed with age, even after four sessions of practice consisting of 480 trials each. Other investigators have identified the rate of accessing and utilizing stored information as a primary locus of age deficits in memory and information processing (Cerella, Poon, & Williams, 1980; Salthouse & Somberg, 1982a; but see Howard, McAndrews, & Lasaga, 1981).

In Card, Moran, and Newell's (1983) recent formulation of the "model human processor," perceptual and cognitive subsystems can operate in either serial (on some tasks such as simple reaction time) or parallel (on tasks such as simultaneous translation). The elementary processes of the model human processor are stated in terms of ten rules, which include: (a) the recognize-act cycle of the cognitive processing system; (b) the perceptual processor rate principle, which suggests that cycle time varies inversely with stimulus intensity; (c) the encoding specificity principle, which states that what is encoded largely determines what information is stored and the retrieval cues that will be effective in accessing stored information; (d) the discrimination principle, which attributes memory retrieval difficulty to the number of items in long-term memory; (e) the variable processor rate principle, which describes a relationship between cycle time and information load such that increased load and practice both serve to reduce cycle time; (f) laws of movement time (e.g., Welford, 1968); (g) the law that the time to perform a task is a power function of the number of practice trials, (h) the uncertainty principle, which stipulates that decision time increases with uncertainty and number of alternatives (e.g., Hick, 1952); (i) the rationality principle, which states that a person acts so as to attain goals or solutions through rational action, given the structure of the task and the limitations of the individual's knowledge and processing ability; and (j) the problem space principle, which states that rational problem solving can be described in terms of a set of states of knowledge, operators for changing one state into another, constraints on applying operators, and control knowledge for applying operators to tasks (see Card, Moran, & Newell, 1980, 1983).

Given the procedural specificity and the apparent general comprehensiveness of this model, it is possible to represent cognitive aging in terms of modal processor theory by describing adult age differences with regard to these principles and parameters. Specifically, the elementary processes of information extraction (Eriksen, Hamlin, & Breitmeyer, 1970), processing rate (DiLollo, Arnett, & Kruk, 1982; Salthouse, 1984), encoding specificity (Craik & Simon, 1980; Perlmutter, 1979; E. Simon, 1979), mental rotation and spatial integration (Cerella, Poon, & Fozard, 1981), memory search and retrieval as a function of load (Anders & Fozard, 1973), decision time under conditions of uncertainty (Hoyer & Familant, 1983; Rabbitt, 1982a), and problem space or working memory (Charness, 1981; Giambra, 1983; Hartley & Anderson, 1983) all tend to be either slower or less efficient in older adults as compared with younger adults.

Individual differences in carrying out complex tasks are in part determined by the efficiency of elementary operations and in part by the efficiency of the sets of rules that are used in combining elementary operations (Posner & McLeod, 1982; Sternberg, 1982). Generally, older adults are at a greater disadvantage compared with younger adults whenever attention has to be distributed among different tasks (Plude & Hoyer, 1981, 1985; Somberg & Salthouse, 1982). It has also been reported that older adults are more easily distracted by irrelevant information in visual search and decision-making tasks, compared with younger adults (e.g., Hoyer, Rebok, & Sved, 1979). With practice, however, dual task performances can be carried out rapidly, accurately, and with little apparent attention demand (e.g., Hirst, Spelke, Reaves, Caharack, & Neisser, 1980).

Developmental differences in control processes

Rabbitt (1982b) has suggested that the locus of adult age differences involves the breakdown of control processes. According to Rabbitt, people rarely behave as passive, externally controlled systems; rather, cognition is an active, self-controlled system which continuously searches for optimal procedures for adjusting cognitive limitations to task demands. Older people select cognitive strategies to attenuate deficits, and Rabbitt argues that there is an age-related loss in the efficiency of self-optimization processes.

The control process function is a prime locus of inter-individual differences on cognitive tasks which require the integration of new information, active memory search, and/or the coordination of other capacity-demanding processes. In contrast to Rabbitt (1982a,b), I suggest that older adults are not at a disadvantage in tasks which do not require controlled processing, or when these operations have become skilled through practice. Asymptotic performance of highly practiced skills is generally unaffected by the age variable, but the sequencing and intertask coordination of highly automated skills can be affected by age-related deficits in control processes. In addition, it is proposed here that intra-individual change in cognitive performance is a function of age-related changes in subject-controlled processes.

We do not yet know *how* the controlled performance of elementary processes becomes more efficient with practice. The controlled-automatic distinction is a descriptive and operational one—not an explanation of how or which mental operations change as processing goes from controlled to automatic. One possible explanation has to do with extending Baddeley's (1982) concept of domain, and the work on automatic semantic activation (e.g., Collins & Loftus, 1975). According to Baddeley (1982) and others, a domain is an area of cognition within which there is an extensive associative network of links and connections. A knowledge domain may consist of particular elementary cognitive processes that, with practice and learning, come to be carried out in a sequence, separately from other processes. It is also reasonable to suggest that there are separable domains or levels of processing analogous to Craik's levels of processing framework (e.g., Craik & Lockhart, 1972; Craik & Simon, 1980; E. Simon, 1979). For example, orthographic processing of words or letters while editing or proof reading a scientific manuscript may be carried out separately from semantic processing, at least with regard to encoding; for example, the skilled reader/editor selectively allocates attentional resources to either domain as needed. Similarly, in automatic semantic priming paradigms, words "automatically" activate a network or related words and meanings—apparently without subject control or mental effort (Howard, McAndrews, & Lasaga, 1981; Neely, 1977).

Integrating new information is a control process (Atkinson & Shiffrin, 1968), whereas various sequences of accessing or executing familiar knowledge can become automatic with practice (Mandler, 1975). Hoyer and Plude (1980, 1982) and others have suggested that the quantity or capacity of cognitive resources available to an individual is limited (in part by age-related factors), but that the allocation of this pool of resources is relatively flexible (e.g., see also Craik & Byrd, 1982); that is, allocation policies can be relatively efficient or inefficient within the individual's limits of mental capacity, independent of the amount of remaining available capacity within that range. Alternatively, one could hypothesize that optimal levels of mental effort and resource allocation are in part a function of capacity limitations. If this were the case, however, cognitive efficiency would be reduced as the limits of capacity were approached. The bulk of the empirical evidence, none of which includes the age factor, supports the first hypothesis (e.g., Miller, 1982).

In studies of the ways children and adults combine multi-dimensional information in choice tasks (e.g., Anderson, 1981), it has been shown that individuals combine information across dimensions rather than compare objects one dimension at a time (as modeled by decision choice trees). According to Anderson, the processes of integration of external information can be represented by simple algebraic rules such as addition and multiplication of the subject-assigned values of stimuli and dimensions.

Even though Anderson's (1981) "cognitive algebra" model of information integration is conceptually and computationally quite simple, there is considerable evidence to suggest that the act of information integration is frequently not "easy" or "automatic" (Schneider & Shiffrin, 1977; Shaw, 1982; Siegler, 1983). Shaw's (1982) findings from visual and auditory detection tasks, for example, indicated that individuals form separate decisions for information sources and then integrate these decisions in order to select a response. Her results reject the notion that one integrates the relevant information from several sources prior to making a decision. One explanation for Shaw's (1982) findings is that the amount of memory or "mental effort" required for processing separable sources of information and for relating this information to current decisions may be less than that required for making decisions based on the integration of raw information,

Development of knowledge structures

The cognitive operations that different individuals use are determined in part by the problems and issues that they "see" or "comprehend." In analyzing individual differences in knowledge use and constraints on learning, Keil (1981) stated: "Undoubtedly there are many important differences between how a theoretical physicist acquires new knowledge about quarks and how a 3-year old learns more about a first language, but in both cases it is necessary to generate rules or hypotheses, test them, and decide whether to discard them in favor of a better alternative" (p. 217).

Related to the notion of domains of knowledge (as discussed in the last section) is the concept of "scripts." The term "script" or "schema" is neither new nor unitary within the study of cognition (e.g., Bartlett, 1932; Piaget, 1928). According to Abelson (1981), *knowledge scripts* contain bits of learned information, such as how to solve arithmetic problems or how to order food in a restaurant, and *action scripts* contain (and control) psychomotor behavior patterns, such as walking or writing. Though scripts are thought to specify a general course of action, they are seen as more than simple mental sequences of knowledge or actions. The script concept incorporates a series of implicit if-then rules that apply, categorically, to a range of circumstances (Schank & Abelson, 1977). For example, scripts may enable an individual to anticipate what is likely to happen in a restaurant, classroom, or sporting event, thus permitting either conscious or automatic preparation of mental resource allocation policies in advance of task demand.

Scripts begin as generalized memory structures, which then become elaborated and transformed into generalized event representations. The construction and elaboration of scripts is considered to be a control process, the efficiency of which varies with age and other ability-related individual difference factors. The efficiency of execution of scripts, when overlearned or well-rehearsed, is unaffected by age-related decrements in elementary processes or in various control functions such as information integration processes. There is empirical evidence to support the distinction between the acquisition and the execution of scripted material (e.g., Alba & Hasher, 1983; Jacoby, 1978; Mandler, 1975). The task of actually computing the product of 12 times 20 is different, for example, than the act of "knowing" or recalling the memorized answer (Jacoby, 1978). Age differences are found mainly in the acquisition or integration of new information and not in execution of well-learned knowledge (see Hasher & Zacks, 1979; Hoyer & Plude, 1982). It has been suggested that the size (or contents) and number of knowledge scripts increase with advancing age in healthy adults, and that scripts become increasingly refined and specialized with age and experience (see Langer, 1980; Wood, 1983), but more empirical evidence bearing on this claim is needed (see Light & Anderson, 1983).

METAPHORS OF ADULT COGNITION

In a discussion of the development of knowledge structures, Klahr and Siegler (1978) noted that "the researcher's decision about how to represent knowledge plays a central role in guiding both the kind of theory that gets formulated and the kind of experiment that gets run" (p. 62). The metaphorical bases of cognition and cognitive development continue to evolve as data and theory are compiled, and as a result of change in the context in which the research enterprise takes place (Gregory, 1981; Riegel, 1972). In Gentner and Grudin's (1985) survey of *Psychological Review* from 1894 to 1982, for illustration, a substantial increase in the prevalence of computational metaphors was found for recent years. The traditional distinctions between organismic and mechanistic metaphors seem less clear in light of new views of cognition (cf. Reese & Overton, 1970). For example, McArthur (1982) noted that current work in the area of computer vision serves to bridge the conceptual gap between mechanistic and constructivist views of perception.

The predominant stereotype of age-related cognitive change in adulthood has been one of irreversible decline with regard to practically all aspects of cognitive function. However, the research indicates a complex pattern of change, and the robustness of many dimensions of cognition during the adult years. There is a need to articulate models of mature cognition which take into account demonstrated gains as well as losses in cognitive function with age (i.e., differential models). In this section, I consider applications of (a) computational modeling, and (b) an expert systems model to the study of cognitive differentiation and aging.

Computational representations of cognitive aging

The descriptive goal of a computational model of adult cognitive development is to (a) represent observed age-related changes in cognitive performance, and (b) to describe by analogy the potentials and limits of cognitive function at various ages. At minimum, the model would represent current understanding of adult cognition in terms of antecedent and consequent functions. That is, the factors affecting knowledge development and elementary and control processes would be represented as inputs (or antecedents) which differentially affect the performance of different aged adults. Though computational models have been constructed mainly on the basis of universal (i.e., nondifferential) rules of problem solving (cf. Ernst & Newell, 1969), recently has there been interest in representing inter-individual differences in mental computations (Chi, Glaser, & Rees, 1982; Simon & Simon, 1978), and in the computational modeling of learning (e.g., Langley & Simon, 1981; Neves & Anderson, 1981; Sutton & Barto, 1981). Computational models of cognitive aging should take into account the changing boundaries of capacity and function by attempting to represent the ways individuals actually perform in adulthood. Ultimately, such description will benefit the explanation of adult cognitive change.

It is important to point out that computational models of cognition are product-oriented, in that simulation programs are written to execute computational routines that yield an outcome or an answer to a particular kind of problem. Ernst and Newell's (1969) "general problem solver," or GPS program, for example, was based on a means-end logic such that problem solving is partitioned into a series of specific sub-problems or sub-goals that are addressed and resolved in a logical order.

In addition to the obvious criticism that humans may be less product-oriented and "logical" than the GPS and other production systems, it may also be that adults give less consistency and quantity of mental effort to carrying out solutions to mental problems than is generally assumed (Hofstadter, 1979; Perkins, 1982; Simon, 1981). It may be that computational programs represent mature cognition in only some domains, and only when conditions encourage or require logical problem solving. Older adults, in particular, may be more concerned with knowing the issues and problem-finding than with problem solving (Arlin, 1975; Kramer, 1983; Sinnott, 1984). At times, even the most logical of reasoners give their attention to mental operations and activities that seem quite nonlogical, and, frequently, there is considerable creative gain from such "jumps out of the system" (Hofstadter, 1979).

If a computational model were developed to emulate "old" cognition, the program would need to be able to "think" differently, not merely slower than a younger adult. As already mentioned, different elementary and control processes exhibit different developmental trends, rate of new acquisition depends on existing knowledge, and some aspects or domains of cognition change rapidly as a function of repeated exposures (e.g., sensory memory), whereas other aspects change relatively slowly with practice or exposure (e.g., semantic knowledge structures). Though programs have been designed to represent incremental improvement with practice and/or sudden improvement with "discovery" in recent years (e.g., Anzai & Simon, 1979; Langley & Simon, 1981; Simon & Simon, 1978), there are few if any programs representing any of the facets of age-related decline in cognitive performance. That is, there are no existing programs to simulate time-related losses of memory, age-related changes in cognitive control processes, or age differences in vigilance and alertness. Obviously, such subprograms would need to be incorporated within a developmental, computational model of adult cognitive behavior.

There are other shortcomings of computational models which need to be addressed before such representations can be usefully applied to the analysis of cognitive aging. Current computational models do not predict the ubiquitous checking and rechecking of answers of some individuals, especially older persons, in problem-solving tasks. Second, existing computational models do not deal with rehearsal, false starts, substitutions, and distractions. Third, they do not take into account inter- and intra-individual variability in memory search times for particular types of items, or rate of processing differences as a function of changing difficulty of the algorithms; solution times cannot be represented as a simple sum of the number of equations to be solved. Fourth, artificial intelligence (AI) models lack the kind of personal goal selection and situation assessment found in everyday human problem solving. For example, chess players pick a goal and then find the move that best achieves that goal, frequently without conducting a blind exhaustive search of all possible moves. Finally, studies of logical reasoning (with syllogisms) have repeatedly found that people are influenced by the way premises are stated and by the affective content of the premises (Bower, 1981; Franks, Bransford, & Auble, 1982); computer representations are not affected by such variables, unless of course they are programmed to emulate variables of this type. These criticisms do not apply to the model of expert cognition discussed below.

Toward an expert systems model of adult cognition

It would be useful to the understanding of adult cognition and its development to provide a model which emulates competent or expert cognitive performance and age-related changes therein. Following Pylyshyn's (1973) notion of competence theory, expert systems models serve to describe the characteristics and boundaries of cognition by representing in some form the types of mental operations that (some) individuals are capable of executing in some conceivable situations. The aim of expert cognition models is to represent what the person is competent to perform, and as such the model is relevant to behavior under idealized and domain-specific conditions where the effects of potentially limiting control operations and processes are discounted. Expert system models have been employed to describe expertise in a wide variety of domains, including skilled game behavior (e.g., chess), designing and writing computer software (e.g., Jeffries, Turner, Polson, & Atwood, 1981; McKeithen, Reitman, Rueter, & Hirtle, 1981), computing and strategic skills in mathematics and physics (e.g., Greeno, 1983; Larkin, 1981, 1983; Sweller, Mawer, & Ward, 1983), and skills involved in identifying and extracting important information in written material (Brown & Day, 1983). There are many applied and basic research areas within cognitive science which could benefit from such analyses, including the study of expertise in compromised cognitive systems such as in stroke or senile dementia patients.

It is proposed here that expert cognition in adulthood is knowledge domain-specific and consists of (a) acquired, rule-based "production systems" or heuristics; (b) control processes, which serve to coordinate rule-based sequences, integrate or restructure knowledge, and create new knowledge; and (c) requisite elementary processes. Individual differences (age-related and age-independent) in the rate of acquisition and development of expert cognition are attributed mainly to the attention-demanding (capacity-limited) control aspects of cognitive systems, whereas individual differences and intra-individual change in the comprehensiveness of expert knowledge or skill are attributed mainly to domain-related cumulative development. It is likely that the control processes required for the acquisition of particular knowledge domains set limits on the range of domains of expert cognition available to particular individuals.

Although there has been much recent work on the characteristics of expert cognitive systems (for a review, see Hayes-Roth, Waterman, & Lenat, 1983), most investigators in this area have paid little or no attention to chronological age differences in the evolution of expertise. Consistent with the classic work on aging and professional achievement (e.g., Cole, 1979; Lehman, 1953), I suggest that there are optimal constellations of changing knowledge structures and control processes which prescribe which age ranges are associated with exceptional performance in particular domains.

Expert systems researchers recognize that the knowledge structures and control processes of expert cognition are largely domain-specific. This observation is supported by research on adult intelligence including (a) studies related to Reinert's (1970) theory of intellectual differentiation, (b) training studies of intellectual performance in late adulthood (e.g., Baltes & Willis, 1982; Labouvie-Vief & Gonda, 1976), (c) investigations of intellectual performance in situations and tasks endogenous to the individual's everyday functioning (e.g., Demming & Pressey, 1957; Kohn & Schooler, 1978; Scheidt & Schaie, 1978), and (d) exemplar (i.e., exceptional cases) studies of cognitive specialization (e.g., Ericsson, Chase, & Faloon, 1980; Hunter, 1977; Luria, 1968). With regard to expert memory, for example, mnemonists such as in the case of Professor Aiken (see Hunter, 1977) exhibit extraordinary memory for numerical information, but ordinary memory for information outside of the numerical domain (see also Luria, 1968).

In highly routinized and structured cognitive tasks, expert performance is procedurally-driven and rule-based (e.g., Card, Moran, & Newell, 1980, 1983), whereas in less structured tasks or situations, cognitive expertise depends on rapid and efficient integrative and inductive skills. Highly skilled older adults clearly continue to function as experts in mastered knowledge domains, but they are less likely, compared with younger adults, to develop proficiency in new domains of expertise which require either underdeveloped control processes and knowledge stores or age-deficient elementary processes. There appears to be little if any correlation between the efficiency of the control processes of working memory, short-term memory span, and the size of the contents of long-term memory (see Dempster, 1981; Klapp, Marshburn, & Lester, 1983). However, the rate and efficiency of the control processes carried out within working memory, and the capacity of the mental "work space" are probably essential to the acquisition, as well as maintenance, of expertise in knowledge domains which require the continuous and rapid integration of large amounts of information (Chi, Glaser, & Rees, 1982; Neves & Anderson, 1981).

Sometimes, the comprehensiveness of an individual's knowledge of some domain appears to be a sufficient criterion for identifying rule-based, cumulative expertise. Rule-based expertise is a function of the comprehensiveness of the rules in the system for handling specific types of problems. Ideally, an expert of this sort possesses all the rules necessary to handle any type of situation within the designated domain. Such expertise is considered to be to a large extent an experience-related acquired skill. Individuals may differ in the rate and level of expert skill acquisition within and across domains. Further, one can infer from the human skills research literature that individual differences are most evident in the rate of acquisition of asymptotic performance and least evident in the fully stablized performance (e.g., Holding, 1981; Welford, 1968).

Although experts presumably possess all the rules necessary to handle problems within the particular domain, they do not necessarily know how they know what they know. Lesgold (1983), for example, has reported that expert radiologists often have difficulty informing novices of diagnostic errors (see also

Lesgold, Feltovich, Glaser, & Wang, 1981). An expert would accurately identify a large white blotch on an X-ray photograph as a collapsed lung, whereas novices (medical residents) diagnose the same stimulus as a large tumor. Further, the expert reports not consciously entertaining the idea that the blotch was a tumor in making the correct diagnosis, although on questioning the expert readily points out in rule form the visual differences between a tumor and a collapsed lung on an X-ray. The expert radiologist reports not having an understanding of what led the novice radiologist to suspect that the blotch was a tumor, suggesting that the expert radiologist's visual diagnostic skills might be a kind of automatic perception—analogous to automatic reading on the part of skilled readers (e.g., Laberge & Samuels, 1974).

Some forms of expert cognition can be carried out at an automatized level of function. Automatic forms of expert skills are often well-rehearsed combinations of motoric, perceptual, and cognitive skills, such as playing a musical instrument or certain sports. Also, knowledge scripts (cf. Abelson's 1981 distinction between knowledge scripts and action scripts) can become highly stabilized with practice, such as the performance of an experienced lecturer in his or her field. In some domains of human function (e.g., reading, language use), it seems that automatization serves to free up capacity-limited control processes for allocation to higher order tasks.

Having a well-learned script or skill sequence for appropriate situations is sufficient for expert cognitive performance *only* when there is no need to construct or integrate new information. Though it may not always be possible to empirically distinguish the products or outcomes of cumulative (acquired) expertise from performance generated by efficient control processes under well-practiced conditions, the products of cumulative experience on the one hand, and effective control functions on the other, are distinguishable under novel and demanding conditions. The active functions of generating new rules as needed, and of integrating vast amounts of information into new and useful knowledge structures, are probably affected by age-related declines in the availability and/or allocation of attentional capacity.

Given the requisite (and sufficient) elementary operations and their control processes, cognitive expertise is a cumulative, time-dependent learning process. In the field of medicine, for example, physicians acquire many rules of the form, "If the symptoms are _____, then the diagnosis is _____," or "If the diagnosis is _____, then the prescription is _____." Medical expert computer programs such as INTERNIST (Pople, 1977), an internal medicine diagnostic program, and MYCIN (Shortliffe, 1976), which diagnoses bacterial diseases, contain several hundred production rules. H. A. Simon (1979) noted that human medical expertise probably consists of thousands of rules related to differential diagnoses, treatment alternatives, and fundamental knowledge of the biochemistry and physiology of the human system.

Although a part of medical expert knowledge can be represented as rule-based, there are many exceptions to the rules in medicine, in part because every patient is different and not all the rules have been formulated. For example, if a patient in not responding satisfactorily to a prescribed drug dosage, the physician draws inferences from a reservoir of acquired experience that is patient-specific and that is generalizable from experience with similarly unique cases. This new knowledge or discovery (e.g., see Pople, 1977; Shortliffe, 1976) can then be formulated as a revision of the original rule. Thus, an expert's ideal response to the exceptional case is integrative and constructive, not strictly rule-based.

The notion of expert cognition rests heavily on the assumption that there is a difference between novices and experts. Based on Larkin's (1983) and Lesgold's (1983) observations of the novice-to-expert shift, it appears that the progression from novice to expert is relatively irreversible and domain-specific. Whether or not a cognitive shift is identified as qualitative depends on the dimensional criteria for measuring and specifying the stage-related components of novice and expert. Evidence for qualitative developmental change depends on having a sufficient number of measures to show a changed pattern of interrelationship among the variables (e.g., see Baltes & Nesselroade, 1973; Harris, 1957). The differences between novice and expert cognition may be qualitative, but the transition may involve incremental, quantitative, and simultaneous change on several cognitive dimensions. There is a need for further research on the novice-to-expert shift aimed at (a) identifying age- and experience-related sources of the shift, and (b) examining how knowledge is restructured within various domains along multiple measures.

With regard to the study of the structure of knowledge, there has been considerable interest recently in the analysis of mental representations (e.g., Fodor, 1983). According to Gentner and Stevens (1983), mental models research is characterized by the careful examination of the way people understand some domain of knowledge. For example, people's representations of physical principles, such as heat and temperature, electricity, evaporation, and space and motion, are studied for their information about human knowledge organizations, structures, and encoding and retrieval strategies.

Knowing how an individual has constructed a system of knowledge, albeit naive or factual, should aid the task of specifying the control processes which contribute to the development of expert cognition. Although verbal reports of mental processes are of questionable utility (Nisbett & Wilson, 1977), it is reasonable to suggest that the same or similar control processes are used by highly skilled experts in highly structured domains of knowledge (e.g., physics), and that different constellations of control processes are possible for expert performance in less structured fields (e.g., creative writing, story telling). I suggest that novices differ from experts across most fields as a function of the well-learned production sequences or heuristics of experts, that experts in highly structured domains (e.g., physics) use similar expert heuristics, that different experts in relatively loosely structured cognitive domains can use a variety of quite different heuristics, and that novices differ from each other in terms of the efficiency and applicability of their heuristic processes.

SUMMARY AND CONCLUSIONS

Research and theory discussed herein indicate the robustness of many of the domains of adult cognition, in spite of age-related and, frequently, disease-related changes in some cognitive processes. The usefulness of an expert system model to represent age-related differentiation of cognitive function is recommended, since the proposed model can take into account the empirically demonstrated gains and losses in various aspects of cognitive function with age.

The proposed model of expert cognition consists of (a) elementary or component information processes; (b) control processes, which serve to coordinate rule-based sequences, transform or restructure knowledge, and integrate new knowledge; and (c) acquired, rule-based production systems or knowledge stores. In new or unfamiliar learning tasks and in cognitively challenging situations, the main source of variance among individuals is with regard to the efficiency of the control processes which coordinate and/or transform existing task-relevant subroutines for processing new information and carrying out particular cognitive operations. In highly practiced and familiar tasks and contexts, adulthood interindividual differences in cognitive performance are attributed primarily to access to accumulated knowledge. This model gives emphasis to the experience-based real knowledge and acquired competencies of older adults, while recognizing that some elementary information processing skills and their control processes may show selective deficits with advancing age.

REFERENCES

Abelson, R. F. (1981). Psychological status of the script concept. *American Psychologist, 36,* 715–729.

Alba, J. W., & Hasher, L. (1983). Is memory schematic? *Psychological Bulletin, 93,* 203–231.

Anders, T. R., & Fozard, J. L. (1973). Effects of age upon retrieval from primary and secondary memory. *Developmental Psychology, 9,* 411–415.

Anderson, N. H. (1981). *Foundations of information integration theory.* New York: Academic Press.

Anzai, Y., & Simon, H. A. (1979). The theory of learning by doing. *Psychological Review, 86,* 124–140.

Arlin, P. K. (1975). Cognitive development in adulthood: A fifth stage? *Developmental Psychology, 11,* 602–606.

Atkinson, R. C., & Shiffrin, R. M. (1968). Human memory: A proposed system and its control processes. In K. W. Spence & J. T. Spence (Eds.), *The psychology of learning and motivation* (pp. 90–195). New York: Academic Press.

Baddeley, A. D. (1982). Domains of recollection. *Psychological Review, 89,* 708–729.

Baltes, P. B., & Nesselroade, J. R. (1973). The developmental analysis of individual differences on multiple measures. In J. R. Nesselroade & H. W. Reese (Eds.), *Life-span developmental psychology: Methodological issues* (pp. 219–251). New York: Academic Press.

Baltes, P. B., & Willis, S. L. (1982). Plasticity and enhancement of intellectual functioning in old age: Penn State's adult Development and Enrichment Project (ADEPT). In F. I. M. Craik & S. E. Trehub (Eds.), *Aging and cognitive processes* (pp. 353–389). New York: Plenum.

Bartlett, F. C. (1932). *Remembering*. London: Cambridge University Press.

Berg, C., Hertzog, C. K., & Hunt, E. (1982). Age differences in the speed of mental rotation. *Developmental Psychology, 18*, 95–107.

Birren, J. E., Woods, A. M., & Williams, M. V. (1980). Behavioral slowing with age: Causes, organization, and consequences. In L. W. Poon (Ed.), *Aging in the 1980s: Psychological issues* (pp. 293–308). Washington, DC: American Psychological Association.

Bower, G. H. (1981). Mood and memory. *American Psychologist, 36*, 129–148.

Brown, A. L., & Day, J. D. (1983). Macrorules for summarizing texts: The development of expertise. *Journal of Verbal Learning and Verbal Behavior, 22*, 1–14.

Card, S. K., Moran, T. P., & Newell, A. (1980). Computer text-editing: An information-processing analysis of a routine cognitive skill. *Cognitive Psychology, 12*, 32–74.

Card, S. K., Moran, T. P., & Newell, A. (1983). *The psychology of human-computer interaction*. Hillsdale, NJ: Erlbaum.

Cerella, J., Poon, L. W., & Fozard, J. L. (1981). Mental rotation and age reconsidered. *Journal of Gerontology, 36*, 620–624.

Cerella, J., Poon, L. W., & Williams, D. M. (1980). Age and the complexity hypothesis. In L. W. Poon (Ed.), *Aging in the 1980s: Psychological issues* (pp. 332–340). Washington, DC: American Psychological Association.

Charness, N. (1981). Aging and skilled problem solving. *Journal of Experimental Psychology: General, 110*, 21–38.

Chi, M. T. H., Glaser, R., & Rees, E. (1982). Expertise in problem solving. In R. J. Sternberg (Ed.), *Advances in the psychology of human intelligence* (pp. 7–75). Hillsdale, NJ: Erlbaum.

Cole, S. (1979). Age and scientific performance. *American Journal of Sociology, 84*, 958–977.

Collins, A. M., & Loftus, E. F. (1975). A spreading activation theory of semantic processing. *Psychological Review, 82*, 407–428.

Craik, F. I. M., & Byrd, M. (1982). Aging and cognitive deficits: The role of attentional resources. In F. I. M. Craik & S. Trehub (Eds.), *Aging and cognitive processes* (pp. 191–211). New York: Plenum.

Craik, F. I. M. & Lockhart, R. S. (1972). Levels of processing: A framework for memory research. *Journal of Verbal Learning and Verbal Behavior, 11*, 671–684.

Craik, F. I. M., & Simon, E. (1980). Age differences in memory: The roles of attention and depth of processing. In L. W. Poon, J. L. Fozard, L. S. Cermak, D. Arenberg, & L. W. Thompson (Eds.), *New directions in memory and aging* (pp. 95–112). Hillsdale, NJ: Erlbaum.

Cunningham, W. R. (1981). Ability factor structure differences in adulthood and old age. *Multivariate Behavioral Research, 16*, 13–22.

Demming, J. A., & Pressey, S. L. (1957). Tests indigenous to the adult and older years. *Journal of Consulting Psychology, 4*, 144–148.

Dempster, F. N. (1981). Memory span: Sources of individual and developmental differences. *Psychological Bulletin, 89*, 63–100.

DiLollo, V., Arnett, J. L., & Kruk, R. V. (1982). Age-related changes in rate of visual information processing. *Journal of Experimental Psychology: Human Perception and Performance, 8*, 225–237.

Dittman-Kohli, F., & Baltes, P. B. (1985). Toward a neofunctionalist conception of adult intellectual development: Wisdom as a prototypical case of intellectual growth. In C. Alexander & E. Langer (Eds.), *Beyond formal operations: Alternative endpoints to human development*. New York: Oxford University Press.

Ericsson, K. A., Chase, W. G., & Faloon, S. (1980). Acquisition of a memory skill. *Science, 208*, 1181–1182.

Eriksen, C. W., Hamlin, R. M., & Breitmeyer, R. G. (1970). Temporal factors in visual perception as related to aging. *Perception and Psychophysics, 7,* 354–356.

Ernst, G. W., & Newell, A. (1969). *GPS: A case study in generality and problem solving.* New York: Academic Press.

Fodor, J. A. (1983). *Modularity of mind.* Cambridge, MA: MIT Press.

Franks, J. J., Bransford, J. D., & Auble, P. M. (1982). The activation and utilization of knowledge. In C. R. Puff (Ed.), *Handbook of research methods in human memory and cognition* (pp. 396–425). New York: Academic Press.

Gentner, D., & Grudin, J. (1985). The evolution of mental metaphors in psychology: A 90-year retrospective. *American Psychologist, 40,* 182–192.

Gentner, D., & Stevens, A. L. (Eds.). (1983). *Mental models.* Hillsdale, NJ: Erlbaum.

Giambra, L. M. (1983). *Complex concept identification in adulthood: An idiographic, in depth, and wholistic approach.* Unpublished manuscript.

Gregory, R. L. (1981). *Mind in science.* Cambridge, England: Cambridge University Press.

Greeno, J. G. (1983). Conceptual entities. In D. Gentner & A. L. Stevens (Eds.), *Mental models* (pp. 227–252). Hillsdale, NJ: Erlbaum.

Harris, D. B. (Ed.). (1957). *The concept of development.* Minneapolis: University of Minnesota Press,.

Hartley, A. A., & Anderson, J. W. (1983). Task complexity, problem representation, and problem-solving performance by younger and older adults. *Journal of Gerontology, 38,* 78–80.

Hasher, L., & Zacks, R. T. (1979). Automatic and effortful processes in memory. *Journal of Experimental Psychology: General, 108,* 356–388.

Hayes-Roth, F., Waterman, D. A., & Lenat, D. B. (1983). *Building expert systems.* Reading, MA: Addison-Wesley.

Hick, W. E. (1952). On the rate of gain of information. *Quarterly Journal of Experimental Psychology, 4,* 11–26.

Hirst, W., Spelke, E. S., Reaves, C. C., Caharack, G., & Neisser, U. (1980). Dividing attention without alternation or automaticity. *Journal of Experimental Psychology: General, 109,* 98–117.

Hofstadter, D. R. (1979). *Godel, Escher, and Bach: An eternal golden braid.* New York: Basic Books.

Holding, D. H. (Ed.). (1981). *Human skills.* New York: Wiley.

Howard, D. V., McAndrews, M. P., & Lasaga, M. I. (1981). Semantic priming of lexical decisions in young and old adults. *Journal of Gerontology, 36,* 707–714.

Hoyer, W. J. (1974). Aging as intraindividual change. *Developmental Psychology, 10,* 821–826.

Hoyer, W. J., & Familant, M. E. (1983). *Adult age differences in the use pre-cue information and attentional set.* Paper presented at the American Psychological Association Meetings, Anaheim, CA.

Hoyer, W. J., & Plude, D. J. (1980). Attentional and perceptual processes in the study of cognitive aging. In L. W. Poon (Ed.), *Aging in the 1980s: Psychological issues* (pp. 227–238). Washington, DC: American Psychological Association.

Hoyer, W. J., & Plude, D. J. (1982). Aging and the allocation of attentional resources in visual information-processing. In R. Sekuler, D. Kline, & K. Dismukes (Eds.), *Aging and human visual function* (pp. 245–263). New York: Alan R. Liss.

Hoyer, W. J., Rebok, G. W., & Sved, S. M. (1979). Effects of varying irrelevant information on adult age differences in problem solving. *Journal of Gerontology, 34,* 553–560.

Hunt, E. (1978). Mechanics of verbal ability. *Psychological Review, 85,* 109–130.

Hunter, I. M. L. (1977). An exceptional memory. *British Journal of Psychology, 68,* 155–164.

Jacoby, L. L. (1978). On interpreting the effects of repetition: Solving a problem versus remembering a solution. *Journal of Verbal learning and Verbal Behavior, 17,* 649–667.

Jeffries, R., Turner, A. A., Polson, P. G., & Atwood, M. E. (1981). The processes involved in designing software. In J. R. Anderson (Ed.), *Cognitive skills and their acquisition* (pp. 255–283). Hillsdale, NJ: Erlbaum.

Keil, F. C. (1981). Constraints on knowledge and cognitive development. *Psychological Review, 88,* 197–227.

Klahr, D., & Siegler, R. S. (1978). The representation of children's knowledge. In H. Reese & L. P. Lipsitt (Eds.), *Advances in child development and behavior* (Vol. 12, pp. 61–116). New York: Academic Press.

Klapp, S. T., Marshburn, E. A., & Lester, P. T. (1983). Short-term memory does not involve the "working memory" of information processing: The demise of a common assumption. *Journal of Experimental Psychology: General, 112,* 240–264.

Kline, D. W., & Scheiber, F. (1981). What are the age differences in visual sensory memory? *Journal of Gerontology, 36,* 86–89.

Kohn, M. L., & Schooler, C. (1978). The reciprocal effects of the substantive complexity of work and intellectual flexibility: A longitudinal assessment. *American Journal of Sociology, 84,* 24–52.

Kramer, D. A. (1983). Post-formal operations? A need for further conceptualization. *Human Development, 26,* 91–105.

Krauss, I. K. (1980). Between- and within-group comparisons in aging research. In L. W. Poon (Ed.), *Aging in the 1980s: Psychological issues* (pp. 542–551). Washington, DC: American Psychological Association.

LaBerge, D., & Samuels, S. J. (1974). Toward a theory of automatic information processing in reading. *Cognitive Psychology, 6,* 293–323.

Labouvie-Vief, G., & Gonda, J. N. (1976). Cognitive strategy training and intellectual performance in the elderly. *Journal of Gerontology, 31,* 327–332.

Langer, E. J. (1980). Old age: An artifact. In J. McGough, & S. B. Kiesler (Eds.), *Aging: Biology and behavior* (pp. 255–281). New York: Academic Press.

Langley, P., & Simon, H. A. (1981). The central role of learning in cognition. In J. R. Anderson (Ed.), *Cognitive skills and their acquisition* (pp. 361–380). Hillsdale, NJ: Erlbaum.

Larkin, J. H. (1981). Enriching formal knowledge: A model for learning to solve problems in physics. In J. R. Anderson (Ed.), *Cognitive skills and their acquisition* (pp. 311–334). Hillsdale, NJ: Erlbaum.

Larkin, J. H. (1983). The role of problem representation in physics. In D. Gentner & A. L. Stevens (Eds.), *Mental models* (pp. 75–98). Hillsdale, NJ: Erlbaum.

Lehman, H. C. (1953). *Age and achievement.* Princeton, NJ: Princeton University Press.

Lesgold, A. M. (1983, May). *Expert systems.* Paper presented at the Cognitive Science 5 Meetings. Rochester, New York.

Lesgold, A. M., Feltovich, P. J., Glaser, R., & Wang, Y. (1981). *The acquisition of perceptual diagnostic skill in radiology* (Tech. Rep.). Pittsburgh: University of Pittsburgh, Learning Research and Development Center.

Light, L. L., & Anderson, P. A. (1983). Memory for scripts in young and older adults. *Memory and Cognition, 11,* 435–444.

Luria, A. R. (1968). *The mind of a mnemonist.* New York: Avon.

McFarland, R. A., & O'Doherty, B. M. (1959). Work and occupational skills. In J. E. Birren (Ed.), *Handbook of aging and the individual* (pp. 452–500). Chicago: University of Chicago Press.

McArthur, D. J. (1982). Computer vision and perceptual psychology. *Psychological Bulletin, 92,* 283–309.

McKeithen, K. B., Reitman, J. S., Rueter, H. H., & Hirtle, S. C. (1981). Knowledge organization and skill differences in computer programmers. *Cognitive Psychology, 13,* 307–325.

Mandler, G. (1975). *Mind and emotion.* New York: Wiley.

Mergler, N. L., & Goldstein, M. D. (1983). Why are there old people. Senescence as biological and cultural preparedness for the transmission of information. *Human Development, 26,* 72–90.

Miller, J. (1982). Divided attention: Evidence for coactivation with redundant signals. *Cognitive Psychology, 14,* 247–279.

Neely, J. H. (1977). Semantic priming and retrieval from lexical memory: Roles of inhibitionless spreading activation and limited capacity attention. *Journal of Experimental Psychology: General, 106,* 226–254.

Neves, D. M., & Anderson, J. R. (1981). Knowledge compilation: Mechanisms for the automatization of cognitive skills. In J. R. Anderson (Ed.), *Cognitive skills and their acquisition* (pp. 57–84) Hillsdale, NJ: Erlbaum.

Nisbett, R. E., & Wilson, T. D. (1977). Telling more than we can know: Verbal reports on mental processes. *Psychological Review, 84,* 231–259.

Perkins, D. N. (1982). *Mind's best work.* Cambridge, MA: Harvard University Press.

Perlmutter, M. (1979). Age differences in adult's free recall, cued recall, and recognition. *Journal of Gerontology, 34,* 533–539.

Piaget, J, (1928). *Judgment and reasoning in the child.* New York: Harcourt, Brace.

Plude, D. J., & Hoyer, W. J. (1981). Adult age differences in visual search as a function of stimulus mapping and information load. *Journal of Gerontology, 36,* 598–604.

Plude, D. J., & Hoyer, W. J. (1985). Attention and performance. In N. Charness (Ed.), *Aging and performance.* London: Wiley.

Plude, D. J., Kaye, D., Hoyer, W. J., Post, T., Saynisch, M., & Hahn, M. (1983). Aging and visual search under consistent and varied mapping. *Developmental Psychology, 19,* 508–512.

Pople, H. (1977). The formation of composite hypotheses in diagnostic problem solving. *Proceedings of the Fifth International Joint Conference on Artificial Intelligence, 2,* 1030–1037.

Posner, M. I., & McLeod, P. (1982). Information processing models—In search of elementary operations. *Annual Review of Psychology, 33,* 477–514.

Pylyshyn, Z. W. (1973). The role of competence theories in cognitive psychology. *Journal of Psycholinguistic Research, 2,* 21–50.

Rabbitt, P. M. A. (1982a). How do older people know what to do next? In F. I. M. Craik, & S. Trehub (Eds.), *Aging and cognitive processes* (pp. 79–98). New York: Plenum.

Rabbitt, P. M. A. (1982b). Breakdown of control processes in old age. In T. M. Field, A. Huston, H. C. Quay, L. Troll, & G. Finley (Eds.), *Review of human development* (pp. 540–550). New York: Wiley.

Reese, H. W., & Overton, W. F. (1970). Models of development and theories of development. In L. R. Goulet & P. B. Baltes (Eds.), *Life-span developmental psychology: Research and theory* (pp. 115–145). New York: Academic Press.

Reinert, G. (1970). Comparative factor analytic studies of intelligence throughout the human life span. In L. R. Goulet & P. B. Baltes (Eds.), *Life-span developmental psychology: Research and theory* (pp. 467–484). New York: Academic Press.

Riegel, K. F. (1972). Time and change in the development of the individual and society. In H. W. Reese (Ed.), *Advances in child development and behavior* (Vol. 7, pp. 81–113). New York: Academic Press.

Salthouse, T. A. (1985). Motor performance and speed of behavior. In J. E. Birren & K. W. Schaie (Eds.), *Handbook of the psychology of aging* (pp. 406–426). New York: Van Nostrand Reinhold.

Salthouse, T. A., & Somberg, B. L. (1982a). Isolating the age deficit in speeded performance. *Journal of Gerontology, 37,* 59–63.

Salthouse, T. A., & Somberg, B. L. (1982b). Skilled performance: The effects of adult age and experience on elementary processes. *Journal of Experimental Psychology: General, 111,* 176–207.

Schaie, K. W. (1979). The primary mental abilities in adulthood: An exploration in the development of psychometric intelligence. In P. B. Baltes & O. G. Brim (Eds.), *Life-span development and behavior* (Vol. 2, pp. 68–115). New York: Academic Press.

Schank, R. C., & Abelson, R. P. (1977). *Scripts, plans, goals, and understanding.* Hillsdale, NJ: Erlbaum.

Scheidt, R. J., & Schaie, K. W. (1978). A taxonomy of situations for an elderly population: Generating situational criteria. *Journal of Gerontology, 33,* 848–857.

Schneider, W., & Shiffrin, R. M. (1977). Controlled and automatic human information processing. I. Detection, search, and attention. *Psychological Review, 84,* 1–66.

Shaw, M. L. (1982). Attending to multiple sources of information: I. The integration of information in decision making. *Cognitive Psychology, 14,* 353–409.

Shortliffe, E. H. (1976). *Computer-based medical consultations: MYCIN.* New York: American Elsevier.

Siegler, R. S. (1983). Five generalizations about cognitive development. *American Psychologist, 38,* 263–277.

Simon, D. P., & Simon, H. A. (1978). Individual differences in solving physics problems. In R. S. Siegler (Ed.), *Children's thinking: What develops?* (pp. 325–348). Hillsdale, NJ: Erlbaum.

Simon, E. (1979). Depth and elaboration of processing in relation to age. *Journal of Experimental Psychology: Human Learning and Memory, 5,* 115–124.

Simon, H. A. (1979). Information-processing models of cognition. *Annual Review of Psychology, 30,* 363–396.

Simon, H. A. (1981). *The sciences of the artificial* (second edition). Cambridge, MA: MIT Press.

Sinnott, J. D. (1984). Postformal reasoning: The relativistic stage. In M. Commons, F. A. Richards, & C. Armon (Eds.), *Beyond formal operations* (pp. 298–325). New York: Praeger.

Somberg, B. L., & Salthouse, T. A. (1982). Divided attention abilities in young and old adults. *Journal of Experimental Psychology: Human Perception and Performance, 8,* 651–663.

Sternberg, R. J. (1982). A componential approach to intellectual development. In R. J. Sternberg (Ed.), *Advances in the psychology of human intelligence* (pp. 413–463). Hillsdale, NJ: Erlbaum.

Sutton, R. S., & Barto, A. G. (1981). Toward a modern theory of adaptive networks: Expectation and prediction. *Psychological Review, 88,* 135–170.

Sweller, J., Mawer, R. F., & Ward, M. R. (1983). Developmental expertise in mathematical problem solving. *Journal of Experimental Psychology: General, 112,* 639–661.

Talland, G. A., & Cairnie, J. (1964). Aging effects on simple, disjunctive, and alerted finger reaction time. *Journal of Gerontology, 19,* 31–38.

Welford, A. T. (1958). *Ageing and human skill.* London: Oxford University Press.

Welford, A. T. (1968). *Fundamentals of skill.* London: Methuen.

Wood, P. K. (1983). Inquiring systems and problem structure: Implications for cognitive development. *Human Development, 26,* 249–265.

Chapter 6

Ecological Validity and Idiography in Developmental Cognitive Science

Jurgis Karuza, Jr.

State University College at Buffalo, and
Western New York Geriatric Education Center

Michael A. Zevon

Roswell Park Memorial Institute

While cognitive scientists have developed sophisticated methodologies and highly articulated, if not overly specialized, models of cognitive functioning, questions can and should be raised about the relevance of the research findings in explaining and predicting practical everyday behavior as it develops over the lifespan. The purpose of the present article is rather modest. First, to remind cognitive scientists of the importance of considering ecological validity both in the design of their research efforts and in the interpretation of the results. Second, to acquaint researchers with the idiographic tradition in the design of experimental methodology, an approach which may be useful in generating a more thorough understanding of cognitive processes as they operate in the world.

ECOLOGICAL VALIDITY

The concept of ecological validity has a long and venerable history (cf. Barker & Wright, 1954), but the term has a variety of connotations which, unfortunately, disguise its relevance to laboratory, experimental methodologies (Bronfenbrenner, 1977; Willems, 1973). Ecological validity has often been taken to be synonymous with nonexperimental field research that stresses naturalistic observation of behavior. There is another sense of ecological validity that focuses on the larger issue of the interdependencies among the organism, its behavior, and its environment. Applying this concern to the scientific enterprise, Bronfenbrenner (1977) defines ecological validity as

> the extent to which the environment experienced by the subjects in a scientific investigation has the properties it is supposed or assumed to have by the investigator. (p. 516)

No matter where the research is conducted, whether the subject perceives and reacts to the setting and task as the researcher anticipated has implications for the interpretation of the results. This should be of equal interest to the laboratory-based cognitive scientist as to the field observer.

Typically among cognitive developmentalists, the concern with ecological validity centers on whether the results of laboratory experiments are descriptive and predictive of individuals' everyday cognitive activities (see Baltes, Reese, & Nesselroade, 1977; Hartley, Harker, & Walsh, 1980). Addressing ecological validity from this perspective highlights the relationship between it and the issue of *external validity* (cf. Cook & Campbell, 1979; Hultsch & Hickey, 1978; Schaie, 1978). While the two terms are related, they should not be treated as synonymous. External validity refers to the extent a study's results are applicable and generalizable to the same or a different population in other settings, and/or in other time periods. It may be best treated as a measurement issue. Ecological validity focuses on the quality of a study's *context,* whether it in fact adequately reflects and operationalizes properties of the environment the researcher seeks to generalize to. Ecological validity is often equated with capturing the tasks and demands of "everyday life," but this may be a limiting definition (see Bronfenbrenner, 1977), since what specific environment is being generalized to depends on the research question asked. The research can focus alternatively on understanding and predicting behavior in community life, a nursing home, a family, or a college classroom. Whether a study is generalizable to a particular environment depends on the study's context containing similar properties as the environment being generalized to, properties which are assumed to trigger in a subject psychological processes and behaviors that are typical of individuals in the environment of interest.

Approaching the point of ecological validity from another direction brings the realization that, in addition to the planned independent variables, the *context* of the research enterprise can affect how subjects interpret and respond to a study. How the context interacts with the independent variable—or is confounded with it—becomes an aspect of the experiment's ecological validity. This sense of ecological validity reflects on the internal and construct validity of the research (Cook & Campbell, 1979). Further, the concept of ecological validity, as applied to laboratory settings, suggests the relevance of some techniques in social psychological research which are used to improve the impact and control of the experimental manipulations. In the sections that follow, we will focus on the specific ways that ecological validity can be important to the developmental cognitive scientist.

Developmental research strategies and ecological validity

As developmental-cognitive scientists describe and assess changes or stability in cognitive performance across two or more age groups, concerns with ecological validity become more complex. The researcher must consider the applicability of the research context, design, and measurement for the various age groups investigated. The study's ecological validity may change across age groups, no matter if the study is longitudinal, cross sectional, or sequential in its data collection strategy. Because of cohort differences, such as formal educational level (cf. Baltes & Schaie, 1976), changes in the historical context over time (cf. Labouvie-Vief & Chandler, 1978), qualitative cognitive changes in the underlying cognitive functioning of individuals, (cf. Labouvie-Vief & Blanchard-Fields, 1982), or quantitative changes in the perceptual and motor systems, subjects of different ages participating in the same study may, quite literally, experience different studies.

If the researcher is following a descriptive strategy (i.e., trying to describe the variations and limits in cognitive functioning across situations and across different ages), then which cognitive tasks are chosen, and when and where they are examined, can become important variables that can determine the informativeness and representativeness of the findings. If the researcher is deductive in his or her approach, then the concern is with matching the cognitive task, the experimental setting, and the dependent measure to the theoretical linkages being tested. Any theoretical cognitive model can be seen as explicitly or implicitly making assumptions about the relevance of environmental or contextual factors to the cognitive processes investigated. For example, as Hoyer in another chapter in this section illustrates, present day computational models of cognitive behavior fail to take into account such factors as alertness, attention, or distraction. These factors largely depend on the context of the cognitive activity. Consider the potential impact of a public competitive chess match, with its distractions and demands, on a player's game—something well known to seasoned masters. In contrast, the currently articulated, top down, and transactional models of cognitive functioning (see Meyer & Rebok's chapter in this volume; Luria, 1976; Meacham, 1982) treat contextual demands and environmental feedback as important influences on cognitive processing.

In cases where a model discounts contextual factors, the environmental and contextual factors must be treated as sources of nuisance error variance. The strategy before the researcher is to avoid systematic variation of these contextual factors, either by holding the context constant across conditions (e.g., using the same sorting task which may be differentially interesting for different age groups), or by assuming the context effects are randomly distributed as error variance (e.g., that no systematic difference can be associated with measuring the cognitive performance of elderly tested in a senior citizen center with friends looking on, and college students being tested alone in a psychology learning laboratory). In both cases, the researcher faces the basic issue of ecological validity even if the researcher is not interested in contextual factors per se.

Traps in ignoring ecological validity

Discounting ecological validity can lead the researcher into traps. If the assumption that differences in experimental context yield random error variance is incorrect, then the experimental adequacy of the research design can be called into question. Some contextual "artifact" that systematically covaried with the experimental manipulation or the age of the subjects may have produced the effect. The safer approach is to "control for" contextual, ecologically based factors by holding them constant over conditions and groups. The danger with this approach is that, in holding the context equivalent, the *external validity* of the study is jeopardized. The context selected may be so artificial (e.g., a sterile laboratory study), and behavior measured so trivial, as to raise doubts about the result's generalizability to everyday world problems and events. Alternatively, a selected context may have high relevance and realism for one age group, but not for another (e.g., the very act of taking a test), thus creating a differential generalizability across age groups. If subjects are differentially captivated by the context or the task, some may respond with their feet, that is, drop out of the study. Differential dropout rates can create problems with the design's *internal validity*.

Compounding these problems for developmentally based cognitive research is the issue of whether the experienced context, the manipulation, and the dependent measure are conceptually equivalent for different age groups (Labouvie, 1980). By making sure that all subjects are exposed to the identical context and manipulations, and are measured using the same dependent measures, the researcher tries to develop an invariant frame of reference that allows comparisons among the different age groups. In such cases, even if a context, manipulation, or dependent measure is identical for all subjects, i.e., formally equivalent, the context, manipulation, or dependent measure may not be functionally equivalent. The study's *construct validity* can be called into question, whether the causes of the obtained differences between age groups or of age group by treatment interactions are correctly identified. Attributing cognitive declines in cognitive processes to maturation may be equivocal when the experimental ecology is interpreted differently by different aged subjects. The declines could be due to noncognitive age-graded differences in motivational level, interest, or familiarity.

Measures

Results could be artifacts of dependent measures that are irrelevant measures of cognitive performance for a given age group. The chosen dependent variables may not typically occur in the generalized environment, or be very low on an individual's response hierarchy. The measures may also be insensitive to changes in the cognitive level of the subjects (Labouvie-Vief, 1985)—akin to measuring locomotive ability of adolescents using a crawling test. A "cohort bias" may exist in the test instruments (Schaie, 1978). An example can be found in a study by Deutscher, Kosierowski, Karuza, and Reid (1979). The performance of elderly relative to young adult subjects significantly improved when the subjects took a 1920s IQ test—which was more cohort-relevant for the elderly subjects, compared to a 1960s IQ test.

Especially important in testing the expert cognition model presented by Hoyer in this volume is the issue of "whose expertise is being studied, the experimenter's or the subject's?" The initial assumption is that the knowledge domains of both subject and experimenter overlap. Historical changes and differences in what information is accumulated and how knowlege is differentiated may make the rules-based sequences of one generation nonequivalent to another. In other words, expertise in many domains is history-relative. Individuals with a long history of experience may have a more articulated knowledge structure and perspective that can affect how the situation is interpreted and what responses are initiated. If the experimenter has a truncated view of a domain, then he or she may misunderstand or misscore the knowledge of an expert that has the benefit of a longer history. Finally, the role of motivational and attentional states in expert models of cognition should not be overlooked. That experts are intrinsically interested in applying and/or expanding their knowledge may not always be true. As in other cognitive research, the subjects' level of involvement and their motivation, products of the ecological demands and social expectations, can directly affect the speed and accuracy of expert performance or acquisition of expert knowlege rules.

Holding aside the issues of the internal and construct validity of cognitive studies, questions should be raised concerning the *functional significance* of experimentally observed cognitive declines to everyday life. Do these declines result in a noticable and meaningful difference? The literature has in the main focused on the causes of declines, and considerably less attention has been paid to how problems resulting from cognitive declines can be solved or *are* solved. Often, developmentalists fail to distinguish the causes of cognitive problems from their solutions, assuming that declines are inevitable by-products of senescent processes and so beyond compensation or rehabilitation. An exception to this has been the literature exploring training and practice on cognitive performance (e.g., Denney, 1979; Labouvie-Vief & Gonda, 1976; Labouvie-Vief, Hoyer, Baltes, & Baltes, 1974).

While organized training programs have been found to be useful, they do not exhaust the possibilities of how individuals cope with cognitive deficits or develop compensatory techniques. In everyday life, organized training or chances for practice trials may not occur very often. When they do occur, their ecology may be different from that found in laboratory studies. Implicit messages about an individual's competency, negative social labels surrounding "being taught," or power differentials between the "teacher" and individual can undermine the intention and benefits of training. Research that examines these contextual and ecological variables in everyday life is important and necessary.

Individuals also may have established a repertoire of alternative strategies that address the dysfunction associated with cognitive deficiencies. Research that evaluates the efficacy of these strategies (e.g., list making, changes in interaction patterns, changes in mode of communication, more realistic goal setting, more efficient scheduling) is warranted. To find age-related changes in cognition, from this perspective, is only the beginning. The focus of the research should broaden, to determine the ecological factors that impede or enhance the functioning of all individuals in everyday contexts and the ways to optimize the level of functioning.

Issues in designing an experiment

The direct examination of the ecological validity of the manipulations and measures can be a key to deriving functionally equivalent and reliable variables. To this end, attempts at developing taxonomies that categorize contexts according to their familiarity, interest, and difficulty to the subject (e.g., Scheidt & Schaie, 1978) may prove useful. Within limits, self reports (see Nisbett & Wilson, 1977), about subjects' experiences in the study, or about how they deal with cognitive problems in daily life (e.g., Hulicka, 1982; Lachman & Lachman, 1980; Meyer & Rebok, in this volume) can be important sources of information, offering leads on developing more ecologically valid designs, setting limits to the generalizability of the results, confirming the adequacy of the manipulations and measures, or fleshing out underlying processes. Practically speaking, this means paying attention to the study's debriefing phase, where opportunities to solicit "meta cognitive" information are possible. It may well be worth it to the researcher to adopt a more social psychological multivariate approach, where the subjects' feelings, evaluations, and opinions are formally solicited and analyzed, in addition to the performance data.

A case in point is the study by Meyer and Rebok in this volume on the development of plans in a sorting task. The self-report data collected about the subjects' intended planning strategy, their satisfaction with the effectiveness of the sorts, and their awareness of the sorting strategy's effectiveness offer compelling evidence for the existence of considerable planning-in-action across the lifespan. These data also help in understanding the age differences found in sorting effectiveness. Specifically, youngsters seem to be less effective in their sorting, because they failed to see the relationship between their plans and subsequent actions, while the elderly seem to suffer from a deficiency in developing fully elaborated plans based on previous sorting experiences.

The mis en scène

In an experiment, the subject is reacting to an environment shaped by the experimenter. To the experimenter, the major component of the experimental environment is the experimental treatment or manipulation, but to the eyes of the subject it is only part of the larger context of "the experiment." The total experimental mis en scène[1] creates for the subject a set of implicit expectations

---

[1]Mis en scène, orginally a French term, refers to the act or art of placing actors, scenery, and props on stage. The term has been adopted by cinema and stage critics in their discussion of a scene's qualities. The term is felt to be particularly descriptive, highlighting the intricacies in properly creating the surroundings, and defining the context of a study.

of what is appropriate behavior, how one is supposed to act and when; e.g., the subject is expected to act like a subject and obey the instructions of the experimenter. The implicit power differential between subject and experimenter, the constraints on what is appropriate behavior, and the limited choice subjects have in an experiment are all reminiscent of the environment found in some institutional settings (Rodin & Langer, 1980). Ironically, laboratory-based studies may be more generalizable to the elderly in institutional settings, where choice is limited and power segregated in the hands of the staff, than to the elderly in community or home-based environments.

A series of studies on cognitive processes across the lifespan illustrate the sensitivity of performance to a host of noncognitive factors, e.g., overarousal (Eisdorfer, Nowlin, & Wilkie, 1970); absence of feedback and reinforcement (Labouvie-Vief et al., 1974; Langer, Rodin, Beck, Weinman, & Spitzer, 1979; Rebok & Hoyer, 1977), familiarity of the task (Demming & Pressey, 1957); disinterest; embarrassment, cautiousness (Canestrari, 1963); lack of practice in orienting to the task, and the techniques of learning (Hultsch, 1974). The experimental mis en scène, things like the rationale (or lack of rationale) offered for the study, the directness and clarity of instructions, the familiarity of the task and surroundings, the amount of feedback given, and opportunities for practice affect the subjects' orientation, attention, involvement, and motivation. Since changes in cognitive processes must be inferred through the subjects' performance, these motivational, attentional, and practice effects can obscure or distort the cognitive processes at work.

At this point, developmental cognitive science may find it useful to borrow a few techniques from social psychological research in creating an appropriate experimental ecology, specifically, through enhancing the study's experimental and mundane realism (Carlsmith, Ellsworth, & Aronson, 1976). When it involves a subject, when it is plausible and realistic to the subject, and when it impacts on the subject, a study is said to have "experimental realism". When what happens or what is expected to happen in an experimental context is analogous to events in the "real world," a study is said to have "mundane realism." The logic is simple: the independent variable has a better chance to have an impact on the subject when he or she is clear about what to do, is familiar with the task, is involved and treats the study seriously, and harbors no suspicion. With subjects truly involved in the study and not playing at being "cooperative experimental subjects," the generalizability of the results to real world situations can be enhanced.

Simply making an experiment high in mundane realism (e.g., using familiar tasks, employing everyday props, running the study in familiar surroundings) by itself may not guarantee ecological validity or generalizable results. Behavior of subjects who are suspicious, overly eager to please, or bored, even when the experimental task is most ordinary and commonplace, will not be representative of the behavior outside an experiment. Further, motivational states, and orientations to the tasks, can differ across subjects even if contexts are familiar and challenging. Ironically, a study which uses a mundane context and task can become ecologically invalid for a group of subjects when trying to explain or predict everyday behavior. One such example is the elderly woman subject in the Meyer and Rebok study who appeared to treat the card sort as a phenomenological exercise, trying different sorting strategies "for curiosity." Contrast that to the dedicated problem-solving orientation of the young adults.

Because of the potential variability in studies, no simple "cookbook" of tested experimental "recipes" can be offered. The study by Meyer & Rebok in the present volume, however, illustrates one promising strategy of enhancing the ecological validity of cognitive studies, that of using tasks and/or materials associated with "gaming." Gaming contexts, such as playing with cards, bingo, guessing games, board games, etc., tend to be familiar, challenging, and interesting to subjects while providing them feedback as the task progresses. Since experience with playing cards cuts across age, questions of the cohort relevance of the task or its equivalence across age groups are less problematic. The process data, wisely collected and reported by Meyer and Rebok, tend to confirm that, in general, subjects of all ages were captivated and intrinsically motivated by the study. Assuming that the theoretical variables of interest can be operationalized adequately, gaming situations and tasks can yield data about the underlying cognitive processes that are less distorted by artifacts such as motivational level or familiarity.

Automatic processing and experimental context

A large part of a study's mis en scène is defined, obviously, by more "macro" aspects of the experimental environment, such as the task being used. Recent work on automatic processing (Shiffrin & Schneider, 1977; Taylor & Fiske, 1978) suggests that subtle variations in the study's context can also contribute to the mis en scène, variations the subject or experimenter may not even be aware of. This literature argues that individuals may often react automatically to salient cues of the environment, or react to situations with reflexive, overlearned cognitive "scripts" (Abelson, 1976; Langer, 1978). How a subject interprets an experimental context, how involved he or she becomes, and when and where his or her attention is directed, may be automatically determined by cues such as brightness, motion or novelty of a stimulus, or the instructional set. Examining the effects of these "micro" cues, and cataloging situational differences, can be important in defining more precisely factors that impact on a study's ecological validity.

Particularly important is determining which situations and environments enhance or suppress the automatic processing mode. Taylor and Fiske (1978) argue that situations that are familiar, frequent, redundant, and boring may, in fact, elicit automatic processing. Accordingly, the extent to which an experimental context enhances the opportunity for automatic processing can be an important consideration for cognitive research, affecting the interpretation and generalizability of a particular study. Research on the expert cognition model is a good example. According to Hoyer, in this volume, the aim of an expert cognition model is

> to represent what the person is competent to perform, and as such the model is relevant to behavior under idealized and domain-specific conditions where the effects of potentially limiting control operations and processes are discounted.

Ecological validity concerns appear to be paramount in testing the expert cognition model. To adequately test the development of expert cognition, selecting contexts that map the correct domain of knowledge that is being studied, and that minimize control processes, is critical. If the experimenter guesses incorrectly in the formulation of the experimental context and choice of task, then control processing effects may masquarade as expert cognition limits. If, as Hoyer suggests, age deficits in cognitive performance are due to control functioning deficits, then generalizing cognitive performance of older subjects in environments that enhance automatic processes to those that do not, becomes problematic. If Taylor and Fiske are correct, then it may be that a boring, less involving environment (e.g., an abstract laboratory setting) may overestimate the effectiveness of expert cognition compared to a more novel, involving real world situation. Examining age related differences in automatic processing phenomena is theoretically and practically interesting.

THE INDIVIDUAL IN COGNITIVE SCIENCE

Thus far, we have argued that the context of the research setting plays an important role in the integrity of developmental cognitive science research. In particular, the cognitive scientist should be aware of potential person-by-environment interactions that could limit the integrity and interpretation of the results. In developmental-based research, individual change becomes intrinsically interesting, unlike traditional experimental approaches where individual differences are sources of error and instability. While the methods of cognitive science have maximized control and precision, we can ask whether the methods are equipped to uncover and fully map individual developmental changes. This leads us to the issue of the status of the individual in cognitive science research.

The typical approach of cognitive science is nomothetic, that is, a level of analysis which seeks to find general principles by examining similarities across individuals. The research strategies treat inter-individual and intra-individual differences as sources of error variance in the experimental design. Methodological techniques, such as large N designs with subjects randomly selected from the target population, and statistical procedures, such as analysis of variance and analysis of covariance, are used to "control" these sources of error variance. The assumption is made that the underlying "essence" of ecological validity, or the principles underlying a cognitive process, can only be found in aggregate data. The individual case is mistrusted, being contaminated with individual differences. The lawfulness of behavior is believed to be more certain when based on many cases (see Lewin, 1931). By computing averages, the data are purified of the "error" of inter-individual differences, since they cancel themselves out. In doing so, the individual is lost. The results from a given nomothetically based study may camouflage divergent streams of behavior that result from individual differences in viewing and reacting to a particular environment and its demands. Borrowing from personality theory, the idiographic, or individual-based, level of analysis can be an effective additional methodological tool for cognitive scientists, not only helping define the parameters of a study's ecological validity but uncovering the development of cognitive processes.

The nomothetic idiographic distinction in psychology

Debate regarding the adequacy of the nomothetic versus the idiographic perspective in science has persisted since Windelband (1904) introduced the terms in an attempt to distinguish scientific enterprises concerned with the identification of general laws (*Naturwissenschaften*) from those that described the unique or particular (*Geisteswissenschaften*). According to this distinction, the role of nomothetic psychology is to search for general laws based on inter-individual comparisons. Idiography, on the other hand, is the study of the unique complexity of the individual case, and is not intent on the discovery of general laws. Allport (1937) has been both credited with and accused of introducing these differing perspectives to American psychology. Allport argued for the necessity of both perspectives and remarked on the neglect of idiography in the scientific psychology of the day. Within psychology, the study of personality has been the arena for the bulk of the methodological debate regarding the idiographic and nomothetic perspectives. The principles being debated are generalizable to many areas of psychology, including the present discussion concerning issues in studying cognitive psychology throughout the lifespan.

A number of theorists have addressed the issue since Allport's introduction. Beck (1953), in an attempted reconciliation of these two perspectives, noted that nomothetic methodologies have held sway and accused these methodologies of reductionism in their "atomization" of the individual. For Beck, the more successful the nomothetic effort, the less satisfactory it became in describing the functioning individual, i.e., the dynamic processes present within the individual escape attention on the level of generalized abstraction. The result of the nomothetically motivated scientific study of the individual has been to "take the person out of the observed datum, and concentrate only on the extraperson event" (Beck, 1953, p. 357). For Beck, the idiographic and nomothetic approaches both represent fundamental approaches to scientific method. Idiographic procedures can yield information which (with the aid of background light provided by previously acquired nomothetic data and insights) illuminate the individual.

Eysenck (1954) responded to Beck's arguments by emphatically declaring that the nomothetic must reign supreme. While welcoming the spirit of Beck's reconciliation, Eysenck stated that Beck had attempted to realign the two perspectives by reducing idiography to a meaningless term, and redefining "nomothetic" so as to include the idiographic. At issue was the claim that the two perspectives have a common methodology (observation, analysis, logical inference, etc.). Eysenck responded to this attempted redefinition of the idiographic domain by declaring that Beck had "surrendered the castle of idiographic beliefs" (p. 339), and broke with the definition advanced by Windelband and Allport.

Falk (1956) addressed the issue by calling for both the evolution of the idiographic perspective and the realization that nomothetically derived laws are potentially capable of dealing with the unique personality. He noted that, in the context of discovery, science often will make inferences regarding constituent elements via the study of the whole. Falk, as Beck, argued against the historically limited conception of idiography as concrete, nonanalytical, intuitive, and molar by attempting to dispel the notion that "the whole must be treated with a different brand of logic, or as a higher-level organization not amenable to reduction" (p. 56). From this basis, Falk extended Beck's position by arguing for the adequacy of general laws for dealing with the unique case, since idiographic methods were reducible to the nomothetic. In an apparent slippage from his evolved definition of idiography, Falk assigned to the idiographic approach the role of novel hypothesis production, while the task of confirmation was left to the nomothetic procedure.

Allport (1962), in addition to calling for the relabeling of the idiographic as "morphogenic," noted that the status of idiographic psychology left much to be desired and called for the evolution of the strategy in order that it might become a significant contributor to the science of psychology. He stated:

> It is not sufficient to intuit the pattern of Bill or Betty. All of their friends do this much, with greater or less success. A science, even a morphogenic science, should be made of sterner stuff. The morphogenic interpretations we make should be testable, communicable and have a high measure of predictive power. (p. 410)

Allport proceeded to catalog those procedures which, while idiographic, fit the scientific criterion he established. While Allport's intent was to give hope to the idiographer, the catalog points clearly to the lack of such techniques. Perhaps the most interesting was a self-anchoring "ladder scale" devised by Kilpatrick and Cantril (1960). Allport noted this ladder scale as an example of an idiographic instrument which has been employed in nomothetic research.

To summarize this section, it appears that attempts to allow for the evolution of idiography have been met with resistance and criticism. Allport's call for the testing of idiographic procedures as scientifically valid, reliable, and predictive seem to have fallen on deaf ears. Meehl (1954), writing on the relative merits of clinical versus statistical prediction in psychology, made several cogent points. When commenting on the propensity of some clinicians to object to the mathematical portrayal of the individual, Meehl stated:

> the indubitable uniqueness of the single case is no more fatal to psychology than it is to physics. To see it as fatal to psychological quantification is to forget that the class character of concepts and dimensions is found in all descriptive enterprises. (p. 129)

Meehl denied the lethality of the unique single case to the nomothetic structure of psychology. Our arguments are based on the similar belief that idiographic and nomothetic analyses represent sequential steps in efforts directed at the understanding of psychological and cognitive processes.

Application of idiographic perspective to cognitive science

In applying the above discussion to the study of cognition across the lifespan, the challange for research is to capture the complexity of the individual's cognitive activity from a nomothetic perspective which allows for the derivation of general laws with wide ranging heuristic relevance.

In an early statement of the issues at hand, Hoyer (1974) indicated that the description of intra-individual stability and change over time had received little attention, relative to the more traditional experimental investigations. He argued for increased attention to the parameters of intra-individual stablity and change as valid topics of scientific inquiry. The challenges inherent to studying age-related cognitive changes relate to the need to capture the often idiosyncratic appreciation of strategies which may be common across individuals. The task is significantly complicated when individuals at varying developmental stages are studied, i.e., developmental stage characteristics add another source of variation which must be captured by the investigator.

While the idiographic/nomothetic approaches to science have historically been viewed as antithetical, a number of recent investigators have demonstrated the power of methodologies which involve intensive idiographic study of several individuals over time (e.g., Zevon & Tellegen, 1982). This modern sense of idiography allows the derivation of clear nomothetic implications by providing an opportunity to confirm principles and laws derived from a single individual through comparisons among individuals (see Lamiell, 1981).

In terms of contemporary cognitive psychology, a number of investigators have noted the de-emphasis of the individual engaged in cognitive processing (e.g., Lamiell, Foss, Larsen, & Hempel, 1983). This criticism echoes earlier debates regarding the role of idiographic and nomothetic methodologies in the scientific study of personality. The overemphasis on input–output mechanization obfuscates the richness of the cognitive processes individuals employ in their daily lives. Capturing underlying cognitive processes and their development is difficult using nomothetic approaches, not only because the process may differentially appear across individuals within conditions, but because nomothetically based analysis, such as analysis of variance, are static, focusing on an average end-product computed from an aggregate frozen at a point in time. The researcher is forced to draw conclusions about a cognitive process based on the hints ongoing processes leave scattered at one, or a few, points in time. A good example of an approach which captures the richness of individuals' cognitive processing is the "transactional opportunistic" planning study of Meyer and Rebok. Their focus on the complexity of the individual's planning strategies, and their use of idiographic data in understanding age differences in sorting effectiveness, illustrates the richness of a sustained focus on the individual who is processing the information. Such a focus, in tandem with well developed hypotheses with clear nomothetic relevance and sophisticated analytic procedures, bode well for the future of idiography in cognitive science.

Ecological validity and idiographic methods

The idiographic level of analysis also suggests a different way to look at the notion of ecological validity. It is not trivial or uninteresting to ask whether ecological validity is best captured as an invarient property of an environment or whether it is *subject-specific*. Expanding on a point made previously, individual differences among subjects can result in the same study taking on different meanings or possessing different properties for different subjects, not only across cohorts but also across individuals. To categorize an environment, task, or situation on the basis of an "average" reaction of several subjects obscures the fact that the environment may be differentially familiar, relevant, interesting or threatening to different subjects, even within the same cohort. A single experimental environment, then, can be differentially ecologically valid across individual subjects. This can be especially problematic among elderly subjects with the assumed increase in variability with age (e.g., Hoyer, 1974). The ecological validity of an experimental setting can also become time bound for each individual subject. *Intra-individual changes,* whether developmentally based or not, may cause the same environment to be seen in a different light by the same subject across time, much as an adult's experience walking through his or her high school halls today is radically different from the experience he or she had when he or she was a teenager. Researchers, by assuming ecological validity is invariant across subjects and ignoring interactions between individual differences and environmental properties, may create a superficial criteria of ecological validity, one that does not generalize well across individuals or across time. As an alternative, developmental cognitive science research may benefit from approaches where the generalizability of environmental properties are also considered across subjects and across time.

While idiographic methods have been proposed as potentially useful in helping cognitive scientists uncover the underlying cognitive processes of individuals, simply employing idiographic techniques in the study of the individual does not guarantee that the study is ecologically valid for the individual, or that the study's results will generalize to other occasions in the individual's life. The pattern of behavior uncovered by an idiographic study may be artificial, because of the obtrusiveness of the data collection procedures (e.g., observation, self-rating forms) and the uniqueness of the experimental task. The ecological validity of an idiographic study hinges on how typical the subject's behavior is in the study, relative to the subject's spontaneous behavior in the context or situation of interest. Cross-subject comparisons would not reveal the ecological validity of an idiographic study, since cross-subject consistency does not indicate how typical the situation or behavior is within the subject's life. Techniques from single case study designs can help determine an idiographic study's ecological validity, e.g., ABAB design and multiple baseline designs (see Kazdin, 1978). The rationale would require observations of the subject in a variety of environments that vary along significant dimensions, e.g., anonymity and formality, while the presence of the independent variable and data collection techniques was systematically varied. By ordering the contexts in terms of their similarity and differences, and comparing the pattern of behavior across the contexts, the researcher can begin to isolate context-specific, measurement-specific, and manipulation-specific influences on the subject's behavior. Of course, the researcher would have to be sensitive to temporally related factors, practice, fatigue, and learning effects in the interpretation of the subject's behavior across conditions.

SUMMARY

It has become a truism among some that research in cognitive science has focused on maximizing precision and control, while downplaying questions of relevance and utility of the research findings. The task before developmental cognitive science is to derive general, parsimonious, and valid models of cognitive processing without losing sight of the fact that the science's basic measure is the extent to which it explains, predicts, and optimizes the cognitive abilities of an individual in his or her quotidian (i.e., daily life) pursuits. Traditionally, concerns with generalizability focus on the representativeness of the findings across people, but our discussions of ecological validity and idiography define two other dimensions of generalizability—generalizability across situations and across time. To be maximally relevant and predictive, results should demonstrate robustness across the three dimensions of generalizability.

Aside from affecting a study's relevance in explaining and predicting everyday behavior, we have argued that ecological validity also affects the control and precision of a study. In many respects, the dialectic between control and relevance, or defining general laws of cognition and describing an individual, is a false one. They should be complementary rather than antagonistic qualities of research. Individuals do not act in a vacuum; rather, they interact with their environment, be it daily life or laboratory experiment. This interaction between context and person can shape a cognitive process, or at least set limits to it. At any rate, the interaction cannot be ignored, especially in developmental research, with its concern with change. Idiography can be a valuable tool in understanding the enactment and development of cognitive process. Idiography offers the insight of an individual perspective, where the lawfulness of behavior can be seen undistorted by the logic of group averages. Cognitive science may benefit from reconceptualizing contextual and individual factors as variables of interest rather than sources of error.

REFERENCES

Abelson, R. P. (1976). A script theory of understanding, attitude and behavior. In J. Carroll & T. Payne (Eds.), *Cognition and social behavior*. Hillsdale, NJ: Erlbaum.

Allport, G. (1962). The general and the unique in psychological science. *Journal of Personality, 30,* 405–422.

Allport, G. (1937). *Personality: A psychological interpretation*. New York: Holt, Rinehart & Winston.

Baltes, P. B., Reese, H., & Nesselroade, J. (1977). *Life span developmental psychology: Introduction to research methods*. Monterey, CA: Brooks/Cole.

Baltes, P. B., & Schaie, K. W. (1976). On the plasticity of intelligence in adulthood and old age: Where Horn and Donaldson fail. *American Psychologist, 31,* 720–725.

Barker, R. G., & Wright, H. F. (1954). *Midwest and its children*. Evanston, IL: Row, Peterson.

Beck, S. J. (1953). The science of personality: Nomothetic or idiographic? *Psychological Review, 60,* 353–359.

Bronfenbrenner, U. (1977). Toward an experimental ecology of human development. *American Psychologist, 32,* 513–531.

Canestrari, R. E. (1963). Paced and self-paced learning in young and elderly adults. *Journal of Gerontology, 18,* 165–168.

Carlsmith, J. M., Ellsworth, P., & Aronson, E. (1976). *Methods of research in social psychology*. Reading, MA: Addison Wesley.

Cook, T. D., & Campbell, D. T. (1979). *Quasi-experimentation: Design and analysis issues for field settings*. Chicago: Rand McNally.

Demming, J. A., & Pressey, S. L. (1957). Tests "indigenous" to the adult and older years. *Journal of Counseling Psychology, 4,* 144–148.

Denney, N. W. (1979). Problem solving in later adulthood: Intervention research. In P. B. Baltes & O. Brim, Jr. (Eds.). *Life-span development and behavior. Volume 2*. New York: Academic Press.

Deutscher, M., Kosierowski, N., Karuza, J., Jr., & Reid, H. (1979, November). *IQ test performance of elderly: Effect of the cohort relevance of the test*. Paper presented Gerontological Society, Washington, DC.

Eisdorfer, C., Nowlin, J., & Wilkie, F. (1970). Improvement in learning in the aged by modification of autonomic nervous system activity. *Science, 170,* 1327–1329.

Eysenck, H. J. (1954). The science of personality: Nomothetic! *Psychological Review, 61,* 339–342.

Falk, J. L. (1956). Issues distinguishing idiographic from nomothetic approaches to personality theory. *Psychological Review, 63,* 53–62.

Hartley, J. T., Harker, J. O., & Walsh, D. A. (1980). Contemporary issues and new directions in adult development of learning and memory. In L. W. Poon (Ed.), *Aging in the 1980s.* Washington, DC: American Psychological Association.

Hoyer, W. J. (1974). Aging as intraindividual change. *Developmental Psychology, 10,* 821–826.

Hulicka, I. (1982). Memory functioning in late adulthood. In F. I. M. Craig & S. Trehub (Eds.), *Advances in the study of communication and affect. Volume 8.* New York: Plenum Press.

Hultsch, D. F. (1974). Learning to learn in adulthood. *Journal of Gerontology, 29,* 302–308.

Hultsch, D. F., & Hickey, T. (1978). External validity in the study of human development: Theoretical and methodological issues. *Human Development, 21,* 76–91.

Kazdin, A. E. (1978). Methodological and interpretive problems of single-case experimental designs. *Journal of Consulting and Clinical Psychology, 46,* 629–642.

Kilpatrick, F. P., & Cantril, H. (1960). Self-anchoring scale: A measure of the individual's unique reality world. *Journal of Individual Psychology, 16,* 158–170.

Labouvie, E. W. (1980). Identity versus equivalence of psychological measures and constructs. In L. W. Poon (Ed.), *Aging in the 1980s.* Washington, DC: American Psychological Association.

Labouvie-Vief, G. (1985). Intelligence and cognition. In J. E. Birren & K. W. Schaie (Eds.), *Handbook of the psychology of aging* (2nd ed.). New York: Van Nostrand.

Labouvie-Vief, G., & Blanchard-Fields, F. (1982). Cognitive aging and psychological growth. *Ageing and society, 2,* 183–209.

Labouvie-Vief, G., & Chandler, M. J. (1978). Cognitive development and life span developmental theory. Idealistic versus contextual perspectives. In P. B. Baltes (Ed.), *Life span development and behavior.* New York: Academic Press.

Labouvie-Vief, G., & Gonda, J. (1976). Cognitive strategy training and intellectual performance in the elderly. *Journal of Gerontology, 31,* 327–332.

Labouvie-Vief, G., Hoyer, W. J., Baltes, M. M., & Baltes, P. B. (1974). Operant analysis of intellectual behavior in old age. *Human Development, 17,* 259–272.

Lachman, J. L., & Lachman, R. (1980). Age and the actualization of world knowledge. In L. W. Poon (Ed.), *New directions in memory and aging: Proceedings of the George A. Talland memorial conference.* Hillsdale, NJ: Erlbaum.

Lamiell, J. T. (1981). Toward an idiothetic psychology of personality. *American Psychologist, 36,* 276–289.

Lamiell, J. T., Foss, M. A., Larsen, R. J., & Hempel, A. M. (1983). Studies in intuitive personology from an idiothetic point of view: Implications for personality theory. *Journal of Personality, 51,* 438–467.

Langer, E. (1978). Rethinking the role of thought in social interaction. In J. Harvey, W. Ickes & R. Kidd (Eds.), *New directions in attribution research. Volume 2.* Hillsdale, NJ: Erlbaum.

Langer, E., Rodin, J., Beck, P., Weinman, C., & Spitzer, L. (1979). Environmental determinents of memory improvement in late adulthood. *Journal of Personality and Social Psychology, 37,* 2003–2013.

Lewin, K. (1931). The conflict between Aristotelian and Galileian modes of thought in contemporary psychology. *Journal of Genetic Psychology, 5,* 141–177.

Luria, A. R. (1976). *Cognitive development: Its cultural and social foundations.* Cambridge, MA: Harvard University Press.

Meacham, J. (1982). A note on remembering to execute planned actions. *Journal of Applied Developmental Psychology, 3,* 121–133.

Meehl, P. E. (1954). *Clinical vs. statistical prediction.* Minneapolis, MN: University of Minnesota Press.

Nisbett, R. E., & Wilson, T. D. (1977). Telling more than we can know: Verbal reports on mental processes. *Psychological Review, 84,* 231–259.

Rebok, G., & Hoyer, W. J. (1977). The functional context of elderly behavior. *Gerontologist, 17,* 27–34.

Rodin, J., & Langer, E. (1980). Aging labels: The decline of control and the fall of self-esteem. *Journal of Social Issues, 36,* 12–29.

Schaie, K. W. (1978). External validity in the assessment of intellectual development in adulthood. *Journal of Gerontology, 33,* 695–701.

Scheidt, R. J., & Schaie, K. W. (1978). A taxonomy of situations for an elderly population: Generating situational criteria. *Journal of Gerontology, 33,* 848–857.

Shiffrin, R. M., & Schneider, W. (1977). Controlled and automatic human information processing: II. Perceptual learning, automatic attending and a general theory. *Psychological Review, 84,* 127–190.

Taylor, S. E., & Fiske, S. T. (1978). Salience, attention, and attribution: Top of the head phenomena. In L. Berkowitz (Ed.), *Advances in experimental social psychology. Volume 11.* New York: Academic Press.

Willems, E. P. (1973). Behavioral ecology and experimental analysis: Courtship is not enough. In J. Nesselroade & H. Reese (Eds.), *Life span developmental psychology: Methodological issues.* New York: Academic Press.

Windelband, W. (1904). *Geschichte und naturwissenschaft.* Strassburg: Heitz.

Zevon, M. A., & Tellegen, A. (1982). The structure of mood change: An idiographic/nomothetic analysis. *Journal of Personality and Social Psychology, 43,* 111–122.

Chapter 7

Reminiscence in Adulthood: A Social-Cognitive Analysis

David J. Sperbeck

Alaska Psychiatric Institute

Susan Krauss Whitbourne

University of Massachusetts at Amherst

Reminiscing in old age is hypothesized to have adaptive value, facilitating the elderly individual's acceptance of past, present, and future accomplishments and disappointments into a unified view of the life span (Butler, 1963; Erikson, 1963). In order to understand more about how this process serves to mediate adjustment in later life, it is first necessary to explore the various elements involved when older adults think about and remember the past. In the present paper, a social-cognitive analysis will be used to provide a framework for this exploration of reminiscence in adulthood.

REMINISCING AS REMOTE MEMORY

The first component of reminiscing to be analyzed is cognitive. By its very nature, reminiscing falls into the category of remote memory, which is variously referred to in the literature as remote, natural, old, autobiographical, or archival memory, and is thought to involve a longer time frame than long term memory. This memory store is generally characterized as containing information acquired in the normal course of life and retained more or less indefinitely. It may be described as "our memory for words, for facts, for names, for places, for events, for procedures, and for that portion of the information we acquired in school and forgot to forget" (Nickerson, 1980, pp. 73–74). Unlike other forms of secondary memory processing which show cross-sectional age declines (Craik, 1977), remote memory seems to be relatively well-preserved in adulthood (Bahrick, Bahrick & Wittlinger, 1975; Botwinick & Storandt, 1974, 1980; Erber, 1981; Franklin & Holding 1977; Klonoff & Kennedy, 1965; Perlmutter, 1978; Warrington & Sanders, 1971).

One possible reason for the superiority of remote memory over secondary memory in the aged is that distant memories involve processes that operate to overcome deficits in cognitive operations, such as being encoded more deeply (Lander & Hoyer, 1980) or being more likely to be encoded with mediators

(Hulicka & Grossman, 1967). Another plausible reason that remote memories are remembered better is because they are rehearsed frequently over the years; rehearsal has been shown to facilitate memory operations in the aged (Howard, Lasaga, & McAndrews, 1980; Kausler & Puckett, 1980). It is also possible that these factors have an interactive effect. Continued reference to remote memories may enhance the number of associations attached to them, simultaneously producing more mediators, and resulting in a deeper level of processing.

It appears, then, that the old memories which would be drawn upon in reminiscing are not impaired by the aging process. This continued accessibility of events from the remote past can provide the content on which reminiscing activity is based.

INFLUENCE OF COGNITIVE BIASES ON REMOTE MEMORY

Whether and how remote memories are retrieved in the process of reminiscing may depend upon the degree to which the individual relies upon cognitive biases. These cognitive biases fall into the category of superordinate activities or motives which influence not only the development of the specific means of operations for remembering, but also help determine the purposes to which remembering abilities can be and are applied (Meacham, 1977). It is assumed that the processing of experience rarely occurs as a wholly rational, nonaffective, and objective process (Abelson, 1976; Pryor & Kriss, 1977). In summarizing a substantial body of social-psychological research on information processing, Greenwald (1980) identified three of these cognitive biases: egocentrism, beneffectance, and cognitive conservatism. Briefly, egocentrism may be defined as recalling events in terms of one's relation to them, beneffectance as viewing oneself as having done well in those events, and cognitive conservatism as the resistance to change of established knowledge structures. Each of these biases may be seen as operating during the reminiscence process.

The significant influence of egocentrism on memory has become apparent from the findings of several studies which have compared memories for material acquired with and without an egocentric perspective. In one such experiment (Brenner, 1973), respondents read aloud in a group context words printed on index cards. Respondents remembered best the words that they themselves had read aloud. Similarly, in studies using both natural and experimental groups, Ross and Sicoly (1979) found that respondents recalled their own contributions to a group effort more readily than they recalled the contributions of other group members. The self-generation effect may also be produced through empathy, such that respondents remembered better the events occurring to characters with whom identification had been induced (Owens, Dafoe, & Bower, 1977).

Extending the findings of these studies to reminiscing, it might be speculated that the remote personal memories recalled during this process are remembered well because they were self-generated. Moreover, beneffectance may operate to distort the way these memories are retrieved, such that the individual manages to emerge as the actor who was behaving in the service of favorable motives, on the side of what is "right," or as having succeeded in important tasks. For instance, as the result of a beneffectance bias, the reasons for breaking up with a romantic partner may be attributed almost entirely to the partner. Over time, it might be expected that selective attention to the personally relevant and self-enhancing aspects of remote memories strengthens them so that they become increasingly resistant to change. Recent work in attributional information processing has shown that, by selectively attending to those stimuli which reinforce existing memory categories, perceivers strengthen stereotypes (Hamilton, 1979), personality prototypes (Cantor & Mischel, 1979), and self-schemata (Markus, 1977). Such findings support the view that cognitive conservatism in remote memory organization can function to influence the reminiscing process.

The underlying incentives for cognitive biases presumably are favorable self-representation, establishing a stable perspective for interpreting future experiences, and maintaining a sense of self-consistency over time, especially around concerns over which ego involvement is high. In terms of reminiscing, the motivation for cognitive biases may be the establishment of a life story in which the individual's previous life is seen as a unified whole. The life story can support identity by virtue of its reinforcement of the indvidual's perception of having accomplished significant life goals. The underlying basis for the life story may be favorable self-representation, but also the establishment of a sense of competence (Whitbourne, 1985).

It seems likely, though, that individuals will vary in the degree to which they bias their reflections on past experiences in order to fit them into a coherent whole in which the rememberers are portrayed in a positive light. Butler's (1963) conception of the life review clearly implies that reminiscing may involve reflections of past experiences in which the individual was behaving in ways that were counter to a positive self-image. The association of reminiscing with negative affect was, in fact, observed by Boylin, Gordon [Whitbourne], and Nehrke (1976). Erikson's (1963) theory as it pertains to ego integrity, in which reminiscing is the predominant activity, includes a description of the unfavorable outcome of despair, in which the individual's past life is viewed as a failure and there is a sense of fragmentation of personal identity. In a test of the construct of ego integrity statuses (Whitbourne & Weinstock, 1985) as representing various styles of resolving the ego integrity versus despair psychosocial crisis, the existence of a group of individuals presently grappling with unpleasant issues from their pasts was demonstrated, as was a "despair" group for whom these issues were unfavorably settled (Walaskay, Whitbourne, & Nehrke, 1984).

From an Eriksonian theoretical perspective, favorable adaptation in old age would be expected to be related to a style of reminiscing in which cognitive biases operate to a minimum degree. In this way, the older individual would be able to incorporate relevant personal information of both a positive and negative nature (in terms of its implications for identity) into a unified view of past life. A working through of the negative self-information would be required, though, in order to achieve a favorable ratio of ego integrity over despair. Accordingly, it may be argued that the ability to interpret past and present experiences in a relatively unbiased way forms the basis for a maximally adaptive identity throughout adulthood (Whitbourne & Weinstock, 1985). Thus, while adults of any age may have the tendency to view past events in an egocentric, beneffectant, and cognitively conservative fashion, it will be those with a more flexible approach to their life experiences who will ultimately adapt most fully to the existential issues faced in old age.

PERSONALITY AND REMINISCING ACTIVITY

The previous discussion leads to the suggestion that the quality of personal flexibility determines how individuals reflect upon their past lives. This quality is best operationalized by Costa and McCrae's (1978) openness to experience construct, defined as the extent to which the individual tolerates and explores the unfamiliar in actions, ideas, and values. The experientially open adult enjoys novel situations, has a playful approach to ideas and problem solving, and appreciates experience for its own sake. The adult who is closed to experience, on the other hand, is behaviorally rigid, has a restricted fantasy and emotional life, and is ideologically dogmatic. The Experience Inventory developed by Costa and McCrae contains six scales to measure the components of openness to: fantasy, esthetics, feelings, activities, actions, and values. The total Openness score can be regarded as a general measure of how the individual subjectively approaches and interprets real and imagined past and present experiences.

It may be predicted that for persons extremely closed to experience, the predominant goal of processing and interpreting personal information into remote memory would be preservation of a stable knowledge base about the self. Conversely, new autobiographical material would be incorporated far more extensively into the identity of the adult who is open to experience. As a preliminary step to investigating the contribution of the open-closed personality dimension to reminiscing activity in adulthood, we conducted a study of the relationship between scores on Costa and McCrae's (1978) Experience Inventory and the number of autobiographical memories recalled in a free association task. It was hypothesized that, regardless of age, adults who were more open to experience would recall more personal events than would experientially closed adults.

As a test of the above hypothesis, 50 adults, ranging in age from 25 to 85 years, were asked to complete the Experience Inventory and an autobiographical memory task. The young adult participants were randomly selected from among the parents of children attending various day care centers located in Western New York state. Middle-aged and older adults were selected randomly from various civic organizations and housing communities in the local area. There were approximately equal numbers of males and females, and the respondents were uniformly distributed across the entire age range. The sample was fairly well-educated (mean= 12.94 years of education) and represented all but the lowest levels of socio-economic status, across all age levels as indicated by: income— 60% reported total annual income in excess of $13,000; and occupation (or former occupation if retired)—30% managers and proprietors, 28% professionals, 16% service workers, 14% clerical and sales, 6% students, 4% craftsmen, and 2% laborers.

In addition to openness to experience, participants were also tested on verbal ability (Gardner & Monge's 1977 multiple-choice vocabulary test) and cognitive flexibility (French, Ekstrom, & Price's 1963 test of ideational fluency) in order to control for the possible contribution of these factors to autobiographical memory. The autobiographical memory task was conducted with the three prompt words used by Robinson (1976): one word for a common object (tree), one for a common activity (fill), and one for a common affect (strong). Instructions for generating free associations were that, for each prompt word presented, participants were to "think of as many experiences as you can which the word reminds you of." It was emphasized that the reported experience must be as specific as possible. Participants were encouraged to continue thinking until a specific incident associated with the word came to mind. It was emphasized that memories could be recent or remote, and of trivial or salient experiences. There were no time restrictions or limits to the number of associations generated. However, it was noted that, even if it seemed to take longer to recover a memory than the respondent felt was acceptable or sufficient, search should continue until a memory which fit the criterion came to mind. Participants were given three practice words (bell, sing, and brave) one at a time, to familiarize them with the procedure and to demonstrate their understanding of it. All responses to the test words were audio-tape recorded. The number of memories generated for each prompt word was the main variable of interest in the present study.

An example from a session with a 28-year old male respondent illustrates the type of material obtained with the autobiographical memory task:

> *E:* The first word which I want you to respond to is "tree." Think of as many experiences that the word "tree" reminds you of.
> *S:* Okay. When I was a little boy, one time I was playing in a tree and it was like a two-trunked tree where there was two trunks that went up like a crotch between the tree. I remember getting my foot stuck in there when I was a little kid and none of my little friends seemed to be able to help me and I remember screaming my head off for my big brother who usually was always antagonizing me. I was screaming for him to help me. I can't remember exactly how old I was, but I know it was- - -
> *E:* Can you estimate approximately?
> *S:* Probably about 6 years old, maybe.

In accordance with the hypothesis, openness to experience was positively associated with the number of memories recalled, $r = .41$, $p < .01$, even with the effect of age partialled, $r = .40$, $p < .01$ (age was not significantly correlated with number of autobiographical memories, $r = .09$, or to openness scores). Of the Experience Inventory subscales, openness to ideas, $r = .44$, and fantasy, $r = .38$, were most highly related to number of memories. Neither verbal ability nor cognitive fluency were related to autobiographical memory recall.

PERSONALITY AND REMINISCING

The present analysis represents the first step in demonstrating the contribution of personality to the process of reminiscing in adulthood. It was shown that the openness to experience personality disposition is positively related to the number of autobiographical memories that adults can retrieve in response to common prompt words. As reported by the subjects, the average age of the memories recalled was approximately 25 years, placing them well into the category of remote storage. The overriding influence of personality compared to age in determining the number of experiences recalled is particularly striking, considering that older adults would potentially have many more experiences to draw upon in completing the autobiographical memory task. On a quantitative basis, then, it appears to be the willingness to become involved in new ideas and events that provides the raw material for reminiscing in adulthood.

The next question to be addressed from the perspective of the influence of cognitive biases on remote memory is whether experientially open adults are less likely than those who are closed to experience to encode and retrieve remote personal memories in such a way that existing views of self are preserved without integrating discrepant information. The answer to this question is beyond the scope of the present analysis, but could be derived from a qualitative analysis of autobiographical memory recall. This qualitative analysis would need to be combined with information on the respondents' identities regarding what qualities in themselves and in their pasts they consider desirable. It would also be necessary to ascertain the veridicality of the events being recalled so that the degree of distortion could be rated. Since over-dependence on cognitive biases leads to "inadequate and maladpative cognitive functioning" (Greenwald, 1980, p. 615), differences would also be expected in the elaborativeness or depth of processing of memories as a function of experiential openness. Furthermore, analyzing the content of experiences recalled with knowledge about other aspects of the individual's life history could yield important information which may explain why particular experiences are recalled and others are not. Rating described experiences for the presence of cognitive biases might help to determine whether material encoded with reference to the "self" is processed more deeply than material encoded with reference to impersonal entities, or the historical context. Such analyses would yield information regarding the self as a memory processing entity (Mancuso & Ceely, 1980; Greenwald, 1980) as well as the presence of scripts (Abelson, 1976) or frames (Minsky, 1976). The influence of these postulated schemas on the organization of remote personal experience should be observable when elaborated responses to prompt words in the autobiographical memory paradigm are content analyzed.

Finally, the adaptive value of an open orientation to favorable resolution of the critical psychosocial issue of later adulthood would need to be assessed by relating to ego integrity the flexible approach of experientially open adults toward their pasts. Demonstration of these interdependent relationships would require a comparison of open and closed individuals, whose autobiographical memories have been found to differ, on an interview (Walaskay et al., 1984) or questionnaire (Boylin et al., 1976) measure of resolution of this psychosocial issue. It would not necessarily be expected, however, that individuals who are more open to past and present experiences score more highly on measures of subjective well-being. In fact, it may very well be that life satisfaction is related in a negative, or complex nonlinear way, to willingness to reflect on the past, inasmuch as such reflections yield memories of accomplishments as well as failures (cf. Campbell, Converse, & Rodgers, 1976). To the extent that experientially open individuals who encounter failures revise their life histories or alter their expectations for the future as coping mechanisms (Whitbourne, 1985), however, both ego integrity and subjective well-being may be maintained at high levels. Conversely, the apparent high life satisfaction of closed adults may reflect an avoidance of potentially ego-threatening issues achieved by "selective forgetting."

The lack of age differences in experiential openness counters the commonly-held notion that older individuals are more rigid than younger persons. Another general belief about the elderly, that they are more involved in reminiscing than are their young adult counterparts, was also dispelled in the present research. It appears, instead, that there are individual differences in personality flexibility throughout adulthood, which would account for variation in the individual's involvement in reminiscing.

AUTOBIOGRAPHICAL MEMORY AS EFFORTFUL PROCESSING

The autobiographical memory procedure used in the investigation reported in this paper yielded results consistent with other studies in the literature in which age was not related to the amount of remote memory recall. This finding can be interpreted in terms of the facilitative effect on memory of self-generation, as described at the outset of this paper. It also raises issues relevant to the distinction between automatic and effortful memory operations, used in recent work on information processing to account for age deficits in cognitive ability (Attig & Hasher, 1980; Hasher & Zacks, 1979). The age-insensitive nature of autobiographical memory retrieval observed in the present study would suggest that perhaps this memory store is being accessed through the use of automatic retrieval operations, which are not impaired by aging. Automatic processes are encoding and retrieval operations that drain minimal energy from the individual's limited capacity attentional resources. These operations do not benefit from experience or practice because they are theorized to occur without intention. Furthermore, automatic processes have been found to mediate judgments of memory remoteness (Perlmutter, Metzger, Miller & Nerzworski, 1980), an operation involved in the autobiographical memory task used here. Participants of all ages had no difficulty completing this aspect of the task.

However, given the elaborative nature of the autobiographical memories recalled, as shown in the example provided earlier, it is more tenable to suggest that these remote memories are retrieved through effortful processing. Since effortful processing requires considerable attentional resources, it is thought to interfere with cognitive activities which demand extensive elaboration and deep processing (Schneider & Shiffrin, 1977; Hasher & Zacks, 1979). In the face of declining attentional resources, the elderly person is considered most vulnerable to effortful processing deficiencies, especially on memory tasks which require substantial capacity, such as free recall of lengthy verbal materials. If this is the case, then the lack of age differences in number of remote memories requires some explanation. One possibility is that, like other effortful processes, remote memory retrieval is sensitive to practice and personality differences (Hoyer & Plude, 1980). Since the present study did not include an investigation of participants' level of rehearsal prior to retrieving autobiographical memories, evidence for the explanation of no age-related deficits in what is presumably effortful processing is tied to the data dealing with personality differences. From a motivational perspective, the personality dimension of experiential openness might be expected to influence the participants' willingness to engage in tasks requiring effortful processing, since open and imaginative individuals might be expected to show more interest in this kind of test situation. In terms of ability, experientially open adults may be expected to accumulate a greater variety of experiences over their lifetimes than their more restricted age-peers, providing them with a larger store from which to draw in the autobiographical memory task (and by inference, for reminiscing activities in general). Consequently, performance on the remote retrieval task would actually be less effortful for the open compared to the closed individuals, thereby enhancing the autobiographical memory scores of those who receive high openness scores.

Other differences in memory processing between the experientially closed and open may depend more on the particular area of openness being measured. A willingness to be open to fantasy and ideas may imply more spontaneous involvement in re-tellings and rehearsals of life histories than a reluctance to generate imaginative thoughts. Familiarity with to-be-remembered material mediates age-related declines in memory scanning (Thomas, Waugh, & Fozard, 1978) and naming latency (Poon & Fozard, 1978). If this phenomenon is operating in the present study, it could be argued that the experientially open on the fantasy and ideas dimensions may produce more autobiographical memories in response to prompt words because these memories have been better rehearsed.

PERSONALITY, EFFORTFUL PROCESSING, AND COGNITIVE BIASES

Inasmuch as the recall of past life experiences constitutes a functional definition of reminiscing, the present paper represents an attempt to account for why some adults reminisce more than others (Merriam, 1980) in terms of cognitive biases whose use in this effortful processing task may depend on openness to experience. It has been proposed that the mediating influence of experiential openness on the original encoding and ultimate retrieval of autobiographical memories is such that open reminiscers have a broader base of experiences encoded in memory, and find the task of generating past events to be less effortful. It may, therefore, be that elderly adults who are closed to experience are faced with the dual deficiencies of not having the base of experiences to choose from, in addition to any age-related deficits in effortful processing skills. As a consequence, individuals closed to experience might be expected to rely on their "revised" personal histories, and therefore become more dependent on cognitive biases, such as egocentrism, beneffectance, and conservatism as predominant modes of maintaining consistency about the self's experiences over time. Given that the requirements of achieving ego integrity in old age include the reworking of one's personal history in an unbiased fashion, it seems likely that the elderly adult who has adopted a restricted approach to experiences for a lifetime will be unable to meet the challenge of this last psychosocial crisis.

REFERENCES

Abelson, R. P. (1976). Script processing in attitude formation and decision making. In J. S. Carroll & J. W. Payne (Eds.), *Cognition and social behavior*. Hillsdale, NJ: Erlbaum.

Attig, M., & Hasher, L. (1980). The processing of frequency of occurrence information by adults. *Journal of Gerontology, 35*, 66–69.

Bahrick, H. P., Bahrick, P. O., & Wittlinger, R. P. (1975). Fifty years of memory for names and faces: A cross-sectional approach. *Journal of Experimental Psychology: General, 104*, 54–75.

Botwinick, J., & Storandt, M. (1974). *Memory related functions and age*. Springfield, IL: Charles C. Thomas.

Botwinick, J., & Storandt, M. (1980). Recall and recognition of old information in relation to age and sex. *Journal of Gerontology, 35*, 70–76.

Boylin, W., Gordon (Whitbourne), S. K., & Nehrke, M. F. (1976). Reminiscing and ego integrity in institutionalized elderly males. *The Gerontologist, 16*, 118–124.

Brenner, M. (1973). The next-in-line effect. *Journal of Verbal Learning and Verbal Behavior, 12*, 320–323.

Butler, R. M. (1963). The life review: An interpretation of reminiscence in the aged. *Psychiatry, 26*, 65–76.

Campbell, A., Converse, P. E., & Rodgers, W. L. (1976). *The quality of American Life*. New York: Russell Sage Foundation.

Cantor, N., & Mischel, W. (1979). Prototypicality and personality: Effects on free recall and personality impressions. *Journal of Research in Personality, 13,* 187–205.

Costa, P. T., Jr., & McCrae, R. R. (1978). Objective personality assessment. In M. Storandt, I. C. Siegler, & M. F. Elias (Eds.), *The clinical psychology of aging.* New York: Plenum Press.

Craik, F. I. M. (1977). Age differences in human memory. In J. E. Birren & K. W. Schaie (Eds.), *Handbook of the psychology of aging.* New York: Van Nostrand Reinhold.

Erber, J. T. (1981). Remote memory and age: A Review. *Experimental Aging Research, 7,* 189–199.

Erikson, E. H. (1963). *Childhood and society* (2nd Ed.). New York: W. W. Norton.

Franklin, J. C., & Holding, D. H. (1977). Personal memories at different ages. *Quarterly Journal of Experimental Psychology, 29,* 527–543.

French, J. W., Ekstrom, R. B., & Price, L. A. (1963). *Manual for kit of reference tests for cognitive factors.* Princeton, NJ: Educational Testing Service.

Gardner, E. F., & Monge, R. H. (1977). Adult age differences in cognitive abilities and educational background. *Experimental Aging Research, 3,* 337–383.

Greenwald, A. G. (1980). The totalitarian ego: Fabrication and revision of personal history. *American Psychologist, 35,* 603–618.

Hamilton, D. A. (1979). A cognitive-attributional analysis of stereotyping. In L. Berkowitz (Ed.), *Advances in experimental social psychology* (Vol. 12). New York: Academic Press.

Hasher, L., & Zacks, R. T. (1979). Automatic and effortful processes in memory. *Journal of Experimental Psychology: General, 108,* 356–388.

Howard, D. V., Lasaga, M. I., & McAndrews, M. P. (1980). Semantic activation during memory encoding across the adult life span. *Journal of Gerontology, 35,* 884–890.

Hoyer, W. M., & Plude, D. J. (1980). Attentional and perceptual processes in the study of cognitive aging. In L. W. Poon (Ed.), *Aging in the 1980's: Psychological issues.* Washington, DC: American Psychological Association.

Hulicka, I. M., & Grossman, J. L. (1967). Age group comparisons for the use of mediators in paired-associate learning. *Journal of Gerontology, 22,* 46–51.

Kausler, D. H., & Puckett, J. M. (1980). Frequency judgments and correlated cognitive abilities in young and elderly adults. *Journal of Gerontology, 35,* 376–382.

Klonoff, H., & Kennedy, M. (1965). Memory and perceptual functioning in octogenerians and nonagenarians in the community. *Journal of Gerontology, 20,* 328–333.

Lander, E. M., & Hoyer, W. J. (1980). *Adult age differences in the effects of word frequency and distinctiveness of encoding on free recall.* Paper presented at the 33rd Annual Scientific Meeting of the Gerontological Society of America, San Diego.

Mancuso, J. C., & Ceely, S. G. (1980). The self as memory processing. *Cognitive Therapy and Research, 4,* 1–25.

Markus, H. (1977). Self-schemata and processing information about the self. *Journal of Personality and Social Psychology, 35,* 63–78.

Meacham, J. A. (1977). Soviet investigations of memory development. In R. V. Kail, Jr., & J. W. Hagen (Eds.), *Perspectives on the development of memory and cognition.* Hillsdale, NJ: Erlbaum.

Merriam, S. (1980). The concept and function of reminiscence: A review of the research. *The Gerontologist, 20,* 604–609.

Minsky, M. L. (1975). A framework for representing knowledge. In P. Winston (Ed.), *The psychology of computer vision.* New York: McGraw-Hill.

Nickerson, R. S. (1980). Motivated retrieval from archival memory. In J. H. Flowers (Ed.), *1980 Nebraska symposium on motivation.* Lincoln, NE: University of Nebraska Press.

Owens, J., Dafoe, J., & Bower, G. H. (1977). *Taking a point of view: Character identification and attributional processes in story comprehension and memory.* Paper presented at American Psychological Association meetings, San Francisco.

Perlmutter, M. (1978). What is memory aging the aging of? *Developmental Psychology, 14,* 230–345.

Perlmutter, M., Metzger, R., Miller, K., & Nerzworski, T. (1980). Memory of historical events. *Experimental Aging Research, 6,* 46–60.

Poon, L. W., & Fozard, J. L. (1978). Speed of retrieval from long-term memory in relation to age, familiarity, and datedness of information. *Journal of Gerontology, 33,* 711–717.

Pryor, J. B., & Kriss, M. (1977). The cognitive dynamics of salience in the attribution process. *Journal of Personality and Social Psychology, 35,* 49–55.

Robinson, J. A. (1976). Sampling autobiographical memory. *Cognitive Psychology, 8,* 578–595.

Ross, M., & Sicoly, P. (1979). Egocentric biases in availability and attribution. *Journal of Personality and Social Psychology, 37,* 322–336.

Schnieder, W., & Schiffrin, R. M. (1977). Controlled and automatic information processing: Detection, search, and attention. *Psychological Process, 84,* 1–66.

Thomas, J. C., Waugh, N. C., & Fozard, J. L. (1978). Age and familiarity in memory scanning. *Journal of Gerontology, 33,* 528–533.

Walaskay, M., Whitbourne, S. K., & Nehrke, M. F. (1984). Construction and validation of an ego-integrity status interview. *International Journal of Aging and Human Development, 18,* 61–72.

Warrington, E. K., & Sanders, H. I. (1971). The fate of old memories. *Quarterly Journal of Experimental Psychology, 23,* 432–442.

Whitbourne, S. K., & Weinstock, C. S. (1985). *Adult Development: The differentiation of experience* (2nd Ed.). New York: Praeger.

Whitbourne, S. K., (1985). The psychological construction of the life span. In J. E. Birren & K. W. Schaie (Eds.), *Handbook of psychology of aging* (2nd ed.). New York: Van Nostrand Rheinhold.

Chapter 8

Social Cognition: A Life Span Perspective

Paul Roodin

State University of New York at Oswego

John Rybash

Mohawk Valley Community College

OVERVIEW

The study of social cognition has expanded exponentially over the past 15 years. It has become the dominant framework within social psychology (Flavell, 1981). In addition, social cognition has become an alternative to traditional trait views of personality (Athay & Darley, 1981; Mischel, 1981), a method of clinical exposition (Meichenbaum, 1977); it is endemic to a variety of concerns in developmental psychology, such as morality (Turiel, 1978), friendship (Berndt, 1981), role-taking (Higgins, 1981; Selman, 1976), and political thinking (Fiske & Kinder, 1981).

Social cognition is defined to include "all intellectual endeavors in which the aim is to think or learn about social or psychological processes in the self, individual others, or human groups of all sizes . . ." (Flavell, 1981, p. 272). With this broad definition, it is clear that social cognition covers a number of widely divergent areas within psychology with a multitude of different approaches, theories, and methodologies. Fitzgerald (1981) notes that such areas, while intellectually stimulating, are particularly frustrating to conceptualize. However, there are two general questions of concern to those studying social cognition from these divergent orientations: (a) how are social cognitions initially formed, created, and later altered; and (b) how are social cognitions utilized developmentally in everyday interactions.

The best description of social cognitions has been provided by Flavell (1977), who used the label "applied cognition." Applied cognition reflects the fact that, over the years, psychologists studying cognitive phenomena have tended to ignore "the social domain in the study of our human capacities for understanding" (Forbes, 1978, p. 123). As anyone who has attempted to control the vagaries of human social interaction in experimental situations can attest, laboratory studies of inanimate subject matter provide a far easier and simpler methodology.

ECOLOGICAL CONSIDERATIONS

Many psychologists have questioned the need for a distinction between social cognitions and cognitions applied to the inanimate world. The social environment and our cognitions *derived* from and *applied* to this domain represent an inherently dynamic process which is not found in exchanges with the world of inanimate objects (cf. Broughton, 1978; Chandler, 1979; Mischel, 1974). Chandler (1977, p. 207) notes that "human construction of knowledge in all of its manifestations entails an interaction of subject and object and can never consist of a purely objective discovery of impersonal, physical reality." Social cognition, through the vehicle of social exchange, represents the essence of the dialectical interactions identified by Riegel (1979). Social cognitions are derived from the matrix of interactions in which we assess the impact of our behaviors on others, others' impact on us, and our continual monitoring of these domains both cognitively and emotionally.

The "constructive" character of adult thinking is well-documented; however, it is also important to recognize that children's social cognitive knowledge is "co-constructed" from their interactions with individuals who are different from themselves and at times more competent (Damon, 1977). These interactions are central forces in Piaget's cognitive developmental stage theory. For Piaget, it is the child's constant give-and-take, as well as sharing of perspectives through peer play and parental interaction, which helps the child to recognize the limits of and dissatisfaction with his or her immature sense of objective reality. Through social interactions, children become increasingly less egocentric and ultimately become capable of more logical forms of thought, according to Piaget. Thus, a more adultlike understanding of the physical world, as well as formal adult cognitive operations, emerge from these early social encounters. For children, knowledge of the social sphere is pivotal in leading to knowledge of the physical sphere—social cognitions are clearly primary in Piaget's view.

Descriptions of this complex process of "social transmission" which triggers young children's cognitive development is a cumbersome task; ultimately it proved even too problematic for Piaget (Damon, 1977). After Piaget's initial descriptions of how social transmission helps children understand and represent adult forms of reality (such as in the *Moral Development of the Child*), he turned his efforts on the simpler, solitary judgments which children make of the non-social world (Damon, 1977). In this change of focus, we find Piaget's assumption that cognitive understanding of the physical world parallels children's developments in social cognition. And, interestingly, recent evidence suggests that children's social cognitive understanding does in fact precede their understanding of the physical domain; Hoffman (1981), for example, notes that, for infants, person permanence precedes object permanence, and that, among preschoolers, social causality is more well understood than physical causality.

Despite the difficulties encountered in studying social cognition, even for Piaget, the problem of "applied cognition" has continued to fascinate psychologists interested in the question: "How is social cognitive understanding derived?" This question is perhaps more closely aligned with the work of ethologists than we realize. Ethologists explore and study those "units of behavior which are meaningful in the lives of animals. Many of these units consist of complex patterns of movements and postures that cannot be isolated from the settings which make them meaningful'' (Buzsaki, Isaacson, & Hannigan, 1981, p. 477). From this perspective, social cognition allows us to function effectively in our exchanges with the social environment, which is an inherent part of our ecological niche.

Humans, like other higher primates, have a social nature and live in a social environment which derives from our genetic heritage. Chimpanzees, for example, share part of our advanced symbolic abilities, which allow the representation of both ''self'' and the perspectives of others. Meddin (1979) notes that chimpanzees in the natural state live in a ''flexible band'' and carve a distinctly social ecological niche in the wild. Their interactions and representational abilities suggest, to naturalistic observers, well-developed social cognitive processes in chimpanzees which allow, for example, the ability to see themselves as objects (Lawick-Goodall, 1975). Experimental tests of the ''sense of self'' have been conducted with both chimpanzees and monkeys (Gallup, 1977). Monkeys respond to their own mirrored reflections as if they are in the presence of another animal, while chimpanzees are able to recognize their own reflections over time, e.g., they gradually engage in appropriate grooming behaviors (Meddin, 1979). When an odorless, tasteless red dye was placed on the heads of anesthetized animals in such a way that it was visible only through a mirror, observers reported an increase in the grooming and orientation to that part of their bodies by the chimpanzees; such changes were not found among lower primates (e.g., monkeys).

Social cognition allows us to function effectively in our social ecological niche. As higher primates, we have basic social drives and a basic social nature which derive from our genetic heritage. Perhaps there are social ''categories,'' which are also part of this heritage, analogous to the work of Rosch and her colleagues (Rosch, Mervis, Gray, Johnson, & Boyes-Braem, 1976). Gelman and Spelke (1981) have addressed this general notion by reviewing the origins of children's concepts of animate and inanimate objects. Such distinctions emerge within the early months of infancy, according to Gelman and Spelke (1981). Trevarthen (1977) notes that not only do 2-month-olds become more ''vocally'' responsive to an adult displaying intensity in social interactions with the infants, but infants also become emotionally upset when adults approach them but remain unresponsive. While learning at this age may be a viable explanation for these findings, it is also possible that young infants may expect social communication from persons in the environment e.g., reflective of a ''natural category'' of social cognition. Another ''natural'' category to which infants are particularly sensitive is crying. Newborn infants have been shown to be sensitive to the crying of other infants. Hearing the crying of other infants evoked emotional distress and similar crying in infants who were initially in a quiet/neutral state and provides tentative support for infants' primitive recognition of social distress (Martin & Clark, 1982).

The social cognitive abilities of preschoolers or toddlers also reflect their burgeoning skills in this domain. Shatz and Gelman (1973), for instance, found that 4-year olds modified their language in response to the age of their intended listener. When asked to describe how to operate a toy to an adult vs. another 4-year-old vs. a 2-year-old, the children made significant modifications in their language complexity reflective of the age of the listener. Such social cognitive competence is quite surprising to see, given our usual "assumptions" of children at this age. Lempers, Flavell, and Flavell (1977) also demonstrated that even 2-year olds, when asked to show a picture to another person, turned the picture towards the person and away from their own gaze. Perhaps equally striking is the work of Muellar and Lucas (1975), and also Mueller and Brenner (1977), demonstrating social cognitive competence in children under 3 years of age. These children, many of whom were preverbal, were able to engage in effective forms of social communication with peers of similar ages and abilities through the use of primitive social cognitive categories. Although such children are typically thought to be lacking in the representation skills necessary for social cognition, Mueller demonstrated that 12 different types of social cognitive forms based on direct action/play served as mechanisms of peer communication. Children appeared to share meaning through such actions as banging on a table, gesturing, or repeating special sound patterns, each of which represented a social cognitive theme (e.g., "chase me and I'll chase you"). Clearly, social cognitions do not require abstract verbal conceptual abilities but may be derived on the basis of actions. Continuation of such observational studies provides a fruitful and important component of our research for better understanding the origins of social cognition.

As children reach school age, investigators of social cognition appear to be concerned with studying *what* children know of their social world and their social interactions. The dominant framework is a comparison with adult social cognitive knowledge. This is clearly one instance in which Piaget's constructivist structuralism continues to direct research. A host of interrelated topics from role-taking, moral judgment, friendship, fairness, and distributive justice have been examined with children between the ages of 4/5 to 11/12 years of age. Research with such Piagetian roots emphasizes again the cognitive consequences of children's social exchanges which promote growth and understanding in these areas. It is important to recall, however, that there are also emotional or affective consequences to such exchanges. In real life, a social exchange produces both social cognitions and socio-emotional judgments of self and other(s). Piaget notes that the child's social judgments are not made solely with respect to isolated actions, but to ". . . personalities that attract or repel him as a global whole" (Piaget, 1932, p.120). Social exchanges, however, have tended to be viewed almost exclusively from the cognitive viewpoint; e.g., social cognitive constructs arise from such exchanges. As we will suggest later, the social cognitive enterprise must begin to assign affect a central role.

SCHEMA THEORY

At the present time, the dominant view regarding social cognition sees these processes within the general concept of schema. Children, in this view, are constructing abstract knowledge structures which, over time, may become firmly entrenched as organizing/processing mechanisms or further altered as a function of additional direct experience. The generic concept of schema was applied to the area of memory, specifically text comprehension (Bartlett, 1932), to offset the associative accounts which failed to explain the complexities of a variety of prose comprehension phenomena (Fiske & Linville, 1980). In essence, simple associ- ate models of memory with direct linear processing assumptions gave way to the more complex, hierarchically arranged views commonly found today. In fact, the processes involve simply "extracting information from the environment and recapturing memory traces" (e.g., encoding and retrieval) since such "percep- tual and memorial operations are better characterized as constructive and recon- structive activities respectively (Bartlett, 1932; Jacoby & Craik, 1979; Jenkins, 1974; Neisser, 1967, 1976)" (Kihlstrom, 1981, p. 127). Current usage finds these hypothetical structures referred to variously as *schemata* (Neisser, 1976; Rumelhart & Ortony, 1977; Tversky & Kahneman, 1973), *scripts* (Abelson, 1981; Schank & Abelson, 1977), *prototypes* (Cantor, 1981; Cantor & Mischel, 1979); and *stereotypes* (Borgida, Locksley, & Bree, 1981). While they are directed at different fields of psychology (e.g., personality, cognition, social psychology), they share a variety of similarities. For instance, schemata assume knowledge structures are constructed and that such constructions place a strong emphasis on the role of direct, personal, concrete experience; once derived, such structures permit inferential processes which allow the child or adult access to "schematic" knowledge; such schematic knowledge expresses hierarchical rela- tionships and a host of "different" relationships which lead to many levels of holistic/schematic relations in a general structure (Nelson, 1981). Our social cognitive knowledge *is* schematic, and not based on limited definitions—such general knowledge has been well delineated (Rumelhart & Ortony, 1977). We will look briefly at these hypothetical structures.

In the application of the "script" construct (Abelson, 1981), it is clear that the schematic, multi-layered type of holistic knowledge is quite similar to the generic schema construct briefly outlined previously. Abelson (1981) notes, for example, the virtual equivalence between his knowledge scripts and cognitive schemata which "do not use sequence information," but merely, "organize expectations or represent different levels of abstract relationships" (Abelson, 1981, p. 717). If event sequencing is an important dimension of a specific knowledge structure, then the coupling of order of information and anticipated events results in an action script. The generic schema construct and script con- struct thus are similar. Abelson (1981) is unique in trying to link scripts of schematic understanding of events to individuals' actual behavior. He highlights the importance of the concept of commitment in which understanding of a social situation may or may not lead to the individuals "performance" of a particular behavior. Such commitment or active involvement derives after the situation has been "understood," after the "choices" of behaviors have been identified, e.g., the situation is related to others in the past, and *then* the individual participates or "enters the script" (Abelson, 1981). There are no other formulations of the relationships of schematic knowledge and "performative structures" than this linkage! Clearly, without the commitment to enter the script there is no behavior which the individual will display. From our perspective, commitment may be one of the more useful ways in which to conceptualize the process.

   In addition to the generic schema and the script, social cognitive processes have also been conceptualized by Cantor (1981) as involving prototypes. Prototypes are considered to summarize the knowledge which we have about various social categories, such as types of personalities (e.g., extraverts) and social settings (e.g., conferences). "Knowledge about the categories may be internally represented and structured in terms of prototypes for the category" (Cantor, 1981, p.27). And prototypes may be identified or defined in a least three basic ways:

1. The central tendency of a set of geometric forms, defined as the mean value of the set of stimulus objects on each relevant feature;
2. a representative set of exemplars of the category; or
3. an abstract set of features commonly associated with members of a category, with each feature assigned a weight according to degree of association with the category (Cantor, 1981, p.27).

In terms of the specific use of these three definitions, we find the central tendency to lead to an "average value" or composite portrait of a particular personality type (using Cantor's illustration, "the criminal type"). Exemplars are instances in which real-life persons fit the category "best." And lastly, according to Cantor (1981), an abstract feature set seems mid-way between each of the other two, since it contains representational information at a variety of abstractions.

   Social stereotypes are also considered to be analogous to the generic schema construct, scripts, and prototypes, since they represent the "products" of our social cognitions which are directed at the social environment (Borgida, Locksley, & Brekke, 1981). Stereotypes allow for the possibility of social inference, judgment, and categorization among others illustrative of the outgrowth of social cognitive processes (Borgida, Locksley, & Brekke, 1981). As can be seen, stereotypes may be viewed as the application of broader classes of social cognitive schemata to larger social groups or categories (e.g., race, ethnicity, or sex). One of the basic measurement operations in assessing social stereotypes has been the *distributional listing* of traits which are thought to be representative of the target social group under study (McCauley & Stitt, 1978). Such a technique is clearly parallel to the use of the average value or central tendency idea underlying certain prototypes.

Hypothetical cognitive constructions like those identified above are at the heart of current explanations of the process of social cognition. Anderson (1976) notes that "no useful theory of representation can be independent of process and it appears that the relationship of the generic schema construct and a model of cognitive processing has largely remained unspecified" (Fiske & Linville, 1980). It appears that, implicitly, a cognitive "developmental" model has been assumed by some, and, in far more instances, a nondevelopmental model has been assumed by default.

The assumption of "nondevelopmental" views of adult cognition suggests a picture of "correct and rational" beings who are precise, exacting, and facile, in their processing. This is the model held up for those to compare the child's incomplete social cognitive understanding. Yet there is ample evidence that adult cognitions, judgments, and inferences are to a degree fallible, error-prone, and "irrational" from time to time. Adults have been found to be inaccurate reporters of complex events which they have witnessed first hand, they tend to fill in gaps of information falsely "remembering" what they did not hear or read, and they are notoriously willing to apply inappropriate normative data or misapply appropriate normative data (Cohen, 1981). Tversky and Kahneman (1974) were among those to discover the errors and bias inherent in adult cognition. In their early work, they found that adult "intuitive judgments of probability are biased towards predicting that outcomes will be similar to the evidence afforded by typical cases" (Cohen, 1981, p. 330). The adults were said to have employed a "representative heuristic" as the basis for their judgments; the heuristic was said to guide adult probabilistic reasoning or the lack thereof. While some have felt that these data suggest a pattern of adult "irrationality," for our purposes it seems sufficient to be able to identify such errors, their potential source(s), and to understand and predict their occurrence. They also reinforce our belief that adult models of social cognitive "competence" are not an appropriate source against which to chart the emergent social cognitive "knowledge" of children.

Moreover, even "developmental" frameworks have made unnecessarily restrictive assumptions about the nature of adult cognition. Adulthood, that "terminal" stage in cognitive development, is never really articulated; its role in cognitive developmental theory often is unclear. In order to provide a complete description of cognitive social development, it is necessary to study these abilities within a general life-span perspective, rather than from the limited child-only views which have dominated past thinking. Thus, the study of adults' social cognitive abilities is an important "developmental" objective. In addition, it is clear both theoretically and empirically that adulthood is *not* a single unitary stage (Chandler, 1975) that is uniformly characterized by ever-present abstract, rational, and logical modes of representation and thought (Baltes & Willis, 1977; Berzonsky, 1978; Dulit, 1972). These latter attainments "are neither as universally achieved, nor as universally practiced by mature adults as theories, such as those of Piaget, are assumed to suppose" (Chandler, 1975, p. 3). We thus need to consider the pluralistic or multilinear view of adulthood (Chandler, 1975) as a model for understanding the social cognitive abilities of mature individuals.

The argument suggested is that adult cognitive abilities (e.g., those needed to construct and/or utilize generic schemas) do not necessarily supplant more basic or earlier modes of processing. Adulthood and adult social cognition is marked by multilinearity, such that skills and abilities acquired earlier in development may coexist with those that emerge later. As Brainerd (1978) and Berzonsky (1978) both suggest, within-stage synchrony in adult cognitive development is difficult to document. Two major conceptual links necessary for understanding social cognition from a *diachronic* perspective appear to be affect and imagery. Each provides an alternative mode of representation utilized in social cognition. And, both may also be linked to the generic schema construct, if we accept that schemata are likely *multi-dimensional* and not necessarily viewed as only cognitive constructions (e.g., affective dimensions).

AFFECTIVE PROCESSING

There are already a number of developmental theorists who subscribe to the notion that schemata can be motoric, imaginal, as well as abstractions based on higher order processes (cf. Piaget, Bruner, Luria, Vygotsky). Such processes and alternative modes of schematic representation, as suggested above, may exist alongside each other. Under certain specified conditions, the more primitive or basic representational modes may be called forth in adulthood. One of the more powerful triggers of basic schematic representation appears to be affect. Kosslyn and Kagan (1981) note with interest that adults encode in vivid rich imagery many of the affect-laden social stimuli which they process. Under conditions of "hot" social cognition, there appears to be a tendency to use imagery-focused schemata rather than the language-based modes typically ascribed to adults as the most efficient for complex representation of information. Kosslyn and Kagan (1981) identify a number of affect laden stimuli (sex symbols, sports cars) to which we can add significant social stimuli (parents, siblings, boss) which may have the necessary emotionality which results in imagery-based representation. Such schemata obviously are not constructed or stored only in this modality, but rather under conditions of strong affect imagery appears to predominate. Given the clear limitations of such types of processing, developmental "differences" may indeed be difficult to document, predict, and understand, since with emotional arousal more mature "adult" processing capabilities are disrupted (Kosslyn & Kagan, 1981). In fact, it is the processing of exactly such affective stimuli that contributes to our interest in social cognition.

Affect can become part of already extant schemata and can also be seen as a viable schema in its own right. Affect is processed as part of the cognitive social environment by young children. In one study, the sensitivity of 5- to 7-year-old children to affect was explored (Rybash, Roodin, & Hallion, 1979). Children heard a set of motivationally ambiguous stories describing different types of damage. They were then shown a picture of the perpetrator who appeared visually to be "happy, neutral, or sad." Across all three ages, children's judgments of the perpetrator's intentions (unintentional vs. intentional) were based on the facial appearance of the central character/perpetrator. Children showed sensitivity to facial cues reflective of affective awareness; happy smiles on the perpetrator indicated to them that the act was intentional, while sad, remorseful appearances indicated to them that the act was unintentional.

How can such schematic components as affect be understood and utilized by young children? One explanation has been derived by Zajonc (1980). Affective stimuli may be processed in a far more efficient manner than other forms of language-related stimuli. Hoffman (1981, p.79) notes that "affective stimuli are remembered longer than cognitive stimuli . . . ." And, according to Zajonc (1980), affect is the more basic, primary mode. Affective evaluations are derived and processed in a more rapid manner than our "cognitive" evaluations or judgments. Affective dimensions most importantly appear then to have both *primacy* and *permanency,* according to Zajonc, who cites research on first impressions and the difficulties in altering such impressions despite new cognitive information (Zajonc, 1980). Affective evaluations appear quite similar to the first dimension of Wundt's tripartite theory of feeling: (a) pleasantness/unpleasantness, (b) strain/relaxation, and (c) excitement/quiescence. The rather controversial aspect of Zajonc's work lies in the assumption that affect and cognition may involve partially separate processing and representational systems, similar to the dual coding hypothesis of Paivio and Csapo (1973) which suggests the existence of discriminably different systems for the processing of words vs. pictures. Thus, it is hypothesized that affective evaluations or pleasant/unpleasant judgments are "carried by affective and motor processes that are closely associated with visual memory representations of things" (Zajonc, 1980, p. 168). Such efficient and rapid processing of imagery-based vs. language-based stimuli is not surprising, if affective evaluations are more directly linked to imagery rather than to words (Zajonc, 1980). Even if such partially separate processing of affective and cognitive evaluations turns out not to be supported, Zajonc presents an impressive case for the fact that affective evaluations typically *precede* cognitive evaluations.

The implications of this position are varied, but one of the most important for our concerns is that affect provides the "glue" or attention for intense social cognitive processing. Without affect, it is likely that processing is rather automatic, superficial (Shiffrin & Schneider, 1977), and not very "deep" (Craik & Lockhart, 1972). Affect helps adult social cognition to be more detailed, deep, and controlled (cf. Shiffrin & Schneider, 1977). Affect may be one antidote to the *mindless* processing of social experience so aptly described by Langer

(1978). Hypothesizing the presence of affect schemata which have primacy over cognitive ones, suggests additional breadth and support for Neisser's contention that "perceivers pick up only what they have schemas for and willy nilly ignore the rest" (1976, p. 90). Thus, the very same social stimuli may be processed using affective schemata and/or cognitive schemata. Affect appears to be one precondition for controlled cognitive processing.

NEUROLOGICAL ASPECTS OF SOCIAL COGNITION

Affect, as a potentially powerful variable in social cognition, needs to be integrated within the holistic framework of this research tradition. It is beginning to be recognized by some as a needed component (Flavell, 1981). With affect, social cognitive phenomena are far more likely to become represented in a variety of different ways within the brain. That is, social cognition is broadened to include both cognitive and affective storage, following Zajonc's speculations, in different projection areas in the brain. Affective processing, according to Zajonc (1980), generally involves the right hemisphere, results in rapidfire judgments without the need for slow autonomic feedback, and uses the same system or neurophysiological mechanism as that involved in excitation. This mechanism suggests that one type of excitatory mechanism is triggered by novel (affective) stimuli, while a different type of excitatory mechanism is triggered by familiar stimuli. While not purely distinct categories, Callaway (1981) suggests different modes of processing/excitation such that cognitive components appear to be aminergic (serial, memory-driven, controlled) and affective components appear to be cholinergic (parallel, data-driven, automatic). Zajonc (1980) suggests the major neurophysiological mechanism underlying affect is the locus coeruleus, which is a major site of norepinepherine in the brain. Its location at the top of the brain stem, its incredibly diffuse pattern of projections of axons to all areas of the neocortex (cf. likely innervating each cortical column; Morrison, Milliver, & Grzanna, 1979), and its rather recently discovered role as a major site of progressive deterioriation/destruction in Korsakoff's syndrome (cf. alcoholism prolonged to the point of producing symptoms including loss of recent memory) serve to provide additional validation to Zajonc's contention. The locus coeruleus may in fact be a basic site which contributes directly to affective processing (Watson, 1981). Affect, from this perspective, is basic and primary in brain phylogeny, and perhaps echoes the theme of this domain having special evolutionary/adaptive significance. The suggestion by Zajonc is that we also consider affect to be primary in social cognitive processing.

There are certainly other models of neurophysiological processing which deserve consideration as well. The recent work of Pribram (1977) devoted to a holographic model of the brain is analogous to the neurophysiological model being presented by Zajonc. The holographic hypothesis is specifically designed to account for the fact that, even with large scale destruction, brain function and memories are generally not drastically impaired. Affect and cognition provide many representational opportunities throughout different brain areas. And, using wave-form analysis of cellular response (e.g., in layers), Pribram has demonstrated the utility of this organizational model of the brain. With Fourier transforms for modeling neural processing, Pribram shows how visual processing can be represented in this holographic fashion. In disagreement with visual processing models which suggest that the cells in the visual system operate as "feature detectors," a novel alternative is provided. Pribram suggests that cells in the visual system act as frequency analyzers "resonating" to the interference pattern of sensory input. In the visual domain, holographic storage is based on the interference patterns of light as reflected from objects; in the holographic model, there is response to patterns of light and dark, which may be represented in terms of spatial frequency. Thus, the cells of the visual system operate as frequency analyzers which respond to the appropriate wave form/spatial frequency (Pribram, 1977).

The concept of resonance appears to provide a processing model of schemata within the domain of social cognition. Both recognition and recall, match or mismatch, and novelty (affect) or familiarity in principal would be amenable to analysis using the Fourier process. By exploring the schematic judgments of persons *across* a wide variety of social cognitive settings, we could identify the "wave forms" to which an individual is sensitive. That is, rather than treating such information in our traditional studies as variance, we could make such variation the focus of our investigations. Analyses and investigations of social perception based on resonance, Fourier process, and holographic models are theoretically useful directions for "schema" theorists to consider. The model provides a *dynamic* method of representing schemata based on different types of activation and the concept of schematic resonance across social settings.

COMPETENT SOCIAL BEHAVIOR

Affect appears to have special importance for those attempting to understand a third question in social cognitive investigations: the relationship between social categorical knowledge and competent social behavior. The question can be phrased in a variety of ways, but it appears that social knowledge and overt social behavior are not always directly related. As the literature in moral development suggests, morality on the highest cognitive-developmental plane is not necessarily transformed into action. Affect appears to provide one critical link between cognitive knowledge and overt behavior. A good example can be seen in the work of Rogers, Kuiper, and Kirker (1977), who studied the recall of adjectives under four different conditions. Two of the conditions required minimum involvement, or minimum affect, since subjects merely had to see if the adjectives were either similar or different in terms of either type of print or rhyming with a comparison set of adjectives. The third condition required subjects to see if the adjectives were similar semantically to a comparison list. And the fourth condition required subjects to identify those adjectives descriptive of the subject (e.g., personal self-reference). Recall was significantly better than all other conditions when self-reference adjective identification was required, even significantly better than the third condition which required semantic processing for identification of equivalence. Similar patterns emerge when other measures of memory are employed (Zajonc, 1980). Personal self-involvement appears to activate affect and provides additional representation and processing power. Such results have been extended to other measures of processing memory-type stimuli with both children and adults.

Evidence of "self-involvement" as a motivator of affective processes producing improvements in cognitive efficiency and overt performance can be found in other areas. Children and adolescents typically provide more advanced moral reasoning when they are asked to assume the role of the central character in moral dilemmas (Keasey, 1977), although college students appear to break this pattern and are much better at judging the morality of others than they are of themselves (Rybash, Roodin, & Lonky, 1981). When adults and elderly subjects are considered, "self-involvement" has been found to be a critical variable in a variety of cognitive tasks and situations. With meaningful stimuli, with situations which are ecologically valid, with minimally anxiety-arousing methods of presentation, and with self-involving methodologies, the greater is the likelihood of investigators finding no age differences between adult and elderly populations of subjects (Botwinick, 1977). In fact, there appear to be fewer "declines" in cognitive processes in recent studies with the elderly. From our perspective, it seems that, with appropriate motivational conditions, such as affective involvement, cognitive processes can be efficiently maintained and enhanced in old age: self-involvement and personal commitment provide this motivation.

Perhaps of far greater interest to cognitive psychologists studying social processes across the life-span, is to consider the range of conditions which impact on aging populations reducing personal involvement in the environment, reducing their affective self-involvement, and limiting their overall cognitive performance. Such patterns are familiar to those studying the aging process and reflect a concern for the situational context in which aging occurs within our society. With affective distance from life and from society, cognitive deficiencies are more likely to emerge. While cognitive declines occur, they rarely impact on the processing of social cognition. That is, affective understanding and social cognitive competence remain basic characteristics of adult/aged subjects populations. This system is rarely influenced at all, except in those cases of extreme pathology . . . senile dementia and other such syndromes, although the relative decline in brain cells in the neo-cortex (Bondareff, 1977) may, for some aged subjects, imply greater reliance on and utility of more basic mechanisms such as the affective sites previously identified.

SELF-APPRAISAL

Consideration of the "self" within cognitive psychology is not yet likely to win accolades; however we are reminded by our information-processing colleagues that the mind is itself a recursive system capable of an endless cycle of self-monitoring, judgmental, evaluative processes of its own productions. We see the need, more importantly, to recognize "self" processes, not only because these appear to provide one manipulable component of affective involvement, but also because the "self" becomes the dominant source of change across the adult years (Neugarten, 1977). The surprising facts emerging in the past decade with elderly subjects in cognitive studies is that decline and decrement are not universal across such populations (Botwinick, 1977). In the writing of contemporary lifespan research investigators, it appears that the "self" undergoes additional elaboration, qualitative change, and increased introspective awareness (Lowenthal, 1977).

Within the emergent life-span tradition, it has become commonplace to note that the adult and aging years involve far more changes in "self" (e.g., changes in restructuring, changes in definition, changes in elaboration, changes in awareness) than in any other domain, including cognition. Thus, a fair description of the social cognitive process must include self-appraisal. The "self" as a social cognitive enterprise suggests challenges for all psychologists. Consider, for instance, the capacity of this system to prepare and plan for future events. Thomae (1970) initially suggested the capacity to engage in anticipatory socialization: e.g., preparing and planning for future events which have not yet been encountered such as retirement, the "empty nest" and even death of a spouse. Or, from the cognitive domain, examine Meacham and Singer's (1977) concept of "prospective memory," which allows for the special effort (affective involvement) needed to retain relevant information which will be necessary to have in the future. Finally, consider the kinds of cognitive restructuring which occur in the face of major life crises. With adequate intellectual abilities, self-reflection, and a degree of "openness" to experience, such opportunities provide the impetus for further growth in numerous domains. Using the logic developed in this paper, it is likely that life crises are vehicles for the creation of new schemata and new resources; yet some adults retreat from such crises and attempt to utilize "old" or inappropriate schemata rather than creatively developing and utilizing new ones. Thus, both our evaluation of the social environment and the self are integral components of adult social cognition.

CONCLUSION

In conclusion, we have emphasized the importance of the process-oriented approach to examining social cognition. This process-oriented approach differs from the schema approach adopted by most social cognitive investigators and presents a broader range of perspectives to be studied. These alternatives include: (a) ecological considerations, (b) affect, (c) neurological foundations, (d) personal competence, and (e) self appraisal. In addition, we considered the importance of personal commitment to action. We believe that, traditionally, psychologists have overemphasized the schema approach. Children's social cognitive abilities have thus been underestimated, and adults' developmental changes in social cognitive abilities have not been fully explored.

Psychologists must further examine these process-oriented perspectives to provide answers to the following basic questions about social cognition, schema, and ultimately overt behavior: (a) are basic schemata modifiable, and if so, how may they be altered? (b) In development, are social cognitive schemata consolidated or is there a possible interference or decay associated with these processes? One area which could be further explored for answers to the above questions is the field of group dynamics. Under careful observation, it may be possible to see the nature of social cognitive behaviors—their relationship with more typical measures of cognitive/affective functioning—and, most importantly, to explore such processes *over time* in a quasinaturalistic research setting. We may be able to intervene and present to such groups "newcomers," friends of oldtimers, and observe the behaviors of those within the group as they deal with the loss of particularly valued members. It is in such life-like situations that we are most likely to see the interactive effects of social cognitive and affective processes on behavior.

While social cognitive schemata provide a useful method of conceptualizing the above processes, the schema concept has not been thoroughly expanded to include the motivational component of affect, nor has it been adequately viewed from the standpoint of "self" knowledge and "self" referent. Schemata have been generally studied from nondevelopmental views, and little information is known about how they directly influence behavior. One of the more intriguing suggestions is that schemata make for more efficient cognitive processing (Mischel, 1981; Kosslyn & Kagan, 1981). They help to simplify the processing of the social environment. The suggestion offered here is that such schemata provide a structure from which the individual can increasingly process the world of social relationships in a successful manner. This type of processing includes both cognitive and affective components. However, individuals are most likely to engage in simple, automatic social cognition which "matches" already extant schemata. New schemata for adults are difficult to develop unless, apparently, an emotional or affective component is involved. With such affect, we find that deeper processing occurs and that such schemata become represented in a variety of ways neurologically.

Social cognition thus must take seriously the recent demands for a psychology with *ecological validity,* given the domain to which we generalize. While such a direction is often given lip-service across many areas of psychology, it is critical in the area of social cognition. Consider for instance, Mischel's work with preschool children, designed to investigate the conditions which facilitate their delay of reward (Mischel & Moore, 1973, 1980). Children were shown color slides of desirable rewards which could only be obtained if they could sufficiently delay or wait. This condition consistently proved to have children who could wait the longest, and clearly employed relevant imagery for its relative success. Yet, in later work (Mischel & Moore, 1980), these effects were disconfirmed when the actual desired rewards were placed in front of the children rather than the color slides of the rewards. Seeing the desired food rewards in front of them (such as marshmallows or pretzels) reduced the amount of time which children could wait for these rewards. Thus, pictures of the rewards enhanced waiting time, while the real objects reduced children's ability to delay receipt of rewards.

Not only does this set of data suggest the need for validation of laboratory studies, it also raises problems for many of our explanatory theories. Mischel (1981) suggested that, perhaps, mode of presentation (pictorial vs. real) activates different kinds of ideation about the rewards. The former condition involves far less affective arousal than the latter and in real life situations, affect is an important variable which impacts on cognitive processing.

Perhaps, most importantly, we need to consider the concept of commitment in order to appreciate fully the relationship of schema and behavior. Across development, increasingly complex social relations require committment to a finite set of schemata which help us negotiate the interpersonal world. These schemata govern our thoughts and feelings about self and others. It is only under apparently intense emotionality that such schemata are created initially, and, following the recent work of Dember (1981), only under parallel conditions that adult cognitive schemata are altered. The intense conditions related to self, self-knowledge, and self-elaboration, may be the life crises of middle and later adulthood.

From Dember's discussion of commitment to ideology, we propose that schemata are derived to help cope with cognitive complexity and provide a method of simplifying (cognitive economy, Mischel, 1981) the social environment. With adequate emotional/affective commitment, these schemata may continue through the lifespan as primary modes of processing social stimuli and situations. With commitment, we showed how the two domains of social cognition can be inter-related.

Reason reveals relations within any given context; it can also compare one context with another on the basis of metacontents established for this purpose. But there is a limit. In the end, reason itself remains reflexively relativistic, a property which turns reason back upon reason's own findings, in even its fartherest reaches then reason will leave the thinker with several legitimate contexts and no way of choosing among them—no way at least that he can justify through reason alone. If he is still to honor reason he must now also transcend it; he must affirm his own position from within himself in full awareness that reason can never completely justify him or assure him. (Perry, 1968, pp. 135–136)

In summary, we have tried to trace the importance of social cognition as in integral part of one's day-to-day functioning in each epoch of human development. Social cognition plays an important role in the integration of cognitive, affective, and behavioral aspects of human potential. Psychologists have often oversimplified the complexities involved in understanding social cognition. Thus, a set of important questions germane to this approach has not been examined fully. It is hoped that others will see the need to extend social cognition within the lifespan developmental approach and begin to focus concern on these processes.

REFERENCES

Abelson, R. P. (1981). Psychological status of the script concept. *American Psychologist, 36,* 715–729.

Anderson, J. R. (1976). *Language, memory, and thought.* Hillsdale, NJ: Erlbaum.

Athay, M., & Darley, J. M. (1981). Toward an interaction - centered theory of personality. In N. Cantor & J. F. Kihlstrom (Eds.), *Personality, cognition, and social interaction.* Hillsdale, NJ: Erlbaum.

Baltes, P. B., & Willis, S. L. (1977). Towards psychological theories of aging and development. In J. E. Birren & K. W. Schaie (Eds.), *Handbook of the psychology of aging.* New York: Van Nostrand.

Bartlett, F. (1932). *Remembering: A study in experimental and social psychology.* Cambridge, England: Cambridge University Press.

Berndt, T. J. (1981). Relations between social cognition, nonsocial cognition, and social behavior: The case of friendship. In J. H. Flavell & L. Ross (Eds.), *Social cognitive development: Frontiers and possible futures.* New York: Cambridge University Press.

Berzonsky, M. D. (1978). Formal reasoning in adolescence: An alternative view. *Adolescence, 13,* 279–290.

Bondareff, W. (1977). The neural basis of aging. In J. E. Birren & K. W. Schaie (Eds.), *Handbook of the psychology of aging.* New York: Van Nostrand.

Borgida, E., Locksley, A., & Brekke, N. (1981). Social stereotypes and social judgment. In N. Cantor & J. G. Kihlstrom (Eds.), *Personality, cognition, and social interaction.* Hillsdale, NJ: Erlbaum.

Botwinick, J. (1977). Intellectual abilities. In J. E. Birren & K. W. Schaie (Eds.), *Handbook of the psychology of aging.* New York: Van Nostrand.

Brainerd, C. J. (1978). *Piaget's theory of intelligence.* Englewood Cliffs, NJ: Prentice Hall.

Broughton, J. (1978). Development of concepts of self, mind, reality, and knowledge. *New Directions for Child Development, 1,* 75–100.

Buzsaki, G., Isaacson, R. L., & Hannigan, J. H. (1981). Behavioral problems related to the interpretation of brain rhythms. *Behavioral and Brain Sciences, 4,* 477.

Callaway, E. (1981). Can the decomposition of attention clarify some clinical issues. *Behavioral and Brain Sciences, 4,* 477–479.

Cantor, N. (1981). A cognitive-social approach to personality. In N. Cantor & J. F. Kihlstrom (Eds.), *Personality, cognition, and social interaction.* Hillsdale, NJ: Erlbaum.

Cantor, N., & Mischel, W. (1979). Prototypes in person perception. In L. Berkowitz (Ed.), *Advances in experimental social psychology* (Vol. 12). New York: Academic Press.

Chandler, M. J. (1979). *Social cognition: A selective review of current research.* Unpublished manuscript.

Chandler, M. J. (1977). Social cognition: A selective review of current research. In W. F. Overton (Ed.), *Knowledge and development*. New York: Plenum Press.

Chandler, M. J. (1975). *Social cognition and life-span approaches to the study of child development*. Unpublished paper, Pennsylvania State University, 1975.

Cohen, L. J. (1981). Can human irrationality be experimentally demonstrated. *Journal of Behavioral and Brain Sciences, 4*, 317–330.

Craik, F. I. M., & Lockhart, R. S. (1972). Levels of processing: A framework for memory research. *Journal of Verbal Learning and Verbal Behavior, 11*, 671–684.

Damon, W. J. (1977). *The social world of the child*. San Francisco: Jossey - Bass.

Dember, W. (1981). *Cognition, complexity, confusion, closure, commitment, conversion*. Paper presented at American Psychological Association Meetings, Los Angeles, California.

Dulit, E. (1972). Adolescent thinking a la Piaget: The formal stage. *Journal of Youth and Adolescence, 1*, 281–301.

Fiske, S. T., & Kinder, D. R. (1981). Involvement expertise, and schema use: Evidence from political cognition. In N. Cantor & J. F. Kihlstrom (Eds.), *Personality, cognition, and social interaction*. Hillsdale, NJ: Erlbaum.

Fiske, S. T., & Linville, P. W. (1980). What does the schema concept buy us. *Personality and Social Psychology Bulletin, 6*, 543–557.

Fitzgerald, J. M. (1981). Research methods and research questions for the study of person-perception in adult development. *Human Development, 24*, 138–144.

Flavell, J. H. (1981). Monitoring social cognitive enterprises: Something else that may develop in the area of social cognition. In J. H. Flavell & L. Ross (Eds.), *Social cognitive development: Frontiers and possible futures*. New York: Cambridge University Press.

Flavell, J. H. (1977). *Cognitive development*. Englewood Cliffs, NJ: Prentice-Hall.

Forbes, D. (1978). Recent research on children's social cognition: A brief review. *New Directions for Child Development, 1*, 123–139.

Gallup, G. (1977). Self recognition in primates. *American Psychologist, 32*, 329–338.

Gelman, R., & Spelke, E. (1981). The development of thoughts about animate and inanimate objects. In J. H. Flavell & L. Ross (Eds.), *Social cognitive development: Frontiers and possible futures*. New York: Cambridge University Press.

Higgins, E. T. (1981). Role-taking and social judgment: Alternative developmental perspectives and processes. In J. H. Flavell & L. Ross (Eds.), *Social cognitive development: Frontiers and possible futures*. New York: Cambridge University Press.

Hoffman, M. L. (1981). Perspectives on the difference between understanding people and understanding things: The role of affect. In J. H. Flavell & L. Ross (Eds.), *Social cognitive development: Frontiers and possible futures*. New York: Cambridge University Press.

Jacoby, L. L., & Craik, F. I. M. (1979). Effects of elaboration of processing at encoding and retrieval: Trace distinctiveness and recovery of initial context. In L. S. Cermak & F. I. M. Craik (Eds.), *Levels of processing and human memory*. Hillsdale, NJ: Erlbaum.

Jenkins, J. S. (1974). Remember that old theory of memory: Well forget it! *American Psychologist, 29*, 785–795.

Keasey, C. B. (1977). Young children's attribution of intentionality to themselves and others. *Child Development, 48*, 261–264.

Kihlstrom, J. F. (1981). On personality and memory. In N. Cantor & J. F. Kihlstrom (Eds.), *Personality, cognition, and social interaction*. Hillsdale, NJ: Erlbaum.

Kosslyn, S. M., & Kagan, J. (1981). Concrete thinking and the development of social cognition. In J. H. Flavell & L. Ross (Eds.), *Social cognitive development: Frontiers and possible futures*. New York: Cambridge University Press.

Langer, E. J. (1978). The thinking of the role of thought in social interaction. In J. Harvey, W. Ickes, & R. Kidd, (Eds.), *New directions in attribution research* (Vol. 2), Hillsdale, NJ: Erlbaum.

Lawick-Goodall, J. (1975). The chimpanzee. In V. Goodall (Ed.), *The quest for man*. London: Phaidon Press.

Lempers, J. D., Flavell, E. R., & Flavell, J. H. (1977). The development in very young children of tacit knowledge concerning visual perception. *Genetic Psychology Monographs, 95,* 3–53.

Lowenthal, M. F. (1977). Toward a sociological theory of change in adulthood and old age. In J. E. Birren & K. W. Schaie (Eds.), *Handbook of the psychology of aging*. New York: Van Nostrand.

Martin, G. B., & Clark, R. D. (1982). Distress crying in neonates: Species and peer specificity. *Developmental Psychology, 18,* 3–9.

McCauley, C., & Stitt, C. L. (1978). An individual and quantitative measure of stereotypes. *Journal of Personality and Social Psychology, 36,* 929–940.

Meddin, J. (1979). Chimpanzees, symbols and the reflective self. *Social Psychology Quarterly, 42,* 99–109.

Meacham, J. A., & Singer, J. (1977). Incentive effects in prospective remembering. *Journal of Psychology, 97,* 191–197.

Meichenbaum, D. (1977). *Cognitive behavior modification*. New York: Plenum Press.

Mischel, W. (1974). Processes in delay of gratification. In L. Berkowitz (Ed.), *Advances in experimental social psychology* (Vol. 7). New York: Academic Press.

Mischel, W. (1981). Personality and cognition: Something borrowed, something new? In N. Cantor & J. F. Kihlstrom (Eds.), *Personality, cognition, and social interaction*. Hillsdale, NJ: Erlbaum.

Mischel, W., & Moore, B. (1973). Effects of attention to symbolically presented rewards on self-control. *Journal of Personality and Social Psychology, 28,* 172–179.

Mischel, W., & Moore, B. (1980). The role of ideation in voluntary delay for symbolically presented rewards. *Cognitive Therapy and Research, 4,* 211–221.

Morrison, J. H., Molliver, M. E., & Grzanna, R. (1979). Noradrenergic innervation of cerebral cortex: Widespread effects of local cortical lesions. *Science, 205,* 313–316.

Muellar, E., & Brenner, J. (1977). The origins of social skill and interaction among playgroup toddlers. *Child Development, 48,* 854–861.

Muellar, E., & Lucas, T. A. (1975). A developmental analysis of peer interaction among toddlers. In M. Lewis & L. A. Rosenblum (Eds.), *Friendship and peer relations*. New York: Wiley.

Neisser, U. (1967). *Cognitive psychology*. New York: Appleton-Century-Crofts.

Neisser, U. (1976). *Cognition and reality*. New York: Appleton-Century-Crofts.

Nelson, K. (1981). Social cognition in a script framework. In J. H. Flavell & L. Ross (Eds.), *Social cognitive development: Frontiers and possible futures*. New York: Cambridge University Press.

Neugarten, B. L. (1977). Personality and aging. In J. E. Birren & K. W. Schaie (Eds.), *Handbook of the psychology of aging*. New York: Van Nostrand.

Paivio, A., & Csapo, K. (1973). Picture superiority in free recall: Imagery or dual coding? *Cognitive Psychology, 5,* 176–206.

Perry, W. G. (1968). *Forms of intellectual and ethical development in the college years*. New York: Holt Rinehart.

Pribram, K. (1977). *Languages of the brain*. Monterey, CA: Brooks Cole.

Riegel, K. F. (1979). *Foundations of dialectical psychology*. New York: Academic Press.

Rogers, T., Kuiper, N., & Kirker, W. S. (1977). Self-reference and the encoding of personal information. *Journal of Personality and Social Psychology, 35,* 677–688.

Rosch, E., Mervis, C., Gray, W., Johnson, D., & Boyes-Braem, P. (1976). Basic objects in natural categories. *Cognitive Psychology, 8,* 382–439.

Rumelhart, D. E., & Ortony, A. (1977). The representation of knowledge in memory. In R. C. Anderson, R. J. Spiro, & W. E. Montague (Eds.), *Schooling and the acquisition of knowledge*. Hillsdale, NJ: Erlbaum.

Rybash, J. M., Roodin, P. A., & Hallion, K. (1979). The role of affect in children's attribution of intentionality and dispensation of punishment. *Child Development, 50,* 1227–1230.

Rybash, J. M., Roodin, P. A., & Lonky, E. (1981). Young adults' scores on the defining issues test as a function of a ''self'' vs. ''other'' presentation mode. *Journal of Youth and Adolescence, 10,* 25–31.

Schank, R. C., & Abelson, R. P. (1977). *Scripts, plans, goals, and understanding.* Hillsdale, NJ: Erlbaum.

Selman, R. L. (1976). Social cognitive understanding: A guide to educational and clinical practice. In T. Lickona (Ed.), *Moral development and behaviors: Theory, research, and social issues.* New York: Holt, Rinehart and Winston.

Shatz, M., & Gelman, R. (1973). The development of communication skills: Modifications in the speech of young children at a function of listener. *Monographs of the society for research in child development, 38,* (2, Serial # 152), 1–37.

Shiffrin, R. M., & Schneider, W. (1977). Controlled and automatic human information processing: II Perceptual learning, automatic attending, and a general theory. *Psychological Review, 84,* 127–190.

Thomae, H. (1970). Theory of aging and cognitive theory of personality. *Human Development, 13,* 1–16.

Trevarthen, C. (1977). Descriptive analysis of infant communication behavior. In H. R. Schaffer (Ed.), *Studies in mother-infant interaction.* London: Academic Press.

Turiel, E. (1978). The development of concepts of social structure: Social convention. In J. Glick & K. Alison Clarke-Stewart (Eds.), *The development of social understanding.* New York: Gardner Press.

Tversky, A., & Kahneman, D. (1974). Judgment under uncertainty: Heuristics and biases. *Science, 184,* 1124–1131.

Vanderwold, C. H., & Robinson, T. E. (1981). Reticulo-Cortical activity and behavior: A critique of the arousal theory and a new synthesis. *Behavioral and Brain Sciences, 4,* 459–514.

Watson, W. C. (1981). *Physiological psychology: An introduction.* Boston: Houghton Mifflin.

Zajonc, R. B. (1980). Feeling and thinking preferences need no inferences. *American Psychologist, 35,* 151–175.

Chapter 9

Personality, Affect, and Cognition: Reflections on Social-Cognitive Development

Royal Grueneich

Hamilton College
Clinton, New York

Cognition about social reality is a central aspect of our intellectual activity in everyday life. We constantly introspect about ourselves, attempting to gain insight into our feelings, our motives, and our reaction to various people and situations. We also continually struggle to understand other people, trying to figure out what their character is really like, how they will respond to us, why they act as they do. Even our institutional forms of activity are based heavily upon ''naive psychology''; for example, modern legal systems at their very core draw upon commonsense notions about the ways in which acts are causally related to consequences, the conditions under which people do or do not have control over their actions, and the sorts of mental elements which must be present for an actor to be held responsible for wrongdoing (Hart, 1968).

Despite the obviously critical role played by social cognition in everyday life, psychological research for too many years largely ignored this topic. In recent years, however, this neglect has been rectified, so that social cognition has become one of the more popular areas of research. The chapters by Roodin and Rybash and by Sperbeck and Whitbourne nicely illustrate the nature and scope of the research in this area. A casual reading of the two chapters might suggest that there is little relationship between them, because they differ so widely in their scope and content. Whereas the chapter by Roodin and Rybash provides a comprehensive survey and critique of the major literature on social-cognitive development, the chapter by Sperbeck and Whitbourne focuses specifically upon the relationship between personality and autobiographical reminiscing in adulthood. Despite this apparent lack of relevance to one another, the chapters do share several important common themes: both place heavy emphasis on ecological validity in research, on the need to give serious consideration to affective or motivational variables, and on the centrality of the self in social cognition. My discussion of the two chapters will concentrate on these shared themes, and it will attempt to highlight some of the chapters' key points while also pointing out some of their possible limitations and offering some additional considerations.

ROODIN AND RYBASH'S CHAPTER

As Roodin and Rybash indicate at the outset of their chapter, social cognition represents a relatively new area of research which has expanded greatly in quantity and scope in the past decade or so. Research areas of which this is true are typically characterized by uneven theoretical and empirical coverage of the important phenomena in the domain. This is brought out clearly by Roodin and Rybash, who emphasize that the current literature on social-cognitive development has some glaring oversights and omissions, and who also suggest some directions researchers might take to redress these problems. I concur with them wholeheartedly in terms of the deficiencies which they identify, but rather than systematically review all of their major criticisms, I wish to focus on three of their main topics: the criterion of ecological validity, identification of the end state in adult social cognition, and the role of affect in social cognition.

Roodin and Rybash's emphasis on the need for greater ecological validity in research echoes a plea which has been voiced frequently in recent years by researchers in a diversity of areas (e.g., Bronfenbrenner, 1974; Neisser, 1976; Willems, 1973). This concern has special relevance in the domain of social cognition, because initial interest in the area was sparked to a substantial degree by the concern over the limited ecological validity of the cognitive research of that time. Thus, Heider's (1958) pioneering work dealt with the belief structure of naive, or everyday, psychology; and early work in social-development was stimulated in part by the perception that Piaget's theory dealt too much with cognition of the physical world and too little with cognition about social reality.

Although I can give full endorsement to Roodin and Rybash's emphasis on ecological validity, I must express some reservations about a couple of their claims. In making the case for the importance of social cognition in human behavior, they suggest that social cognition precedes physical cognition in development, citing, as an example, evidence that person permanence is achieved before object permanence. It is not clear to me whether Roodin and Rybash wish to claim that social cognition *always* precedes physical cognition, or only that it *usually* does. I am extremely skeptical that it always does, and uncertain even about whether it usually does. Kohlberg's theory of moral development, for example, takes the opposite view by arguing that level of cognitive development is necessary, though not sufficient, for level of moral reasoning; thus, formal operational reasoning ability is held to be a prerequisite for post-conventional moral reasoning (Kohlberg, 1976). Further, this is not just an empty theoretical claim as there is some empirical evidence in its support (Walker & Richards, 1979). One also has to take account of the fact that our level of knowledge is much more advanced in the physical sciences, which deal with the physical world, than it is in the social sciences, which deal with social reality. Although this involves historical development in intellectual disciplines rather than ontogenetic development, and thus may not be applicable to the issue, it is suggestive and does call into question assertions about the general priority of social cognition over physical cognition.

I am somewhat confused by the section which attempts to draw an analogy between certain types of innate social knowledge and the categories studied by Rosch and her colleagues (Rosch, Mervis, Gray, Johnson, & Boyes-Braem, 1976). My confusion stems from the fact that, in this part of their discussion, Roodin and Rybash seem to be exclusively concerned with aspects of social-cognitive development which may be innate, such as infants' apparent sensitivity to distress in others. Rosch's work, on the other hand, says little about the issue of innate knowledge, but rather concentrates on the notions of basic object level categories and prototypes. More precisely, the argument of Rosch et al. (1976) is that the principles of category formation are universal, whereas the content of the categories are not. Since Roodin and Rybash make no reference to the concepts of basic object level categories or prototypes in this section of their chapter, I am unable to see a clear connection between their remarks and the work of Rosch and her colleagues.

In making my final remarks on the issue of ecological validity, I wish to reinforce and elaborate Roodin and Rybash's point that the literature on social cognition to date has not done justice to the breadth and diversity of social knowledge possessed by humans. There has been an unfortunate tendency to focus on a few areas of knowledge, such as role-taking or attributions, which has resulted in a biased and incomplete picture of the domain of social cognition. Consider for a moment what kinds of knowledge and skill must be possessed by a salesperson to convince a customer to buy a product, by a trial lawyer to sway a jury's opinion, by a parent to persuade a child to share toys with a sibling, or by a politician to get the support of his or her colleagues for a bill. I know of almost nothing in the psychological literature which sheds light on these fascinating areas of social cognition. This lacuna in our research knowledge is highlighted by Gardner (1983) in his recent book, where he argues that knowledge about the self and other persons, which he terms "personal intelligence," is distinct from other kinds of intelligence, and that people differ considerably in their level of personal intelligence, as is the case for the type of intelligence that is assessed by IQ tests.

A concrete example of unusually keen personal intelligence is given in Ken Follett's (1983) book, *On wings of eagles,* which is a real-life account of the successful attempt by an American company to free two of its business executives from a jail in Tehran during the time of the recent Iranian revolution. One of those involved in the rescue effort was an Iranian native named Rashid, who possessed unusual insight into the psychology of human behavior. At one point, the rescue team was stopped by a group of revolutionary guards:

Rashid asked himself: What will be the psychology of the leader of the revolutionary committee?

He has a million things to do, Rashid thought. He has just taken control of this town, and he has never been in power before. He must deal with the officers of the defeated army, he must round up suspected SAVAK agents and interrogate them, he must get the town running normally, he must guard against a counterrevolution, and he must send troops to fight in Tabriz.

All he wants to do, Rashid concluded, is *cross things off his list.*

He has no time or sympathy for fleeing Americans. If he must make a decision, he will simply throw us in jail for the time being, and deal with us later, at his leisure. Therefore, I must make sure that he does not decide.

Rashid was shown into a schoolroom. The leader was sitting on the floor. He was a tall, strong man with the thrill of victory on his face, but he looked exhausted, confused, and restless.

Rashid's escort said in Farsi: "This man comes from Mahabad with a letter from the mullah—he has six Americans with him."

Rashid thought of a movie he had seen in which a man got into a guarded building by flashing his driving license instead of a pass. If you had enough confidence you could undermine people's suspicions.

"No, I come from the Tehran Revolutionary Committee," Rashid said. "There are five or six thousand Americans in Tehran, and we have decided to send them home. The airport is closed, so we will bring them all out this way. Obviously we must make arrangements and set up procedures for handling all these people. That is why I am here. But you have many problems to deal with—perhaps I should discuss the details with your subordinates."

"Yes," said the leader, and waved them away.

It was the technique of the Big Lie, and it had worked. (p. 336)

Most people in this type of situation would be overwhelmed and baffled about what to do; yet, as the episode indicates, some people are able to handle it because they possess both an unusual degree of insight into human behavior (though not of the textbook sort) and the audacity to act on the basis of their insight.

I see no reason why the vast amount of knowledge about human behavior possessed by successful salespeople, politicians, doctors, etc. could not be systematically investigated and uncovered. For example, people who seem to possess great insight into behavior in a particular area could be interviewed to determine what techniques and what knowledge they are using. Or, psychologists could make a systematic review of relevant material in other disciplines, such as literature, government, or law, because these often provide codifications of common-sense knowledge about behavior. The legal literature, for instance, is filled with tantalizing references to concepts and notions relevant to everyday action and social intercourse, such as notions about the conditions for making someone responsible for wrongdoing, about what serves as fair compensation for a broken promise, and about what obligations are implicitly undertaken when using someone else's property. Once knowledge of this sort is identified and mapped out, research on individual and developmental differences could be conducted by testing subjects on their awareness of this knowledge and their ability to apply it in relevant situations. Such research could make a refreshing contribution to the social cognition literature.

Returning to the points made by Roodin and Rybash, one of their major themes is the failure of the literature to clearly define and articulate the nature of adult social cognition. This is a particularly serious problem for researchers who operate within a developmental framework, where it is essential to identify the forms which development may take. To elaborate on their remarks, there are at least three general possibilities with respect to the endpoint of adult social cognition. One is that there is a definite, identifiable stopping point which tends to be reached at some common point in adulthood. If this is the case, then social-cognitive development involves progression toward this single common endpoint (and possible regression from it during late adulthood). This, in essence, is how Piaget views cognitive development; formal operational thinking, which is achieved during adolescence or possibly adulthood, is the final, highest possible level of thought toward which all development proceeds, though, of course, not everyone actually reaches this point. A second possibility is that there is continual development during adulthood but that this occurs through a sequence of several more or less universal stages. In this case, people typically do not reach a stopping point in their social-cognitive development, but they do proceed through a common pathway of development. A third possibility involves an individual difference rather than a developmental stage model. According to this model, in adulthood people acquire or possess different types and/or levels of cognitive skills which are not ordered in any developmental sequence. (Roodin and Rybash also mention the possibility of multilinearity, which is the notion that earlier and later developing skills can co-exist and be used simultaneously by an individual. Multilinearity is not necessarily incompatible with any of the models described above unless one holds a very strict view of these models.)

Which of these possibilities (or combination thereof) is true in reality? Roodin and Rybash are skeptical that the first model, which represents the traditional cognitive-developmental view, actually holds, and I am inclined to agree with them. However, I have to say that I do not think we know enough yet about social-cognitive development to answer this question with any authority. For instance, in presenting his stage account of development in the realm of physical cognition, Piaget relied upon relatively explicit theoretical criteria and a broad set of systematically collected empirical evidence to support his claims to have identified four distinct types of logico-mathematical reasoning. It is true that these claims have generated considerable opposition and controversy, and may eventually be completely overturned, but there was *some* reasonable theoretical and empirical basis for them. In contrast, no comprehensive program of this sort has yet been attempted for the social-cognitive realm, so I think it is premature to make firm judgments at this time. Rather, researchers need to explore the content of adult social cognition more thoroughly and extensively, and at the same time, to give more careful thought about the forms this cognition may take over the course of adult development.

Another major thrust of Roodin and Rybash's chapter is that the literature on social cognition has largely neglected the role of affect. This is a curious oversight; intuitively, it is apparent that one of the features which makes social cognition special or unique is its emotionally engaging nature. But despite being in complete sympathy with Roodin and Rybash in their emphasis on the centrality of affect, I take exception to some of their statements about its role in cognition. Specifically, I question their equation of "cognitive schemata" with automatic and superficial processing and "affective schemata" with controlled, deep processing. First, the terminology is somewhat misleading; contrary to what the terms might imply, both "cognitive" and "affective" schemata involve knowledge, or cognition; the difference between them is that the former involves little or no emotional arousal, whereas the latter does involve significant affective arousal. More substantively, I doubt whether processing which lacks a significant affective component is necessarily shallow, and whether processing which possesses substantial affect is always deep. It is not obvious to me that knowledge which is free of personal affect is superficial, or restricted only to old and familiar schemata. Is it not possible, for example, to achieve a reasonably good understanding of, say, statistics or micro-economic theory, while simultaneously being quite bored by the subject? (In fact, this may be the norm rather than the exception for college students, though I would not want to overestimate the profundity of the knowledge which is typically achieved.) Similarly, is it not possible to achieve some pretty shrewd insights into the character and behavior of someone in whom we have little interest? Conversely, is it really the case that heavily affect-laden processing always leads to deep understanding? Or is it possible that affect which is too intense will disrupt processing and lead to excessive reliance upon old and familiar schemata? Hoffman (1983), in fact, makes this point when he stresses that affective arousal plays a critical role in the impact of inductive discipline upon children. He argues that, if children are too little aroused, they are not likely to pay attention to their parents' reasoning, whereas, if they are too highly aroused, their attention will be disrupted and they will not be able to process the content of their parents' reasoning effectively. Thus, optimal processing of the information conveyed by the induction will occur when the child is at a moderate, rather than high, level of arousal.

SPERBECK AND WHITBOURNE'S CHAPTER

Sperbeck and Whitbourne's chapter is a report and discussion of their investigation of the relationship between autobiographical memory and personality. The major hypothesis which they tested was that individuals who are open to experience, in the sense of tolerating and exploring unfamiliar actions, ideas, and values, will incorporate new autobiographical material more extensively into their identity. The hypothesis was supported by the finding of a significant correlation ($r = +.41$) between scores on the inventory measuring openness to experience and number of autobiographical memories recalled. The magnitude of this correlation is impressive, considering that the openness measure appears to be representative of standard paper-and-pencil personality scales, with their notorious reputation for having low correlations with external measures (Mischel, 1968). Further, the authors ruled out some plausible sources of artifact in this finding by demonstrating that the correlation between openness and autobiographical memory was not mediated by any relationship between these variables and the factors of age, verbal ability, and cognitive flexibility. It is also of note that the study measures favorably with the standards established in Roodin and Rybash's review, with its emphasis upon ecological validity, affective variables, and self schemata.

Despite its considerable positive features, there are some potential limitations and unexplored issues in the research which merit some attention here. One problem, which is recognized clearly enough in the chapter, is that the measure of autobiographical memory, number of personal experiences recalled, was strictly quantitative. However, the major hypothesis—that openness affects the nature of personal reminiscing—clearly requires more than a demonstration that individuals with greater openness to experience can recall more autobiographical memories. Given the openness to experience construct, it is reasonable to predict, for example, that people who are more, as opposed to less, open to experience would: (a) recall a relatively greater proportion of negative reminiscences, (b) recall a greater number of experiences which are incongruent with their self concept, and (c) have more accurate autobiographical memories. In admitting the inadequacy of a strictly quantitative measure of autobiographical memory, Sperbeck and Whitbourne suggest analyzing the content of the subjects' reported memories in terms of factors such as veridicality, desirability, depth of processing, and relevance to the self. Although there may be nearly insurmountable obstacles in deriving good measures of some of these factors (e.g., the only possible way to assess veridicality that I can think of is to check with other sources, such as written records or people who know the subject), it should be relatively straightforward to have subjects rate items in terms of other features such as how pleasant was an experience, how relevant was it to the self, and how much was it seen to reflect accurately a feature of the self. This could be done using some form of rating scale, such as a semantic differential scale. Consider, for instance, the protocol provided by Sperbeck and Whitbourne for the subject who recalled getting stuck in a tree as a child. This subject would likely rate this experience as being at least somewhat unpleasant, and he might also rate it as being highly relevant to himself and as being very characteristic of his self if he views himself as a relatively helpless person who is dependent on other people who frequently let him down. On the other hand, he might view this as a traumatic but isolated incident which occurred a long time ago in early childhood, and so he might rate it as being not very accurate in expressing his real self as he perceives it. Whatever additional measures are developed, the study would be enhanced by the finding of a qualitative as well as quantitative relationship between openness and autobiographical memory.

A second limitation is that the chapter does not clearly specify the locus of the effects of openness to experience on autobiographical memory. That is, in terms of a simple stage model of memory, openness could have its effects on input (or encoding), on consolidation (or storage), or on output (or retrieval) of autobiographical items. Thus, openness might affect input by influencing the extent to which an individual exposes himself or herself to different experiences, or by influencing how much attention he or she pays to the experiences. Or openness could affect the extent to which he or she rehearses, or elaborates upon, the events which he or she has experienced. Finally, openness might affect the extent to which he or she is able, or actively attempts, to retrieve personal experiences in memory. Of course, openness could, and probably does, affect two, or even all three, of these stages in combination. Sperbeck and Whitbourne do explicitly suggest in a couple places that openness has its effects on encoding and retrieval, and they hint elsewhere that it might also affect rehearsal or elaboration of autobiographical items. However, their treatment of this issue is not systematic, and they do not explain in any detail why openness might be expected to have an effect at various stages of memory. It is true that the issue of locus of effects does not affect the basic finding of the study, which is that openness to experience and autobiographical memory *are* related, but it is still important to inquire into the possible mechanisms which underly this relationship.

The chapter's treatment of automatic versus effortful processing leaves me a bit uneasy. While this is a critical distinction which has much precedent in the literature, Sperbeck and Whitbourne fail to propose any clear criteria that could be used for making this distinction in their data. Because they do a fair amount of speculation about how much of the subjects' reminiscing might have involved effortful as opposed to automatic processing, but do so without being able to draw upon unambiguous information from their data, they end up going through a tortuous and inconsistent chain of reasoning.

They begin by noting that the age-insensitive nature of the subjects' autobiographical memories suggests access through use of automatic retrieval operations, which are not affected by aging. However, given the elaborative nature of the autobiographical memories which were recalled by subjects, Sperbeck and Whitbourne think it necessary to postulate that these memories were retrieved through effortful processing, which typically shows age effects. If so, then the lack of age differences in memory requires explanation. The authors suggest, as one possibility, that recall is related to personality factors; in their study, they speculate, openness might be such a relevant factor. They further suggest that individuals who are open to experience will accumulate more experiences; accordingly, recall will be less effortful for them, and they will recall more items. But here is where the reasoning breaks down. Note that, to explain the lack of age differences in the presumed effortful processing, two opposing trends must be posited: (a) impairment of effortful processing with age, and (b) enhanced recall with age due to greater openness, which leads to accumulation of more experiences and easier recall. However, to explain the lack of age differences, we have to assume that the two trends exactly cancel each other, and, more problematically, that openness increases with age. This last assumption is flatly contradicted by the data, which showed no significant correlation between the openness measure and age. Given these problems, it might be better to admit simply that although the issue of automatic versus effortful processing is important, it is impossible to resolve to any degree of satisfaction in this study.

Though they do not elaborate on the topic a great deal, Sperbeck and Whitbourne's remarks concerning the possible relationship between autobiographical memory and personal identity are very intriguing. Their basic thesis is that autobiographical memory is functionally related to the individual's self concept, or sense of identity, such that he or she will attempt to integrate autobiographical memories into a coherent personal account or life story. Thus, autobiographical memory is susceptible to a number of cognitive biases, such as establishment of a favorable self-representation, maintenance of a sense of self-consistency over time, especially around concerns of high ego involvement, establishment of a stable framework for examining future experiences, and reinforcement of the belief of having realized significant life goals. Given these suggestions by Sperbeck and Whitbourne, a reasonable prediction is that individuals who are open to experience are willing to tolerate a more "ragged" personal account (i.e., one that is more likely to include experiences which contradict each other or which are discrepant with central features of the self concept). In addition, it seems likely that the relationship between autobiographical memory and self concept is reciprocal rather than unilateral, that is, that memories influence the type of self concept which is formed, as well as being affected by the self concept.

My thoughts having been stimulated by these intriguing ideas, I would like to propose a few simple and general principles which might govern the relationship between autobiographical memory and self concept. First, if it is assumed that there is a tendency to form a coherent personal identity (i.e., one in which various themes are inter-related to form an organized pattern), then it readily follows that people will tend to select and emphasize those autobiographical items which are illustrative of and consistent with those themes and how they are organized. For example, if success as an academic psychologist is central to an individual's self concept, then specific events which mark major successes, failures, and turning points in her career pathway should be prominent in her autobiographical memory. Thus, this person might have especially strong memories concerning the times when she took her introductory psychology course (because this is when she decided to major in psychology), received a letter of acceptance from the graduate school of her first choice, got negative comments on her first research project in graduate school (which led her to believe that she had no talent for research), received substantial praise for her second project (which made her believe that there might be hope after all), and went on the job interview which helped to get her first job.

A second principle, derived again from the assumption that there is a tendency to form a coherent and organized life story, is that personal experiences will tend to be reorganized in memory into a form which preserves a coherent narrative sequence. This principle, which is not simply a tautological restatement of the assumption, implies the operation of at least two processes: (a) a tendency for events which are experienced at different points in time but which reflect the same identity theme to be stored together with each other in memory, and (b) a tendency to order events which are subsumed by a common theme into a coherent temporal sequence. These processes are of interest because they suggest that autobiographical items are not stored simply according to the order in which they occurred, but rather are organized in terms of the aspects of personal identity which they represent. Thus, even though event A (e.g., getting an A in statistics) and event B (e.g., making the varsity soccer team) occurred simultaneously or close to each other in time, they may not be recalled together in reminiscing because they are relevant to different themes.

My third and final suggestion is that selection and emphasis of items in autobiographical memory may be influenced by the representativeness and availability heuristics as described by Tversky and Kahneman (1974). Briefly, the representativeness heuristic stipulates that, in making a judgment of whether an object or event is a member of a category, people assess the degree to which the salient features of the object or event are similar to, or representative of, the features presumed to be characteristic of the category. Thus, an individual may assume that his fear of authority figures was caused by an incident in early childhood when he was deeply humiliated by his mother because of the apparent similarity between the presumed causal event in childhood and the adult trait. The availability heuristic is the tendency of people, when they are required to judge the relative frequency or likelihood of a particular event, to be influenced by the relative accessibility of the event in perception, memory, or imagination. To use again the example just cited, an individual may relate his fear of authority to the childhood experience of parental humiliation because the experience is so strong in his memory that it readily comes to mind when he searches for the causes of his fear of authority.

For a specific real-life illustration of how the representativeness and availability heuristics might elucidate the relationship between autobiographical memory and personal identity, consider the following recollection by Ulysses S. Grant of an incident from his boyhood. The incident appears in Grant's memoirs and is reproduced here from McFeely's (1981) biography of Grant:

. . . a Mr. Ralston living within a few miles of the village. . . owned a colt which I very much wanted. My father had offered twenty dollars for it, but Ralston wanted twenty-five. I was so anxious to have the colt, that after the owner left, I begged to be allowed to take him at the price demanded. My father yielded, but said twenty dollars was all the horse was worth, and told me to offer that price; if it was not accepted I was to offer twenty-two and a half, and if that would not get him, to give the twenty-five. I at once mounted a horse and went for the colt. When I got to Mr. Ralston's house, I said to him: "Papa says I may offer you twenty dollars for the colt, but if you won't take that, I am to offer twenty-two and a half, and if you won't take that, I am to give you twenty-five." It would not require a Connecticut man to guess the price finally agreed upon. . . . . I could not have been over eight years old at the time. This transaction caused me great heart-burning. The story got out among the boys of the village, and it was a long time before I heard the last of it. (pp. 10–11)

According to McFeely, this experience haunted Grant all his life, and he repeated it often. Given that one of the major themes of Grant's life was his complete failure as a businessman, and that this failure bothered him greatly, we can assume with some degree of confidence that this failure was a major negative component of his self concept. Then, applying the representativeness and avail- ability heuristics in conjunction with this assumption, it may be possible to shed some light on how the boyhood memory just cited came to play such a prominent role in Grant's memory. The representativeness heuristic is relevant because there is an obvious similarity between the salient feature of the boyhood memo- ry—lack of business acumen—and the acute sense which Grant had as an adult that he was a failure as a businessman. In other words, in searching for causes or reasons for his business difficulties, Grant might have focused on a boyhood incident that seemed to be the epitome of this problem.

Similarly, the availability heuristic may also be relevant for explaining the strength of Grant's memory. The experience obviously generated a great deal of emotion for Grant when it occurred, and because of this he may have formed a particularly strong and readily accessible memory of the experience. Since it came so readily to mind, Grant might naturally have relied upon it whenever he tried to understand why he was such a failure as a businessman. It should be realized that this is not an attempt to explain the strength of this particular memory but rather the prominence it held in Grant's overall reminiscing. Fur- ther, the explanation is predicated on a relationship between a feature of the memory (its accessibility) and a feature of Grant's self concept (his concern about his failure as a businessman).

Of course, it is impossible to know with certainty the exact role which this particular boyhood memory played in Grant's personal identity, or what mecha- nisms accounted for this role, and so the interpretations which have just been offered could very well be inaccurate or irrelevant. Still, they may help to illuminate to some extent the relationship between autobiographical memory and self concept.

CONCLUSION

The two chapters which have been discussed here do an excellent job of identifying the blind spots in the current literature on social cognition, and in suggesting the directions which future research might profitably take. But whatever weaknesses and limitations may exist in the field as it currently stands, and however slow the progress of research might turn out to be, the future prospects are bright because social cognition concerns the fascinating topic of how we go about trying to understand the behavior of ourselves, of others, and of human groups and institutions. As long as people remain curious about themselves and about others, they will continue to strive to make sense of human behavior, and there will continue to be good reason to study social cognition.

REFERENCES

Bronfenbrenner, U. (1974). Developmental research, public policy, and the ecology of childhood. *Child Development, 45,* 1–5.

Follett, K. (1983). *On wings of eagles.* New York: William Morrow.

Gardner, H. (1983). *Frames of mind.* New York: Basic Books.

Hart, H. L. A. (1968). *Punishment and responsibility.* New York: Oxford University Press.

Heider, F. (1958). *The psychology of interpersonal relations.* New York: Wiley.

Hoffman, M. L. (1983). Affective and cognitive processes in moral internalization. In E. T. Higgins, D. N. Ruble, & W. W. Hartup (Eds.), *Social cognition and social development.* Cambridge, England: Cambridge University Press.

Kohlberg, L. (1976). Moral stages and moralization. In T. Lickona (Ed.), *Moral development and behavior.* New York: Holt, Rinehart, & Winston.

McFeely, W. S. (1981). *Grant: A biography.* New York: W. W. Norton.

Mischel, W. (1968). *Personality and assessment.* New York: Wiley.

Neisser, U. (1976). *Cognition and reality.* San Francisco: W. H. Freeman.

Rosch, E., Mervis, C. B., Gray, W. D., Johnson, D. M., & Boyes-Braem, P. (1976). Basic objects in natural categories. *Cognitive Psychology, 8,* 382–439.

Tversky, A., & Kahneman, D. (1974). Judgment under uncertainty: Heuristics and biases. *Science, 185,* 1124–1131.

Walker, L. J., & Richards, B. S. (1979). Stimulating transitions in moral reasoning as a function of stage of cognitive development. *Developmental Psychology, 15,* 95–103.

Willems, E. P. (1973). Behavioral ecology and experimental analysis: Courtship is not enough. In J. R. Nesselroade & H. W. Reese (Eds.), *Life-span developmental psychology.* New York: Academic Press.

Chapter *10*

Examining Reading Problems as a Means to Uncovering Sex Differences in Cognition

Myra Okazaki Smith

Colgate University

SOME PRELIMINARY REMARKS

To inquire whether there are sex differences in cognitive functions is to raise a politically sensitive issue. Those psychologists who are influenced by radical feminism are fearful that an examination of sex differences may result in a setback in progress towards equal rights and opportunities for women. In part their anxiety has a realistic basis, for in the past, on the rare occasions when scientists took note of sex differences, they regarded them as confirmation of the intellectual inferiority of women. Nevertheless, I believe that the subject of sex differences in cognitive styles and strategies is a legitimate scientific concern. The danger of such research lies not in any discovery of differences but in their misinterpretation and misapplication. Sex differences have been documented for dyslexia, performance on tests of spatial relations, and achievement in mathematics. It is, in my opinion, as unproductive to deny that these differences exist or to attribute them a priori to socialization pressures as it is to assume that they are genetically mediated and therefore irreversible. It is important to inquire further into these differences, to ask what specific skills are involved, and to search for the conditions that foster or are inimical to their cultivation. Only in this way can effective programs be developed to train individuals in skills the relative lack of which put them at a disadvantage socially, politically, and economically.

INTRODUCTION

In examining sex differences, we should be mindful that differences in performance do not necessarily signify inequalities in abilities. They may be the culmination of attempts to adapt to different environmental circumstances. To the extent that males and females have had to cope with different tasks or situations in the course of evolutionary and ontogenetic development, there may have evolved sex-specific modes of cognitive functioning. These differences would offer testimony to the versatility of human behavior, and would pose a problem only when they are directed towards a specific task for which the cognitive style characteristic of one sex is not appropriate. Thus, it may be that a strategy that enables males successfully to manipulate objects in a three-dimensional world may handicap them when they must process the two-dimensional visual forms that constitute the elements of our writing system. Differences, in other words, need not imply superiority–inferiority in an absolute sense but only in relation to a specific task. And even in the latter sense, inequality in accomplishment is not immutable, for once we have analyzed the appropriateness and inappropriateness of various strategies for a particular task, it should be possible to plan an effective remedial program that would benefit either sex.

In my examination of sex differences in perception and cognition, I have chosen to focus on reading for the following reasons: (a) It is an activity that brings into play skills that vary widely in kind and complexity; (b) in literate societies, it is an activity that members of both sexes are expected and given equal opportunity to learn; and (c) it is an activity for which sex differences in failure rate have been documented.

The magnitude of sex differences that has been reported in the United States has varied depending upon the sample of reading disabled children examined, e.g., whether drawn from the early elementary or more advanced grades and whether selected from referrals to a reading clinic or from children who, on the basis of standardized reading tests, are judged to be below grade level. The ratio of boys to girls with reading problems that is commonly reported varies between 6:1 and 4:1 (Benton, 1975; Finnuci & Childs, 1981). Not only is the incidence of reading disability higher in boys than girls, but it is also the case that reading problems generally are both more severe and persist to a much later age in boys (Finnuci & Childs, 1981). However, any attempt to interpret these observations must take into account evidence that sex differences in reading problems may occur only among those children struggling to master an alphabetic as compared to a syllabic or logographic writing system (Makita, 1968).

TYPES OF WRITING SYSTEMS

Two broad classes of writing systems currently exist: Phonographic and logographic (Kandel, Tsao, & Smith, 1981). Phonographic systems consist of visual symbols that are mapped to units of speech. In the case of the alphabet, visual symbols are mapped to phonemes, while in the case of a syllabic system, graphic symbols are mapped to syllables. In a logographic system, each character represents a word or concept. The principal difference between the two classes of writing systems is in accessibility of meaning: In the phonographic system, meaning awaits decoding of the graphic symbol to sound; in the logographic system, meaning is directly represented by the visual symbol. Thus, it is possible for two people who speak very different languages to communicate by means of logographs. Such in fact is the case for the Japanese and Chinese. The spoken languages of these peoples belong to different linguistic families, Sinitic in the case of the Chinese and Ural-Altaic in the case of the Japanese. The Japanese adopted the Chinese writing system centuries ago, and, although in their hands it underwent modification, there are enough residual similarities that make it possible for a Japanese-speaking and a Chinese-speaking person to "converse" through writing.

At first thought, because the alphabet and syllabary are both phonologically based and logographs are semantically based, one may conclude that the first two require cognitive skills that are more alike than those tapped by the latter. In fact, this is the assumption made by psychologists who have compared the different writing systems (Gibson & Levin, 1975; Gleitman & Rozin, 1977; Paivio & Beggs 1981; Rozin & Gleitman, 1977). I believe, however, that, compared to the other two, the alphabetic system requires perceptual and cognitive skills that are inordinately complex. The issue "Why Johnny can't read (or spell)" appears not to be raised in Hong Kong, where children as young as 3 years are introduced to logographs (Butler, 1976) and in Japan (Makita, 1968), where 5- and 6-year-olds begin their career in literacy with learning of not one, but two different syllabaries (here I should add that all Japanese children are schooled in the two syllabaries, katakana and hiragana, and the logographic script).

SKILLS REQUIRED BY ALPHABETIC SYSTEM

Because alphabetic writing is intimately linked to speech, all the capacities necessary for proficiency in speech comprehension and production are essential to successful decoding. These include phonemic discrimination, well-developed auditory short-term memory, perception of temporal order, and at least tacit knowledge of phonological rules. McGuinness (1976, 1981) has reviewed studies that point to female superiority in auditory-linguistic skills, a superiority that is most evident in the first 5 years of life. It is reasonable to conclude that, at the time of entry into elementary school, boys are less prepared than girls to benefit from phonics instruction.

Understanding the principle behind the alphabet requires sophisticated linguistic knowledge beyond that necessary for speech comprehension and production. While phonemic discrimination has been found in infants as young as 1 month old and is an ability that is developmental in nature, appearing universally with a predictable age of onset and course (see, for example, Cutting & Eimas, 1975; Eimas, 1974), phonemic segmentation, or analysis, requires explicit awareness of the phonemic structure of language and appears not to come naturally to all children (Liberman, Shankweiler, Liberman, Fowler, & Fischer, 1977). Indeed, the level of metalinguistic sophistication required for phonemic analysis may explain why the alphabetic writing system was invented only once, while ideographic forms were independently developed many times. For the child of 5 or 6 years, the phoneme has little psychological reality, and yet it is this abstraction that, in theory, is the referent of the letter. The child discriminates between spoken words on the basis of phonemes, and he or she produces them in the process of saying a word, but except for vocalic ones, he or she never hears or pronounces them in isolation. Yet he or she is expected to segment continuous speech flow into phonemes so that he or she can match letters to them. Upon being presented with a string of letters, such as "cat," he or she is instructed to voice their phoneme equivalents in the order in which they are symbolized, which is impossible to do in the case of consonants without also adding a vowel, and then he or she is to blend them into a sound that matches a word he or she knows. The outcome is usually an utterance that is quite foreign and unrecognizable. Even if the relationship between grapheme and phoneme were truly isomorphic, the task of reconstructing a spoken word from sequentially arranged letters would tax the understanding of many novices.

Despite the fact that the alphabet was developed to represent phonemes, it is possible to focus the child's attention on another level of the relationship between writing and speech. Liberman and her colleagues (Liberman, Shankweiler, Fischer, & Carter, 1974) have demonstrated how much easier it is for 5- and 6-year-olds to segment words into syllables than into phonemes. It is reasonable, then, to begin reading instruction by pointing to the correspondence between grapheme and grapheme clusters on the one hand, and syllables on the other (the beauty of the alphabetic system lies in its hierarchical structure). However, while doing so eases the phonological analysis, it increases the difficulty of the visual task. It places greater demands on visual processing. The reader must analyze the printed word into segments of variable length without aid of physical boundaries. How should he or she segment "signing"? What about "signature"? What are the visual cues that direct the reader to confer syllable status to "sign" in the first instance and "sig" in the second? Moreover, within a grapheme cluster, he or she must be attentive to the spatial order of letters. His or her performance would be considerably facilitated if each syllable were represented by a single, unique visual symbol. He or she would then be deciphering symbols from a syllabic writing system.

The advantage of the syllabary, in my opinion, lies in its visual simplicity. Because each character stands for a syllable, there are clear-cut visual boundaries that demarcate the latter, and, moreover, the problem of spatial order of elements disappears. The character is perceived in its entirety and immediately evokes an image of its phonological counterpart. There is no need for mental analysis or restructuring of the printed word.

Logographs share the same advantage as syllabaries in that they require only minimal visual analysis and integration. Each visual symbol stands alone and is apprehended globally. Of course, it has the further advantage that, because it is directly mapped to meaning, the reader is spared the necessity of phonological analysis and integration. Logographs can be visually complex from the point of view of the number of strokes that produce them. However, as Rozin and Gleitman (1977) have indicated, ". . . Chinese symbols have more coherence and distinctiveness than our written words. Brooks (1977) has shown that it is easier to learn to identify complex symbols than their spatially sequenced component parts" (p. 66).

To summarize the present discussion: I am proposing that alphabetic script requires sophisticated levels of auditory *and* visual processing. Moreover, I should like to suggest that it is the demand for visual as well as auditory analysis that presents an especially difficult challenge to boys. I state this in spite of Liberman and Mann's (1981) and Vellutino's (1979) dismissal of graphic analysis as a problem to poor readers, the great majority of whom are males.

ARGUMENTS AGAINST VISUAL ANALYSIS AS A PROBLEM

Liberman, Shankweiler, Orlando, Harris, and Berti (1971) reported a study in which third graders pronounced 60 monosyllabic words so chosen as to maximize opportunity for errors in letter orientation and sequencing. Examination of the errors made by 18 children whose reading performance placed them in the lowest third of their class indicated that reversals and orientational confusions accounted for 25% of the total mistakes. Moreover, the commission of these errors was not consistent for any particular child. The "low" frequency of these errors, and their lack of stability, led the investigators to reject problems in visual analysis as a contributing factor in poor reading performance. I should like to point out the unlikelihood that the so-called poor readers were truly reading impaired. While estimates of incidence of dyslexia varies, in any unselected school population it would fall below 10% and probably below 5% (Benton, 1975). In any case, it is hardly likely to be as large as 33%. Moreover, the inconsistency in occurrence of orientational and sequencing errors is insufficient grounds for dismissing them as being irrelevant to reading performance.

In reference to sex differences, Liberman and Mann (1981) suggest that the greater difficulty experienced by boys in learning to read is due specifically to a problem in linguistic analysis. They argue that it cannot be visual-perceptual, because of the frequently superior performance of dyslexic boys on tests of spatial relations. Vellutino (1979) has also remarked that poor reading performance may be associated with excellent visual spatial processing ability. As evidence, both groups of authors refer to the report of Symmes and Rapoport (1972). Finally, Rozin and Gleitman (1977) make the point that, since poor readers are readily able to learn to associate Chinese logographs with English words, visual discrimination is not at the root of their problem.

I should like to rephrase the issue of visual analytic processing in the hope that another perspective might emerge. Instead of thinking in terms of deficiencies in visual perception, we might consider differences in visual processing strategy. In doing so, the suggestion that a child can excel at perception of visual spatial relations and still struggle with visual analysis of the printed word ceases to be self-contradictory.

EVIDENCE FOR VISUAL ANALYSIS AS A PROBLEM

Most tests of spatial relations involve mental rotation and other transformations of internal representations of three-dimensional objects. They require assumption of a dynamic attitude that permits objects to retain shape constancy over a number of different spatial orientations. Reading, on the other hand, involves perception of two-dimensional nonsense shapes that have no three-dimensional equivalent. A static attitude is encouraged in that the letters must be apprehended in constant spatial relationship to each other and to the specific visual framework provided by the edges of the page. It is possible that boys generally surpass girls on spatial relations tasks, because their mental representations of form are higher order abstractions of relationships that are invariant across perspective transformations. Just as Witkin and his associates (1962) discovered that men's perception of the vertical is field independent, so it may be with their perception of form. In other words, the internal geometry of objects may be sufficient for form identification. On the other hand, for this very reason they may not perform as well as girls when confronted with letters, whose identity is linked to the visual upright. To test this possibility, the following study was conducted.

Blindfolded college students (12 men and 12 women) were instructed to palpate a standard nonsense form with their left or right index finger, and to select its match from among five comparison stimuli. Three of the latter were the same form in different spatial orientations, a fourth the same form in an identical orientation, and a fifth a form that differed from the standard in one distinctive feature other than orientation (for convenience, selection of any of the first three as a match for the standard will be referred to as a rotational match, the fourth as the correct match, and the fifth as a distractor match). As expected, women demonstrated greater accuracy in form matching than men $F(1, 22) = 7.48$, $p < .025$. Of special interest is the three-way interaction of sex, hand, and stimulus choice $F(2, 44) = 3.43$, $p < .05$, which is related to the observation that, among male subjects, the pattern of stimulus choice did not vary with hand, whereas among females there was a significant interaction between these two variables $F(2, 22) = 6.39$, $p < .01$. The pattern of match selection for the left hand of women was the same as for either hand of men, consisting of comparable numbers of correct, orientational, and distractor matches. In contrast, the right hand of women not only made more correct choices relative to their left $F(1, 11) = 4.82$, $p < .05$, but also fewer orientational choices $F(1, 11) = 14.44$, $p < .01$. The frequency of distractor stimulus choice was the same for both hands. On the basis of these results and studies by Bradshaw (1978) and by Levy,

Trevarthen, and Sperry (1972), demonstrating that form is processed by the left hemisphere according to distinctive features and by the right hemisphere according to gestalt qualities, we concluded that the left hemisphere of women processes orientation as a distinctive feature of form.

The tendency of female subjects to treat object orientation as a distinctive feature of form may be one manifestation of a more general disposition to attend to differences between objects rather than to their similarities. Such a strategy would favor identification of similar and complex forms such as letters. To test this hypothesis, Laurie Jackson and I (Jackson & Smith, 1981) conducted a study that compared the effectiveness of two instructional methods for form discrimination. The forms were letter-like nonsense patterns and two variants of each pattern. In the learning trials, six pairs of variants were projected onto a screen, one pair at a time. In the distinctive features condition, which was designed to draw attention to differences between similar shapes, the variants paired were of two similar forms having different names. In the prototype condition, which focused subjects' attention on similarities between forms, two variants of the same form were paired together on a slide. In both conditions, subjects were told to remember the names of the forms as the experimenter pointed to each variant in a pair and called out its name. After each pair had been presented five times, the effectiveness of instructional methods was tested by projecting one at a time the original forms, only the variants of which subjects had seen during learning trials, and having the subjects name each.

With college students as subjects, a significant main effect of sex was found, with women performing better than men $F(1, 36) = 15.635, p < .01$. More relevant to our present interest was the significant interaction between instructional method and sex $F(1, 36) = 5.18, p < .05$, which revealed that the superior performance of women was due to proficiency under both conditions of learning. Men, in contrast, performed discrepantly under the prototype and distinctive features condition $F(1, 18) = 7.2, p < .05$, scoring as high as women only in the former. In an attempt to determine how early in ontogeny this interaction became evident, we repeated the experiment on beginning kindergarteners, increasing the interslide interval during learning trials from 5 seconds, used with college subjects, to 10 seconds. We uncovered no significant main effect or interaction with these children. On the other hand, repetition of the study with fifth graders, using the same interslide interval as with kindergarteners, revealed a pattern of results similar to that obtained from college students. Their overall performance, collapsed across sex and instructional method, fell between that of the kindergarteners and the college students, and was significantly better $F(1, 108) = 4.53, p < .05$ than that of the former. Even more noteworthy was the suggestion of different rates of improvement with age for males and females under the two conditions. While, at each age level, female subjects performed equivalently under the two conditions, in the post-kindergarten years males showed increasing divergence in performance under the two conditions, which reached statistical significance in the college age group. Although direct age comparisons are not in order, because stimulus intervals used during training were different for the children and college students, the fact that, at each age level, the PT scores for males were comparable to both PT and DF scores for females and, except for kindergarten boys, were superior to their own DF scores, permits one to infer that in boys, the development of distinctive features detecting skills lags behind PT formation in the elementary school years. These results suggest that, beyond kindergarten age, females are more easily able to switch perceptual strategies, i.e., to decenter in Piagetian terminology. Males, on the other hand, appear to rely on a strategy that focuses on the gestalt qualities of stimuli, even when attention to details enhances task performance.

A strategy that results in the detection of distinctive features should facilitate not only letter but word identification to the degree that the latter requires sensitivity to recurrent orthographic patterns in which letter order serves as an important distinctive feature (e.g., as in the confusable pair "loin" and "lion"). Proficient reading involves immediate detection of key graphemes and grapheme clusters that are regularly mapped to speech units, and the ability to generate the printed word from them. The greater salience of distinguishing elements for girls than boys is observed in the graphic productions of children. Upon inspecting drawings of people by 4½- to 7½-year-olds, Willsdon (1977) concluded that boys cling longer than girls to tadpole figures, and are generally less attentive to details of body parts and clothing. Waber (1977) observed that, when asked to copy complex geometrical figures, 5- to 6-year-old girls included more discrete parts in their drawings than their male age-mates.

By emphasizing visual analysis, I do not mean to suggest that holistic perception is an inappropriate strategy at all stages of reading acquisition. Certainly, when one becomes a fluent reader, the object of perception is the word or even the phrase. Even then, however, when an experienced reader encounters a new and difficult word, he or she may have to pause to segment the words into graphemic units.

ORIGINS OF STRATEGY DIFFERENCES

The difference in visual processing strategies of boys and girls may be rooted in differing rates of linguistic development. The earlier verbal development and fluency of girls has been well documented (see, e.g., Maccoby & Jacklin, 1974). Precocious linguistic competence, along with girls' greater affiliative needs (Oetzel, cited in Frieze, Parsons, Johnson, Ruble, & Zellman, 1978, p. 56), may result in lessened motivation to explore their physical environment, for knowledge of objects and three-dimensional space can be acquired second hand through social interaction involving verbal inquiry. This reliance on verbal communication as the dominant mode of knowing requires correct use of labels that, in turn, demands attention to distinguishing features of similar objects assigned different names. Inquiring about rather than manipulating objects retards the detection of invariant features of form undergoing perspective change as a result of the viewer's own actions. A consequence is the development of static images of objects that are rigidly linked to the visual upright.

Boys, because they lag behind in verbal development, may depend upon their own actions as a means of acquiring knowledge of the world. The physical operations performed on objects may produce internal representations that are holistic, dynamic, and free of the constraints of a visual spatial framework.

VISUAL-AUDITORY INTEGRATION

It is conceivable that a child may possess good visual and auditory discrimination abilities and still encounter problems in learning to read. The difficulty may reside in the formation of associative links between graphic and phonetic units. Birch and Belmont (1964), for example, argued that intersensory integration was deficient in dyslexics. Assuming that this is the case for at least some reading disabled children, what would be a cause, and how would it account for sex differences in reading performance? One possible explanation may lie in the nature of the associative bonds, whether these are intra- or interhemispheric. Masland (1970) has proposed that intrahemispheric links are more easily established than interhemispheric ones, which must involve the corpus callosum. There is universal agreement that speech discrimination and memory for speech sounds are mediated by the left hemisphere. There is considerably less agreement concerning the site of processing of visual symbols. Cioffi and Kandel (1979) report that consonant bigrams were more accurately perceived by girls when they were palpated with their right than left hand, while, among boys, they were better perceived when they were presented to the left hand. Our own studies mentioned earlier (Jackson & Smith, 1981; Smith, 1981) point to the effective use by girls of a strategy (distinctive features detection) that has been associated with the left hemisphere, and by boys of a strategy (holistic) that has been associated with the right hemisphere (Bradshaw, 1978; Levy, Trevarthen, & Sperry, 1972). It may be, then, that visual-auditory connections are formed within the left hemisphere in girls, while in boys they may involve visual processing in the right hemisphere and auditory processing in the left hemisphere. The observations that boys and poor readers of English find logographs easier to decode than alphabetic representations of words may be due to the likelihood that the former involve visual-semantic associations in the right hemisphere. Sasanuma and his colleagues (Sasanuma, Itoh, Kobayashi, & Mori, 1980) have in their tachistoscopic studies demonstrated greater right hemisphere involvement in the processing of logographs than phonologically based characters, and Zaidel (1983) has concluded from his studies of commissurotomized patients that the right hemisphere possesses a "rich lexical semantic system" (p. 544).

CONCLUSION

In concluding, I would like to say that I have attempted to examine reading problems from the point of view of overreliance upon perceptual and cognitive strategies that have been developed in the apprehension of objects and object relations in three-dimensional space. I would also like to acknowledge my limited treatment of the processes involved in reading. In focusing on visual analysis and integration, I have not intended to suggest that phonological knowledge is not essential to learning to read alphabetic script. It received scant treatment by me only because its role in reading has received abundant attention by others. Nor have I meant to suggest that problems in adopting the appropriate visual perceptual strategy underlie all or even most reading disorders. Unlike those who have felt compelled to uncover a single, unitary deficiency to explain all cases of dyslexia, I believe that we are dealing with a heterogeneous group, the problems of subgroups of which have varying etiologies.

REFERENCES

Benton, A. L. (1975). Developmental dyslexia: Neurological aspects. In W. J. Friedlander (Ed.), *Advances in neurology* (Vol. VII). New York: Raven Press.

Birch, H. G., & Belmont, L. (1964). Auditory-visual integration in normal and retarded readers. *American Journal of Orthopsychiatry, 34,* 852–861.

Bradshaw, J. L. (1978). Human cerebral asymmetry. *Trends in Neurosciences, 1,* 113–116.

Brooks, L. (1977). Visual pattern in fluent word identification. In A. S. Reber & D. L. Scarborough (Eds.), *Towards a psychology of reading.* Hillsdale, NJ: Erlbaum.

Butler, S. R. (1976). Reading problems of Chinese children. In L. Tarnopol & M. Tarnopol (Eds.), *Reading disabilities: An international perspective.* Baltimore: University Park Press.

Cioffi, J., & Kandel, G. (1979). Laterality of stereognostic accuracy of children for words, shapes, and bigrams: A sex difference for bigrams. *Science, 204,* 1432–1434.

Cutting, J., & Eimas, P. D. (1975). Phonetic feature analyses and the processing of speech in infants. In J. F. Kavanagh & J. E. Cutting (Eds.), *The role of speech and language.* Cambridge, MA: M.I.T. Press.

Eimas, P. D. (1974). Auditory and linguistic processing of cues for place of articulation by infants. *Perception and Psychophysics, 16,* 513–521.

Finucci, J. M., & Childs, B. (1981). Are there really more dyslexic boys than girls? In A. Ansara, N. Geschwind, A. Galaburda, M. Albert, & N. Gartrell (Eds.), *Sex differences in dyslexia.* Towson, MD: The Orton Dyslexia Society.

Frieze, I. H., Parsons, J. E., Johnson, P. B., Ruble, D. N., & Zellman, G. L. (1978). *Women and sex roles: A social psychological perspective.* New York: Norton & Co.

Gibson, E. J., & Levin, J. (1975). *The psychology of reading.* Cambridge, MA: M.I.T. Press.

Gleitman, L. R. & Rozin, P. (1977). The structure and acquisition of reading I: Relations between orthographics and the structure of language. In A. S. Reber & D. L. Scarborough (Eds.), *Towards a psychology of reading.* Hillsdale, NJ: Erlbaum.

Jackson, L., & Smith, M. O. (1981). *Prototype vs. distinctive features learning in pattern identification: Sex differences and age trend.* Paper presented at Eastern Psychological Association, New York.

Kandel, G., Tsao, Y. C., & Smith, M. O. (1981). Neuropsychological theory and sex differences in cognitive style: Implications for reading instruction. In R. Malatesha & L. Hartlage (Eds.),

N.A.T.O.A.S.I. *Neuropsychology and cognition* (Vol. II). Amsterdam: Martinus and Nijhoff International Publishers.

Levy, J., Trevarthen, C., & Sperry, R. W. (1972). Perception of bilateral chimeric figures following hemispheric deconnexion. *Brain, 95,* 61–78.

Liberman, I. Y., & Mann, V. A. (1981). Should reading instruction and remediation vary with the sex of the child? In A. Ansara, N. Geschwind, A. Galaburda, M. Albert, & N. Gartrell (Eds.), *Sex differences in dyslexia.* Towson, MD: The Orton Dyslexia Society.

Liberman, I. Y., Shaukweiler, D., Fischer, F. W., & Carter, B. (1974). Explicit syllable and phoneme segmentation in the young child. *Journal of Experimental Child Psychology, 18,* 201–212.

Liberman, I. Y., Shankweiler, D., Liberman, A. M., Fowler, C., & Fischer, F. W. (1977). Phonetic segmentation and recoding in the beginning reader. In A. S. Reber & D. L. Scarborough (Eds.), *Toward a psychology of reading.* Hillsdale, NJ: Erlbaum.

Liberman, I. Y., Shankweiler, D., Orlando, C., Harris, K. S., & Berti, F. B. (1971). Letter confusions and reversals of sequence in the beginning reader: Implications for Orton's theory of developmental dyslexia. *Cortex, 7,* 127–142.

Maccoby, E. E., & Jacklin, C. N. (1974). *The psychology of sex differences.* Stanford, CA: Stanford University Press.

Makita, K. (1968). The rarity of reading disability in Japanese children. *American Journal of Orthopsychiatry, 38,* 599–614.

Masland, R. L. (1970). Implications for therapy. In F. A. Young & D. B. Lindsley (Eds.), *Early experience and visual information processing in perceptual and reading disorders.* Washington, DC: National Academy of Sciences.

McGuinness, D. (1981). Auditory and motor aspects of language development in males and females. In A. Ansara, N. Geschwind, A. Galaburda, M. Albert, & N. Gartrell (Eds.), *Sex differences in dyslexia.* Towson, MD: The Orton Dyslexia Society.

McGuinness, D. (1976). Sex differences in the organization of perception and cognition. In B. B. Lloyd & J. Archer (Eds.), *Exploring sex differences.* New York: Academic Press.

Paivio, A., & Begg, I. (1981). *Psychology of language.* Englewood Cliffs, NJ: Prentice-Hall.

Rozin, P. & Gleitman, L. R. (1977). The structure and acquisition of reading II: The reading process and the acquisition of the alphabetic principle. In A. S. Riber & D. L. Scarborough (Eds.), *Towards a psychology of reading.* Hillsdale, NJ: Erlbaum.

Sasanuma, S., Itoh, M., Kobayashi, Y., & Mori, K. (1980). The nature of task stimulus interaction in the tachistoscopic recognition of kana and kanji words. *Brain and Language, 9,* 298–306.

Smith, M. O. (1981). Sex differences in perceptual and cognitive skills essential to reading acquisition. In A. Ansara, N. Geschwind, A. Galaburda, M. Albert, & N. Gartrell (Eds.), *Sex differences in dyslexia.* Towson, MD: Orton Dyslexia Society.

Symmes, J. S., & Rapoport, M. D. (1972). Unexpected reading failure. *American Journal of Orthopsychiatry, 42,* 82–91.

Vellutino, F. R. (1979). *Dyslexia: Theory and research.* Cambridge, MA: M.I.T. Press.

Waber, D. P. (1979). Cognitive abilities and sex-related variations in the maturation of cerebral cortical functions. In M. A. Wittig & A. C. Petersen (Eds.). *Sex-related differences in cognitive functioning.* New York: Academic Press.

Willsdon, J. A. (1977). A discussion of some sex differences in a study of human figure drawings by children aged four-and-a-half to seven-and-a-half years. In G. Butterworth (Ed.), *The child's representation of the world* (pp. 61–71). London: Plenum Press.

Witkin, H. A., Dyk, R. B., Faterson, H. F., Goodenough, D. R., & Karp, S. A. (1962). *Psychological differentiation.* New York: Wiley and Sons.

Zaidel, E. (1983). A response to Gazzaniga: Language in the right hemisphere, convergent perspectives. *American Psychologist, 38,* 542–546.

Chapter 11

Sex Related Differences and Cognitive Skills

Jane M. Connor

State University of New York at Binghamton

In putting together the material for this chapter, I found myself asking the question, "Why should the reader be interested in sex differences in cognitive skills?" Somewhat surprisingly, since I, myself, have been an active researcher in the field for over 10 years, I found that I had a great deal of difficulty answering this question. In fact, I found that I was able to come up with more answers to the question, "Why should the reader *not* be interested in sex differences in cognitive skills?" than to the first question. The reason for this is that research on sex differences cannot be separated from the historical and social context of the research. Indeed, without certain social context, most sex differences research would never have been conducted. To my knowledge, for example, no one is conducting research on differences in cognitive skills between people with curly hair and people with straight hair, or between people with round faces and those with more square faces. These physical differences, like the physical differences between men and women, are genetically determined, and are easily observable. However, they are not considered to be socially relevant in the same way as gender is, and are not a salient category for classifying people. With these thoughts in mind, I would first like to examine the historical and social context in which sex difference research has been conducted. This will be followed by a review of some research findings. Lastly, recommendations for future research directions will be made.

SEX-DIFFERENCE RESEARCH IN CONTEXT

As stated earlier, sex difference research cannot be viewed apart from the social and historical context, because the research would never have been conducted without certain supports from the social climate. In addition, the direct and indirect influence of the social climate on the conduct and interpretation of the research has been more pervasive and pernicious in this area than in probably any other field of psychological research. In this section, I will amplify upon these ideas.

Some of the early research on sex differences was conducted at the end of the nineteenth century and the beginning of the twentieth century. As carefully described by Shields (1975) in her scholarly and eloquent article "Functionalism, Darwinism, and the psychology of women: A study in social myth," it was the purpose of this early research on sex differences to determine which neurophysiological differences between the sexes explain the intellectual inferiority of women. What was self-evident to the early researchers was that women were, in fact, intellectually inferior. What needed research was the physiological basis of this inferiority. It was at first hypothesized that the basis for the inferiority was the fact that women's brains were smaller and weighed less. However, research revealed that brain weight was not predictive of intellectual performance. It was then hypothesized that perhaps the frontal lobe was the seat of intelligence and, hence, it must be true that in females the frontal lobe was smaller than in males. This did not turn out to be true. It was then posited that the parietal lobe was the locus of intellectual performance, and sex differences in the size of the parietal lobe were thought to explain intellectual differences. At no point did the empirical results of the research lead the researchers to question either the assumption that women are intellectually inferior to men, or that behavioral differences in intellectual achievement might be due to factors such as gender-related differences in opportunities for schooling and intellectual pursuits.

The possibility that the greater accomplishments of, and recognition received by, men in the sciences, the arts, politics, and law might be due to the proscriptions of a patriarchal society, rather than to inherent biological differences in men and women, was unexplored by these researchers. This possibility was unexplored because the researchers themselves were an integral part of the social network of the time—the same network that took as an unexamined assumption the belief that women are inherently intellectually inferior to men. This was also the same network which determined what was a suitable or researchable scientific question. Just suppose, for example, that empirical research had demonstrated that women had larger brains than men. If this had been clearly determined, there is no doubt in my mind that this would have had to be interpreted as support for the notion that larger brains lead to lower, rather than higher, intellectual performance. The historical record indicates clearly that no data would have seriously threatened the assumption of women's intellectual inferiority; it would merely have served to "clarify" the specific physiological basis for the inferiority.

Nevertheless, many female psychologists did try to collect data to challenge the established beliefs of that time. Leta Hollingworth, in particular, spent years trying to disprove the hypothesis that males are superior intellectually because there is greater variability among males than among females. (Rosenberg, 1984, describes these efforts in a fascinating chapter.) Hollingworth worked as a tester of the retarded for New York City in 1913. She noted that the preponderance of males among the retarded was primarily due to disproportions among those under the age of 16. She observed that the behavior of retarded girls was less likely to come to the attention of authorities, because of society's different expectations of boys and girls. As adults, women would be brought to institutions for the retarded when they became widows or, if they were prostitutes, when they became ill. She concluded that "There seems to be no occupation which supports feeble-minded men as well as housework and prostitution supports feebleminded women" (quoted in Rosenberg, 1984, p.92).

At the other end of the intellectual spectrum, the small representation of women among lists of geniuses and accomplished people was used as evidence of the inferiority of women and as a reason for discouraging their further education. For example, James McKeen Cattell wrote,

> I have spoken throughout of eminent men as we lack in English words including both men and women, but as a matter of fact women do not have an important place on the list. They have in all 32 representatives in the thousand. . . . Women depart less from the normal than men—a fact that usually holds throughout the animals series. (quoted in Rosenberg, 1984, p. 93)

Edward Thorndike wrote,

> Not only the probability and the desirability of marriage and training of children as an essential feature of women's careers, but also the restriction of women to the mediocre grades of ability and achievement should be reckoned with our educational systems . . . postgraduate instruction, to which women are flocking in large numbers is, at least in the higher reaches, a far more remunerative investment in the case of men. (quoted in Rosenberg, 1984, p. 83)

Hollingworth (1916, 1918) published major reviews of the research evidence on the sex differences in intelligence and sex differences in variability in mental performance, and found no support for the variability hypotheses. Meanwhile, Hollingworth and other women were still not receiving the recognition and employment opportunities that men of similar accomplishment were. Hollingworth herself was not able to obtain support for her research, despite its quality. As her husband writes, "No one will ever know what she might have accomplished for human welfare . . . if some of the sponsorship freely poured out on many a scholarly dullard had been made available for her own project" (quoted in Rosenberg, 1984, p. 95). Despite the clarity and throughness of Hollingworth's work (1916, 1918), the hypothesis of greater male variability as an explanation of male intellectual superiority has been advanced time and time again (Lehrke, 1972, 1974; Terman, 1925). The popularity of this hypothesis appears unrelated to the lack of empirical support for either the premise of greater male variability or male intellectual superiority.

Although most of the research reviewed in this paper up to this point was done at the turn of the century, I would not wish to leave the reader with the belief that the imposition of strong, socially-determined stereotypical beliefs on sex-difference research is a relic of the distant past. Approximately 15 years ago, Broverman, Klaiber, Vogel, and Kobayishi (1968) published a literature review and a theory of sex differences in cognitive skills in one of the most highly regarded psychological journals, *Psychological Review.* As is convincingly analyzed by Parlee (1972), the thesis of the authors that women are generally superior at routine tasks, while men are superior at intellectually difficult and creative tasks, has so little relationship to the objective data cited by Broverman et al. that one seriously questions the process by which this thesis was developed. Would reading, for example, generally be considered an easy, rote task or a difficult one? Teachers of reading would be interested to know that Broverman et al. classify it as a simple task. This is because reading is a cognitive skill in which sex differences, when they are found in an American society, favor females. In order for this finding to be consistent with the Broverman et al. thesis, reading must be classified as an easy task. Let us suppose that all of the sex difference findings cited by Broverman et al. had been in the opposite direction of what was reported. It seems very unlikely that the authors would have then proposed that men are superior at easy, routine cognitive tasks and that women are superior at the really difficult, challenging ones!

One characteristic of the vast majority of the theoretical and empirical research on sex-related differences in cognition is that biological factors have been emphasized. In addition to the theories already mentioned in this paper, it has also been hypothesized that important cognitive differences may be due to earlier dominance of the left hemisphere in females (Buffery & Gray, 1972), higher levels of uric acid in the blood of men (Hyde & Rosenberg, 1976), hormonal differences (Broverman et al., 1968), and the X-linkage of cognitive skills (Stafford, 1961, 1972). Although many, many words have been printed elaborating on these theories and reporting minimal amounts of data, the amount of knowledge gained in this area has been extremely small. In her thorough and careful review of this work, Sherman (1977) concludes, "It would be difficult to find a research area more characterized by shoddy work, over-generalization, hasty conclusion and unsupported speculation" (p. 183). Why the popularity of this type of work? Why, even in a recently published volume dedicated to the topic of sex-related cognitive differences (Wittig & Petersen, 1979), a volume in which approximately 80% of the authors are females, is the biological viewpoint the overwelmingly dominant one? One reason, as Sherif (1979) points out, is that biological perspectives are accorded more respect and weight, and are considered more "basic," by the psychological establishment. How shall we increase our understanding of sex-related differences in mathematics achievement? Shall we look to chromosomes, or shall we consider the popular portrayals of women as incapable of balancing a checkbook? The fact that psychologists, female as well as male, have turned to physiological and biochemical explanations to such a great extent reflects the greater prestige accorded these fields as compared to history, anthropology, or sociology, rather than the amount of enlightment they shed.

It is also fascinating to me that biological explanations are seen somehow as more objective than culturally-based ones. A colleague of mine once challenged me, "How can we trust your work and conclusions when you obviously have a point of view that you are interested in advancing?" The implication, of course, was that this was not the case for nonfeminist researchers.

As the writings of Shields (1975), Rosenberg (1984) and Sherman (1977) clearly show, sexist bias permeated all aspects of research on sex differences. The only reason that it is not more noticeable and objectionable to my colleagues, to reviewers, and editors is that the sexist assumptions are an integrated part of our whole culteral milieu. Just as a fish would have difficulty recognizing that it swims in water without the experience of being out of water, so we remain unaware of the sexist foundation of much of the research on sex differences until we are confronted with a different set of assumptions.

SEX-RELATED DIFFERENCES AND COGNITIVE SKILLS

As indicated in the preceding section, most research on sex differences would never have been conducted without the support, approval, and biases of the social and political establishment. Nevertheless, it is possible to examine the empirical findings that have been obtained in this area, and consider what directions these findings suggest for future research.

In this section, I would like to review some of the research on sex differences in the areas of mathematics achievement and visual-spatial skills. These are the two areas in which sex-related differences, when they are observed, most typically favor males. I will be examining these differences with the specific purpose of evaluating (a) the reliability, replicability, and robustness of these differences; and (b) the modifiability of such differences, when they are observed.

In the late 1970s and early 1980s, there was a flurry of research in the area of sex-related differences in mathematics achievement. This research was stimulated by the contemporary interest in increasing women's career opportunities, and by the observation that relatively few women were entering the sciences such as mathematics, engineering, and physics. Prior to this time, it was commonly accepted that a major reason for this disparity was related to the fact that men were simply more skilled in such fields. However, in 1976 Lucy Sells presented a paper that pointed out the huge disparity in mathematical background in men and women by the time they finished high school. She referred to the lack of mathematics background as a "critical filter" which limits the choices of females in college majors. As Fox (1976) concluded in her cogent review, there are many reasons for this difference in backgrounds. Teachers, parents, and peers all have more negative feelings about mathematically talented girls than mathematically talented boys (Fox, 1976). Childrens books, textbooks, the popular media, and even mathematics textbooks, all present females in stereotypic manners (Fox, 1976). Whereas males are shown solving problems, working with laboratory equipment, and exploring, females are frequently shown sitting and watching. It is also relevant that in our society both males and females consider mathematics to be a male domain, and males perceive mathematics as more useful and relevant than females do (Fennema & Sherman, 1977).

Most older studies of mathematic achievement did not take into account the number of formal mathematics courses taken by the research participants (Fennema, 1976). When differences in course taking are considered, sex-related differences either vanish or are exceedingly small (Fennema & Sherman, 1977). Recently, a great deal of media attention (including articles in the *New York Times, Time,* and *Newsweek*) was given to reports heralding males as being biologically more able in mathematics. The research that stimulated this attention was reported by Benbow and Stanley (1980) in *Science.* They summarized data from a series of very highly selected samples of seventh and eighth grade students. These students, who scored in the top 2, 3, or 5% on standardized achievement tests, were given the Scholastic Aptitude Test, designed for college bound high school seniors. In each of the 6 years of the talent search, the mean performance of the boys was higher than that of the girls, the highest scorer was a boy, and the percentage of students scoring above 600 was higher for boys than for girls. Since boys and girls did not differ in the number of mathematic courses taken at this point, Benbow and Stanely reject the hypothesis of differential course-taking as explaining the results. From this conclusion, which is certainly inescapable, Benbow and Stanley leap to the conclusion that the differences in performance "result from superior male mathematical ability" (p. 1264), which is due, at least in part, to biological factors. They present no evidence for this conclusion other than the consistency of the pattern observed. However, the culture that male and female students were exposed to during the years of the project was also a relatively consistent one. Parents of mathematically talented females do not encourage the study of mathematics as much as the parents of mathematically talented boys, and are less likely to buy scientific types of toys (Astin, 1974). There is, further, no evidence that the differences that Benbow and Stanley report have any general applicability to the bottom 95–98% of the population (Tobias, 1982; Tooney, 1981). Although the data reported by Benbow and Stanley was not new data, and their conclusion of a biological bases of sex differences was not supported by the data (nor was it disconfirmed), the presentation of the data and its associated conclusion was featured prominently in *Science.* The popularity of biological theories of sex differences is reflected in this decision, as well as the decisions of numerous popular magazines, to give ample play to what was purported to be evidence for male genetic superiority in mathematics.

Sex-related differences in visual-spatial skill have frequently been referred to as one of the few sex-related differences that "really" exists (Maccoby & Jacklin, 1974). Indeed, some researchers have even accepted the presence of a sex difference in favor of males as a marker for the visual-spatial content of a test (Smith, 1964, p. 210). The results of some recent research, however, involving over 1200 subjects, reveal a great deal of inconsistency in the findings regarding sex differences in visual-spatial skill (Connor & Serbin, 1984). In one study, seventh grade boys obtained a higher mean score on the Differential Aptitude Test(DAT)-Space Relations Test than girls did, but there were no sex-related differences in this group on five other measures of visual-spatial skill. (These measures were the Cube Comparisons Test, the Hidden Pattern Test, the Gestalt Completion Test, the Paper Folding Test, and the Card Rotations Test.) In a close replication of the procedures of this study with an independent sample, a mean difference favoring seventh grade males was obtained on the Form Board Test, but not on the DAT-Spatial Relations Test or on four other measures of visual-spatial skill. (Connor & Serbin, 1984) These comparisons among the seventh-graders are particularly interesting, because the courses taken by boys and girls do not differ at this point (although other kinds of experience that might be related to the development of visual-spatial skill clearly do. See Sherman, 1967). Differences favoring males were somewhat more apparent among the tenth-graders, but even here no significant difference was found on five of the six visual-spatial measures in one study, and on two of the six measures of the second study. The DAT-Spatial Relations Test was the most consistent differentiator of mean performance. Males obtained a higher mean than females in three of the four relevant comparisons. It is important to note, however, that this difference averaged one fifth of one standard deviation for both the seventh and tenth graders. This difference means that 58% of the males obtained a score that was the same or greater than a score that was also exceeded by 50% of the females. There was, in other words, a great deal of overlap in the distribution of scores of males and females. There were no consistent differences in either the range or variability of scores obtained by males or females.

Our understanding of sex-related differences in visual-spatial skill has also been furthered by research on the trainability or modifiability of performance on tests of visual-spatial skill. One of the earliest reports of training effects on visual-spatial skill is a report of the effect of 1 year's experience in engineering school on performance on the College Entrance Examination Board Space Relations Test (Blade & Watson, 1955). Despite the lack of a true control group (i.e., random assignment was not used), the use of reasonable comparison groups and the existence of independent replications (see also Myers, 1953) lend support to the findings and interpretations made by the authors. Students in two engineering programs were observed to improve an average of one standard deviation in performance on the DAT Space Relations Test between the time they entered the program and the beginning of their second year. Students in two nonengineering programs showed a gain of half as much during the same period. The improvement made by the engineering students is substantial in view of their already high level of performance on the first test administration, approximately one-half a standard deviation above the norm.

The effectiveness of a more systematic visual-spatial training program is described by Brinkmann (1966). Brinkmann developed a short course in elementary geometry emphasizing visual-spatial problem solving and using programmed instruction techniques. (He cites the results of three unpublished studies showing that more traditional geometry courses which emphasize formal proofs have no effect on visual-spatial performance.) Extensive discrimination training was provided, as well as practice with the visual and physical manipulation of geometric shapes. Twenty-five eighth-grade students who participated in this training program once a day for 3 weeks showed an average increase of 18 raw score points, or approximately 1½ standard deviations, on the Space Relations part of the Differential Aptitude Test. The control group, which participated in standard math classes during the training period, showed an increase of only 3 raw score points. There was also evidence of a significant increase in knowledge of geometry as a result of the program. There was no evidence of poorer performance by females on the post-test (in fact, females averaged two points higher than males on the Spatial Relations post-test). Unfortunately, Brinkmann did not report separate means for males and females on the pre-test, so that it is not clear if a sex-related difference was apparent in his sample prior to training. However, Brinkmann's (1966) conclusion that females can at least maintain parity with males, when given appropriate training does appear to be reasonable interpretation of these data.

A small number of studies have investigated sex-related differences in response to training. Goldstein and Chance (1965) gave adult males and females extensive practice on the Embedded Figures Test and additional comparable stimuli. They found that both males and females reduced their discovery time substantially over the series of trials. However, while females responded significantly more slowly than males in the first block of trials, by the last block of trials there were no significant sex-related differences.

In more recent research (Connor, Schackman, & Serbin, 1978; Connor, Serbin, & Schackman, 1977), sex differences in the response of children to training or practice on a visual-spatial test have been found. The first study involved the random assignment of first, third, and fifth graders to either one of two training conditions, which were designed to teach visual-spatial disembedding, or to a control group. One of the training procedures (the overlay condition) consisted of practice locating a diamond shape in each of five specially constructed complex pictures. After a few moments exposure to the complex figure (in which few of the children were able to locate the diamond), an overlay was removed from the picture which decreased the amount of complexity and detail in the picture. Shortly thereafter a second overlay and a third overlay were removed, at which point the diamond, with few extraneous details, was readily apparent to all children. The overlays were then repositioned so that the child could observe changes in the appearance of the diamond shape as more details were added. This procedure was followed with all five pictures. The second training procedure (the flat figures condition) consisted of practice in locating the diamond in identical pictures without the overlays.

The results of this study indicated that girls who received the overlay procedure before being tested on the Children's Embedded Figures Test scored significantly higher on the test than girls in the Flat Figures and the Control conditions. The test performance of the boys was not affected by either type of training. Comparing the performance of the two sexes, there was a tendency for boys in the control condition to receive higher scores than girls in the control condition, while, among the children receiving the overlay training, no sex differences were observed. It appeared, in other words, that the slight deficiencies girls sometimes show in visual-spatial disembedding during the elementary school years are readily changed with even a brief amount of appropriate training.

In a second study with first graders, Connor, Schackman, and Serbin (1978) explored these findings further with a pre-test post-test design and a measure of generalization to a related test. This design permitted the evaluation of both practice and training effects. On the pre-test, girls tended to score slightly less than boys. This tendency was not observed on the post-test, which was given 4 days later, for either the control or the training group. Thus, the effect of the pre-test (i.e., practice) was to eliminate the sex difference as well as to increase the scores of both boys and girls. In addition to the practice effect, an effect of training was found for both boys and girls. However, there were no significant differences between the training and control group on the generalization measure, which consisted of an adaptation of the DAT Space Relations test appropriate for use with young children (Sternglanz, 1977).

In a related study in this series Connor, Serbin, and Freeman, (1978) employed the identical procedures with a group of educable retarded children whose performance and verbal I.Q.s on the Wechsler Intelligence Scale for Children were both below 80. On the pre-test, the performance of these children was similar to that of children of comparable mental age rather than comparable chronological age. On the post-test, the children in the control condition showed no significant increase in performance, while the children in the overlay training condition were performing at age-appropriate levels, an increase greater than one standard deviation. No sex differences were observed in this study for either mean level of performance or response to training. The implication that visual-spatial training is particularly effective in increasing the performance of students who initially obtain relatively low scores on tests of visual-spatial skill is consistent with our other findings.

Most recently, Connor and Serbin (1984) evaluated the effectiveness of five newly developed sets of visual-spatial training materials, each employed in one 30-minute session. Despite a substantial amount of preliminary work in the development of these materials, only two of the five sets were found to increase performance on the visual-spatial skill they were designed to improve. However, the widely used Differential Aptitude Test-Spatial Relations Test was one of the tests that did show a significant training effect.

There was no indication in this study (as opposed to the findings of Connor et al., 1977, 1978) that females profited more from training than males. In fact, the only treatment by sex interaction that was obtained was in the opposite direction; i.e., on the Card Rotations Test males profited from the training while females did not. It is interesting to note, however, that in this case the males in the control group were performing less well than the females in the control group. What these findings suggest is that the sex which is performing less well without training is likely to benefit more from training.

In sum, the results of these studies indicate that visual-spatial skill is trainable at a variety of age levels. Beneficial effects of training have been found in elementary school children (Connor et al., 1977, 1978), junior high school students (Brinkmann, 1966), and college students (Blade & Watson, 1955; Goldstein & Chance, 1965; Myers, 1953). Such procedures have been found effective both with students relatively high in visual-spatial skill (Blade & Watson, 1955) as well as with students relatively low in visual-spatial skill (Connor, Serbin, & Freeman, 1978). Some studies have found that training and/or practice effects are relatively stronger for females than for males (Connor et al., 1978; Goldstein & Chance, 1965), but in other cases males and females benefit a similar amount from training (Connor & Serbin, 1984).

RECOMMENDATIONS

What conclusions can we draw from this brief survey of some of the sex-differences literature? It is useful to consider the "ostensible objectives" of such researchers, and compare them with what Bernard (1976) has referred to as the "latent function" of the research. The ostensible objectives include the desire to answer practical questions such as "Are there major differences in cognitive functioning between males and females?", "Are certain modes of thinking or processing information more typical of males or females?", and "Are males or females more suitably matched with certain occupations or vocations because of differences in cognitive functioning?"

The sex difference research has, in my opinion, yielded no affirmative answers to any of these questions. There is no evidence whatsoever that males and females differ qualitatively in any cognitive function; sex-related differences in performance, when they are found, typically consist of small differences in mean performance. Sex-related differences in visual-spatial skill, which are the most pronounced differences found in the literature, are not extremely robust. A significant sex-related difference in visual-spatial skill may or may not be observed in any given study depending, in unknown ways, on the test used, the age group used, and major sample-to-sample variations. As previously discussed, when a significant difference in visual-spatial is obtained, it is typically a relatively small difference in means, and the variability observed within each sex is much greater than the between sex variability. Lastly, such differences are likely to disappear after small amounts of practice or training with suitably chosen materials.

Given the small and unstable differences observed in the mean performance of males and females, it is extremely difficult to see any possible practical implication of this research. Further, even if a larger and more stable mean difference were found, one would still not want to make recommendations for the education and guidance of individuals on the basis of a broad group membership rather than the skills of that specific individual. This is especially true when the correlation between group membership and performance is as low as it is in the sex difference literature.

A second ostensible objective of sex-difference research is to increase our knowledge of how individual differences arise. If, for example, it could be determined that a sex-related difference in visual-spatial skill existed and its pattern was consistent with patterns predicted by X-linked inheritance, then this could, theoretically, further our understanding of factors leading to the development of visual-spatial skill. This objective has, in my opinion, also not been fulfilled by sex-difference research. Typically, biologically based theories have been proposed and widely accepted on the basis of very little supporting data. The theories have not been politically neutral. As Shields (1975) points out, the findings of psychology and biology have replaced religion as justifiers for the inferior status of women. The "latent function" of sex difference research has been to rationalize the status quo and more of the same. For example, Nash (1970) writes,

> It is a plain corollary of the argument put forward here that males and females differ in certain important respects and that these differences require them to have distinct child rearings or, at least, to be reared in manners more distinct than is customary in our society. Not only, it is suggested, do boys and girls react differently to the same experience, but they also require some different experiences with differing emphases. (p. 210)

> . . . cultures have different expectations of males and females because man's observations of the natural world show him that males and females *are* [italics added] different. These expectations are not some arbitrary imposition perpetuated throughout history by cultural inertia but a dynamic expression of a biological fact inherent in the nature of men and women. (p. 438)

Societal understandings and expectations of sex-roles are inextricably a part of the research that has been conducted and of the theories that have been proposed. Bias has been reflected in the choice of research hypotheses (e.g., the study of brain weight and its relation to sex-differences in intelligence) and the phrasing of the research question (e.g., "Why are men better at mathematics?" as opposed to "Why is the proportion of men who excel at mathematics greater than the proportion of women who excel?"). Bias has also been apparent in the labeling of skills. (For example, why have sex-related differences in performance on the Rod and Frame Test been interpreted to show that females are less "field independent" than males, instead of revealing that males are less "field aware" or that they are "field ignorant"?) Bias has also been a part of decisions about the materials and setting that are part of the data collection process (See Frieze, Parsons, Johnson, Ruble, & Zellman, 1978, chapter 2). Perhaps most imporantly, sexist bias has been a part of data interpretation, theory-building and the uses to which the data has been put.

What directions, if any, I now find myself wondering, should sex-difference research take? Or, as posed at the beginning of this chapter, "Why should the reader be interested in sex differences in cognitive skills?" First, I believe it is crucial for researchers in this field to re-examine their assumptions about sex differences. To what extent are stereotypic assumptions about what females are supposed to be skilled at influencing the formation of hypotheses and tests of these hypotheses? To what extent are the questions we ask and do not ask about sex differences influenced by our "nonconsious ideology" of male and female roles (Bem, 1970)?

I also believe, as does Bernard (1976), that we are giving a disproportionate amount of emphasis to between-sex differences rather than within-sex differences. It is not enough to simply state "between-group exceeded within-group differences," and then proceed to ignore the latter and give all the attention to small differences in means.

I would also like to see more research investigating the belief in sex differences, or what Grady (1979) calls "the illusion of sex differences." Where do these beliefs come from, what are their effects on performance and behavior in general, and what relation, if any, do they have to what Unger and Sitter (cited in Grady, 1979) call the "grain of truth regarding sex differences" (p. 175).

Lastly, I believe that researchers in the field of sex differences must, if they are to make meaningful contributions, have suitable background in the fields of anthropology, society, history and literature, as much as biology, chemistry, and physics. It is not sufficient to the understanding of potential sex-related differences in behavior to imply, as Benbow and Stanley (1980) do, that if seventh grade males and females have taken the same academic courses, then any difference in their cognitive behavior must be for genetic reasons. Such an implication reveals an apalling lack of understanding of societal and familial socialization practices as they relate to males and females. The noted and recently honored biologist Barbara McClintock speaks of her approach to research as "letting the material speak to you" and having "a feeling for the organism" (quoted in Bleier, 1984, p. 205). Good science requires such a listening attitude, a willingness to learn from the subject matter being studied. Furthermore, Bleier states:

> It [good science] has to do with not imposing the ego in the form of preconceived, unalterable, unacknowledged, and constraining belief systems on the subject matter, but rather creating the circumstances that permit the matter to reveal some of its characteristics to you. This means the courageous and difficult task of examining and questioning all of our assumptions and the very structure of our thought processes, all clearly born and bred within a profoundly stratified, hierarchical, patriarchal culture. These include assumptions about dominance and subordinance, women and men, objectivity and subjectivity; about causation, truth and reality; about what is 'normal' and 'natural'; about power; about reproduction and motherhood. Doing good science involves an appreciation of the complexity of all phenomena and the constancy of only the process of change. (p. 206).

REFERENCES

Astin, H. S. (1974). Sex difference in mathematical and scientific precocity. In J. C. Stanley, D. P. Keating, & L. H. Fox (Eds.), *Mathematical talent: Discovery, description and development.* Baltimore, MD: Johns Hopkins University Press.

Bem, D. (1970). *Beliefs, attitudes, and human affairs.* Belmont, CA: Brooks/Cole Publishing Company.

Benbow, C. P., & Stanley, J. C. (1980). Sex differences in mathematical ability: Fact or artifact? *Science, 210,* 1262–1264.

Bernard, J. (1976). Sex differences: An overview. In A. G. Kaplan & J. P. Bean (Eds.), *Beyond sex-role stereotypes: Readings toward a psychology of androgyny* (pp. 9–26). Boston, MA: Little, Brown.

Blade, M. F., & Watson, W. S. (1955). Increase in spatial visualization test scores during engineering study. *Psychological Monographs, 69*(12), 13.

Bleier, R. (1984). *Science and gender: A critique of biology and its theories on women.* New York: Pergamon.

Brinkmann, E. H. (1966). Programmed instruction as a technique for improving spatial visualization. *Journal of Applied Psychology, 50*(2), 179–184.

Broverman, D. M., Klaiber, E. L., Kobayashi, Y., & Vogel, W. (1968). Roles of activation and inhibition in sex differences in cognitive abilities. *Psychological Review, 75,* 23–50.

Buffery, A. W. H., & Gray, J. A. (1972). Sex differences in the development of spatial and linguistic skills. In C. Ounsted & D. C. Taylor (Eds.), *Gender differences: Their ontogeny and significance.* Baltimore, MD: Williams & Williams.

Connor, J. M., Schackman, M., & Serbin, L. A. (1978). Sex-related differences in response to practice on a visual-spatial test and generalization to a related test. *Child Development, 49,* 24–29.

Connor, J. M., Schackman, M., & Freeman, M. (1978). Training visual-spatial ability in EMR children. *American Journal of Mental Deficiency, 83,* 116–121.

Connor, J. M., & Serbin, L. A. (1984). Mathematics, visual-spatial ability and sex roles. In S. Chipman (Ed.), *Women and mathematics: Balancing the equation,* Hillsdale, NJ: Erlbaum.

Connor, J. M., Serbin, L. A., & Schackman, M. (1977). Sex differences in response to training on a visual-spatial test. *Developmental Psychology, 13,* 293–295.

Fennema, E. (1976). *Influences of selected cognitive, affective, and educational variables on sex-related differences in mathematics learning and studying.* Madison, WI: University of Wisconsin, Department of Curriculum and Instruction.

Fennema, E., & Sherman, J. (1977). Sex-related differences in mathematics achievement, spatial visualization and affectie factors. *American Educational Research Journal, 14,* 51–71.

Fox, L. H. (1976). *The effects of sex role socialization on mathematics participation and achievement.* Baltimore, MD: The John Hopkins University Press.

Frieze, I. H., Parsons, J. E., Johnson, P. B., Ruble, D. N., & Zellman, G. L. (1978). *Women and sex roles: A social psychological perspective.* New York: Norton.

Goldstein, A. G., & Chance, J. E. (1965). Effects of practice on sex-related differences in performance on embedded figures. *Psychonomic Science, 53,* 361–362.

Grady, K. (1979). Androgyny reconsidered. In H. Williams (Ed), *Psychology of Women.* New York: W. W. Norton & Company, 172–177.

Hollingworth, L. (1916). Sex differences in mental traits. *Psychological Bulletin, 13,* 377–385.

Hollingworth, L. (1918). Comparison of the sexes in mental traits. *Psychological Bulletin, 25,* 427–432.

Hyde, J. S., & Rosenberg, B. G. (1976). *Half the human experience: The psychology of women.* Lexington, MA: D. C. Heath.

Lehrke, R. (1972). A theory of x-linkage of major intellectual traits. *American Journal of Mental Deficiency, 76,* 611–619.

Lehrke, R. (1974). *X-linked mental retardation and verbal disability.* New York: Intercontinental Medical Book Corporation.

Maccoby, E., & Jacklin, C. (1974). *The psychology of sex differences.* Palo Alto, CA: Stanford University.

Myers, C. T. (1953). A note on spatial relations pretest and posttest. *Educational and Psychological Measurement, 13,* 596–600.

Nash, J. (1970). *Developmental psychology.* Englewood Cliffs, NJ: Prentice Hall.

Parlee, M. B. (1972). Comments on "Roles of activation and inhibition in sex differences in cognitive abilities" by D. M. Broverman, E. L. Klaiber, Y. Kaobayski, & W. Vogel. *Psychological Review, 79,* 180–184.

Rosenberg, R. (1984). *Beyond separate spheres: Intellectual origins of modern feminism.* New Haven, CT: Yale University Press.

Sells, L. W. (1976). *The mathematics filter and the education of women and minorities.* Paper presented at the annual meeting of the American Association for the advancement of Science, Boston, Massachusetts.

Sherif, C. W. (1979). Bias in psychology. In J. A. Sherman & E. T. Beck (Eds.), *The prism of sex: Essays in the sociology of knowledge* (pp. 93–113). Madison, WI: University of Wisconsin Press.

Sherman, J. A. (1967). Problem of sex differences in space perception and aspects of intellectual functioning. *Psychological Review, 14,* 290–299.

Sherman, J. A. (1977). Effects of biological factors on sex related differences in mathematics achievement. In *Women and mathematics: Research perspectives for change.* Washington, D.C.: National Institute of Education.

Shields, S. A. (1975). Functionalism, darwinism, and the psychology of women: A study in social myth. *American Psychologist, 30,* 739–54.

Smith, I. M. (1964). *Spatial ability, its educational and social significance.* San Diego, CA: Robert Knapp.

Stafford, R. E. (1961). Sex differences in spatial visualization as evidence of sex-linked inheritance. *Perception and Motor Skills, 13,* 428.

Stafford, R. E. (1972). Hereditary and environmental components of quantitative reasoning. *Review of Educational Research, 14,* 183–201.

Sternglanz, S. (1977). *A study of sex and age differences on a spatial relations test in elementary school children*. Paper presented at the meeting of the Society for Research in Child Development, New Orleans.

Terman, L. M. (1925). *Genetic studies of genius*. Palo Alto, CA: Stanford University Press.

Tobias, S. (1982). Sexist equations. *Psychology Today, 15,* pp. 14,16,18.

Tooney, N. (1981). The "math gene" and other symptoms of the biology backlash. *Ms., 10,* 56,59.

Wittig, M. A., & Petersen, A. C. (1979). *Sex-related differences in cognitive functioning: Developmental issues*. New York: Academic Press.

Chapter *12*

Sex Differences in Cognition: The Nature–Nurture Controversy Revisited

Carolyne M. Weil

University of Massachusetts at Amherst

Few other issues are as emotionally charged as the discussion of possible sex-related differences in human functioning. The reasons for this are obvious and have been discussed by both Smith and Connor in the preceding chapters: the history of the treatment of women in our society as a result of such views, the relative focus on the heritability of such differences in much of the research literature, particularly in the realm of "cognitive science," and the political implications of the acceptance of such sex-difference theories regarding the current and future status of women in our culture.

It is with these rather weighty considerations in mind that I will discuss the preceding Smith and Connor chapters. I will not even pretend to take a neutral stance; however, I will discuss each position within the context of the general research literature regarding sex differences in cognition, in order that the particular views of both authors can be considered from a broader perspective.

First, perhaps a brief historical sampling of attitudes towards women's intellect might elucidate how we have arrived at our current state of affairs. I would like to acknowledge Julia Sherman's (1967, 1971, 1974, 1978) work here which, in addition to providing a number of the following quotes, also helped to crystallize my thoughts in this area. Hers is the most parsimonious, not to mention palatable, view of cognitive sex differences in the extant research literature.

The roots of "sexism" (regarding women's intellect) have been traced back at least as far as Aristotle, who is oft quoted as having stated "the female state is . . . as it were a deformity" (as quoted in Sherman, 1978, p.4), referring to the cursed-by-the-sins-of-Eve, crooked-rib syndrome, which was the prevailing view during the Middle Ages. Women were by nature depraved creatures, who needed to be tamed by their husbands.

Later, Darwin's theory of evolution postulated an increasing sexual differentiation, with the characteristics most suited to the role and function of each sex being gradually perfected. For males, such traits were courage, intelligence, and resourcefulness, while the traits for females were generally geared towards passivity and maternalism (Fee, 1976). This view was later expanded by Herbert Spencer, who in his 1873 article on the "Psychology of the Sexes" stated that since intellectual attributes were not necessary for child-rearing purposes, such characteristics had not been developed in women during the course of evolution (cited in Fee, 1976). Women were thus viewed as an instance of arrested evolutionary development (Sherman, 1978)!

Next, Lambroso, a nineteenth-century Italian criminologist, suggested that this evolutionary sex differentiation is evidenced in what he saw as the similarities between women and children. Women, he said, "have many traits in common with children; that their moral sense is deficient; that they are revengeful, jealous, inclined to vengeance of a refined cruelty . . . . In ordinary cases, these defects are neutralized by piety, maternity, want of passion, sexual coldness, by weakness and an undeveloped intelligence" (as quoted in Sherman, 1978, p.7).

It has even been suggested by Paul Mobius, a late nineteenth-century German physiologist, that the "mental incapacity" of women might even be *adaptive* in an evolutionary sense, as it would thus ensure the survival of the species: "If woman was not physically and mentally weak, if she was not as a rule rendered harmless by circumstances, she would be extremely dangerous" (as quoted in Sherman, 1978, p.7).

It is important to keep in mind that evidence suggesting sex differences in *general* intelligence was then and still is, virtually nonexistent (Maccoby & Jacklin, 1974). However, there do appear to be some rather well-documented *specific* ability differences between the sexes, which have been discussed in both the Smith and Connor chapters. That is, males are generally found to be superior in spatial and mathematical abilities, while females are found to be superior in verbal abilities (Maccoby & Jacklin, 1974). The general question that is being raised by both Smith and Connor (and in the research literature in general) is the degree to which such sex-related differences are attributable to genetic and constitutional factors on the one hand, and to social/environmental factors on the other—the ubiquitous "nature–nurture controversy."

Before we examine the research evidence regarding this controversy as presented by Smith, Connor, and others, a few words of caution are in order; i.e., caution regarding the *interpretation* of research findings related to sex differences. As has been suggested by numerous researchers in this area, we need to be extremely careful in drawing conclusions on the basis of *published* research findings of sex differences. As all researchers are perhaps painfully aware, journal publishers are generally not interested in findings of "no differences," or "failure to reject the null hypothesis" in our jargon. The end result is that the published literature tends to be unrepresentative and biased. This is obviously a problem in all areas of research, but perhaps particularly so in the area of sex differences, given the tremendous political and social implications of the findings.

A related methodological issue in the interpretation of research related to sex differences is the problem of *measurement* per se. It has been suggested (e.g., Donlon, Ekstrom, & Lockheed, 1976; Sherman, 1967, 1974) that many of the tasks that have been used to measure sex differences are in fact "sex-typed" or "sex-biased"; witness the Rod and Frame Test and the Block Design subtest of the Wechsler Intelligence Scales, both of which are frequently utilized to measure spatial abilities and which are obviously composed of *male*-preferred activities. Should anyone be surprised (or interested) if women do not fare as well on such tests, and what conclusions can be drawn from such findings?

With these cautions in mind, let us consider the evidence presented by Smith and Connor within the context of the research literature in general. Myra Smith's hypothesis regarding observed sex differences in reading abilities represents another in a series of biologically-based views of sex differences in cognitive functioning. It has been previously suggested that males lag behind females in the development of verbal activities because of greater prenatal and perinatal complications in male babies (McKeever, 1981), possible maturational lags due to hormonal differences (Hier, 1981; Waber, 1976), and/or X-linked inheritance of cognitive skills (Maccoby & Jacklin, 1974). With respect to possible brain lateralization differences between males and females, researchers have alternatively suggested that the brains of females may become lateralized (i.e., left-hemisphere dominant) at an earlier age than those of males (Harshman & Remington, 1976), they may be more bilateralized for verbal abilities relative to males (Levy, 1972), and/or they may be less bilateralized for spatial abilities relative to males (Buffery & Gray, 1972). The evidence presented in support of these views has been fairly minimal and highly speculative (Sherman, 1978).

Smith's hypothesis is a relatively new variation on this biological theme. Her basic underlying assumption is that early genetically-determined brain lateralization differences between males and females lead to female superiority in verbal abilities and, almost by default, male superiority in spatial abilities. In an interesting twist, she proposes that it is these superior spatial abilities in boys that actually *interfere* with the process of learning to read; i.e., because their internal representations of form are holistic, dynamic, and 3-dimensional, boys are actually impeded in the process of learning to read, which, according to Smith, requires the visual processing of 2-dimensional forms that are "rigidly linked to the visual upright." Girls, in her view, because of their precocious linguistic development, greater affiliative needs, and "lessened motivation to explore their physical environment,"(!) acquire knowledge about objects and 3-dimensional space through inquiry about, rather than manipulation of, objects. Such knowledge leads to internal representations of form that are static and 2-dimensional, and in which orientation in space is processed as a distinctive feature of form.

The data Smith presents in support of her hypothesis neither supports the notion of early sex differences in spatial abilities, nor does it even address the issue of reading ability per se. In fact, the only developmental study she presents (Jackson & Smith, 1981) actually refutes her hypothesis, as she found no difference in the detection of distinctive features of form in male and female kindergarten children. Smith's hypothesis is also difficult to reconcile with a large body of data which suggests that male superiority in spatial abilities does not reliably emerge until *adolescence* (Maccoby & Jacklin, 1974; McGee, 1979). This is not to deny that there is something different in the early strategies that some male and female children employ in the process of learning to read. It is, however, to suggest that the difference may be more of a *semantic* than a visual one (e.g., Liberman & Mann, 1981) and that it might be more fruitful to focus future research on the development of linguistic strategies in male and female children.

In light of the paucity of data supporting biological explanations of sex differences in cognitive functioning, it is curious that they have remained the prevailing viewpoint. As Connor notes, perhaps this is because biological explanations are generally accorded greater respect and prestige than historical, social, or cultural explanations, and are seen as somehow being more "objective" than the latter.

Such biological explanations, according to Jane Connor, ignore the tremendous role that the extremely powerful vehicle known as *socialization* plays in the determination of sex-related differences in human functioning. I shall now look at the evidence presented by Connor in the context of the general research literature concerning sociocultural determination of cognitive sex differences.

One such line of evidence can be derived from studies on cultural variations in sex differences. For example, while many studies indicate that, in general, girls read earlier than boys and attain higher levels of reading achievement (Maccoby & Jacklin, 1974), some cross-cultural studies have demonstrated an actual male superiority in reading achievements. Johnson (1973–1974) found that girls were superior to boys in the United States and Canada; however, in England and Nigeria, boys were superior to girls. It should be noted that all four countries are English-speaking and thus use an "alphabetic" writing system as described by Smith and which, according to her hypothesis, is more difficult for boys to learn to decode. Similarly, Preston (1962) found American girls to be superior to American boys in reading achievement; however, German boys were superior to German girls. Preston attributes this difference to the predominance of female teachers in the United States and male teachers in Germany. Smith's assertion, that cross-cultural differences in reading failure rates for boys and girls are due to the types of *writing* systems particular to the cultures, completely ignores the tremendous cultural influences on the development of sex-appropriate behavior.

In the area of spatial abilities, cultural variations have been found as well. Among the Eskimos, who are depicted as having less traditional sex role socialization than in the continental United States (e.g., girls are permitted to go on hunting trips with the boys), studies have reported *no* sex differences in spatial abilities (Berry, 1966; McArthur, 1967). In contrast, Mexican children, who are reared in a culture which has been credited with originating the concept of "machismo," evidence even *greater* sex differences on spatial tasks than American children (Mebane & Johnson, 1970). While this is not conclusive evidence that the obtained findings are due to cultural variations alone, it is rather compelling evidence that biological explanations are insufficient, and suggests that more definitive research is needed in this area.

A second line of evidence regarding possible socialization effects in the determination of cognitive sex differences can be derived from studies concerning sex-role effects in spatial abilities and perception. Nash (1975) found that male gender preference was correlated with spatial ability in both sexes. Similarly, when traditionally male sex-typed measures are translated into more *female* sex-typed activities, females are often found to perform better than males. Naditch (1976) modified the traditional Rod and Frame task, in which the subject is required to align a rod in a vertical position relative to a bent frame, into an "empathy task," with the rod representing a person. Males were found to perform superior to females under the traditional conditions; however, females *surpassed* males under the empathy conditions.

The role of practice in determining sex differences in spatial abilities has been investigated in a number of studies, including several conducted and discussed by Connor. In her studies on visual-spatial training in elementary school aged children (e.g., Connor, Schackman, & Serbin, 1978; Connor, Serbin, & Schackman, 1977), females were found to evidence more of a facilitation from pre-test to post-test performance as a result of training relative to males. In another study concerning pre-schoolers' performance on a field articulation task (Coates, Lord, & Jakabovics, 1975), the authors reported that increased levels of block play by girls was correlated with higher performance on the field articulation task. Similar findings have been reported in spatial training with older (i.e., college-age) women as well (e.g., Fennema & Sherman, 1977).

A final group of factors that have been hypothesized as potentially determining sex differences in academic performance are related to the "sexist" nature of schooling in general. It has been frequently suggested that many aspects of traditional schooling are geared towards, and thus reinforce, traditionally "feminine" types of behavior: docility, passivity, dependency and so on (Feshbach, 1969). In fact, schools have been characterized as being "against boys" in many respects, which calls into serious question Smith's assertion that boys and girls have equal access to learning to read.

Indeed, the very materials which are used to teach reading have been criticized as being female- rather than male-oriented, and thus may be less challenging and motivating to boys (e.g., Heilman, 1967). In addition, boys may have difficulty identifying and interacting with predominantly female teachers, who have been found to respond differentially towards male and female students (e.g., Brophy & Good, 1970). Dwyer (1973) concluded that schools place boys in a situation of "conflicting demands," where reading is actually *incompatible* with the developing male sex role and appears to have little real-world relevance. Several studies have demonstrated that both boys and girls, from grades two through twelve, view reading as a feminine activity (e.g., Stein & Smithells, 1969) and that the degree to which one considers reading to be appropriate to one's own sex is correlated with reading achievement scores (Dwyer, 1974; Mazurkiewicz, 1960). As Connor has asserted, the frequently observed sex differences in math and science abilities (favoring boys, this time) are presumably determined in much the same fashion.

My intent here has not been to deny totally the possibility of biological contributions to sex differences; however, I feel that they have been over-emphasized in the research literature and have lended credence to the various myths and stereotypes regarding the biological origins of "male" and "female" behavior. As we have seen here, there is substantial evidence that a number of sex differences that have been presumed to be biologically determined, may in fact be more a result of environmental (i.e., sociocultural) influences.

In this vein, Sherman (1967, 1971) has offered what she calls the "bent twig hypothesis," which suggests that early maturational differences favoring the physical development of girls, and which perhaps account for very early differences in speech production, "bend" girls toward verbal (i.e., left-hemisphere) processing, which is then facilitated by the environment. The development of visual-spatial skills is *not* similarly facilitated in girls, as such activities have been sex-typed male by our culture. Males excel in visual-spatial skills, as they tend to engage in those activities that are probably highly related to their development. In Sherman's view, then, overall sex differences in cognitive functioning are primarily *environmentally* determined. As previously discussed, evidence supporting the biologically-based view of sex differences in reading to which Myra Smith subscribes appears to be extremely lacking.

In closing, it might be useful to inquire as to the practical significance of statistical significance in sex difference research, particularly in light of the minimal amount of the variance accounted for by such differences in many studies. In addition, as has been previously mentioned by Connor and others, differences *between* the sexes on measures of cognitive abilities tend to be small relative to the variability *within* each sex. Both of these findings suggest that the generalizability and even validity of obtained sex-related differences in cognitive functioning is dubious at best. And, given the political implications of such findings, to suggest that we should be *extremely* careful in their interpretation is indeed an understatement.

REFERENCES

Berry, J. W. (1966). Temne and Eskimo perceptual skills. *International Journal of Psychology, 1*, 207–229.

Brophy, J., & Good, T. (1970). Teachers' communication of differential expectations for children's classroom performance: Some behavioral data. *Journal of Educational Psychology, 61,* 365–374.

Buffery, A. W. H., & Gary, J. A. (1972). Sex differences in the development of spatial and linguistic skills. In C. Ounsted & D. C. Taylor (Eds.), *Gender differences: Their ontogency and significance.* Baltimore, MD: Williams & Wilkins, 1972.

Coates, S., Lord, M., & Jakobovics, E. (1975). Field dependence-independence, social–nonsocial play and sex differences in preschool children. *Perceptual and Motor Skills, 40,* 195–202.

Connor, J. M., Schackman, M., & Serbin, L. A. (1978). Sex differences in response to practice on a visual spatial test and generalization to a related test. *Child Development, 49,* 24–29.

Connor, J. M., Serbin, L. A., & Schackman, M. (1977). Sex differences in children's response to training on a visual-spatial test. *Developmental Psychology, 13,* 293–294.

Donlon, T. F., Ekstrom, R. B., & Lockheed, M. (1976, September). *Comparing the sexes on achievement items of varying content.* Paper presented at the annual meetings of the American Psychological Association, Washington, DC.

Dwyer, C. A. (1973). Sex differences in reading: An evaluation and critique of current theories. *Review of Educational Research, 43,* 455–467.

Dwyer, C. A. (1974). Influence on children's sex role standards on reading and arithmetic achievement. *Journal of Educational Psychology, 66,* 811–816.

Fee, E. (1976). Science and the woman problem: Historical perspectives. In M. S. Teitelman (Ed.), *Sex differences.* Garden City, NY: Anchor.

Fennema, E., & Sherman, J. (1977). Sex-related differences in mathematics achievement, spatial visualization, and affective factors. *American Educational Research Journal, 14,* 51–71.

Feshbach, N. D. (1969). Student teacher preferences of elementary school pupils varying in personality characteristics. *Journal of Educational Psychology, 60,* 126–132.

Harshman, R. A., & Remington, R. (1976). Sex, language, and the brain, part 1: A review of the literature on adult sex differences in lateralization, *UCLA Working Papers in Phonetics, 31,* 86–103. (Cited in Sherman, 1978).

Heilman, A. W. (1967). *Principles and practices of teaching reading* (2nd ed.) Columbus, OH: Charles Merrill.

Hier, D. B. (1981). Sex differences in brain structure. In A. Ansara, N. Geschwind, A. Galaburda, M. Albert, & N. Gartrell (Eds.), *Sex differences in dyslexia.* Towson, MD: The Orton Dyslexia Society.

Jackson, L., & Smith, M. O. (1981). *Prototype vs. distinctive features learning in pattern identification: Sex differences and age trend.* Paper presented at the Eastern Psychological Association, New York.

Johnson, D. D. (1973–1974). Sex differences in reading across cultures. *Reading Research Quarterly, 9,* 67–86.

Levy, J. (1972). Lateral spacialization of the human brain: Behavioral manifestation and possible evolutionary basis. In J. A. Kiger (Ed.), *The biology of behavior.* Corvalis, OR: University Press.

Liberman, I. Y., & Mann, V. A. (1981). Should reading instruction and remediation vary with the sex of the child? In A. Ansara, N. Geschwind, A. Galaburda, M. Albert, & N. Gartrell (Eds.), *Sex differences in dyslexia.* Towson, MD: The Orton Dyslexia Society.

Maccoby, E. E., & Jacklin, C. N. (1974). *The psychology of sex differences.* Palo Alto, CA: Stanford University Press.

McArthur, R. (1967). Sex differences in field dependence for the Eskimo: Replication of Berry's findings. *International Journal of Psychology, 2,* 139–40.

McGee, M. G. (1979). *Human spatial abilities.* New York: Praeger.

McKeever, W. F. (1981). Sex and cerebral organization: Is it really so simple? In A. Ansara, N. Gerschwind, A. Galaburda, M. Albert, & N. Gartrell (Eds.), *Sex differences in dyslexia.* Towson, MD: The Orton Dyslexia Society.

Mazurkiewicz, A. J. (1960). Social-cultural influences and reading. *Journal of Developmental Reading, 3,* 254–263.

Mebane, D., & Johnson, D. L. (1970). A comparison of the performance of Mexican boys and girls on Witkin's cognitive tasks. *International Journal of Psychology, 4,* 227–239.

Naditch, S. F. (1976). *Sex differences in field dependence: The role of social influence.* Paper presented at the annual meetings of the American Psychological Association, Washington, DC.

Nash, S. C. (1975). The relationship among sex-role stereotyping, sex-role preference, and the sex difference in spatial visualization. *Sex Roles, 1,* 15–32.

Preston, R. C. (1962). Reading achievement of German and American children. *School and Society, 90,* 350–354.

Sherman, J. (1967). Problem of sex differences in space perception and aspects of intellectual functioning. *Psychological Review, 74,* 290–299.

Sherman, J. (1971). *On the psychology of women: A survey of empirical studies.* Springfield, IL: C. C. Thomas.

Sherman, J. (1974). Field articulation, sex, spatial visualization, dependency, practice, laterality of the brain and birth order. *Perceptual and Motor Skills, 38,* 1223–1235.

Sherman, J. (1978). *Sex-related cognitive differences: An essay on theory and evidence.* Springfield, IL: C. C. Thomas.

Stein, A. H., & Smithells, J. (1969). Age and sex differences in children's sex role standards about achievement. *Developmental Psychology, 1,* 252–259.

Waber, D. P. (1976). Sex differences in cognition: A function of maturation rates? *Science, 192,* 572–574.

Chapter 13

Ape Language: Communication Problems Among Researchers

Carol A. Vázquez

State University of New York at New Paltz

In what may be taken as an indictment of the field of psychology, Nessel (1982) revealed an embarrassing lack of agreement in what "11 of the best minds in the field" consider to be the most important contributions to psychology in the past 15 years. B. F. Skinner, for example, cited progress in the behavioral areas, while Jerome Bruner celebrated the "continued movement away from the restrictive shackles of behaviorism. . . ." And while a few did refer to the discovery of endorphins, i.e., endogenous opiates—a discovery which some affirm should be credited to pharmacologists—still others seemed to have difficulty citing any specific contribution to the field.

The topic of this paper, research on animal language, was also raised and described as both an achievement and a failure. Stanley Milgram: "Finally, psychologists have learned to . . . communicate better with animals. By teaching primates elements of sign language . . . we've . . . gained new insights into animal congnition" (p.50).

Ulric Neisser:

> Language is especially important for our conception of human nature because language is uniquely our own. This point has sometimes been disputed, but recent research has put it beyond doubt. There have been several concerted attempts to bestow sign language on apes, for example, and they have essentially failed. (p. 45)

This lack of consensus proved too irresistible for Nicholas Wade (1982) to let pass without comment. In a *New York Times* editorial entitled "Smart Apes, or Dumb?" the science critic catalogued the disparate and sometimes self-serving opinions of pundits in the field and asked, "Can psychology be taken seriously if even its leading practitioners cannot agree on its recent advances?" (p.30).

The concern in this chapter is not with the state of psychological science as a whole, but rather with the specific area of animal language research. Wade's editorial underscores the controversial state of the field and the need to evaluate where animal language research stands as a science. Though some have declared the field dead, others are still actively engaged in research. It will be argued that the animal language field is a new and vital composite of several older, established disciplines, and is plagued by the crises and the myriad of problems attending any young science.

THE REVISIONIST VIEW

One of the reasons the ape language literature is controversial is the revisionist interpretation of early animal studies proffered by critics such as Thomas Sebeok (Sebeok & Sebeok, 1980) and Herbert Terrace (Terrace, Pettito, Sanders, & Bever, 1979; Terrace, 1981). After trying to teach sign language to a male chimpanzee named Nim Chimpsky, Terrace eventually concluded that the project was a failure. Moreover, after scrutinizing videotapes of other animals' signing, he arrived at the same conclusion regarding all animal language projects and thus, what some had taken as evidence of linguistic abilities in apes was now seriously in question.

Much of the revisionist interpretation hinges on the Clever Hans effect. Clever Hans was a horse that could do arithmetic computations, among other things by clopping its foot on the ground. It was soon discovered that the horse was not really capable of such things, but was instead relying on inadvertent cues from its owner to signal when it should stop clopping.

The term Clever Hans has become the battle-cry of the revisionists. The classic literature on animal language, and more recent research, including Terrace's work with Nim (Terrace, 1979) were reexamined and dismissed as artifacts of Clever Hans or experimenter bias effects. Often expressed in vehement and scathing terms, this criticism, once the focus of an entire conference sponsored by the New York Academy of Sciences (Sebeok & Rosenthal, 1981), has provoked considerable debate.

CAN SCIENTISTS COMMUNICATE WITH EACH OTHER?

Controversial in nature, research on animal communication is an especially multidisciplinary effort. While other areas in cognitive science may be seen as blends of psychology and related disciplines (e.g., information processing and computer science or mathematics, psychology of language and linguistics), this particular area of research has attracted the attention of scholars from many diverse disciplines, e.g., psychologists, linguists, biologists, anthropologists, philosophers, and at least one magician. Like the blind man and the elephant metaphor, it may be that diversity of disciplines which is responsible, to some extent, for the diversity of opinions on animal communication. Because many disciplines are focusing on the problem in terms of their own perspectives, they are unable to deal with issues in an integrative fashion.

According to Kuhn (1962), communication among proponents of competing scientific communities can be "incommensurable," not unlike the difficulties experienced by speakers of foreign tongues. Communication problems abound *within* established fields, with the result that theoretical arguments are inevitable; there are, therefore, "significant limits" to what proponents of different theories can communicate to each other (Kuhn, 1977).

Sigmund Koch (1975) extends Kuhn's idea on an almost Whorfian level, suggesting that scientific "languages" have a deterministic effect on the speaker's perspective:

> . . . single minds can 'speak' and understand several (sometimes many) such languages, in some degree. That does not mean that the speaker has integrated or can integrate these asystematically different languages. When 'speaking' each (at any level) there is a change of perspective. A perspective is not the kind of thing that can fuse. Perspectival knowledge multiplies, but the nature of a human universe and our resources for ordering that universe are such that attempts toward large integrations or fusions can make no sense. (p. 543)

The language problems inherent within a scientific community are much more acute in a situation requiring cross-disciplinary communication. And, predictably, much of the difficulty in animal communication research concerns the very definition of language. The problems involved in defining language are certainly not specific to the ape literature; this has been a traditional polemic in linguistics and is not likely to be resolved in the near future. But as Roger Brown (1973) pointed out, it is impossible to evaluate the apes' capacity for human language without taking a specific position on the nature of language.

Among the many different denotations and operational definitions of language are Hockett's (1963) design features of language (e.g., vocal/auditory channel, semanticity, displacement, productivity), in various forms, and Terrace's criterion, sentence creation (Terrace et al., 1979). Some of the definitions offered would, a priori, excude animals. More than 10 years later, there is still no agreement on what constitutes language. So, the research continues in the absence of a consensus, thus fueling controversy.

If debate concerning the definition of language is to be expected, there is one issue that should be, but is not, beyond debate; that is the particular language that was used in the sign language research projects. We have been told repeatedly by the Gardners (Gardner & Gardner, 1980), by Patterson (Patterson & Linden, 1981) and by Terrace (1979), for example, that the apes were taught American Sign Language, also referred to as Ameslan and ASL. In his book, entitled *Nim,* Terrace clearly states that it was his goal to teach a chimp ASL, and he further asserts that the Gardners taught Washoe ASL. Accordingly, Terrace devotes a

33-page appendix to a description of the features of the language. Now, however, Terrace (1981) contends that none of the animals was taught American Sign Language; he states categorically that they all, even Washoe, learned pidgin sign language instead. But while the Gardners have already admitted that Washoe was not really taught ASL, it seems that not everyone agrees or understands. For example, referring to the Gardners' work, Seidenberg & Pettito (1981) state, "At this time . . . we have no detailed information concerning the nature of their sign code" (p. 121).

What language was actually used? If it was not American Sign Language, then why was the term ever used and why is it still being used by some? Did Terrace originally think he was teaching Nim ASL and only subsequently realize that what he did use could be better described as a pidgin? What is pidgin sign, and does it make any difference?

Part of the confusion stems from the fact that it has taken years for sign language to be recognized as a legitimate language, and, as such, it has only recently been subjected to the rigorous linguistic analyses that are routinely performed on spoken languages. Nevertheless, there seems to be some agreement that sign language can be best characterized as a continuum, with ASL at one end and manually coded English at the other (Woodward, 1980). As a gestural language, manually coded English is, in terms of "word" order, the closest to spoken English, and ASL is the furthest. That is, the word order of spoken English can be very different from the sign order of ASL. Pidgin sign falls in the middle on this continuum. Pidgin languages, in general, are hybrids of at least two languages, and thus, the term "pidgin sign" refers to a gestural language containing some of the features of ASL and English. Though pidgin sign has been described as a combination of English word order with sign vocabulary, Woodward asserts that there is no good definition of pidgin sign, that there is, in fact, a variety of intermediate pidgins, e.g. Ameslish, Signed English and Pidgin Sign English. Thus, the classification of the apes' communication as pidgin sign language is not as definitive as Terrace implies. For example, according to Woodward, Pidgin Sign English retains certain grammatical features (i.e., word or sign oder) of both American Sign Language and English.

Moreover, there are ramifications for the interpretation and evaluation of the apes' performance insofar as word order or sign order has been a *critical* criterion. As Seidenberg & Pettito (1981) point out, most discussions of signing order in apes' utterances are based on the following assumption: that the apes learned a code closer to English than to American Sign, with respect to word order. The problem is that the assumption may not be justified. Even if we assume the apes were taught a pidgin sign, not ASL, if we do not know the nature of that pidgin, i.e., the extent to which the sign order used in the research projects conformed to the word order of spoken English, we cannot easily or objectively evaluate the apes' success on this dimension. The task of evaluation is even more difficult when an ape has an excessive number of teachers (as did Nim) whose signing, in terms of order, may fall at different points along that continuum.

Ironically, such problems represent a pronounced lack of communication among researchers in the area of animal communication. While the concern about the possibility of Clever Hans effects may be valid, it should be equally important that professionals explicitly and effectively report their methods and assumptions. At this point, it is not clear to what extent the controversy over ape language is independent of the apes' actual utterances and generated, instead, by faulty communication among researchers.

In order to understand thoroughly the ape language literature, and ideally, in order to carry out such research, one should have a command of traditional learning theory, ethology, theoretical linguistics, and a thorough knowledge of normal language acquisition in the deaf child, as well as a working knowledge of sign language. Understandably, not many can claim mastery of all these areas. Problems in the evaluation of the apes' performance can occur when an outside evaluater or the trainer is not proficient in an area, or simply chooses to emphasize one area over another. The confusion over what type of sign language was used is a case in point. The question of the appropriateness of the sign order criterion is another example. Indeed, the Clever Hans Conference itself seemed to be based, in part, on the assumption that some investigators in the field were ignorant of certain facts relating to animal behavior, and that, after being apprised of the secrets and insights of professional animal tamers and prestidigitators, they would be in a better position to dismiss the animals' performance as semiotic illusion.

Another example of how individuals, because of bias or limited expertise in an area, are focussing on different parts of the elephant is evident in the ethological view of ape language research. Typically, the concern has been with the relevance of linguistic tasks to apes' ethograms, or the apes' natural behavioral repertoire. In two papers given at the Clever Hans Conference, Hediger (1981) and Bouissac (1981) discussed, at some length, some entertaining examples of how animal trainers found out the hard way that it is difficult, if not impossible, to train an animal to do a trick that is not part of its ethogram, and conversely, that, when a trainer appears to have taught an animal a trick, he has probably just managed to elicit a behavior that the animal would have naturally performed in a given set of circumstances. For example, as astute circus performer will capitalize on the fact that young tigers and adult tigresses naturally roll over as a sign of submissiveness, though adult male tigers rarely do so. Though fascinating, these insights are disappointing in that the notion of an ethogram was not applied in a substantive analysis of the apes' putative linguistic behavior. In fact, Bouissac made no attempt to discuss the animal language literature other than his mention that Karl Pribram's finger was bitten by Washoe. Such contributions are highly idiosyncratic and of limited value in determining whether apes have language. These papers and the one given by the Amazing Randi (1981), the magician, fall short of being the definitive exposé of animal language research anticipated by the Sebeoks in the introduction to *Speaking of apes* (Seabeok & Sebeok, 1980).

At the top of the phylogenetic scale, humans are, without argument, linguistic creatures. One fairly well-documented case of a deaf child taught gestural communication offers some uncanny analogies to recent work with animals, the case of Helen Keller (Keller, 1954, 1955; Lash, 1980). Like the result of the ape studies, there were many perspectives on Helen Keller's linguistic accomplishments.

At the age of 12, Helen Keller was accused of plagiarism and suffered a Clever Hans crisis of her own. The matter was never really resolved, but according to Keller's own version of the incident, she recalled and unconsciously plagiarized a short story her teacher, Anne Sullivan, had told her years before.

By this time, Helen was an international celebrity. After her story, "The frost king," was published in the newspaper as evidence of her miraculous abilities, someone discovered the plagiarism and published the original story alongside Helen's. Needless to say, it was a terrible scandal that the story was not a genuine, spontaneous act of creativity but a rehash of a story fed to her by her teacher (it is still a point of contention whether Sullivan was aware of the plagiarism).

Even before the incident, in addition to those who were awe-struck by Helen's abilities, there were skeptics who believed Helen to be some sort of automaton who, under Sullivan's control, mechanically performed her tricks without any real comprehension of what she was doing. Some of Sullivan's worst critics were her peers, teachers of the deaf who, based on their own experience, claimed that Sullivan's accomplishments were impossible.

When the scandal broke, Helen, who later graduated cum laude from Radcliffe and who wrote several books, was attacked as a fraud, as was her teacher. Since the story was considered by many to be a hoax, doubts about her other documented progress were raised and the two women were subjected to considerable public ridicule. This incident only served to confirm suspicions that Helen was a fraud or an automaton. However, there were those who supported Helen through the crisis and dismissed the incident as an unfortunate and embarrassing exaggeration of their real abilities. So, at the same point in time, Helen Keller was considered a genius, a fraud, and a robot.

We can go back and substitute Washoe's name for Helen's, the Gardners' for Sullivan's, and let Terrace be the critic. Most of the passage would still make sense. Is it only coincidence?

Alas, Washoe will never make it to Radcliffe, while Helen Keller did eventually dispell most—though not all—doubts about her linguistic abilities. This is not to say that Washoe will some day be vindicated; nor should it be taken as proof of the futility of teaching animals to communicate. The intention is merely to describe the similarities between a child, whose linguistic ability is, in retrospect, virtually unimpeachable, and an ape who is still the focus of a heated debate. Each is an example of how a single phenomenon can be interpreted in very different ways.

APE COMMUNICATION AS A SCIENCE

The disparate perspectives and the consequent communication problems among scholars in the area of animal language are, in large measure, a reflection of a more general issue that should be raised, namely the maturity of the science. How far has the study of animal language progressed? How do we identify progress? The major concern here is not with the animals' performance, but with the developmental nature of the field itself.

In evaluating the social sciences in general, Kuhn (1970), whose graduate training was in physics, used the term "proto-science", i.e., fields which he claims can generate testable hypotheses but are more akin to philosophy and the arts than to the established sciences; as a consequence, they suffer "incessant criticism and continued striving for a fresh start . . . and will not result in clear-cut progress any more than in philosophy or the arts" (p. 244). Furthermore, he offers no helpful advice to accelerate the maturation process from a proto-science to a science: ". . . maturity comes most surely to those who know how to wait" (p. 245).

As previously discussed, Sigmund Koch's (1975) view is no more encouraging. He seems to recognize sub-areas of psychology as true sciences if they sound like the natural sciences, e.g., biological psychology, physiological psychology, and he relegates cognitive psychology to the humanities: the use of the word "science" to refer to such areas is a "deadly form of role-playing" beset with "incredible expectations" (p. 494).

Highly debatable when applied to cognitive psychology as a whole, the above views are, in a limited sense, descriptive of the animal language field. Linguistics is subsumed under the humanities. It is, however, the experimental investigation of linguistic functions which characterizes animal language research as a science. And, currently, it is the incessant criticism and the lack of clear progress which make it a proto-science.

Adducing methodological problems and a lack of universally accepted evidence of linguistic abilities among apes, in spite of approximately 15 years of intensive research, the revisionists have already rung the death knell for research on ape language. Methodological flaws are a legitimate concern in this area of research, as they are in any other; it should go without saying that sound design and data analyses are minimal requirements of good research.

But is it really the case that "the data are in"—particularly if the studies are as flawed as critics claim? The revisionists' tacit deadline of 10 or 15 years to resolve the issue of linguistic capacity in animals seems arbitrary in light of the disordered state of the literature. What is lacking in animal language research is a sense of coherence. As previously discussed, the field is currently devoid of agreement about what apes have accomplished linguistically or what would be considered an accomplishment; there is no consensus concerning the appropriateness of the techniques that are classified as linguistic (sign language, computer teletype, etc.). The methods and goals are different, the analyses varied, and the definitions of language open to interpretation. Replete with methodological weaknesses, dogmatism and a sprinkling of ad hominem attacks, the literature on animal language confuses more than it enlightens.

As a mature science, we should be able to predict where the field is going. At the very least, we should be able to discern where it has been. As Wade (1981) states, mature science is characterized by an important dimension, i.e., an agreement about what has been accomplished in a field and what are considered appropriate research goals. Using this criterion, research on animal communication is still in an early stage of development. Methodological rigor practiced in the absence of this dimension would still be immature science.

IS THERE A FUTURE FOR APE LANGUAGE RESEARCH?

If, in spite of its chronological age, the animal language field is developmentally young, it would seem premature to decide that the question of linguistic capacity in apes has already been resolved (and unfortunate if research funds were to dry up). The methodological problems and the contradictory nature of the literature, which are seen by some as evidence of the futility of the research, may also be seen as the inevitable growing pains of a new scientific field.

There are indications that the field has made some progress insofar as there is agreement on one issue. In terms of approach, most now concede that it is not fruitful to pursue the question of whether animals really have *human language*. Instead, researchers seem concerned with examining animals' linguistic or cognitive abilities, such as they are. These investigations may, for example, take a developmental approach, or they may be justified for the applications they would have for teaching retarded humans. In any case, the research is increasingly an investigation of animal cognition and less an attempt to impose human language on another species.

This evolution of approach is partly due to the problems encountered in trying to define language, and partly due to a change in the expectations that some had for the field. The original hope was that apes would someday be able to converse freely with humans, about everything that humans normally discuss. Accordingly, the researchers' hypotheses were rather straightforward: either apes had human language, or they did not. In retrospect, the expectations seem naive, and the hypotheses simplistic. But, while these realizations have forced some, like Terrace, to abandon the field, they have also given way to a new perspective on the area, one which emphasizes the importance of animals' inherent cognitive abilities, as well as the relationship of human and animal.

We may encourage progress in the field by making a few changes. First, for reasons that should be apparent by now, this area has been plagued by more viciousness than most areas of current psychological research. For example, the Clever Hans Conference, sponsored by the New York Academy of Sciences, was described as a "witch hunt" (Rumbaugh, 1981). The Sebeoks's (1980) reference to Francine Patterson and Koko as beauty and the beast is another not-so-isolated example of the emotional undercurrent in scholarly exchanges. While it is impossible to mandate tolerance and professional courtesy, it is hoped that the research atmosphere in the future will be less emotionally charged. To this end, it is suggested that critics take advantage of invitations to research laboratories, in order to observe the animals first hand and to exchange views with researchers in a nonconfrontational manner.

More importantly, it is suggested that those involved in the field—researchers, critics, and supporters—make a more concerted effort to familarize themselves with the methods, goals, assumptions, and "language" of the various disciplines involved in animal communication. The diversity of disciplines which is currently responsible for so many communication problems has the potential to facilitate and enrich this area of research which is, perhaps only accidentally, anchored in psychology.

REFERENCES

Bouissac, P. (1981). Behavior in context: In what sense is a circus animal performing? In T. Sebeok & R. Rosenthal (Eds.), *The Clever Hans phenomenon: Communication with horses, whales, apes and people. Annals of the New York Academy of Sciences, 364,* 18–25.

Brown, R. (1973). *A first language:* Cambridge, MA: Harvard University Press.

Gardner, R. & Gardner, B. (1980). Comparative psychology and language acquisition. In T. Sebeok, & J. Sebeok (Eds.), *Speaking of Apes,* (pp. 287–330). New York: Plenum Press.

Hediger, H. (1981). The Clever Hans phenomenon from an animal psychologist's point of view. In T. Sebeok & R. Rosenthal (Eds.), *The Clever Hans phenomenon: Communication with horses, whales, apes and people. Annals of the New York Academy of Sciences, 364,* 1–17.

Hockett, C. (1963). The problem of universals in language. In J. Greenberg (Ed.), *Universals of language.* Cambridge, MA: M.I.T. Press.

Keller, H. (1954). *The story of my life.* Garden City, NY: Doubleday & Co.

Keller, H. (1955). *Teacher: Anne Sullivan Macy.* Garden City, NY: Doubleday & Co.

Koch, S. (1975). Language communities, search cells, and the psychological studies. *Nebraska Symposium on Motivation, 23,* 477–559.

Kuhn, T. (1962). *The structure of scientific revolutions.* Chicago: University of Chicago Press.

Kuhn, T. (1970). Reflections on my critics. In I. Lakatos, & A. Musgrave (Eds.), *Criticism and the growth of knowledge,* (pp. 231–278). London: Cambridge University Press.

Kuhn, T. (1977). *The essential tension.* Chicago: University of Chicago Press.

Lash, L. (1980). *Helen and teacher: The story of Helen Keller and Anne Sullivan Macy.* New York: Delacorte Press.

Nessel, J. (1982). Psychology today: The state of the science. *Psychology Today, 16,* 41–59.

Patterson, F. & Linden, E. (1981). *The education of Koko.* New York: Holt, Rhinehart, & Winston.

Randi, J. (1981). Semiotics: A view from behind the footlights. In T. Sebeok, & R. Rosenthal (Eds.), *The Clever Hans phenomenon: Communication with horses, whales, apes and people. Annals of the New York Academy of Sciences, 364,* 291–296.

Rumbaugh, D. (1981). Who feeds Clever Hans? In T. Sebeok, & R. Rosenthal (Eds.), *The Clever Hans phenomenon: Communication with horses, whales, apes and people. Annals of the New York Academy of Sciences, 364,* 26–34.

Sebeok, T., & Rosenthal, R. (Eds.). (1981). *The Clever Hans phenomenon: Communication with horses, whales, apes and people. Annals of the New York Academy of Sciences, 364.*

Sebeok, J., & Sebeok, T. (1980). Introduction: Questioning apes. In T. Sebeok, & J. Sebeok (Eds.), *Speaking of apes,* (pp. 1–59). New York: Plenum Press.

Seidenberg, M. & Pettito, L. (1981). Ape signing: Problems of method and interpretation. In T. Sebeok, & R. Rosenthal (Eds.), *The Clever Hans phenomenon: Communication with horses, whales, apes and people. Annals of the New York Academy of Sciences. 364,* 115–129.

Terrace, H. (1979). *Nim: A chimpanzee who learned sign language.* New York: Washington Square Press.

Terrace, H. (1981). A report to an Academy. In T. Sebeok, & R. Rosenthal (Eds.), *The Clever Hans phenomenon: Communication with horses, whales, apes and people. Annals of the New York Academy of Sciences, 364,* 94–114.

Terrace, H., Pettito, L., Sanders, R. & Bever, T. (1979). Can an ape create a sentence? *Science, 206*(4421), 891–906.

Wade, N. (1982). Smart apes, or dumb? *New York Times,* April 30, p. A 30.

Woodward, J. (1980). Some sociolinguistic aspects of French and American sign languages. In H. Lane, & F. Grosjean (Eds.), *Recent perspectives on American sign language.* Hillsdale, NJ: Erlbaum.

Chapter 14

Cross-Linguistic Perspective on Cognitive Development*

Richard M. Weist

State University of New York College at Fredonia

LANGUAGE AND THOUGHT

Some alternative hypotheses

Language acquisition is one of the few domains of cognitive psychology in which at least some investigators have brought cross-cultural perspective to bear in their quest to explain developmental processes (cf. Dasen, 1977). A decade ago, for example, Roger Brown (1973) put his analysis of the first stages of language acquisition in the following diverse linguistic perspective: (a) Indo-European; e.g., Swedish (Germanic family) versus Russian (Slavic family), and (b) Outside Indo-European; e.g., Finnish (Uralic family) versus Samoan (Austro-Tai family). More recently, Martin Braine (1976) included an equally far reaching perspective in his study of the early word patterns in child language. In spite of this tradition of scholarship, psycholinguists have not escaped the affliction of viewing child language through English-tinted glasses. Only recently have we had a broadly based, penetrating cross-linguistic analysis of child language (Slobin, in press a).

As this is a chapter in a book which deals with the broad scope of cognitive psychology, we might start by asking: Why should a cognitive psychologist who is working in areas such as memory processes, problem solving, or pattern recognition be interested in the insights gained from cross-linguistic analysis? At one level, the answer is obvious. Since our capacity to process linguistic information is one of the most pervasive areas of the overall perceptual–conceptual information processing capabilities of the species, any adequate explanation of the mental processes which are involved in this domain will have relevance to other problems. But, more to the point, why should the cognitive psychologist be concerned with such matters as the way in which Turkish children code the

---

* This project was supported by NSF Grant No. BNS 8121133, and a SUNY Fredonia small grant program. My thanks to Katarzyna Witkowska-Stadnik for her helpful comments on the manuscript.

concepts of "agent" and "patient," or the way in which Polish children talk about time? More generally, why should the cognitive psychologist be concerned with linguistic relativity in the acquisition process?

Let us assume for the sake of argument that we can take the set of mental operations and partition them into linguistic and nonlinguistic subsets. There are at least two reasons why we might be concerned about the linguistic subset. First of all, the two subsets may interact, with one set of mental operations influencing (or determining) the form of the other. Radically different and opposite hypotheses have been proposed on this issue, ranging from the Sapir-Whorf hypothesis of linguistic determinism to the "neo-Piagetian" hypothesis of cognitive determinism. These hypothesis and their implications are as follows: (a) Linguistic determinism—language structure shapes cognitive structure. Language structure varies from language to language. Hence, children learning different languages will develop different thought processes (cf. Whorf, 1956; Sapir, 1968). (b) Cognitive determinism—cognitive structure shapes language structure. Cognitive structures change as children develop. Hence, as thought processes develop, the nature of child language will change (cf. Cromer, 1974; Sinclair-de-Zwart, 1973). Obviously, if the linguistic determinism hypothesis was correct, the cognitive psychologist would have to be deeply concerned with linguistic relativity. However, this hypothesis is not very influential. While some contemporary psycholinguists ascribe to the strong view of *cognitive* determinism, none argue for linguistic determinism, and most take an interactionist position (see reviews by Bowerman, 1976; Cromer, 1974). Varying degrees of linguistic influence have been claimed ranging from a small amount to a moderate amount, e.g., see Cromer's position cited below.

There is a second way of looking at the potential relevance of linguistic relativity. Instead of looking at linguistic and nonlinguistic mental operations as separate subsets which may or may not interact, the human's capacity to process linguistic information (and thereby construct the schemata which structure communication) may be viewed as an integrated subset of a more general set of mental operations. When we learn about the form of the mental operations in the subset, we have an opportunity to learn something about the superset. We know that the principles of language processing are integrated at the conceptual level (see Newport, 1982), and they may reflect general cognitive universals. Bever (1970) proposed, for example, that "the universality of the noun/verb distinction in language might be explained as the linguistic reflection of the general cognitive distinction between objects and relations between objects" (p. 351). In order to determine what is universal about language processing, a cross-linguistic analysis is necessary (see Comrie, 1981a, chap. 1). Hence, cognitive psychologists may be interested in this chapter because language processing may have a moderate influence on other perceptual–conceptual processes and/or because language processing is highly integrated into overall perceptual–conceptual processes.

I will start my discussion of child language and conceptual development where Cromer (1974) left off 10 years ago. Cromer ended his paper with the following "weak" version of the cognitive determinism hypothesis: "We are able to understand and productively to use particular linguistic structures only when our cognitive abilities enable us to do so. Our cognitive abilities at different stages of development make certain meanings available for expression. But, in addition, we must also possess certain specifically linguistic capabilities in order to come to express these meanings in language" (p. 246). The linguistic capabilities which Cromer had in mind were the operating principles proposed by Slobin (1973). According to Slobin (most recently, in press b), operating principles are the initial procedures or strategies which children use to construct a basic grammar. These strategies guide the perception, storage, analysis, and organization of stored information. While cognitive development may "make certain meanings available," the relationship between the child's information processing strategies and the structure of the target language controls the ultimate utilization and expression of available meanings in the child's language. The availability of a concept is a relative matter, and the early utilization of a concept in a child's language may increase its availability (see Brown, 1956), and may influence the role of the concept in the reorganization of language structures (see Bowerman, 1982). If a language codes some concept in a manner which is compatible with the child's information processing strategies, the concept will be transparent. If there is a mismatch between linguistic codes and processing strategies, the concept will be opaque. As a consequence of variations in the degree of opacity, conceptual breakthroughs may be left undetected in one culture because the children are unable to express key relationships, yet, in a different linguistic environment, transparent coding may lead to early expression.

While Slobin (1973, 1982, in press b) has provided numerous examples of this relationship between the form of linguistic coding and the precocity of acquisition, his comparison of Turkish and Serbo-Croatian is the most relevant to my discussion later. Slobin (1982) argued that the case system is acquired more rapidly in Turkish than in Serbo-Croatian, because in Turkish (among other reasons) there is a one-to-one relationship between the semantic concepts underlying the case distinctions and the morphemes which express these distinctions (see Table 1 in the next section for a contrast between agglutinating and fusional languages). In contrast to the acquisition of case systems, the capacity to formulate relative clause constructions takes Serbo-Croatian speaking children less time to acquire than Turkish speaking children, because Serbo-Croatian (unlike Turkish) provides cues which clearly segment the clause structure and holds constant the form of nouns and verbs in the subordinate and superordinate clauses. Slobin (1982, p. 166) concluded with the speculation that "languages may not differ considerably, overall, in ease of acquisition. The Turkish advantage in morphology is balanced by a disadvantage in syntax. On the other hand, the ease with which Yugoslav 2-year-olds produce relative clauses suggests that their disadvantage in morphology is compensated for by an advantage in syntax.''

In this paper, I will try to show how a wide ranging cross-linguistic perspective improves our understanding of two problems: (a) the level of complexity in sentence processing, and (b) the evolution of the capacity to conceptualize temporal relationships. In my discussion of sentence processing, I intend to show that sentence processing during early patterned speech involves a relatively complex morphological analysis and a syntactic-semantic function mapping.[1] I will argue that this explanation of sentence processing has important implications for the more general picture of perceptual-conceptual processes. In the second part of the paper, I will trace the evolution of increasingly complex configurations of time concepts, and the implications that these changes in child language have for the overall course of conceptual growth.

Language typology

In order to discuss cross-linguistic perspective, a few remarks about language typology are needed. The concepts "agent," "patient," and "subject" are essential for this discussion. Agent and patient are semantic functions. Agent is the active element which initiates action. The agent function is inherently potent, and may also have the property of living. The patient is the passive element which is affected by the action in some way, such as changing states or location (cf. Nilsen, 1972; Weist, 1982). Thus, in the sentence, *The mailman jumped,* the *mailman* is the agent, and in the sentence, *The snowman melted,* the *snowman* is the patient. In the transitive context, the action is transferred from agent to patient, e.g., *I cracked the dish.* Subject is a syntactic function with properties such as priority of position (i.e., subject precedes object), case identification, agreement with the verb, etc. (see Keenan, 1976).

The dimensions analytic–synthetic and agglutinating–fusional can be used to classify morphological language types and hence to show us the kinds of coding patterns with which children have to deal (see Comrie, 1981a; Lyons, 1968). In the prototypical analytic language (also called isolating), there is a one-to-one correspondence between morphemes and words, whereas, at the other end of the continuum, highly synthetic languages have a many-to-one relationship. At the synthetic extreme (in polysynthetic languages), the entire sentence may consist of one word made up of many morphemes. Sentence 1 provides an example from the highly analytic language of Vietnamese, and sentence 2 shows the morphological pattern of the highly synthetic language of Eskimo (Siberian-Yupik). The examples were taken from Comrie (1981a, pp. 40, 42):

---

[1] To appreciate the level of complexity that I am proposing, it might be helpful to look at MacWhinney's (1982) review of six information processing strategies which ranged in complexity from "rote" to "class bound patterns" (see also Maratsos & Chalkley, 1980). My argument here is that sentence processing strategies go beyond the scope of the most complex strategies reviewed by MacWhinney.

1. Khi tôi dên nhà ban tôi, chúng tôi bắt dâu làm bài. When I come house friend I
   PLURAL I begin do lesson 'when I came to my friend's house, we began to do
   lessons.'

2. angya   —ghlla   —ng   —yug   —tuq
   boat —AUGMENTATIVE—ACQUIRE—DESIDERATIVE—3 SINGULAR
   'He wants to acquire a big boat.'

In the ideal isolating language, the ratio of the number of morphemes to the
number of words would be 1.00. The ratio is 3.72 for the highly synthetic
language of Eskimo, and it is 1.68 for the relatively analytic language of English
(Lyons, 1968, p. 188). As the target language moves from analytic to synthetic,
there is more pressure on the language learner to break down word segments into
their meaningful morpheme components.

The agglutinating–fusional dimension identifies the way in which grammatical categories such as case, gender, number, etc. are coded in the morphology. For the prototypical agglutinating language, there is a one-to-one mapping of grammatical categories onto their morphological surface realizations. In
fusional languages, a single surface realization will express a combination (or a
fusion) of grammatical categories. To the extent to which one-to-one mappings
are easier for children to learn, the agglutinating system will facilitate the identification of grammatical categories. Table 1 contains examples of the agglutinating morphology of Turkish and the fusional morphology of Polish (a Slavic

Table 1. Agglutinating Versus Fusional Morphology

Agglutinating—Turkish[a]			
Number	Possessive	Case	
-ø Singular	-im 1st person	-i accusative	-de locative
-ler Plural	-in 2nd person	-e dative	-den ablative
		-le instrumental	

Fusional—Polish[b]					
	Accusative Case			Genitive Case		
	Masculine	Feminine	Neuter	Masculine	Feminine	Neuter
Singular	-a/-ø	-ę	-o/-e	-a	-y/-i	-a
	Virile	Nonvirile		Virile	Nonvirile	
Plural	-ów	-y/-i		-ów	-ø	

[a]A consideration of vowel harmony has been omitted (see Underhill, 1976, p. 23).
[b]This is a simplified version of 2 of the 7 cases (cf. Schenker, 1973, p. 386).

langauge similar to Serbo-Croatian). Turkish nouns are not inflected for gender, and the concepts of number and case (as well as possession) are specified independently by distinct morphemes. Hence, the form of the accusative case morpheme remains the same regardless for example of number, e.g., *ev-ø-i* house-SINGULAR-ACCUSATIVE 'house' versus *ev-ler-i* house-PLURAL-ACCUSATIVE 'houses'. In Polish, however, the concepts of gender, number, and case are fused together, producing a different form of the morpheme depending on the combination, e.g., *ps-a* dog—MASCULINE & SINGULAR & ACCUSATIVE 'dog' versus *ps-y* dog—MASCULINE & PLURAL & ACCUSATIVE 'dogs'.

Another source of language variation which will be important for this discussion is the order of syntactic functions in the basic (or canonical) sentence pattern. There is a universal trend for the subject function to precede the object function, which is only violated by about 1% of the extant languages. The most frequent patterns are SOV, SVO, and VSO (see Greenberg, 1966). It is for this reason that we can say that priority is a subjecthood property. Some languages such as English rely heavily on word order to express syntactic functions, while other languages use the inflectional morphology. Hence, in one language the position of a word provides the most information for the identification of syntactic functions, while in another language the form of a word is most informative. The more clearly synthetic the language, the greater the dependence on the form of words and the less the importance of word order for coding syntactic functions.

Yet another important source of language variation is derived from a relationship between transitivity and case marking. The highly transitive configuration contains a verb, an agent, and a patient, e.g., *The child spilled the milk* (see Hopper & Thompson, 1980). The intrasitive configuration contains a subject and a verb where the subject may be an agent, e.g., *John is running*, or a patient, e.g., *John is dying*. The concept of transitivity is integrated into the case marking system of languages. The two systems which are found most frequently are nominative (NOM)–accusative (ACC) and ergative (ERG)–absolutive (ABS). In the nominative–accusative system, the case of the agent in the transitive pattern is the same as case of the subject of the intransitive pattern, e.g., *He pushed him* versus *He sang*. In the ergative–absolutive system, the case of the patient in the transitive pattern is the same as the case of the subject of the intransitive pattern, e.g., if English was an ergative language, then it would have the pattern, *He pushed him* versus *Him sang* (see Comrie, 1981a, for ergative languauge examples). Sentences 3 and 4 demonstrate the ergative case marking pattern of the Polynesian language of Tongan (these examples were taken from Anderson, 1976, p. 384).

3.   na'e lea 'a elalavou
     past speak ABS young-man
     'The young man spoke'.

4. na'e tamate'i 'a kolaiate   'e tevita
    past Kill   ABS Goliath ERG David
    'David killed Goliath'.

Obviously, children will have to learn to discriminate transitive and intransitive sentence patterns in order to retrieve and express agent and patient relationships in a manner which corresponds either to their nominative–accusative or to their ergative–absolutive system of case marking.

SENTENCE PROCESSING AND PERCEPTUAL-CONCEPTUAL COMPLEXITY

Linear conceptual structure

Given this background, we can rephrase the first problem concerning the level of complexity in sentence processing as: how do children comprehend and produce agent and patient functions? In an early phase of child language (around 1½ years), children appear to be able to understand and express these semantic functions (or their equivalents). As Brown, Cazden, and Bellugi (1969, p. 118) observed, the child ". . . seems to express the relations he means to express from the start. At any rate there are few detectable errors in all the records." One simple explanation is that children have (by nature or nurture) a conceptual structure in which semantic functions are organized in a linear manner. Comprehension and production involve direct one-to-one mappings of the units in the semantic structure onto positions in the utterance. According to Bruner (1975, p. 17), for example, ". . . a concept of agent-action-object-recipient at the prelinguistic level aids in grasping the meaning of *appropriately ordered* utterances" (stress mine), and, in a similar vein, Osgood and Tanz (1977, p. 537) propose that "the most basic simple cognition would be Actor/Instrument—Action—Recipient/Object for action relations and Figure—State—Ground for stative relations. Even the not-so-astute reader will recognize these simple cognitions as characterizing SVO languages."

At first, this proposal appears to be contradicted by the basic facts of language typology, such as variations in canonical word order, i.e., SVO, VSO, SOV, etc. However, the argument was (still is) that child language differs from adult language. Osgood and Tanz (1977, p. 540) conjectured that ". . . in the process of language development in children there is initially a relatively fixed SVO ordering in 'sentence' productions." Parenthetically, it is important to note that the syntactic functions subject (S) and direct object (O) are likely to correspond to the semantic functions agent and patient in the canonical sentence form. To complete the argument about child language, it was proposed that the inflectional morphology of highly synthetic languages is either absent or nonfunctional in the child's version. Hence, children must use word order as opposed to case affixes to express basic relationships. Word order would then mediate the acquisition of the inflectional system; for example, in his discussion, "Fodor proposed that case rules were acquired first by assigning positions to parts of speech and then by marking inflections on the basis of position" (Smith & Miller, 1966, p. 151). More recently, Braine (1976) has put the ultimate emphasis on the role of position information, claiming that "All early learning can then be interpreted as a learning of positional patterns" (p. 66).

Perspective from synthetic languages

Cross-linguistic analysis shows that the idea that comprehension and production in child languages can be explained by the one-to-one mapping of an agent–action–patient concept onto a position 1–position 2–position 3 sentence pattern is *false*. The best evidence to the contrary comes from two synthetic languages of which one is an agglutinating language, i.e., Turkish, and the other is a fusional language, i.e., Polish (see Table 1). In their overview of the acquisition of Turkish, Aksu and Slobin (in press) point out that ". . . the entire set of noun inflections and much of the verbal paradigm is mastered by 24 months or earlier. Both noun and verb inflections are present in the one-word stage, and there is some evidence for productive use as young as 15 months," and later, "word order is used flexibly for pragmatic function, as in the adult language." In comprehension tests where children ranging in age from 2.0 to 4.4 were asked to act out the meaning of transitive sentence patterns with toys, e.g., *The squirrel scratches the dog,* the youngest children showed that they could accurately use the case system (i.e., inflectional information) to recover the agent and patient relationships. While the children produced their best performance when presented the canonical SOV pattern for Turkish, alternative patterns, e.g., SVO or VOS, did not create much interference (see Slobin, 1982; Slobin & Bever, 1980). The SVO arrangement was clearly *not* the most "natural" order to process. Hence, in child Turkish, inflectional information is more important than word order, and there is no evidence that position information mediates the acquisition of inflectional morphology.

Polish is a good language to contrast with Turkish because it is also relatively synthetic but primarily fusional as opposed to agglutinating. To give some idea what this typological contrast means to the child, let us consider one component of the declension systems in these languages. Reviewing what was said earlier in reference to Table 1, Turkish has a unique suffix which identifies the accusative case, and this provides the child with unambiguous access to the patient function. In Polish, the concepts of gender, case, and number are combined to produce a single suffix (not to mention other complications). Hence, the actual surface realization which identifies a specific case, such as the accusative case, will vary depending on the components of the conceptual mix, e.g., feminine, accusative, and singular. In spite of the apparent opacity of this inflectional system, Polish children learn to express and retrieve agent–patient relations at a relatively precocious age. At least for the singular, it is safe to say that the seven cases within the Polish system emerge between about 1.6 and 2.0 (see Smoczyńska, in press), which gives us clear evidence that case distinctions such as nominative and accusative are productive. For Zarębina's (1965) Hanna, the last two cases to be utilized were dative at 1.8 and locative at 1.10, and for Bartosz (a child in my Poznań project) the last two cases were instrumental at 1.8 and dative at 1.9. Smoczyńska (in press) pointed out that, while many components of the case system "are used correctly from the very first moment of emergence of a given category," some properties of the fusional system (plus certain irregularities) produce predictable errors.

Case is only one of a set of subjecthood properties which can play an important role in the retrieval of semantic functions. In Polish, verbs are inflected for aspect, tense, gender, mood, person, and number. In the indicative mood at least, agreement in person and number is always found, and gender agreement is specified in the past and future tense. The morphology in the verb system is acquired equally as rapidly, and with the same precision, as in the noun system. Hence, the typical child can use agreement as well as case to establish basic relationships prior to the age of 2. Weist (1983) has shown that children who are 2½ years old can use priority of position as well as case in comprehension, but that case is the dominant subjecthood property when case and priority are in conflict (cf. Slobin & Bever, 1980, on Serbo-Croatian).

Szwedek (1976) has proposed that word order in Polish has a discourse function, with the basic positional pattern being given–new. Katarzyna Witkowska-Stadnik and I are working on this problem now. We are finding that children use all possible arrangements of given–new and subject–object with equally variable stress patterns. At the present moment, we will have to agree with Smoczyńska (in press) that "as for the pragmatic use of word order by Polish children, it needs further detailed study." One thing is clear. The typical child learning Polish can express and interpret agent–patient relationships by processing the inflectional morphology without reference to word order. We can not find any evidence to support Radulović's (1975) claim about Serbo-Croatian (also a Slavic language), that "Coordination of SVO word order is a prerequisite to the recognition of structural relationships which may be varied in productive language by the use of inflections" (p. 117).

The claims made by Radulović (1975) about the acquisition of Serbo-Croatian deserve a second look since they have tended to perpetuate a distorted view of the relationship between word order and affix processing in child language. According to Radulović, "a young child readily ignores inflectional morphemes" (p. 117), and exhibits a "tendency to first perceive word stems or bare forms as basic psychological units" (p. 144). Furthermore, the young child expresses the basic relations "subject/object" by assigning the bare word stems which carry these syntactic functions "to *slots* in a fixed word order" (p. 98; emphasis mine). While there is a period (about 1.0 to 1.6) in which children learning Slavic languages use frozen forms such as the third singular present imperfective form of verbs, or the feminine nominative singular form of nouns, there is never a period during which bare stems appear. When Radulović began to observe Ana at 1.8 and Damir at 2.0, the distinct inflectional patterns of nouns, verbs, and adjectives were clearly attested in the corpora. In the first observational period from 1.8 to 1.10, Ana used six of the seven cases correctly. In the verb system, she used indicative and imperative mood, imperfective and perfective aspect, and past, present, and future tenses. While Damir used only three of seven cases during the initial 2.0 to 2.2 period, he used a similar variety of verb forms. Obviously, these children were not ignoring the inflectional morphology. Damir (but not Ana) produced relatively frequent and persistent errors by using the nominative form of nouns as opposed to the correct accusative, genitive, or locative forms. This kind of behavior would be very unusual for a normal child learning Polish (see Smoczyńska, in press), and it is probably rare in other Slavic languages.

Furthermore, Ana and Damir did not use an inflexible word order which could be described as having slots for nouns with the syntactic functions subject and object. During the 2.0 to 2.2 period, when utterances combining the three components subject, object, and verb were still infrequent, Damir produced the following two-component arrangements: SV - 22%, VS - 34%, VO - 26%, and OV - 11% (cf. the Polish child, Bartosz, at 1.7 to 1.8: SV - 20%, VS - 19%, VO - 16%, and OV - 45%). When both subject and object functions were expressed, Ana and Damir produced primarily SVO arrangements and secondarily VSO and SOV.[2] Instead of rigid slots, Radulović found that children almost always express the subject prior to the object. Subject function priority in child Serbo-Croatian is not all that surprising, in light of the fact that Radulović also showed that adults speaking to children seldom reverse the subject–object order.

Verb concepts as mediators in syntactic-semantic function mapping

The view of sentence processing that I would like to develop here involves three components. I assume that semantic functions such as agent and patient are the basic relations of the semantic component of child language. Since a great deal has been written to support this claim (see Braine & Hardy, 1982; Golinkoff, 1981), I will not review arguments here. The second part of my argument is that children can and do process the subjecthood properties case, agreement, priority, and animacy. This claim can be supported by comprehension research

---

[2] In fact, Radulović (1975) classified a variety of oblique objects as object, including the following: stative and directional locatives, indirect objects, instrumentals, and objects of prepositions taking varied cases. Even if we imagined some abstract slot for the second noun in the sequences which Radulović described as S-O, this slot could not be viewed as mediating the acquisition of inflectional morphology.

in a diverse set of languages. Using a test which requires children to act out reversible transitive sentences with toys, the following properties of the syntactic function of subject were utilized in comprehension: (a) Case (e.g., Slobin, 1982, with Turkish & Serbo-Croatian; Weist, 1983, with Polish), (b) Agreement (e.g., Frankel, Amir, Frenkel, & Arbel, 1980, with Hebrew), (c) Subject–Object positional priority (e.g., deVilliers & deVilliers, 1973, with English; Segalowitz & Galang, 1978, with Tagalog), and (d) Animacy (e.g., Bates, MacWhinney, Caselli, Devescovi, Natale, & Venza, 1983, with Italian and English; Chapman & Kohn, 1978, with English). Some research shows that a combination of these properties is very important, e.g., case and positional priority (Hakuta, 1982, with Japanese).

The third component of the argument is that the process of mapping syntactic onto semantic functions (or vice versa) is mediated by the child's understanding of verb concepts. My research has shown that, at the earliest age tested, i.e., 2.0, children learning English show a clear understanding of the distinction between verbs which have agents as inherent functions (action verbs) versus verbs which have inherent patient functions (process verbs) (Weist, 1982). The capacity to process subjecthood properties may be a necessary condition for sentence processing, but it is not a sufficient condition. In a highly transitive sentence, the noun with the subject function is likely to be the agent. In the sentence, *The knight slew the dragon,* there is little doubt that the knight initiated the action and that the transfer of action was from knight to dragon. However, in the intransitive sentences *We are jumping* versus *He is dying,* the component which is unmistakably the subject (i.e., having the properties of nominative case, preverbal position, agreement in number, and animacy) is an agent in the first sentence and a patient in the second. In the intransitive context, children do *not* use some simple rule like, If it is a subject, make it an agent. Children must know something about the inherent semantic functions of verbs like *jump* versus *die,* and in fact children as young as 2 years old begin to make the discrimination.

While a number of different investigators have been concerned with the development of predicate types (e.g., Antinucci & Miller, 1976, with Italian; Bloom, Lightbown, & Hood, 1975, with English; Stephany, 1981, with Greek; Weist, Wysocka, Witkowska-Stadnik, Buczowska, & Konieczna, in press, with Polish; Wells, 1974, with English), only Erbaugh (1982) has used a classification system which yields a direct comparison of action verbs and process verbs. Working with Mandarin, Erbaugh found that, during the period from 1.10 to 2.4, the most frequent type of verb was the type which occurs with both an agent and a patient function, e.g., *kāi* 'open' and *dài* 'carry'. Chafe (1970) called these "action-process" verbs. Another relatively high frequency category was the simple action verbs, such as *kū* 'cry' and *fēi* 'fly'. During this same period, the relative proportion of process verbs, e.g., *pò* 'break' and *diào* 'fall', was quite low (only 4 to 6%).

While there is no parallel analysis in Polish, the contrast between action verbs and process verbs is evident in the early phase of predicate development, and process verbs are more visible than in some other languages, e.g., Marta (1.7) (*dziewczynka*) *skacze* '(girl) jumps/is jumping' versus *Kapie deszczyk* 'drips/is dripping rain' or *Kwiaty rosną* 'flowers grow.' At 1.8 and 1.9, Marta produced process verbs marked with *się*[3] such as *przewróciła się* '(Marta) got knocked down' and (*Woda*) *wylewa się* '(water) pours/is pouring out', and Marta even invented the collocation, *Wszystkie dzieci kwaszą się* 'all children become sour', where the verb *kwasić się* normally takes an inanimate patient. At 1.7, Bartosz produced action verbs such as *pacze* (=*płacze*) *Martusia* 'cries/is crying Marta', and process verbs such as (*zegarek*) *spadł* '(watch) fell' and *tu uderzyłem się* 'here (I) got hit.'

The next problem is to show how the concept of transitivity becomes integrated into the child's verb system. While cross-linguistic perspective forces a relatively eclectic analysis, it obviously does not guarantee a unique explanation, and, on this next point, my argument contrasts with Slobin's (1981, in press b). The difference is critical to my overall argument that the syntactic to semantic function mapping is mediated by the knowledge of verb concepts. Slobin (in press b) proposed that children "are not grammaticalizing the notion of actor in general, but are only grammatically marking manipulative activities," i.e., components of "manipulative activity scenes." Slobin's argument was based in part on a developmental pattern in the case marking of ergative languages. Slobin pointed out that children do not overextend the ergative case from the subject of a transitive sentence to the subject of an intransitive sentence even when the semantic function is an agent in both environments. In order to explain this finding, let us pretend that English is an ergative language. If English were ergative, here is the pattern we would find: *He + ERG hit him + ABS* and *Him + ABS ran,* but not *He + ERG ran.* Slobin argued that this failure to make overextension errors such as *He + ERG ran* means that grammatical marking is limited to prototypical scenes and is not being applied to the semantic functions agent and patient.

A parallel developmental pattern is found in the accusative language of Polish. Children learning Polish do not overextend the accusative case from the direct object of transitive sentences to the subject of intransitive sentences, even when the semantic function is a patient in both environments. Using a direct analogy to English, we find the patterns *He + NOM hit him + ACC* and *He +*

---

[3] The particle *się* has a number of functions in Polish including the specification of so called "inchoative" verbs (see Kubiński, 1982). Inchoative verbs represent a subset of process verbs which take a *się* deleting causative derivation (see Antinucci & Gebert, 1977). We are not attributing an understanding of this derivational relationship to children in the initial process verb stage, because there isn't sufficient evidence for contrasting verb pairs.

NOM died, but not *Him + ACC died.* This failure to overextend the accusative case could also be interpreted as evidence for Slobin's manipulative activity scenes. However, there is an alternative explanation for both of these failures to make overextension errors. In her analysis of a variety of clause types in Polish, Smoczyńska (1978) has shown that the first two clause types to become productive are transitive and intransitive at the following ages: Inka (1.6), Kasia (1.5), Jaś (1.9), Basia (1.8), and Tenia (1.8). It is possible that the distinction between transitive and intransitive in the child's verb system blocks the overextension of case marking in both nominative–accusative and ergative–absolutive languages.

Furthermore, Slobin's argument for restrictive scenes was also based on the fact that Gvozdev's son (cited by Slobin, 1981), who was learning the nominative–accusative language of Russian, limited his direct objects to recipients of direct physical action. However, we must be careful how far we generalize from a single informant. Many children learning Polish (another nominative–accusative and Slavic language) extend their initial uses of the accusative case to low transitive environments where direct physical action does not pertain. The following are examples of some high and low transitive sentences produced by two children in our Poznań project: Marta (1.7 and 1.8) *dzieck-o narysowa (narysuje) słoni-a* 'child-NOM (will) draw elephant-ACC' versus *Krasnoludk-i mają brod-ę* 'elves-NOM have beard + ACC', and Bartosz (1.8) *mieli kaw-ę* '(He) grinds/is grinding coffee + ACC' versus *baczymy (= zobaczymy) dzidziusi-a* '(We) (will) see the baby'. The same contrast between high and low transitivity can be found with Smoczyńska's (1978) informants Kasia, Inka, and Jaś, but not Basia and Tenia (as far as one can tell from her Tables 13d & 13c). Furthermore, both high and low transitive sentences are found at a similar phase in the development of Serbo-Croatian (Radulović, 1975). The only safe generalization which might be made at this point is that early transitive sentences are *more likely* to be high in transitivity. However, this generalization is quite consistent with the claim that children discriminate transitive from intransitive predicate types, and that the semantic functions agent and patient are utilized with both predicate types.

In conclusion, cross-linguistic perspective shows that children are not limited to the use of some simple mapping rules, such as "put semantic function X in some position Y" or "identify semantic function X with some affix Y." It becomes obvious that the first of these simple rules is inadequate when we contrast analytic with synthetic languages, and the inadequacy of the second simple rule appears when we contrast ergative with accusative languages. In order to explain how children *can* adapt to the variety of languages which they *do* adapt to, we need an explanation which combines an understanding of the child's knowledge of semantic functions, operating principles, and lexical concepts.

I have argued that, when sentence processing is analyzed in a cross-linguistic context, we gain a new appreciation for the overall complexity of the child's information processing capabilities. This view of sentence processing is consistent with Piaget's (1954, p. 293) observations of sensorimotor development. Piaget argued that, by the sixth stage, the child is capable of "reconstructing causes in the presence of effects alone" and "foreseeing and representing to himself" the future effects of some potential action. This knowledge of cause and effect may very well provide the conceptual substance upon which semantic functions and transitivity relations are built (see Sinclair-deZwart, 1973). In spite of this *consistency,* my sentence processing argument does not change our understanding of the child's capacity to construct reality.

TEMPORAL SYSTEMS AND THE CONCEPTUALIZATION OF TIME

In contrast to insights gained from a cross-linguistic evaluation of sentence processing, a cross-linguistic perspective on the evolution of temporal systems has a direct impact on estimates of the course of conceptual growth with regard to concepts such as displacement, decentration, and seriation. Any insights into the development of time concepts which can be obtained from child language should be a welcome sight to developmental researchers, since the period of maximum change in linguistic temporal systems (i.e., 1½ to 4½ years) corresponds to the period of minimum research on the development of time concepts. In a recent review of the research on developing time concepts, Friedman (1978) pointed out that "In fact, there is no research that fills the gap between Piaget's infant work and his studies of the temporal seriation of 6- to 10-year-olds" (p. 274). While today we know that this gap is being narrowed by the work of people like Levin (1982) and Friedman himself (1982b), the gap is far from being closed.

Let me take Friedman's (1978) review article as a point of departure for my analysis of the relationship between a cross-linguistic perspective on the emergence of temporal systems and the development of time concepts. Friedman organized the research on time concepts in children into the three categories logical time, conventional time, and experiential time, and he categorized the development of tense in child language under conventional time. After a brief discussion of some research concerning the initial appearance of temporal adverbs in English, Friedman arrived at the following far-reaching conclusion: "In general, the claims for an orderly emergence of tense reference are dubious. It is more likely . . . that this time system is not embedded in the intuitions of early language learners but is acquired later as an aspect of conventional time" (p. 281). It is difficult to imagine a statement about the temporal systems in child language which could be further from the truth. It shows how one can be misled by focusing on one phase in the development of one language. In the next two sections, I will outline a cross-linguistic perspective on this problem and then discuss its relevance for conceptual development in general.

The concepts of tense and aspect

In order to understand the system of temporal relationships which exists within a language and which varies from one language to another, we must begin with the two fundamental concepts of aspect and tense[4] (see Comrie, 1976, in press, for additional perspective on these concepts). Aspect has to do with the temporal (or dynamic) properties of situations, such as completion, repetition, and duration. Hence, an aspectual distinction might specify if a situation is complete versus incomplete, punctual versus moderately long lasting, a single event versus a series of events, etc. Tense is a relational (i.e., deictic) concept, and it specifies relationships between intervals in time. Following Smith's (1980) lead, I have found it very useful to analyze the evolution of temporal systems in child language within the framework of an updated (e.g., Comrie, 1981b) version of Reichenbach's (1947) theory. Within this framework, the intervals in time which are related by tense are: (a) speech time (ST)—the time interval of the speech act, (b) event time (ET)—the time relative to ST which is established for a specific situation, and (c) reference time (RT)—the temporal context which is identified. The following qualitative relationships exist for these time concepts: (a) simultaneous (=), (b) prior to (←), and (c) subsequent to (→). These time concepts are also related quantitatively by degree of remoteness. Two of the many temporal configurations which can be expressed are demonstrated by sentences 5 and 6.

5. Ewa arrived at midnight. (RT = ET ← ST)

6. Adam will arrive before midnight. (ST → ET → RT)

In sentence 5, the past tense establishes ET ← ST, and the temporal expression *at midnight* provides a point of reference for the event which occurs precisely at that point. In sentence 6, the future tense specifies the ST → ET relationship, the reference time is *midnight,* and the temporal preposition *before* indicates that ET → RT.

Evolution of temporal systems

I have argued elsewhere (Weist, in press) that temporal systems in child language evolve through a sequence of increasingly complex configurations of temporal concepts. The systems were identified as the speech time (ST) system, the event time (ET) system, the restricted reference time (RT$_r$) system, and the free reference time (RT$_f$) system. Since these systems were described in detail in Weist (in press), they will only be summarized in this section. Initially, child

---

[4] A more complete discussion would also integrate the concept of modality (see Stephany, in press).

language is primarily a here-and-now communication system. Children do not code deictic relationships between ST and ET. The temporal system contains only the concept of speech time. Children make reference to objects which are not within the confines of the immediate perceptual environment (giving evidence for object permanence), but they do not place ET prior to or subsequent to ST. Aspectual relationships are also not coded during this period. During the period from 1.6 to 2.0, children typically break out of the constraints of the ST system and begin to contrast present with past tense. Depending on the language, they also contrast present with future tense either immediately or after a short delay. The emergence of deictic relations signals the onset of the ET system. Within the ET system, the aspectual properties "complete" and/or "continuous" (depending on the language) are typically coded.

The point at which the ET system emerges is very important, because the establishment of the ET system provides a *sufficient* condition to argue that children can think abstractly about time. Primarily due to research on Romance languages (Antinucci & Miller, 1976; Bronckart & Sinclair, 1973), the argument was presented that the initial tense morphology is defective in its function, coding aspect rather than tense. It was argued that children do not express the deictic ET ← ST relations, because they are not yet conceptually capable of dealing with displacement in time. However, a broad cross-linguistic perspective including Slavic, Finno-Ugric, and Altaic languages shows that tense is seldom (if ever) defective in the initial phase (Weist, in press; Weist, Wysocka, Witkowska-Stadnik, Buczowska, & Konieczna, in press). We now know that children can think abstractly about events in time a full year (or more) earlier than the most precocious of prior estimates (cf. Smith's 1980 remarks on more conservative prior estimates).

While the ET system is characterized by deictic relations, the point of temporal reference is frozen at ST. At about 2½ to 3 years of age, children begin to show at least a limited capacity to more RT away from ST. Children use temporal adverbs and adverbial clauses to establish a point of reference. However, RT corresponds either to ET or to ST, for example, RT=ET *Yesterday something happened* or RT=ST *Something has happened*. Hence, the child's temporal system is still limited to time configurations which relate only two intervals of time, e.g., ((RT=ET) ← ST) or ET ← (RT=ST)).

Some languages such as English code a temporal concept called perfect. The perfect is a complex concept because it has some properties which are tense-like and some properties which are aspect-like. With regard to tense, perfect codes the relationship ET ← RT. We can consider any tense relationships which is anchored at ST, e.g. ET ← ST, as an *absolute* tense relation (see Comrie, in press), and, in contrast, the relation ET ← RT may be called a *relative* tense relation. Perfect can be past, present, or future, in which case RT is either prior to, simultaneous with, or subsequent to speech time. Thus, perfect has the properties of both relative and absolute tense. Furthermore, perfect sometimes codes a resultative aspectual property. When this property is added, we derive a configuration in which the result of some situation at ET continues to be relevant during the RT interval; e.g., present perfect produces present relevance for a past situation, *Tom can't ski today. He HAS BROKEN his leg.*

The evolution of the perfect in child language provides a prototypical example of the importance of cross-linguistic perspective on conceptual development. In his analysis of two American children, Cromer (1968) observed that the present perfect does not emerge until about 4½ years of age at the earliest. Based on this observation in conjunction with a number of other factors, Cromer argued that children go through a process of temporal decentration which allows one "to free oneself from the immediate situation" (p. 165). However, it is clear from cross-linguistic perspective that the conceptual process of temporal decentration, which Cromer correctly described, must evolve almost 2 years earlier, with the onset of the restricted reference time system. Temporal adverbs such as 'yesterday' are found in Italian at 3.0, French and Spanish at 2.6 (see Clark, in press), Polish at 2.8 (Weist, in press), and Mandarin at 2.3 (Erbaugh, 1982). In 1974, after arguing to his satisfaction that the delay of the present perfect was not a linguistic coding problem, Cromer proposed "that the ability to use the perfect tense property rests on a late-developing ability to consider the relevance of another time to the time of the utterance" (p. 223). There are a variety of reasons to suspect that there is something wrong with Cromer's argument, but the most poignant reason derives from an examination of child Finnish. The majority of the children studied by Toivainen (1980) contrasted the simple past form (i.e., preterite) with the present perfect form (i.e., perfect) prior to 2.6. Part of Cromer's problem was that he did not have enough perspective on English (much less cross-linguistic perspective) since Wells (1979) has shown that half of the 60 children in his sample used the perfect by 2.3 (see Fletcher's 1981 remarks on the discrepancy).

The development of more abstract temporal systems is surely regulated in part by the emergence of such major conceptual breakthroughs as displacement and decentration, but development is also regulated by the complexity of the temporal configurations which characterize the system. It appears that what I have called "the free reference time system" does not emerge until about 4 to 4½ years of age. At this age, children begin to establish ST, ET, and RT at different intervals in time. The evidence for this comes primarily from use of 'before' and 'after' as temporal prepositions. While we have some evidence on the aspectual properties which are integrated into the event time system, we do not know how aspectual distinctions evolve as ST, ET, and RT become integrated into more complex systems.

Temporal systems and time concepts

Granting that there is a research gap from about 2 to 5 years, the purpose of this section is to selectively review some of what is known about the child's conception of time just prior to 2 years of age and just subsequent to about 5 years of age, and then to insert the implications of child language research in the gap. Piaget's work on sensorimotor knowledge remains the most relevant to the early period. Piaget (1954, p. 348) summarized the status of temporal develop-ment in the sixth stage (1.6–2.0) as follows: "the objectification of the temporal series extends to representation, that is, the child, becoming capable of evoking memories not linked to direct perception, succeeds by that very fact in locating them in a time which includes the whole chronology of his universe." This argument was supported by the following observation: "At 1.7 (25) Jacqueline picks up a blade of grass which she puts into a pail as if it were one of the grasshoppers a little cousin brought her a few days before. She says, 'Totelle (sauterelle, or grasshopper), totelle, jump, boy (her cousin)'" (p. 346). The example has three interesting properties: (a) it refers to an activity (or atelic situation), and while the memory is cued, it does not rely on some speech time product of the prior situation; (b) it is a moderately remote reference; and (c) trusting the translation, the child's word is not inflected for tense. This is the kind of past reference which some investigators have claimed that children are not capable of making even after the initial tensing emerges. Ironically, the same investigators cite Piaget to support their claims.

On the other side of the 2-to-5 years research gap, investigations have focused on the concepts of duration, succession, and cyclic time (see the collection of papers in Friedman, 1982a). When children are asked to make judgments about duration in the absence of logical or conventional cues, Friedman (1978) classi-fies this as the knowledge of experiential time. In their reviews, both Fraisse (1963, 1982) and Friedman (1978) agree that 4- to 6-year-old children can make accurate judgments of brief intervals, but only after sufficient training. At this age, children are also subject to time illusions typical for adults, such as the overestimation of filled intervals and the underestimation of empty intervals.

Levin (1977, 1982) has shown what happens to the child's judgments of duration when cues (or components) of logical time such as succession, speed, and distance must be considered. Levin (1977) contrasted still time and rotational time judgments with judgments in a standard Piagetian linear time problem. In the still time problems, two dolls started and/or stopped sleeping simultaneously, and in the rotational problems the cue of variable spinning time was added to variable starting and/or stopping times. Children of approximately 5, 7, and 9 years of age were required to judge duration and explain their answers. Their explanations were scored for information about succession, e.g., "the red doll slept longer because it went to sleep first." While none of the children excelled on the linear time problems, the 5-year-old children did reasonably well on the still time problems, and the 7- and 9-year-olds showed the capacity to integrate speed in the rotational problems. Hence, the reserach shows that 5-year-old children can infer duration from information about succession. When required to integrate speed, distance, and duration, 5-year-olds use a different set of rules than adults (see also Wilkening, 1982).

As far as the conceptualization of cyclic time is concerned, much of the recent work has been done by Friedman (e.g., Friedman, 1982b). In Friedman's simplest task, 3- to 10-year-old children were given four pictures and asked to put them "the way you think they go." The daily cycle pictures were of waking, school, eating, and sleeping, and the annual cycle pictures were of seasonal activities as well as other cyclic events. Three-year-old children did not exceed chance expectations on the daily cycle problem, but older children were successful. However, it is not until after 5 years of age that children begin to solve cyclic problems with arbitrary starting points. Annual cycle problems were difficult for children until about 6 or 7. The capacity to judge the acceptability of permutations of daily or annual cycles does not develop until about 8 years.

The research on conceptual development indicates that children begin to make displaced temporal references prior to 2 years of age, and they have difficulty making inferences about temporal phenomena at 5 years of age. Research on the evolution of temporal systems in language can shed some light on the conceptual transition from 2 to 5 years of age. To facilitate this analysis of conceptual development, I will start by proposing a model of time flow which is relevant to both a theory of tense and the psychological representation of time. The model of time flow is based on the concept of a helix. Time is viewed as a point moving along the arc of a helix and the helix itself is viewed as recoiling. The helical model preserves the relationships of anteriority, simultaneity, and posteriority which can be established by a linear model, and the helix adds the important property of cyclicity. While the helical model adds cyclicity, it avoids the problems produced by a circular model.

In language, the major motivation for the helical model comes from the fact that, for languages with remote tenses, the cut-off points frequently refer to cyclical periods such as days and years (see Comrie, in press, chap. 4; Hyman, 1980). The Dschang dialect of the Bantu language Bamileke, for example, has a relatively symmetrical system in the past and future, with the following five levels of remoteness: immediate, today, 1 day from today, within a period from 2 days to several days from today, and a year or more. Taking just the third level of remoteness, for example, Bamileke-Dschang has a past tense form implying yesterday and a future form implying tomorrow. From the psychological point of view, man is genetically equipped with a physiological clock which is partially calibrated into 24 hour periods by circadian rhythms. Other cyclic physiological changes partition time into longer intervals, such as the menstrual cycle. Meanwhile, the species must adapt to cyclic environmental phenomena such as days and seasons.

Children have clearly achieved object permanence by the one-word phase of language, 1.1 to 1.6 (Corrigan, 1978), or earlier (see Bower, 1974, chap. 7), and the first conceptual development of concern here is displacement. When the ET system emerges in child language (about 1.6 to 3.0), children can code the properties of anteriority, simultaneity, and posteriority which are expressed in many languages by absolute tense. This represents an understanding of the succession of events which is tied to the speech time situation as the deictic center. During this phase of development, there is no indication that children can conceptualize cyclic temporal properties, and the child's concept of time flow could be represented by a linear (in contrast to a helical) model of time flow. At this phase in development, children learning languages with remote past tenses would not be expected to discriminate levels of remoteness with cyclic cut-off points. However, children learning languages without absolute tenses would be expected to use the aspectual and/or modal properties of the language to code anteriority and posteriority.

Just as tenses can be considered to be absolute (i.e., related to the deictic center), or relative, so also can temporal adverbs be defined as absolute or relative. Hence, the temporal adverbs 'yesterday', 'today', and 'tomorrow' are absolute in the sense that they define a deictic relationship between RT and ST, and temporal expressions 'in a little while', 'on Monday', and 'in winter' are relative in the sense that the temporal context referred to is not tied to ST. Some temporal adverbs are cyclic in nature, e.g., 'yesterday', and some are not, e.g., 'later'. Given the state of the art, any remarks about specific trends in the development of temporal adverbs will have to be tentative. When the restricted RT system emerges (about 2.6 to 2.0), children begin to demonstrate a relative sense of time and a conceptualization of first order cyclic phenomena. The temporal adverbs which are most commonly cited in the cross-linguistic literature are both deictic (or absolute) and cyclic, such as 'yesterday'. When children begin to use temporal adverbs, they often use them in ways which do not correspond to the adult's usage. A number of investigators have observed that children will use a single expression to mean some degree of remoteness either in the past or the future, e.g., 'yesterday' could refer to either the prior or the subsequent cycle. This creates superficial tense-adverb mismatches in the child's speech, and this may cause some observers to view the child's conception of time as being confused at this phase in development. In point of fact, the child has demonstrated the capacity to move reference time away from the deictic center and to enlist the concept of daily cycles. Unfortunately, we do not have data from languages with remote tenses to support the argument that cyclicity is a property of child language at this phase of development.

The restricted RT system spans a period of conceptual transition from egocentric to objective temporal reference. We might expect to find that children gradually shift from absolute to relative temporal adverbs, and from first order cyclic adverbs to higher order cyclic time expressions such as 'in summer'. When the free RT system evolves (about 4.0 to 4.6), children show the capacity to make inferences about the succession of events which are independent of the deictic center of ST. Hence, children can establish summer vacation as a point of reference and then locate events either before or after the time of reference. There is a parallel development of aspectual concepts, but since the research on the development of aspect in child language is in its infancy, we do not know when such distinctions as durative aspect emerge. Further research on aspect will provide important insights into the child's developing ability to conceptualize time properties such as duration.

Cross-linguistic perspective on child language reveals a gradual and systematic sequence of conceptual breakthroughs. A similar argument has been made by other reviewers of the child language literature, e.g., Kuczaj and Boston (1982) and Harner (1982). The major shift over the 1½-to4½-year time interval is from an egocentric to an objective concept of time reference, and from a linear to a cyclical representation of time flow. The conceptualization of time which children are acquiring during this period should probably be described as personal (Kuczaj & Boston, 1982) and logical rather than cultural and conventional (Friedman, 1978).

CONCLUDING REMARKS

In this chapter, I have taken a relatively conservative position on the issue of linguistic versus cognitive determinism. I have demonstrated that cross-linguistic perspective makes us more sensitive to the language acquisition process, hence more aware of the evolution of supporting conceptual processes and schemata. This position gives language only the role of a barometer on the developing conceptual climate. However, I would go further than this and propose that language has at least the effect Roger Brown (1956) proposed of altering the availability of concepts. I do not think (nor does anyone else) that tense distinctions in language cause children to think abstractly about time, or that the gender distinctions produce the concept of gender identity. It appears that the structure of language forces children to pay attention to certain distinctions and this changes their level of awareness.

In Hebrew, for example, Berman (in press) explains that the "child has no basic or citation form of verbs which he can resort to until he reaches the point where he is ready to encode tense-distinctions, so that his language forces him to make a choice from very early on." In Polish, the distinction between perfective and imperfective aspect is at the core of the verb system, and, more often than not, one can not produce a sentence in Polish without making a choice between the perfective and the imperfective form of the verb. The imperfective aspect is neutral (i.e., the unmarked form) and perfective aspect specifies the concept of a complete situation, i.e., a situation with a beginning, middle, and end. In Polish, just as in Hebrew, there are no citation forms (i.e., bare stems) in the verb system, and children are forced to pay attention to aspect. The fact that children pay attention to this property of situations may produce an increased awareness of the concept of completion. The potential influences on the child's awareness of conceptual distinctions extend beyond the domain of space and time all the way to awareness of such concepts as social relationships. As a consequence of the way in which sociolinguistic factors are integrated into the morphology of the verb system, "every predicate one utters in Japanese necessarily reflects the nature of the social relationship between the speaker and the hearer" (Clancy, in press). Clancy has argued that, as a result of acquiring this type of language, "Japanese children are exposed to linguistic differences correlated with social variables from a very early age, and are probably *more sensitive* to the social factors which trigger linguistic differences in Japanese, such as relative age, sex, and status of speaker and hearer, than are American children of comparable age" (emphasis mine).

Most cross-linguistic investigators who are willing to speculate about the potential effects of language on the availability of various concepts in early childhood are aware that we lack the experiments on cross-cultural conceptual development which are required to confirm these speculations (cf. Rosch, 1973, on color concepts). Despite the fact that we are forced to remark that further research on conceptual development is needed to resolve these speculations, we now have ample cross-linguistic data to dispense with some of the myths about the acquisition of language and correlated conceptual structures. In this chapter, I have presented data from a variety of diverse languages which disconfirm earlier arguments about the importance of linear predispositions in sentence processing, and I have shown that the evolution of temporal systems in child language is an orderly process which reveals the systematic development of a sequence of conceptual discoveries.

While the process of cross-linguistic comparison has been a part of the psycholinguistic tradition, the data basis for penetrating scientific analysis is still limited. We don't have acquisition projects designed specifically to contrast child language in a variety of typological categories such as ergative versus accusative and aggulatinating versus fusional, and we don't have data on such interesting phenomena as O-S canonical order or remote tense systems. Those of us who take the cross-linguistic approach to cognitive psychology think that these kinds of comparisons are needed to understand conceptual development. Furthermore, it is our bias that fixating on the study of a single language will not produce an adequate understanding of developmental conceptual processes.

REFERENCES

Aksu, A. A., & Slobin, D. I. (in press). Acquisition of Turkish. In D. I. Slobin (Ed.), *The crosslinguistic study of language acquisition*. Hillsdale, NJ: Erlbaum.

Anderson, S. R. (1976). On the notion of subject in ergative languages. In C. N. Li (Ed.), *Subject and Topic* (pp. 1–24). New York: Academic Press.

Antinucci, F., & Gebert, L. (1977). *Semantyka aspektu czasownikowego* [Semantics of verbal aspect]. *Studia Gramatyczne I*, Polska Akademia Nauk Instytut Języka Polskiego, Wrocław.

Antinucci, F., & Miller, R. (1976). How children talk about what happened. *Journal of Child Language, 3*, 167–189.

Bates, E., MacWhinney, B., Caselli, C., Devescovi, A., Natale, F., & Venza, V. (1983). *A cross-linguistic study of the development of sentence interpretation strategies*. Unpublished manuscript.

Berman, R. A. (in press). Acquisition of Hebrew. In D. I. Slobin (Ed.), *The crosslinguistic study of language acquisition*. Hillsdale, NJ: Lawrence Erlbaum Associates.

Bever, T. G., (1970). The cognitive basis for linguistic structure. In J. R. Hayes (Ed.), *Cognition and the Development of Language* (pp. 279–352). New York: Wiley.

Bloom, L., Lightbown, P., & Hood, L. (1975). Structure and variation in Child Language. *Monographs of the Society for Research in Child Development, 40*, No. 2.

Bower, T. G. R. (1974). *Development in Infancy*. San Francisco: Freeman.

Bowerman, M. (1976). Semantic factors in the acquisition of rules for word use and sentence construction. In D. M. Morehead & A. E. Morehead (Eds.), *Normal and Deficient Child Language* (pp. 99–179). Baltimore, MD: University Park Press.

Bowerman, M. (1982). Reorganizational processes in lexical and syntactic development. In E. Wanner & L. R. Gleitman (Eds.), *Language Acquisition: The State of the Art* (pp. 319–346). Cambridge, England: Cambridge University Press.

Braine, M. D. S., (1976). Children's first word combination. *Monographs of the Society for Research in Child Development, 41*, 1–97.

Braine, M. D. S., & Hardy, J. A., (1982). On what case categories there are, why they are, and how they develop: an amalgram of a priori considerations, speculations, and evidence from children. In E. Wanner & L. R. Gleitman (Eds.), *Language Acquisition: The State of the Art* (pp. 219–239). Cambridge, England: Cambridge University Press.

Bronckart, J. P., & Sinclair, H. (1973). Time, tense, and aspect. *Cognition, 2*, 107–130.

Brown, R. (1956). Language and categories. In J. S. Bruner, J. J. Goodnow, & G. A. Austin (Eds.), *A Study of thinking* (pp. 247–312). New York: Wiley.

Brown, R. (1973). *A first language: the early stages*. Cambridge, MA: Harvard University Press.

Brown, R., Cazden, C. B., & Bellugi, U. (1969). The child's grammar from I to III. In J. P. Hill (Ed.), *Minnesota Symposium on child psychology, Vol. 2* (pp. 28–73). Minneapolis, MN: University of Minnesota Press.

Bruner, J. S., (1975). The ontogenesis of speech acts, *Journal of Child Langauge, 2*, 1–19.

Chafe, W. L. (1970). *Meaning and the structure of language*. Chicago: University of Chicago Press.

Chapman, R. S., & Kohn, L., (1978). Comprehension strategies in two and three year olds: Animate agents or probable events? *Journal of Speech and Hearing Research, 21*, 746–761.

Clancy, P. M. (in press). Acquisition of Japanese. In D. I. Slobin (Ed.), *The crosslinguistic study of language*. Hillsdale, NJ: Erlbaum.

Clark, E. V. (in press). Acquisition of Romance, with special reference to French. In D. I. Slobin (Ed.), *The crosslinguistic study of language acquisition*. Hillsdale, NJ: Erlbaum.

Comrie, B. (1976). *Aspect: an introduction to the study of verbal aspect and related problems*. Cambridge, MA: Cambridge University Press.

Comrie, B. (1981a). *Language universals and linguistic typology: Syntax and morphology*. Chicago: Chicago University Press.

Comrie, B. (1981b April–May). On Reichenbach's approach to tense. *Chicago Linguistic Society Annual Meeting, 17*, 24–30.

Comrie, B. (in press). *Tense*. Cambridge, England: Cambridge University Press.

Corrigan, R. (1978). Language development as related to stage 6 object permanence development. *Journal of Child Language, 5*, 173–189.

Cromer, R. F. (1968). *The development of temporal reference during the acquisition of language.* Unpublished doctoral dissertation, Harvard University.

Cromer, R. F. (1974). The development of language and cognition: the cognitive hypothesis. In B. Foss (Ed.), *New perspectives in child language* (pp. 184–252). Harmondsworth, England: Penguin Books.

Dasen, P. R. (1977). *Cross-cultural contributions.* New York: Gardner Press.

de Villiers, J. G., & de Villiers, P. A., (1973). Development of the use of word order in comprehension, *Journal of Psycholinguistic Research, 2,* 331–341.

Erbaugh, M. S. (1982). *Coming to order: natural selection and the origin of syntax in the Mandarin-speaking child.* Unpublished doctoral dissertation in linguistics, University of California, Berkeley.

Fletcher, P. (1981). Description and explanation in the acquisition of verb forms. *Journal of Child Language, 8,* 93–108.

Fraisse, P. (1963). *The psychology of time.* New York: Harper & Row.

Fraisse, P. (1982). The adaptation of the child to time. In W. J. Friedman (Ed.) *The developmental psychology of time* (pp. 113–140). New York: Academic Press.

Frankel, D. G., Amir, M., Frenkel, E., & Arbel, T., (1980). The developmental study of the role of word order in comprehending Hebrew. *Journal of Experimental Child Psychology, 29,* 23–25.

Friedman, W. J. (1978). Development of time concepts in children. In H. W. Reese & L. P. Lipsitt (Eds.), *Advances in child development and behavior* (*Vol. 12*) (pp. 267–298). New York: Academic Press.

Friedman, W. J. (1982a). *The developmental psychology of time.* New York: Academic Press.

Friedman, W. J. (1982b). Conventional time concepts and children's structuring of time. In W. J. Friedman (Ed.), *The developmental psychology of time* (pp. 171–208). New York: Academic Press.

Golinkoff, R. M. (1981). The case for semantic relations: Evidence from the verbal and nonverbal domains. *Journal of Child Language, 8,* 413–438.

Greenberg, J. H. (1966). *Language Universals.* The Hague: Mouton.

Hakuta, K., (1982). Interaction between particles and word order in the comprehension and production of simple sentences in Japanese children. *Developmental Psychology, 18,* 62–75.

Harner, L. (1982). Talking about the past and future. In W. J. Friedman (Ed.), *The developmental psychology of time* (pp. 141–170). New York: Academic Press.

Hopper, P. J., & Thompson, S. A. (1980). Transitivity in grammar and discourse. *Language, 56,* 251–299.

Hyman, L. M. (1980). Relative time reference in the Bamileke tense system. *Studies in African Linguistics II,* 227–237.

Keenan, E. L., (1976). Towards a universal definition of "Subject." In C. N. Li (Ed.), *Subject and Topic* (pp. 303–334). New York, Academic Press.

Kubiński, W., (1982). Polish *się* constructions and their English counterparts. *Papers and Studies in Contrastive Linguistics, 15,* 55–65.

Kuczaj, S. A., & Boston, R. (1982). The nature and development of personal temporal-reference systems. In S. A. Kuczaj II (Ed.), *Language Development* (Vol. 2) (pp. 365–395). Hillsdale, NJ: Erlbaum.

Levin, I. (1977). The development of time concepts in young children: Reasoning about duration. *Child Development, 48,* 435–444.

Levin, I. (1982). The nature of development of time concepts in children: The effect of interfering cues. In W. J. Friedman (Ed.), *The developmental psychology of time.* New York: Academic Press.

Lyons, J. (1968). *Introduction to theoretical Linguistics.* Cambridge, England: Cambridge University Press.

Mac Whinney, B., (1982). Basic syntactic processes. In S. Kuczaj (Ed.), *Language acquisition: Syntax and semantics* (pp. 73–136). Hillsdale, NJ: Erlbaum.

Maratsos, M., & Chalkley, M., (1980). The internal language of children's syntax: The ontogenesis and representation of syntactic categories. In K. Nelson (Ed.), *Children's Language* (Vol. 2) (pp. 127–214). New York: Gardner Press.

Newport, E. L., (1982). Task specificity in language learning? Evidence from speech perception and American Sign Language. In E. Wanner & L. R. Gleitman (Eds.), *Language acquisition: the state of the art* (pp. 450–486). Cambridge, England: Cambridge University Press.

Nilsen, D. L. F. (1972). *Toward a semantic specification of deep case.* The Hague: Mouton.

Osgood, C. E., & Tanz, C., (1977). Will the real direct object in bitransitive sentences please stand up? In A. Juilland (Ed.), *Linguistic studies offered to Joseph Greenberg* (pp. 537–590). Saratoga, CA: Anma Libri.

Piaget, J. (1954). *The construction of reality in the child,* New York: Basic Books.

Radulović, L. (1975). *Acquisition of language: studies of Dubrovnik children.* Unpublished doctoral dissertation, University of California, Berkeley.

Reichenbach, H. (1947). *Symbolic logic.* Berkeley: University of California.

Rosch, E. (1973). On the internal structure of perceptual and semantic categories. In T. E. Moore (Ed.), *Cognitive development and the acquisition of language* (pp. 114–144). New York: Academic Press.

Sapir, E. (1968). Language and environment. In D. G. Mandelbaum (Ed.), *Selected Writings of Edward Sapir in language, culture and personality.* Berkeley: University of California Press.

Schenker, A. M. (1973). *Beginning Polish, Vol. 2.* New Haven: Yale University Press.

Segalowitz, N. S., & Galang, R. G., (1978). Agent-patient word-order preference in the acquisition of Tagalog, *Journal of Child Language, 5,* 47–64.

Sinclair-de Zwart, H. (1973). Language acquisition and cognitive development. In T. E. Moore (Ed.), *Cognitive development and the acquisition of language* (pp. 9–26). New York: Academic Press.

Slobin, D, I., (1973). Cognitive prerequisites for the development of grammar. In C. A. Ferguson & D. I. Slobin (Eds.), *Studies of child language development* (pp. 175–208). New York: Holt, Rinehart & Winston.

Slobin, D. I., (1981). The origins of grammatical encoding of events. In P. J. Hopper & S. A. Thompson (Eds.), *Syntax and Semantics, Vol. 15: Studies in Transitivity* (pp. 409–422). New York: Academic Press.

Slobin, D. I. (1982). Universal and particular in the acquisition of language. In E. Wanner & L. R. Gleitman (Eds.), *Language acquisition: State of art* (pp. 129–172). Cambridge, England: Cambridge University Press.

Slobin, D. I. (in press a). *The cross-linguistic study of language acquisition.* Hillsdale, NJ: Erlbaum.

Slobin, D. I. (in press b). Crosslinguistic evidence for the language-making capacity. In D. I. Slobin (Ed.), *The cross-linguistic study of language acquisition.* Hillsdale, NJ: Erlbaum.

Slobin, D. I., & Bever, T. G. (1980). *Children use canonical sentence schemas: A cross-linguistic study of word order and inflections.* Unpublished manuscript.

Smith, C. S. (1980). The acquisition of time talk: Relations between child and adult grammars, *Journal of Child Language, 7,* 263–278.

Smith, F., & Miller, G. A. (1966). *The genesis of language.* Cambridge, MA: MIT Press.

Smoczyńska, M. (1978). *Wczesne studia rozwoju składni w mowie dziecka.* [The early phase of development of syntax in the speech of children.] Unpublished dissertation, Uniwersytet Jagielloński, Kraków.

Smoczyńska, M. (in press). Acquisition of Polish. In D. I. Slobin (Ed.), *The crosslinguistic study of language acquisition.* Hillsdale, NJ: Erlbaum.

Stephany, U. (1981). Verbal grammar in Modern Greek early child language. In P. S. Dale & O.

Ingram (Eds.), *Child language: An international perspective* (pp. 45–57). Baltimore, MD: University Park Press.

Stephany, U. (in press). Modality. In P. Fletcher & M. Garman (Eds.), *Language acquisition: Studies in first language development*. Cambridge, England: Cambridge University Press.

Szwedek, A. (1976). *Word order, sentence stress, and reference in English and Polish*. Edmonton, Canada: Linguistic Research.

Toivainen, J. (1980). *Inflectional affixes used by Finnish-speaking children aged 1–3 years*. Helsinki, Finland: Suomalaisen Kirjallisuuden Seura.

Underhill, R. (1976). *Turkish grammar*. Cambridge, MA: MIT Press.

Weist, R. M., (1982). *Verb concepts in child language: acquiring constraints on action role and animacy*, Tübingen, Germany: Gunter Narr Verlaq.

Weist, R. M., (1983). The word order myth. *Journal of Child Language, 6*, 97–106.

Weist, R. M. (in press). Tense and aspect: Temporal systems in child language. In P. Fletcher & M. Garman (Eds.), *Language acquisition: Studies in first language development*. Cambridge, England: Cambridge University Press.

Weist, R. M., Wysocka, H., Witkowska-Stadnik, K., Buczowska, E., & Konieczna, E. (in press). The defective tense hypothesis: on the emergence of tense and aspect in child Polish. *Journal of Child Language*.

Wells, G. (1974). Learning to code experience through language. *Journal of Child Language, 1*, 243–269.

Wells, G. (1979). Learning and using the auxiliary verb in English. In V. Lee (Ed.), *Language development* (pp. 250–270). London: Croom Helm.

Whorf, B. (1956). Linguistic relativity and the relation of linguistic process of perception and cognition. In J. Carroll (Ed.), *Language, thought, and reality* (pp. 207–219). Cambridge, MA: MIT Press.

Wilkening, F. (1982). Children's knowledge about time, distance, and velocity interrelations. In W. J. Friedman (Ed.), *The developmental psychology of time* (pp. 87–112). New York: Academic Press.

Zarębina, M. (1965). *Kształtowanie się systemu językowego dziecka*. [The formation of the language system of a child.] Kraków: Wydawnictwo Polskiej Akademii Nauk.

Chapter 15

Current Issues in Psycholinguistics

Margaret W. Matlin

State University of New York at Geneseo

The section on psycholinguistics included chapters on two topics, language acquisition and animal communication. Both of these topics are central to the current concerns of psycholinguistics. I would like to comment upon these chapters and then address two issues related to this volume: (a) Psycholinguistics in real-life settings, and (b) The influence of language on thought.

The topics of language acquisition and animal communication have attracted both scholarly and popular attention for many centuries. For example, Saint Augustine remarked in *The Confessions,*

> . . . for I was no longer a speechless infant, but a speaking boy. This I remember; and have since observed how I learned to speak. It was not that my elders taught me words . . . in any set method; but I, longing by cries and broken accents and various motions of my limbs to express my thoughts, that so I might have my will, and yet unable to express all that I willed, or to whom I willed, did myself, by the understanding which Thou, my God, gavest me, practise the sounds in my memory. . . . And thus by constantly hearing words, as they occurred in various sentences, I collected gradually for what they stood; and having broken in my mouth to these signs, I thereby gave utterance to my will. Thus I exchanged with those about me these current signs of our wills, and so launched deeper into the stormy intercourse of human life. . . . (c. 397/1949, p. 11)

An ancient Child ballad, called "The Outlandish Knight," enthusiastically describes a parrot who has mastered not only language but prevarication. This particular parrot hears its mistress returning late at night and calls to her:

> The parrot being in the window so high,
> Hearing the lady, did say:
> "I'm afraid that some ruffian has led you astray,
> That you have tarried so long away."

> "Don't prittle nor prattle, my pretty parrot,
> Nor tell any tales of me;
> And thy cage shall be made of glittering gold
> And the door of the best ivory.

The king being in the chamber so high,
And hearing the parrot, did say—
"What ails you, what ails you, me pretty parrot
That you prattle so long before day?"

"It's no laughing matter," the parrot did say
That so loudly I call unto thee;
For the cats have got into the window so high,
And I'm afraid they will have me."

"Well turned, well turned, my pretty parrot,
Well turned, well turned for me;
Thy cage shall be made of the glittering gold
And the door of the best ivory."

REVIEW OF WEIST'S AND VÁZQUEZ'S CHAPTERS

Saint Augustine's remarks and the Child ballad relate to the issues discussed in Weist's chapter on language acquisition and Vázquez's chapter on animal communication, respectively. These two psycholinguistic areas are highly important ones in current psycholinguistic research and are topics which do not have any easy answers, clearcut theories, or consistent empirical results. Even though neither topic deals with well-formed adult human speech, both may provide insights into adult speech. Research on children's language and apes' language will also help cognitive scientists to appreciate the enormous complexity of adult speech in terms of its semantic, syntactic, and social richness. Weist's chapter is discussed first, followed by a discussion of Vázquez's chapter.

Weist: language acquisition

Richard Weist's purpose, in his paper on language acquisition, is to focus on two issues: (a) How do children understand the difference between agent and patient functions? and (b) How do children capture time relationships in their language? Before discussing these two issues, however, I would like to address a more general question that Weist mentions concerning the relationship between language and cognition.

There is a sentiment that language is a system that is quite separate from other cognitive processes. For example, when I was preparing an undergraduate cognition textbook (Matlin, 1983), one anonymous reviewer argued that a chapter on language had no place in the textbook. This view, probably an extreme one, may have its origins in the school of psycholinguistics, dominant in the 1960s, that proposed that children have an innate knowledge about language, perhaps a Language Acquisition Device (e.g., McNeill, 1970). This LAD, according to McNeill and his supporters, is specifically tailored for mastering language, so that language acquisition accelerates ahead of the other cognitive skills with which the child is struggling.

The cognitive approach to language acquisition represents a contrasting view. One of the most persuasive forms of this cognitive approach was provided by John Macnamara (1972). Macnamara's primary thesis, consistent with Piaget's (e.g., 1963) and even elements of Saint Augustine's, is that young language learners are quite worldly wise by the time they begin to speak. They use meaning as a clue to language, rather than using language as a clue to meaning. Thus, children figure out the meaning that a speaker wants to convey to them, and then they figure out how that meaning is related to the language they hear. Children, according to Macnamara, master language in the same way they master other skills. They have an impressive ability to make pattern and order out of situations that involve human interactions.

More specifically, children rely on their previous learning of vocabulary. They hear a sentence, take the main lexical items in that sentence, and then use their knowledge of the referents to decide what semantic structures the speaker intends. Finally, they figure out what syntactic devices—such as word order and affixes—are correlated with the semantic structures they have derived. Cognitive processes therefore aid young children in unraveling the mysteries of language.

Weist continues in the same tradition as Macnamara. Weist points out that issues in psycholinguistics are relevant to cognitive scientists because cognitive processes and linguistic processes may influence one another. Furthermore, an understanding of linguistic processing may afford us a better understanding of how cognitive processes operate. It is interesting that cognitive psychologists often need to be persuaded that linguistic processing is relevant to their areas of interest. They would probably not need to be similarly persuaded about the relevance of areas such as memory or problem solving.

Let me return to the first major topic in Weist's chapter, which expands on the relationship between language and thought. This topic investigates children's appreciation of agent (or action-initiating) and patient (or action-affected) functions. Weist argues that a cross-linguistic approach to this problem is useful, because children in different linguistic communities differ in the kind of linguistic information they use in order to decode semantic relationships. In some languages, children use word-order information; in other languages, they use inflectional information; in most languages, verb information is useful.

An English-based approach to the problem of children's understanding of agent and patient functions encourages us to conclude that word order information is always of primary importance. Recall, for example, Braine's (1976) strongly worded claim that positional patterns are responsible for all early language learning. According to this view, the agent appears first in an utterance, the action second, and the patient last (that is, a SVO order). Word order may indeed be important in English. However, Weist cites Slobin's data that young Turkish children exploited inflectional information more than word order information in order to understand semantic relationships in simple sentences. Furthermore, young Polish children can understand semantic relationships by using inflectional information. Again, word order information is *not* required for children to properly understand which items in a sentence are agents and which are patients. Thus, a cross-linguistic approach offers convincing evidence that word-order information is not universally crucial in the child's mastery of semantic relationships.

Weist argues that children gain an additional source of information about semantic relationships through their understanding of verb concepts. By two years of age, they appreciate the distinction between action verbs (which involve an agent) and process verbs (which involve a patient). Children seem to be remarkable strategists who use whatever syntactic cues are available in their language in order to discover meaning.

The second topic in Weist's paper focuses on another dimension of the relationship between thought and language: How is a child's conceptual understanding of time related to her or his linguistic representation of time? Weist traces children's language development from an early stage in which language typically encodes only the present time frame. Shortly before 2 years of age, however, their language can encode the concept that an event being discussed may occur either before or after the present moment. Their linguistic competence in describing time demonstrates that they must now be able to think about time relationships (although Weist suggests that their cognitive processes reach that degree of sophistication up to a year before time relationships are evidenced in sentence production).

An even more complex linguistic accomplishment is the representation of a third dimension of time—namely reference time—that may differ from both speech time and event time. Studies based on English, such as the one by Cromer (1968), suggest that children do not develop an appreciation for this time relationship until they are almost school-aged. However, Weist cites cross-linguistic evidence from Romance languages, Polish, Mandarin, and Finnish that demonstrate an elementary understanding of these more abstract time relationships at an even earlier age.

Weist also discusses children's conceptions of time and their use of time-related adverbs. It seems to me that this topic offers rich possibilities for future research. For example, it would be interesting to know more details about how children's linguistic competence with respect to time is related to their conceptual competence. I wonder, for instance, whether 3- and 4-year-olds who perform at above-chance levels on Friedman's (1982) daily cycle task, of placing events in order, show more accurate use of linguistic time-related terms than their peers who perform at chance levels.

More generally, it seems necessary to develop tasks that assess children's conceptual understanding of time relationships. Psychologists have been very inventive in devising methodology that permits neonates to "tell" us what they know about topics such as object permanence, color categories, and size constancy. Psychologists have been less industrious about constructing methods of assessing conceptual knowledge in preschool children. More specific conclusions about the interrelationship of language and thought in young children may depend upon developing appropriately valid tasks.

Weist's information on children's language is a compelling illustration that children's linguistic skills are far from primitive. They are impressive strategists who use their cognitive skills to provide information about linguistic concepts as diverse as agent/patient functions and time relationships. A few decades ago, many psycholinguists were similarly optimistic about the cognitive skills underlying the linguistic performance of apes. However, as Carol Vázquez's paper illustrates, that optimism has withered appreciably.

Vazquez: animal communication

Carol Vázquez, in her discussion of the ape-language literature, suggests that the researchers in this area—like the legendary blind men—are focussing on different parts of the elephant. This characterization of the state of the literature seems quite accurate. We seem to have many perspectives on the same problem, and these perspectives bear little resemblance to one another. The researchers cannot even agree about what the apes are being taught, standard ASL or a pidgin variety. The controversy is fanned into a roaring blaze by emotional exchanges, such as Allen Gardner's evaluation of Terrace's work, "It is the shoddiest piece of work I have ever seen in this area" (cited in Marx, 1980, p. 1330).

The pattern of events in the ape-language literature reminds Vázquez of the sequence of events involving Helen Keller. A single situation can be interpreted in a variety of ways, so that it is simultaneously an indication of profound accomplishment and an indication of a relatively primitive kind of learning. In addition, it seems to me that the pattern of events in this literature is reminiscent of the trend we have seen so many times in the infant perception and cognition literature.

Some decades ago, infants were credited with the perceptual and cognitive skills of, perhaps, an old tennis shoe. Then researchers, led by T. G. R. Bower (1966), claimed to have demonstrated size constancy in infants who were just a few weeks old. (A statistician friend, having read one of Bower's books, remarked that his infant daughter might be expected to begin solving differential equations momentarily.) More recent evidence has cast suspicion on this assertion; it now seems that infants do not achieve substantial constancy until they are somewhat older (Day & McKenzie, 1977).

Similarly, psychologists were at one time very pessimistic about infants' skills in the area of olfaction. Then Macfarlane claimed that infants as young as 6 days of age could discriminate between a pad that their mothers had worn, in contrast to a pad that a stranger had worn (reported in Macfarlane, 1977). In contrast, Russell (1976) found no difference in reactions to mothers' pads versus strangers' pads until infants had reached 6 *weeks* of age. It is tempting to remark, "Oh, well, 6 weeks—that's fairly old." We can no longer refer to the "Amazing Newborn," but instead to the "Somewhat Amazing Newborn."

The analogy with the ape literature is clear. It had been previously maintained that apes were completely incapable of language. Then the Gardners' reports encouraged the belief that "The Planet of the Apes" was not far off. Other researchers also shared their imaginative visions with the scientific community. For example, Savage and Rumbaugh (1977) speculated that in the future, language-trained apes might accompany humans in field research projects in order to provide interpretations for apes' signal systems, perhaps resulting in coauthorship struggles.

Herbert Terrace has introduced skepticism; apes are probably not as proficient as a 3-year-old child, he claims. The apes have not been conversing, according to Terrace (1981). Instead, they have merely been attempting to communicate their demands quickly, in a nonconversational manner so that various rewards can be obtained with little delay. Many psychologists concur with Terrace's assessment, as in Neisser's statement that the apes "do *not* have language in any reasonable sense of the term" (Neisser, 1983, p. 130). However, many of us are impressed that the apes' linguistic skills are sophisticated enough to be compared with those of a 3-year-old human.

I would like to summarize some of the major points of the ape-language controversy, particularly with reference to Terrace's Nim project. First of all, let us consider the reasons that Terrace (1981) and other skeptics believe that the development of Nim's language differed from the development of a child's language.

1. Though Nim's vocabulary increased as he grew older, there was no substantial increase in the length of his utterances. Nim's mean length of utterance fluctuated between 1.1 and 1.6 signs during the last 2 years of the project. In contrast, the spoken language of hearing children and the signed language of deaf children increase rapidly during language acquisition, with a mean length of utterance that grows from about 1.5 to 4 or more in a 2-year period. Furthermore, Nim's utterances that were long were not very informative, as in Nim's classic 16-sign command, "Give orange me give eat orange me eat orange give me eat orange give me you" (Terrace, 1981, p. 101). In addition, Nim's three-word combinations were rarely more informative than his two-word combinations, for example, "play me Nim" versus "play me."

2. Most combinations contained just a few central words, such as "point," "Nim," or "you," in contrast to the richness of children's language.

3. Relatively few of Nim's utterances were spontaneous. Only 12% were not preceded by a teacher's signs. In contrast, children's utterances are mostly spontaneous, by some estimates about 80%.

4. As children grow older, their imitation of parental utterances decreases systematically. In contrast, Nim's imitation of his teachers increased over time.
5. As children's language grows more sophisticated, it shows a marked increase in the percentage of utterances that are expansions of an adult's speech. In contrast, Nim's expansion percentage remained stable at less than 10%.
6. Nim frequently interrupted his teachers' signs, whereas children do not. Children master the pragmatics of language; they realize that conversationalists must take turns in speaking.

Furthermore, there are several reasons why the apes' linguistic abilities may not be as impressive as was originally claimed:

1. Terrace's subsequent analyses revealed that the teachers prompted Nim more than had been originally noted.
2. Terrace also analyzed some of the Gardner's data on Washoe and crushed several of the findings for which some of us had deep affection. For example, Washoe's sentence that ends the Nova-produced film, "First Signs of Washoe" is "Baby in my drink." According to Terrace, this sentence appears to have been a run-on sequence with little connection between the elements in the utterance.
3. About 60% of Washoe's signs could be classified as highly iconic (for example, curved fingers drawn over the hair to indicate combing). In contrast, the ASL used by fluent humans involves primarily noniconic gestures (Savage-Rumbaugh & Rumbaugh, 1980).
4. Washoe's excellent performance on the Gardner's presumably "double blind" vocabulary tests is open to interpretation. Her correct performance could have been elevated by the order of stimulus presentation, the nature of the feedback, and so forth (Seidenberg & Petitto, 1981).
5. Although the Gardners reported that Washoe had a large receptive vocabulary, there were apparently no formal tests of context-free comprehension (Seidenberg & Petitto, 1981).

In defense of those who argue that apes have mastered language, we should consider some reasons why Terrace's work with Nim may have been executed in less than ideal circumstances.

1. As even Terrace acknowledges, Nim had about 60 different trainers, hardly a situation that approximates the environment of a normal human child learning to speak. Affective relations were no doubt impaired.
2. Many of those 60 trainers were not fluent in ASL.
3. The classroom setting in which Nim was taught was far removed from the home environment of human children.
4. Nim may have been taught using operant conditioning techniques, though

this point is as unclear as the nature of the language Washoe was taught. At any rate, critics of the Nim project believe that operant conditioning techniques produce passivity and imitation, rather than spontaneity.

5. Critics argue that Terrace evaluated children and chimps by different criteria, taking context into consideration in the case of children but not in the case of chimps.

Before we approach the more general question of whether apes have language, let us first consider some of the linguistic attributes that apes have not mastered (Savage & Rumbaugh, 1977; Stahlke, 1980). Apes cannot use the vocal modality, embedded clauses, and tenses. They cannot acquire language spontaneously. Their language is not used beyond achieving immediate gratification of some physical need or in responding to a human's inquiry. In addition, mature humans can talk about their language. No ape has yet shared his or her metalinguistic observations with us.

Ultimately, we must grapple with the central issue in the controversy: Do apes have language? Naturally, the answer to this question depends upon one's definition of the term. Of the numerous definitions cited for language, the most frequently mentioned involves Hockett's "design features" (e.g., Hockett, 1963). These design features are a set of properties characterizing communication in humans, and the specificity of each of these features is superficially appealling. However, the strength of specificity is simultaneously its weakness. For example, Stahlke (1980) discusses one of these features, which is termed "rapid fading of the message." Sumerian is a language preserved almost entirely in dried clay. Because it does not meet the criterion of rapid fading, must it be disqualified as a language?

The attempt to find definitions that are general enough to include all languages and yet specific enough to be useful is reminiscent of Eleanor Rosch's discussion of natural categories (e.g., Rosch, 1977). A defining-features approach to category membership would state that every item that meets the specified requirements belongs to a given category; items that lack one or more requirements belong to another category. Just as Hockett's design-features approach encounters problems, such as Sumerian's failure to meet the criterion of rapid fading, the defining-features approach encounters problems when we inspect the essential features for a natural category, such as "bird," and find that penguins don't really fly, and yet they are birds.

According to Rosch, a more useful approach to category membership is that we decide whether a given item belongs to a category by comparing the item with a prototype, a best example of the category. Thus, a robin is an excellent bird, whereas a penguin is a rather feeble example of that category. Similarly, using a prototype approach, the language demonstrated by Washoe, Nim, and other illustrious apes would constitute "penguins" rather than "robins" with respect to its similarity to prototypical language.

Savage and Rumbaugh (1977) remind us that it is unwise to conclude that there is a wide gap between the nonverbal communication of nonhuman primates and the language of humans. An evolutionary framework suggests that it would be heresy "for a communicative system as complex and pervasive as language to have suddenly appeared with a complicated grammar and unique internal structure, completely independent of the former highly elaborate and effective nonverbal communicative mode" (p. 288).

Thus, it seems appropriate to propose that there is a continuum from nonprototypical language, such as that demonstrated by the apes, to prototypical language. Given the complexity of the definitions of language, it seems highly unlikely that we will be able to propose what Malmi (1980) calls a "linguistic Rubicon" that will neatly separate those blessed with language from those unfortunate apes who can only communicate demands.

PSYCHOLINGUISTICS IN REAL-LIFE SETTINGS

Another issue I would like to address in this chapter concerns the settings in which psycholinguistics research is conducted, since this is a theme that runs through many of the chapters in this volume. To some extent, psycholinguistics has always exploited real-life settings to a greater extent than have other disciplines within cognition. One early example is Haggerty's (1930) recording, "What a Two-and-one-half-year-old Child Said in One Day." The naturalistic research tradition continued on through the 1960s with numerous publications on language acquisition by psycholinguists such as Martin Braine, Roger Brown, and Dan Slobin. A glance through recent issues of *Journal of Child Language, Child Development,* or *Journal of Psycholinguistic Research* will reassure any skeptic who might suspect that naturalistic research on children stopped with Adam, Eve, and Sarah. The research that Weist has summarized is an example of how this tradition has been applied cross-linguistically.

For several decades, psycholinguists interested in children's language have pursued their subjects with tape recorders and videotape equipment. In contrast, psycholinguists interested in adults' language confined their investigations to the laboratory until rather recently. Adult subjects memorized embedded sentences, judged the relative position of stars and pluses, and recalled complex transformed sentences without ever leaving the basements of psychology buildings throughout the nation.

In recent years, however, researchers have shown an increased enthusiasm for capturing their adult subjects' utterances in real-life settings. For example, in order to examine sex differences in interruption patterns, Zimmerman and West (1977) recorded conversations in coffee shops, drug stores, and other public places near a university, and Brooks (1982) observed female and male graduate students in the classroom.

Perhaps the most common setting for these real-life investigations is a professional one. Consider the psychotherapeutic setting, for example. Phoenix and Lindeman (1982) examined how various schools of therapy differ in the way they use verb tense during the therapy session. Similarly, Leaffer (1982) investigated the use of linguistic negatives in clinical denial.

The medical setting provides a wealth of information about real-life discourse. Some researchers analyze the patients' speech to their doctors. For example, Bonanno (1982) discovered that female patients frequently used hedges (qualifiers such as *sort of*), tag questions (questions at the end of sentences, such as "It's difficult, *isn't it?*"), and euphemisms in medical interviews, though the frequency of each of these devices depended upon the sex of the physician. Other researchers examine the linguistic interactions between doctors and patients (for example, Fisher, 1982; Tannen & Wallat, 1982). Still others study conversations of physicians with each other; for example, Prince, Frader, and Bosk (1982) observed that physicians use hedges frequently when speaking with one another. A prototypical sentence fragments contains four such hedges:

> . . . *I had to believe* he was hypovolemic, and he *seemed to* correct them awfully quickly, um and *I was wondering whether* there was any . . . any renal problems, but uh . . . basically *hard to say*. (p. 89; emphasis in the original)

Legal settings have also attracted the attention of psycholinguists. The variety of issues that have been addressed is impressive. For example, O'Barr and Atkins (1980) found that male and female witnesses showed greater sex similarities than sex differences in their language usage. Walker (1982) discovered that the disruptive and nondisruptive speech patterns used in legal depositions follow rules that are different from the ones that govern "normal" interactions. The linguistic structure of lies were examined by Epstein (1982), using testimonies provided by John Ehrlichman, John Dean, and Richard Nixon. Written language in legal documents inspired several papers (e.g., Arena, 1982; Finegan, 1982).

An excellent book edited by Di Pietro (1982) entitled *Linguistics and the professions* describes numerous other real-life examinations of discourse. Included among these topics are the psycholinguistics of advertisement, language choice in a bilingual community, communication patterns at the reference desk of the library, and pragmatic features of bureaucratic documents such as I.R.S. forms.

There is one profession that seems to have been seriously underrepresented in psycholinguists' explorations of real-life settings: the academician. Swacker (1979) has examined sex differences in verbal behavior at professional conferences. However, I am not aware of an enormous literature on the discourse patterns of academicians. If such exists, I am hopeful that they provide more optimistic assessments of the linguistic capacities of these professionals than was offered by Maclay and Osgood (1959). These authors recorded the speech of 13 professionals who attended a conference at University of Illinois. The following passage, with ellipses representing the pauses, illustrates speech errors committed by academicians:

> As far as I know, no one yet has done the in a way obvious now and interesting problem of . . . doing a in a sense a structual frequency study of the alternative . . . syntactical . . . in a given language, say, like English, the alternative . . . possible structures, and how what their hierarchal . . . probability of occurrence structure is. Now, it seems to me you w-w-will need that kind of data as base line. . . . (p. 25)

Naturally, there are many kinds of linguistic interactions in everyday life that have not yet been explored. For example, psycholinguists have demonstrated an obvious elitism in their choice of work settings. What kinds of verbal interactions occur on the assembly line or among cafeteria workers? Social settings have also received insufficient attention. What kinds of conversations take place at Rotary lunches, at county fairs, and at midtown Manhattan restaurants? Obviously, the opportunities for psycholinguistics research in real-life settings are abundant. Further research in these areas may help us understand how language is influenced by the cognitive context in which the language occurs.

THE INFLUENCE OF LANGUAGE ON THOUGHT

The previous section touched on the influence of social and cognitive context upon language. Now I would like to conclude this chapter by approaching the relationship between cognition and language from the opposite direction. In particular, let us return to the topic introduced in the discussion of Weist's paper: How does language influence thought? This question, like the ones of animal language and child language acquisition that were considered earlier in this chapter, has been scrutinized for centuries. For example, Aristotle wrote:

> Words are spoken symbols or signs of affections or impressions of the soul . . . speech is not the same for all races. . . . But the mental affections themselves, of which the words are primarily signs, are the same for all of [humanity], as are also the objects of which those affections are representations or likenesses, images, copies. (Dinneen, 1967, p. 80)

For Aristotle, the languages that we speak may differ, but our thoughts about the obejcts, described in our various languages, are universal.

The Sapir-Whorf hypothesis, which probably had its beginnings in 18th century Germany (Stam, 1980), provides an opposing viewpoint. Edward Sapir was a professor of anthropology and linguistics, and mentor to Benjamin Lee Whorf, a fire-prevention inspector who devoted his spare time to his hobby, linguistics.

According to the Sapir-Whorf hypothesis,

We dissect nature along lines laid down by our native languages. The categories and types that we isolate from the world of phenomena we do not find there because they stare every observer in the face; on the contrary, the world is presented in a kaleidoscopic flux of impressions which has to be organized by our minds—and this means largely by the linguistic systems in our minds. We cut nature up, organize it into concepts, and ascribe significances as we do, largely because we are parties to an agreement to organize it in this way—an agreement that holds throughout our speech community and is codified in the patterns of our language. (Whorf, 1956, p. 213)

There are two components to the Whorfian hypothesis: (a) linguistic determinism, which is the idea that the structure of language determines the structure of thought, and (b) linguistic relativity, which is the idea that speakers of different languages have different thought structures. Our primary concern here is the linguistic determinism component, though linguistic relativity is occasionally relevant. Let us first consider several ways in which language does *not* influence thought, and then we will turn to several ways in which language *might* influence thought. The organization for this topic is primarily derived from Steinberg's (1982) *Psycholinguistics: Language, mind, and world.*

How language doesn't influence thought

According to one view, speech production is the very basis of thought. Watson (1924), for example, argued, *"what the psychologists have hitherto called thought is in short nothing but talking to ourselves . . ."* (p. 238; emphasis in the original). This view has frequently been promoted by behaviorists who prefer observable behaviors, such as speech, to covert cognitive activities.

However, there are a number of problems with this viewpoint, as Steinberg notes. For example, in normal children, speech understanding precedes speech production. A child can understand the sentence, "Go over and put your coat on the hook" many months before he or she can produce this same sentence. Furthermore, we can speak one series of words while thinking about something unrelated (Furth, 1966), as countless hymn-singers and Pledge-of-Allegiance-reciters can testify. Naturally, this feat would be impossible if thought were simply speech.

According to a second view about the influence of language on thought, language is the fundamental basis of thought; Sapir and Whorf would endorse this position (Steinberg, 1982). Whereas the first view emphasizes the physical act of producing spoken language, this second view emphasizes the influence of a language system, which does not necessarily need to be spoken.

Again, however, there are problems with this approach. For example, some deaf children, whose parents do not know sign language, do not begin to learn language until they are school-aged. Nonetheless, Furth (1966) has demonstrated that normal and deaf persons do not differ in their intelligence. A second problem concerns multilinguals. A Swiss person who is fluent in French, German, and English should theoretically form three independent systems of thought, an arrangement that would surely produce cognitive deficits. However, there seems to be no evidence for malfunctioning thought processes among multilinguals. A third problem with this approach, as Glucksberg and Danks (1975) point out, is that nonlinguistic animals show relatively complex thought processes, without the benefit of language capacities. (However, I would like to note a question raised by Limber in 1980 that is relevant to Vázquez's paper: Would a chimpanzee who had learned to sign the names of objects have an edge over a similar but untutored chimp in a problem-solving task that involved those objects?)

Slobin (1979) reminds us of further evidence for the independence of thought from verbal formulation: Thoughts are frequently nonverbal in their format. Remember Kekulé's vision of the snakelike chain leaping into a closed loop, which provided him an insight about the structure of benzene (Ghiselin, 1955), or Einstein's remark about the importance of visualization rather than verbalization. The current research on the analog basis of mental imagery (e.g., Kosslyn, 1980) offers further testimony about thought without linguistic involvement.

A third possibility for the influence of language on thought is that the language system itself provides the specifics for our view of nature (Steinberg, 1982). This interpretation exploits the linguistic relativity component of the Sapir-Whorf hypothesis. The explorations into this third possibility have generally examined whether color terminology influences color memory. At one time it seemed that, when subjects undertook challenging memory tasks, those colors for which we have ready names in English were also the easiest to remember (Brown & Lenneberg, 1954). Presumably, other languages would "dissect nature" along other boundaries to create different color terms, and patterns of recall would be different in these other languages. However, subsequent research determined that those colors that were memorable to speakers of English were also memorable to speakers of dramatically different languages, such as the Dani of New Guinea, who have only two color names (Heider, 1972; Heider & Olivier, 1972). It is possible that language can influence thought processes that are less physiologically based than color perception, but this issue has not been satisfactorally researched.

A fourth possibility regarding language's influence on thought is that a language system provides specifics about our culture (Steinberg, 1982). In the words of Sapir (1929), "We see and hear and otherwise experience very largely as we do because the language habits of our community predispose certain choices of interpretation" (p. 209). However, the *same* language may produce *different* world views. At a peace rally, the demonstrators and the counter-demonstrators may all nominally speak English, yet their world views are vastly different from each other. Furthermore, different languages may produce the same world views. A demonstrator at a peace rally in Upstate New York probably has a world view that is more similar to the world view of a German demonstrator than it is to the world view of his or her flag-waving neighbor. As Steinberg adds, evidence against this fourth possibility includes: (a) the unified world view of multilinguals, and (b) a changing world view in a country such as China where the language remains relatively stable.

How language may influence thought

In the 1980s, the strong version of the Sapir-Whorf hypothesis is not faring well. The structure of language does not seem to be a powerful determinant of the structure of thought. Nonetheless, language may influence the content of particular thoughts. I would like to examine several ways in which this influence operates, paying particular attention to the generic masculine issue with respect to the influence of sex-biased language on thought.

First, as Weist points out in his paper in this volume, the structure of language forces children who are acquiring language to pay attention to certain distinctions. Thus, to repeat Weist's useful analogy, language is more than a barometer that reveals a child's developing conceptual climate. A decision regarding which verb form to employ, for example, forces the child to contemplate conceptual distinction about tense. During the week in which I read Weist's discussion of this issue, my 11-year-old daughter provided me with an illustration of his point. She was learning two past tenses in Spanish and remarked that she had never before noticed that the simple past tense, such as *ate,* meant something different from the other past tenses, such as *was eating* or *had eaten.* Thus, the acquisition of a second language—as well as one's first language—requires us to rearrange concepts about the thoughts we want to express. Similarly, experienced language-users are forced to contemplate conceptual distinctions when they are mastering the vocabulary of a new discipline. For example, incipient opera enthusiasts must attend to the kinds of distinctions that separate a *basso cantate* from a *basso profundo.*

Secondly, as Steinberg (1982) notes, language can provide new ideas. It is difficult to envision how readers of this volume could be provided non-linguistically with the thoughts that the authors wish to convey.

Third, language can change our beliefs and values. Throughout the nation, as I prepared this chapter, the supporters of the two candidates in the Presidential election were feverishly printing position papers aimed at persuading the voters. A representative brochure from Committee for a Sane Nuclear Policy, for example, attempts to change beliefs and values regarding Ronald Reagan with arguments such as, "Ronald Reagan has stated that he is for arms control and peace. But did you know that he has opposed every major nuclear arms control ever negotiated? Every one."

Two other ways in which language may influence thought return us to the more traditional areas of cognitive research. Glucksberg and Danks (1975) point out the role of language in problem solving. For example, if an electrical circuit cannot be completed because of insufficient wire, people will be more likely to realize that a screwdriver blade can provide the missing link if that object is called by a nonsense name *jod* rather than by its traditional name, *screwdriver,* which promotes functional fixedness. As Weist commented in connection with language acquisition, language changes the availability of concepts. In this case, the label *screwdriver* lowers the availability of the concept "metal blade."

In addition, language influences memory. Sometimes language distorts memory. Recall the classic experiment by Carmichael, Hogan, and Walter (1932) in which an ambiguous figure was distorted in the direction of the label that had originally been applied to the object. For example, the straight, narrow line that connected two circles was recalled as bent when that figure had been labeled "eyeglasses," but that same line was recalled as straight and wide when the figure had been labeled "dumbbells." More recently, Loftus (1975) produced distortions in recall for automobile speed by varying the verb used in the question; describing the incident in terms of *smashed* produced higher estimates than *collided, bumped, contacted,* and *hit.* Also, Snyder and Uranowitz (1978) showed distortions in recall among students who had been provided with the label "lesbian" for a woman named Betty whose life history they had just read. These students were more likely to report that Betty had never dated men and was unattractive, in contrast with other students who had received a "heterosexual" label for Betty.

Clearly, languages may aid memory as well as impede it; words help us remember when we use verbal mnemonics. We may use chunking, thereby grouping a sequence of numbers, letters, or words together into a verbal unit. Also, we may use organization by grouping together conceptually related items, as demonstrated by studies on clustering in free recall. Furthermore, we may use a variety of mediation techniques, such as generating an English word to help us remember a nonsense syllable, developing a narrative to string together unrelated words, or forming a word or a sentence out of the first letter of each item that we must recall.

One additional topic has been repeatedly linked with the Sapir-Whorf hypothesis, in both psychological and sociological research, and I would like to discuss this topic in greater detail. This topic has been referred to by many names, but I will use Martyna's (1980) term, "the generic masculine." A problem arises in English because words such as *he, his,* and *man* have been playing two roles, the first referring specifically to males, and the second referring generically to all human beings, both males and females. In this final section of the chapter, I will examine the linguistic status of the generic masculine, the relationship of the generic masculine to the Sapir-Whorf hypothesis, and research on the generic masculine.

The use of a word such as *man* to refer to both males and females is an instance of a linguistic phenomenon known as "marking." There are many pairs of words, most commonly adjectives, in which one member of the pair can be used in a neutral or generic sense to refer to an entire dimension as well as to one pole of the dimension. For example, the word *big* is used to refer to the entire big–small dimension, as well as to one pole of that dimension. Thus, a person might ask "How big is your foot?" to refer to a very small foot as well as to a very large foot. The responses "very small" and "very big" would be equally probable. In contrast, the question "How small is your foot?" implies that the response "very small" is much more probable than the response "very big." In linguistics, the member of the pair that can be used in a neutral sense is called *unmarked,* whereas the other member is called *marked.* In our example, *big* is unmarked, and *small* is marked.

On the surface, pairs of words such as *he–she, his–her,* and *man–woman* seem to operate like unmarked and marked words (Moulton, Robinson, & Elias, 1978). That is, the words *he, his,* and *man* are similar to unmarked adjectives because they are used to refer to both males and females, as well as to males alone. All of us learned from our fifth-grade teachers that in the sentence, "Each student took his pencil," the word *his* refers to both genders. In contrast, the words *she, her,* and *woman* are similar to marked adjectives because they are used to refer only to females. Our fifth-grade teachers, who had never been exposed to the occasional current use of the generic feminine, would surely conclude that "Each student took her pencil" referred exclusively to female students.

Many people maintain that words such as *he, his,* and *man* truly operate like unmarked words. For example, the biology department at S.U.N.Y. Geneseo offers a course called "Biology of Man," and they see no paradox in the fact that a major portion of the course is devoted to the female reproductive system. *Man,* they argue, refers equally to men and women, just as the question "How big is your foot?" could elicit a response from either the big or the small pole of the big–small scale.

However, as any devotee of the fine points of A.P.A. style knows, psychology manuscripts must no longer use a word such as *man* in a generic sense (American Psychological Association, 1983), and numerous commercial publishing houses concur. Their rationale is that these words are sex-biased, imprecise, and misleading when used to refer to both sexes. At the time "Guidelines for Nonsexist Language in APA Journals" (American Psychological Association, 1977) was originally published, few studies had been conducted to determine whether generic masculine terms were indeed misleading. However, the conclusion now seems to be justified.

The nature of the current literature on the generic masculine is truly interdisciplinary, for it represents researchers from disciplines such as psychology, sociology, speech communications, women's studies, philosophy, and linguistics. The model that investigators in this area use most frequently is the Sapir-Whorf hypothesis. As applied to the generic masculine, the sex-bias in these linguistic terms predisposes people to think in sex-biased ways. In particular, sex-biased language produces sex-biases in a wide variety of cognitive processes, such as mental imagery, search patterns, and decision making.

Some theoreticians have proposed that sex-biased thinking produces sex-biased language, rather than the reverse. According to this view, language is merely a barometer that reflects the dominant thoughts of society. Lakoff (1975) proposes, for example, that the use of masculine terms in the generic masculine sense is simply a historical consequence of the superior role of men. If sex-biased language is just an epiphenomenon of a sex-biased society, then all the elaborate attempts of the American Psychological Association and others to change language can only offer symptomatic relief. Language change would not have any consequential influence on sex-biased thinking.

The dominant view, however, is that the process is bidirectional. A sex-biased culture no doubt produced masculine terms to refer to both sexes. However, the further use of these masculine terms to refer to both sexes helps to perpetuate sex-biased thinking. As Dayhoff (1983) points out, "relatively subtle linguistic features not only reflect but also help enforce social attitudes and stereotypes. . . . The subtle message is that the male is associated with the universal, general, the subsuming; the female with the more excluded, deviant, or special case" (pp. 544–545).

A number of studies demonstrate that generic masculine terms are more likely than gender neutral terms to produce male-oriented thoughts. It appears that the most effective way to categorize the research on the generic masculine is in terms of the dependent variable used to measure thought processes. In each case, the independent variable is the kind of linguistic terms used, either generic masculine or gender neutral. I located six classes of dependent variables: picture choice, decisions about sentence/picture compatability, judgments about professions, recall, subsequent word choice, and ratings on semantic differential scales.

Some of the earliest studies on the generic masculine employed picture choice as the dependent variable. Schneider and Hacker (1973), for example, asked students to choose pictures that could be used to represent chapters for an introductory sociology textbook. Chapter titles sometimes included a generic masculine term, such as "Social Man" or "Industrial Man," and sometimes included a gender neutral term, such as "Society" or "Industrial Life." A significantly larger number of pictures of men only were selected in the generic masculine condition, in contrast to the gender neutral condition.

Harrison (1975) instructed junior high students to draw pictures to illustrate assorted human activities. The stimulus sentence was identical in three conditions except for the key term. In one condition, the key term included a generic masculine word, for example "early man" or "mankind," whereas in two other conditions, the terms were gender neutral, such as "early people" or "men and women." Students in the generic masculine condition drew a greater proportion of males to females than students in the two gender neutral conditions.

A second class of studies involves decisions about the compatibility between a sentence and a picture, using a variant of the typicality paradigm. Martyna (1980), for example, constructed a number of sentences referring to a hypothetical neutral person, such as "When someone prepares for an exam, —— must do some studying." One of three terms was inserted in place of the blank: *he, they,* and *he or she.* Students were shown a sentence and a picture of someone performing the appropriate activity, in this case, studying, but the sex of the person was sometimes male and sometimes female. In each case, they were asked to decide whether the sentence applied or did not apply to the picture. How did people respond to a picture of a woman studying and the sentence, "When someone prepares for an exam, he must do some studying"? When the picture followed the sentence, the sentences containing the generic masculine *he* were judged not to apply about 20% of the time. When the picture and the sentence were presented simultaneously, the generic masculine sentences were judged not to apply about 40% of the time.

Silveira (1978) employed a similar design but focused on reaction times for those subjects who judged that a picture of a woman *was* appropriate for sentences such as "Man is mortal." Her results showed that the reaction times were significantly slower when a picture of a woman followed the sentence "Man is mortal" than when a picture of a man followed that same sentence. In contrast, reaction times to the two pictures were similar to each other when they followed the sentence "People are mortal."

To review, we have seen in two different classes of studies that, when people encounter a sentence containing a generic masculine term, they appear to create masculine mental representations. These masculine mental representations guide them in their selection of pictures that are more likely to show males than females. These masculine mental representations are also judged to be less compatible with pictures of women than with pictures of men.

A third class of studies on the generic masculine involve judgments about the attractiveness or appropriateness of various professions. In an early study, Bem and Bem (1973) found that women were more likely to express an interest in jobs when they were described in gender neutral terms than when they were described in generic masculine terms.

However, Gottfredson (1976) did not find that linguistic terms influenced judgments; this study and one other are the only ones I was able to locate in the published literature that failed to differentiate between the two kinds of terms. Gottfredson administered vocational interest inventories to female students in a private, college-preparatory school. These inventories used either gender-neutral terms or generic masculine terms to describe assorted vocations. The young women were no more likely to express an interest in a profession if it was described in gender-neutral terms than if it was described in generic masculine terms. Todd-Mancillas and Meyers (1980) speculate that the nature of the subject population in Gottfredson's study may have influenced the outcome.

More recently, two additional studies confirm the influence of linguistic terms on judgments. Stericker (1981) found that undergraduate women were more likely to express an interest in a social-work-related occupation if the occupation had been described in "he or she" terms rather than in exclusively "he" terms.

In addition, Briere and Lanktree (1983) showed different versions of a paragraph to undergraduate men and women. The paragraph was based on a description of psychologists found in the 1972 APA "Ethical Standards of Psychologists." The generic masculine version began, "The psychologist believes in the dignity and worth of the individual human being. He is committed to increasing man's understanding of himself and others. . . ." Two other versions were gender neutral. Subjects were asked to rate psychology in terms of its attractiveness as a future career for men and for women. The results demonstrated that subjects who had seen the generic masculine version rated a career in psychology as less attractive for women than did subjects who had seen either of the gender neutral versions.

In this third class of studies, the research by Bem and Bem (1973), Stericker (1981), and Briere and Lanktree (1983) suggests that generic masculine descriptions of vocations produce a more masculine mental representation of these vocations, in contrast to gender-neutral descriptions. Consequently, it is more difficult to envision these vocations as being appropriate for women. Gottfredson's study demonstrates, however, that the effect is not inevitable; some subjects in some conditions are not influenced by the choice of linguistic terms.

A fourth class of studies uses recall as the dependent measure. Crawford and English (1984) prepared a gender-neutral and a generic masculine version of a 400-word essay describing the professional activities of psychologists. Two days later, they were tested for recall. These authors found a significant interaction between sex of subject and linguistic terms. That is, male subjects had higher recall scores with the generic masculine version, whereas female subjects had higher recall scores with the gender-neutral version. Their results were also replicated with a different essay. It seems, then, that men perform better when the text favors a masculine mental representation, whereas women perform better when the text favors a mental representation that includes women.

A fifth class of research uses subsequent word choice as the dependent measure. The studies belonging to this category are the ones with which psychologists are most familiar, because they were both published in the *American Psychologist*. In one of these papers, Moulton, Robinson, and Elias (1978) asked male and female undergraduates to write stories based upon a topic sentence. For example, some students were given the generic masculine topic sentence, "In a large coeducational institution the average student will feel isolated in his introductory courses" (p. 1034). Other students were given two kinds of gender-neutral topic sentences. The authors examined the paragraphs to discover whether the subsequent text used feminine pronouns or female names. They found that paragraphs written in response to the generic masculine "his" produced stories about females 35% of the time, in contrast to an average of 51% in the two gender-neutral conditions.

Mackay (1980) selected paragraphs from a textbook on writing and prepared four versions of these paragraphs. One version used the generic masculine *he* and its variants, whereas the other three versions used gender-neutral neologisms, *E, e,* or *tey.* (Each of these neologisms has been suggested as an alternative to the awkward ''he or she.'') After reading one version of the paragraph, subjects were asked a number of multiple-choice questions designed to test comprehension. The target question asked whether the person discussed in the paragraph was male, female, or either male or female. The subjects who had read the generic masculine paragraph had a 50% error rate; half of the time, they believed that the paragraph referred only to a male rather than to either a male or a female. In contrast, the subjects who had read the gender-neutral versions had a 13% error rate overall. Thus, both studies involving subsequent word choice as the dependent measure have demonstrated that the generic masculine *he* is associated with males to a greater degree than assorted gender-neutral words.

The sixth and final class of studies uses ratings on a semantic differential scale as the dependent measure. Cole, Hill, and Dayley (1983) felt that many of the earlier studies used a procedure that was rather obvious to subjects, so that demand characteristics might contaminate the results. Furthermore, they were concerned that subjects in the Moulton et al. study may have merely repeated the pronoun from the topic sentence. Thus, a student who continues, in response to the topic sentence listed above, by writing, ''He may feel that the instructor doesn't even know his name,'' may simply echo the same masculine pronoun. This student may not actually have a masculine representation for the sentence. Accordingly, Cole and her coauthors conducted a series of five experiments. In several of these studies, a job description used either generic masculine pronouns or one kind of gender-neutral pronoun. Subjects were then asked to visualize the person in the job and to rate this person on semantic differential scales that tapped masculinity-femininity, such as ''very active–very passive'' and ''very tactful–very blunt.'' In general, sentences that used generic masculine pronouns received ratings that were just as feminine as sentences that used gender neutral pronouns. However, in one experiment, the generic masculine pronoun ''he'' was used in the same sentence as the generic masculine noun ''man.'' The combined effect was decidedly masculine. When people read a description ''The man for this job must have a bachelor's degree. . . . He . . . ,'' their mental representation was male.

In summary, most of the studies reviewed here demonstrate that generic masculine terms lead to thoughts about males, rather than gender-neutral thoughts. (The exceptions were Gottfredson's study on the attractiveness of professions and several of Cole's studies.) Naturally, many people are concerned that the generic masculine may have an important implications. An article in the APA Monitor summarized this position:

> We do not know, but can guess at the psychological costs of being a nonperson in one's own language. What message is presented to young girls about their present

and future status as human beings, when it is constantly drummed into their heads that they must refer to themselves and others of their sex as males.

As psychologists, we have come to recognize that the seemingly "trivial" is in fact of utmost importance in the conduct of human behavior—the slight nod and smile when someone says or does what we want may through conditioning determine that person's behavior far into the future; the failure to touch or give even the briefest eye contact when it's expected may create deep feelings of rejection. To say that subtleties of language are trivial and thus can't affect us, is to fall into the trap of psychological ignorance. (Association for Women in Psychology Ad Hoc Committee on Sexist Language, 1975, p. 16)

Thus, it seems likely that the generic masculine is more than a linguistic curiosity. In fact, it may play a part in sex-role socialization. However, the task of specifying in real-life settings how the generic masculine contributes to sex-biased cognitive structures (and ultimately, perhaps, to sex-biased behaviors) seems infinitely complex. In contrast, other challenging topics, such as the relationship between children's conceptions of time and their linguistic competence, look extremely approachable.

FUTURE DIRECTIONS

In this paper, I have discussed four topics of research: (a) language development, (b) animal communication, (c) psycholinguistics in real-life settings, and (d) the Sapir-Whorfian hypothesis. The area of children's language development is the one with the longest tradition, and research will doubtlessly continue at a steady pace on this complex topic. Animal communication, more specifically ape language, has had a relatively short history. Furthermore, if the financial backing essential for this kind of research were to evaporate—a reasonable possibility as Vázquez suggests—this area will be short-lived. I suspect that research on psycholinguistics in real-life settings will expand as it seems likely that there will be an increasing emphasis on the social and contextual determinants of language. With respect to the work on the influence of language on thought, we can safely conclude that a strong interpretation of the Sapir-Whorf hypothesis has been abandoned. However, I would hope to see more extensive examination of the idea that the language system provides the specifics for our view of nature. As mentioned in the discussion of this topic, research has focused almost exclusively on color perception, and work on a less physiologically based area would be welcomed. Thus, I expect that all four of these psycholinguistic research areas will represent genuine directions in the future of psycholinguistics.

Another issue discussed in this chapter which will probably be a direction within the topic of language and thought is the research on the generic masculine question. This reserach is barely more than a decade old, and the current enthusiasm for research on sex roles and psychology of women would seem to guarantee more work in this area. However, I hope that future work would not merely demonstrate more instances of the generic masculine terms leading to thoughts of males. Instead, it would be useful to examine what factors are related to the strength of this effect. For example, are there consistent sex or age differences, and is the effect related to the respondents' views about women? In addition, as mentioned earlier, it would be valuable to find out how the use of generic masculine terms might ultimately produce sex-biased behaviors and might contribute to the acquisition of sex roles.

Looking more generally at the area of psycholinguistics, it is difficult to predict in which direction this discipline will proceed. For example, will we have an all-encompassing theory of language comprehension and language production, widely accepted by psycholinguists, prior to the 21st century? Consistent with the arguments of Vázquez, it seems likely that, for decades to come, psycholinguists will be using language—the very tools of their trade—to argue the relative merits of various alternatives.

REFERENCES

American Psychological Association. (1977) *Guidelines for nonsexist language in APA Journals*. Washington, DC: Author.

American Psychological Association. (1983). *Publication Manual of the American Psychological Association* (3rd ed.). Washington, DC: Author.

Arena, L. A. (1982). The language of corporate attorneys. In R. J. Di Pietro (Ed.), *Linguistics and the professions* (pp. 143–153). Norwood, NJ: Ablex.

Association for Women in Psychology Ad Hoc Committee on Sexist Language. (1975, November). Help stamp out sexism: Change the language! *APA Monitor, 16*.

Augustine, Saint. (1949). *The confessions of Saint Augustine*. (E. B. Pusey, Trans.). New York: The Modern Library.

Bem, S. L., & Bem, D. J. (1973). Does sex-biased job advertising "aid and abet" sex discrimination? *Journal of Applied Social Psychology, 3*, 6–18.

Bonanno, M. (1982). Women's language in the medical interview. In R. J. Di Pietro (Ed.), *Linguistics and the professions* (pp. 27–38). Norwood, NJ: Ablex.

Bower, T. G. R. (1966). The visual world of infants. *Scientific American, 215* (6), 80–92.

Braine, M. D. S. (1976). Children's first word combination. *Monographs of the Society for Reserach in Child Development, 41*, 1–97.

Briere, J., & Lanktree, C. (1983). Sex-role related effects of sex bias in language. *Sex Roles, 9*, 625–632.

Brooks, V. R. (1982). Sex differences in student dominance behavior in female and male professors' classrooms. *Sex Roles, 8*, 683–690.

Brown, R., & Lenneberg, E. H. (1954). A study in language and cognition. *Journal of Abnormal and Social Psychology, 49*, 454–462.

Carmichael, L., Hogan, H. P., & Walter, A. A. (1932). An experimental study of the effect of language on the representation of visually perceived form. *Journal of Experimental Psychology, 15*, 454–462.

Cole, C. M., Hill, F. A., & Dayley, L. J. (1983). Do masculine pronouns used generically lead to thoughts of men? *Sex Roles, 9*, 737–750.

Crawford, M., & English, L. (1984). Generic versus specific inclusion of women in language: Effects on recall. *Journal of Psycholinguistic Research, 13*, 373–381.

Cromer, R. F. (1968). *The development of temporal reference during the acquisition of language.* Unpublished doctoral dissertation, Harvard University.

Day, R. H., & McKenzie, B. E. (1977). Constancies in the perceptual world of the infant. In W. Epstein (Ed.), *Stability and constancy in visual perception: Mechanisms and processes.* New York: Wiley.

Dayhoff, S. A. (1983). Sexist language and person perception: Evaluation of candidates from newspaper articles. *Sex Roles, 9*, 543–555.

Dinneen, F. P. (1967). *An introduction to general linguistics.* New York: Holt, Rinehart & Winston.

DiPietro, R. J. (Ed.). (1982). *Linguistics and the professions.* Norwood, NJ: Ablex.

Epstein, J. J. (1982). The grammar of a lie: Its legal implications. In R. J. DiPietro (Ed.), *Linguistics and the professions* (pp. 133–142). Norwood, NJ: Ablex.

Finegan, E. (1982). Form and function in testament language. In R. J. DiPietro (Ed.), *Linguistics and the professions* (pp. 113–120). Norwood, NJ: Ablex.

Fisher, S. (1982). The decision-making context: How doctors and patients communicate. In R. J. DiPietro (Ed.), *Linguistics and the professions* (pp. 51–81). Norwood, NJ: Ablex.

Friedman, W. J. (1982). Conventional time concepts and children's structuring of time. In W. J. Friedman (Ed.), *The developmental psychology of time* (pp. 171–208). New York: Academic Press.

Furth, H. (1966). *Thinking without language.* New York: Free Press.

Ghiselin, B. (1955). *The creative process.* New York: Mentor Books.

Glucksberg, S., & Danks, J. H. (1975). *Experimental psycholinguistics: An introduction.* Hillsdale, NJ: Erlbaum.

Gottfredson, G. D. (1976). A note on sexist wording on interest measurement. *Measurement and Evaluation of Guidance, 8*, 221–223.

Haggerty, L. C. G. (1930). What a two-and-one-half-year-old child said in one day. *Journal of Genetic Psychology, 37*, 75–101.

Harrison, L. (1975, April). Cro-magnon woman—in eclipse. *Science Teacher, 42*, 8–11.

Heider, E. R. (1972). Universals in color naming and memory. *Journal of Experimental Psychology, 93*, 10–20.

Heider, E. R., & Olivier, D. C. (1972). The structure of the color space in naming and memory for two languages. *Cognitive Psychology, 3*, 337–354.

Hockett, C. F. (1963). The problem of universals in language. In J. H. Greenberg (Ed.), *Universals of language* (2nd ed.). Cambridge, MA: M.I.T. Press.

Kosslyn, S. M. (1980). *Image and mind.* Cambridge, MA: Harvard University Press.

Lakoff, R. (1975). *Language and woman's place.* New York: Harper & Row.

Leaffer, T. (1982). Applications to psychoanalysis and psychotherapy. In R. J. DiPietro (Ed.), *Linguistics and the professions* (pp. 13–25). Norwood, NJ: Ablex.

Limber, J. (1980). Language in child and chimp? In T. A. Sebeok & J. Umiker-Sebeok (Eds.), *Speaking of apes* (pp. 197–220). New York: Plenum Press.

Loftus, E. F. (1975). Leading questions and the eyewitness report. *Cognitive Psychology, 7*, 560–572.

Macfarlane, A. (1977). *The psychology of childbirth.* Cambridge, MA: Harvard University Press.

Mackay, D. G. (1980). Psychology, prescriptive grammar, and the pronoun problem. *American Psychologist, 35*, 444–449.

Maclay, H., & Osgood, C. E. (1959). Hesitation phenomena in spontaneous English speech. *Word, 15*, 19–44.

Macnamara, J. (1972). Cognitive basis of language learning in infants. *Psychological Review, 79*, 1–13.

Malmi, W. A. (1980). Chimpanzees and language evolution. In T. A. Sebeok & J. Umiker-Sebeok (Eds.), *Speaking of apes* (pp. 191–196). New York: Plenum Press.

Martyna, W. (1980). Beyond the "He/Man" approach: The case for nonsexist language. *Signs, 5,* 482–493.

Marx, J. L. (1980). Ape-language controversy flares up. *Science, 207,* 1330–1333.

Matlin, M. W. (1983). *Cognition.* New York: Holt, Rinehart & Winston.

McNeill, D. (1970). The development of language. In P. H. Mussen (Ed.), *Carmichael's manual of child psychology* (3rd ed., Vol. 1). New York: Wiley.

Moulton, J., Robinson, G. M., & Elias, C. (1978). Sex bias in language use: "Neutral" pronouns that aren't. *American Psychologist, 33,* 1032–1036.

Neisser, U. (1983). Dialogue IV. Ulric Neisser's views on the psychology of language and thought. In R. W. Rieber (Ed.), *Dialogues on the psychology of language and thought* (pp. 123–141). New York: Plenum.

O'Barr, W. M., & Atkins, B. K. (1980). "Women's language" or "powerless language?" In S. McConnell-Ginet, R. Borker, & N. Furman (Eds.), *Women and language in literature and society* (pp. 93–110). New York: Praeger.

Phoenix, V. G., & Lindeman, M. L. (1982). Language patterns and therapeutic change. In R. J. DiPietro (Ed.), *Linguistics and the professions* (pp. 3–11). Norwood, NJ: Ablex.

Piaget, J. (1963). Le langage et les operations intellectuelles. In *Problemes de Psycho-linguistique (Symposium de l'association de psychologie scientifique de langue francaise)* (pp. 51–72). Paris: Presses Universitaires de Frances.

Prince, E. F., Frader, J., & Bosk, C. (1982). On hedging in physician-physician discourse. In R. J. DiPietro (Ed.), *Linguistics and the professions* (pp. 83–97). Norwood, NJ: Ablex.

Rosch, E. H. (1977). Human categorization. In N. Warren (Ed.), *Advances in cross-cultural psychology* (Vol. 1). London: Academic Press.

Russell, M. J. (1976). Human olfactory communication. *Nature* (London), *260,* 520–522.

Sapir, E. (1929). The status of linguistics as a science. *Language, 5,* 207–214.

Savage, E. S., & Rumbaugh, D. M. (1977). In D. M. Rumbaugh (Ed.), *Language learning by a chimpanzee* (pp. 287–309). New York: Academic Press.

Savage-Rumbaugh, E. S., & Rumbaugh, D. M. (1980). Language Analogue Project, Phase II: Theory and tactics. In K. E. Nelson (Ed.), *Children's language,* volume 2 (pp. 267–307). New York: Gardner Press.

Schneider, J. W., & Hacker, S. L. (1973). Sex role imagery and use of the generic "man" in introductory texts: A case in the sociology of sociology, *American Sociologist, 8,* 12–18.

Seidenberg, M. S., & Petitto, L. A. (1981). Ape signing: Problems of methods and interpretation. In Sebeok, T., & Rosenthal, R. (Eds.), *The Clever Hans phenomenon: Communication with horses, whales, apes and people. Annals of the New York Academy of Sciences, 364,* 115–129.

Silveira, J. (1978). *Women on the fringes: Generic masculine words and their relation to thinking.* Unpublished manuscript.

Slobin, D. I. (1979). *Psycholinguistics* (2nd ed.). Glenview, IL: Scott, Foresman and Company.

Snyder, M., & Uranowitz, S. W. (1978). Reconstructing the past: Some cognitive consequences of person perception. *Journal of Personality and Social Psychology, 36,* 941–951.

Stahlke, H. F. W. (1980). On asking the question: Can apes learn language? In K. E. Nelson (Ed.), *Children's language* (Vol. 2, pp. 309–329). New York: Gardner Press.

Stam, J. H. (1980). An historical perspective on "linguistic relativity." In R. W. Rieber (Ed.), *Psychology of language and thought* (pp. 239–262). New York: Plenum.

Steinberg, D. D. (1982). *Psycholinguistics: Language, mind, and world.* London: Longman.

Stericker, A. (1981). Does this "he or she" business really make a difference? The effect of masculine pronouns as generics on job attitudes. *Sex Roles, 7,* 637–651.

Swacker, M. (1979). Women's verbal behavior at learned and professional conferences. In B. L.

Dubois & I. Crouch (Eds.), *The sociology of the languages of American women* (pp. 155–160). San Antonio, TX: Trinity University.

Tannen, D., & Wallat, C. (1982). A sociolinguistic analysis of multiple demands on the pediatrician in doctor/mother/child interaction. In R. J. DiPietro (Ed.), *Linguistics and the professions* (pp. 39–50). Norwood, NJ: Ablex.

Terrace, H. S. (1981). A report to an Academy, 1980. In Sebeok, T., & Rosenthal, R. (Eds.), *The clever Hans phenomenon: Communication with horses, whales, apes and people. Annals of the New York Academy of Sciences, 364,* 115–129.

Todd-Mancillas, W. R., & Meyers, K. A. (1980). *The effects of inclusive/exclusive language on reading comprehension, perceived human interest, and likelihood of inclusive pronoun usage.* Paper presented at the International Communication Association.

Walker, A. G. (1982). Patterns and implications of cospeech in a legal setting. In R. J. DiPietro (Ed.), *Linguistics and the professions* (pp. 101–112). Norwood, NJ: Ablex.

Watson, John B. (1924). *Behaviorism.* New York: Norton.

Whorf, B. L. (1956). Science and linguistics. In J. B. Carroll (Ed.), *Language, thought and reality: Selected writings of Benjamin Lee Whorf.* Cambridge, MA: M.I.T. Press.

Zimmerman, D. H., & West, C. (1975). Sex roles, interruptions and silences in conversation. In B. Thorne & N. Henley (Eds.), *Language and sex: Difference and dominance.* Rowley, MA: Newbury House.

Chapter 16

Can Involuntary Slips Reveal One's State of Mind?—With an Addendum on the Problem of Conscious Control of Action*

Bernard J. Baars

University of California, San Francisco

The idea that, in unguarded moments, we may involuntarily express thoughts which we normally keep private is not new. It may be a part of linguistic folklore all over the world, and Freud, whom we credit with its modern version, was happy to quote from Schiller and Shakespeare on the subject (Freud, 1901/1938; 1920/1966). In *The Merchant of Venice*, Portia's husband is to be chosen by lot; but Portia is in love with Bassanio, though she cannot tell him this outright. Instead, her declaration of love "slips out" involuntarily. She begins by denying her love:

> There's something tells me (*but it is not love*)
> I would not lose you. . . .

. . . then contemplates how she cannot tell Bassanio the secret solution to the lottery:

> I could teach you how to choose right, but then I am forsworn.

Her love makes her want to give Bassanio the solution to the problem, so that she can be his; but she is sworn to keep the secret, and inclined anyway to deny her love. This is her inner conflict. One part of her stands against another, and the struggle triggers a revealing slip of the tongue:

* The development of this paper and some of the research cited has been supported by NSF Grant BNS-7906024 to the author. I am grateful also to Michael T. Motley, Carl Camden, and Mark E. Mattson for their support in this collaborative effort.

The addendum was written after Gelfand completed his chapter.

The author is currently visiting scientist at the Langley Porter Psychiatric Clinic, UCSF.

Beshrew your eyes
They have o'erlooked me, and divided me;
One half of me is yours, the other half yours,—
Mine own, I would say; but if mine, then yours,
And so all yours. (Emphasis added)

Triumphantly, the poet concludes his conceit by having Portia recognize her slip as an admission of love: "but if mine, then yours/And so all yours." Thus Shakespeare captures all the elements of conflict and involuntary self-revelation in a half dozen lines. First, love; then, denial of love; hence, conflict, leading to an involuntary expression of love; the slip is corrected; and finally, the tension is resolved by Portia's recognition that her slip has revealed her true feelings.

So much for poetry. What about science? Is there any evidence that such things happen in the real world? And if there is, do we have the theoretical tools to represent these commonsensical ideas in an explicit way? Until recently, the only evidence for the "Freudian hypothesis" about slips was anecdotal (e.g., Ellis, 1980). That situation has now changed, since we now have experimental methods for eliciting predesigned, involuntary slips in the laboratory. At this point, there are six different tasks that elicit predictable slips, including spoonerisms, word-blends, word-exchanges in sentences, and slips of typing (Baars, 1980a). Given these methods, we can manipulate contextual information to see if slips expressing some idea are more likely to occur in the appropriate context, and we can even select subjects who appear to be in some conflict, and see if the conflict will increase the likelihood of a revealing slip (Motley, 1980). This evidence is detailed below.

But how do the ideas expressed by Shakespeare and Freud relate to our current concepts of human functioning? I agree with Erdelyi (1974) and others that we can indeed represent such commonsense notions as "state of mind," "inner conflict," and "involuntary slip" in a straightforward way with the theoretical tools that are in common use today (viz. Boden, 1977).

Let's take these ideas one by one.

States of mind

By a "state of mind" I mean a rather global pattern of cognitive activation, including unconscious processes as well as conscious thoughts, feelings, and images. This whole constellation is what social psychologists commonly mean by "attitude" or "belief system" (Abelson, 1981), and what social and clinical psychologists have taken to calling "self-schemas" (e.g., Markus & Sentis, 1980). Thus, any pervasive emotional or motivational state may be called a state of mind, whether it is need for power or achievement, love, anxiety, or depression. Lately a number of neurophysiological correlates of such states have been found (McClelland, Davidson, Saron, & Floor, 1980; Reuter, Lorenz, & Davidson, 1981; Weinberger, Schwartz, & Davidson, 1979). Further, I want to include the possibility of *conflicted* states of mind, where one intention or goal may be contradicted by another roughly equal salience. In a theory, such states of mind would typically be represented as a pattern of activation in a complex network of concepts. Such semantic networks have been widely used by artificial intelligence workers and cognitive psychologists to represent common-sense knowledge of the world, visual information, game playing, natural language simulation, and even psychopathology (e.g., Boden, 1977; Schank & Colby, 1973). Both cognitive psychologists and artificial intelligence workers have found it increasingly useful to model processing in such a network by the spread of "activation." That is, all the nodes in the network are assigned numbers, and high-activation nodes spread their activation by raising the values associated with adjacent nodes (e.g., Anderson, 1983). There are several ways of representing a conflict between different intentions or goal-systems, but perhaps the simplest is to permit nodes representing different intentions to have equal activation in the network, although only one intention can be executed.

Cognitive psychologists in general would predict that such pervasive states will have widespread measurable consequences. Thus, if words expressing sadness were flashed tachistoscopically to a depressed person, we would expect a lower detection threshold for those words, faster reaction time, higher confidence levels, and the like (Bruner, 1957). In memory tasks, depressed people should have better recall for sad stories, and worse recall for happy stories. Immediate pragmatic inferences made during the process of reading a story can be assessed by later false recognition tests (viz. Bransford, 1979), and, in depressed subjects, more immediate inferences are likely to be unhappy as well. Consider the following ambiguous sentences.

1. The entire office of the President is a mess.
2. She could not bear children after the accident.
3. My ex-wife hates spinach as much as me.

Given sentences like these, one would expect that depressed people would be more likely to interpret (1) as referring to the presidency, rather than the room; (2) as referring to an injury to a woman's reproductive organs rather than a feeling of annoyance after an irritating mishap caused by children; and (3) as hatred for "me," rather than "my hatred for spinach." One can think of many other tasks in which depressed people can be expected to interpret the world or their memories along depressed lines. The same goes for any other powerful state of mind.

Generally, we can say that *states of mind work globally to structure information processing in the nervous system, such that given a choice between two interpretations of any material, the interpretation that fits a prevalent state of mind is more likely to be chosen.* (See addendum for further discussion.)

Note that this generalization also suggests a way of assessing someone's state of mind: namely, if we can find a *choice-point* where a person must select one of two possible interpretations of an ambiguous stimulus, between two relevant elements in memory, or between two plausible actions. Such choice-points occur with great frequency, and, in general, we are likely to choose whichever alternative corresponds best with some pervasive state of mind.

Nor is this idea new. It is implicit in all projective tests. But there is an important difference from classical projective tests, in that we now have the ability to present such material to people in a very precise way so that there is no doubt about the meaning of their choices. The ambiguous sentences cited above are an example of this. Each sentence permits at least two interpretations, one of which is negative or saddening. There is good evidence that our choice of a conscious interpretation results from unconscious processes in normal sentence comprehension, so that we can be quite sure that the subject cannot deliberately manipulate the outcome of the test. Thus, we avoid the typical problems of interpretation with standard projective tests.

But are not ambiguities—or choice-points in processing—artificial? Neisser (1976) makes the case that too many of our cognitive procedures have no clear relation to the things that people do in everyday life. I would claim, however, that resolving ambiguities of various kinds is ecologically natural and important. Life presents us with numerous natural ambiguities. Language is rife with it, as we can see simply by looking at a dictionary, where almost every entry has multiple meanings. Further, in the first instant of perceiving anything unpredictable—immediately after opening a door, lifting the telephone, or turning on the television—we need to resolve numerous perceptual choices. Then there are noisy perceptual conditions: listening to a conversation at a crowded cocktail party, or trying to see traffic at night or in the rain. Finally, one important domain for human beings is almost entirely ambiguous—namely, the social domain. We can never be entirely sure whether someone likes and respects us, and we care about that sort of thing quite a lot. Much of the time we are left guessing. Here, too, our state of mind may be revealed by the way in which we interpret inadequate information (e.g., Sherwood, 1981). So the need to make a choice in the face of ambiguity is not at all unnatural.

Slips reflect ambiguities in speech production

What do ambiguities have to do with slips? I have argued elsewhere that slips reflect *choice-points* in speech production, just as ambiguous sentences create choice-points in language comprehension (Baars, 1980b). One kind of choice-point in speech production might involve actual competition between different ways of saying something, and, in fact, all of our techniques for inducing involuntary slips make use of competition to induce the slips (Baars, 1980a). Thus, we can create a spoonerism like *bad goof–gad boof* by leading people to expect a word-pair that resembles the slip. Their expectations are controlled by first showing "phonological bias" pairs like *gas balloon/get booze/got book* and the like, all of which begin with /g/ and /b/; the resulting expectations conflict with the target word pair *bad goof,* and people will occasionally slip and say "*gad boof.*"

Each word pair is presented for about 1 second, using a microcomputer or a memory drum. Subjects are told to read the word pairs silently, but to be prepared to say any word pair quickly, immediately *after* it has been presented, on cue. Thus, subjects must be constantly prepared to repeat any word pair which they have just read. Under these conditions, "phonological bias" creates a readiness to say a word pair that differs from the target word pair in its initial consonants, and subjects commit unintentional spoonerism in about 20–30% of the trials. The effect is very robust across subjects, meaning of the slip, contextual conditions, and modes of stimulus presentation.

Other techniques create order-competition between words or phrases. For instance, we can ask people to answer a question like:

"Is the blue sky below the grey sea?"

with the proviso that their answer must contain the same words as the question. About 20% of the time, they will make a slip like:

"No, the blue sea is below the gray sky"

or even the truth-violating slip:

"Yes, the blue sky is below the grey sea"

(Baars & Mattson, 1981). In this case, there is competition between the order of adjective-noun pairs in the question (*blue sky >> grey sea*) and in the correct answer ("No, the *grey sea* is below the *blue sky*"). From previous research, we know that competition of order between higher-level chunks will often lead to an exchange of lower elements, and this is what we find: order competition between two adjective-noun constituent units leads to an exchange of adjectives or nouns between the constituents (cf. Baars & Motley, 1976).

Competition between alternative speech plans requires the speaker to resolve ambiguity, just as a person confronted with an ambiguous sentence or a vague memory must resolve ambiguity. Generally speaking, we resolve ambiguity by bringing in additional information from a great variety of other knowledge sources *including our biases, expectations, or states of mind.* Thus, it is not surprising that states of mind affect the way in which we interpret ambiguous stimuli. Similarly, we would expect states of mind to affect the likelihood of our making a slip expressing the state of mind. (The addendum to this paper suggests a theoretical explanation for these properties.)

What is meant by "involuntary"?

There is only one more term to clarify, and then we can re-examine the evidence for Shakespeare's (and Freud's) account of Portia's slip. How do we know that the slips induced in the laboratory are genuinely involuntary slips, such as people make in the real world? What does the term "involuntary" mean anyway?

Baars and Mattson (1981) suggest that the most satisfactory operational definition of "involuntary" involves *the speaker's surprise at his own utterance.* This can be assessed by spontaneous exclamations of surprise, spontaneous self-correction, voluntary reports of surprise, and the various measures of the Orienting Reaction, including a rapid increase in the skin conductivity. Further, we may call an action involuntary if it resists deliberate attempts to control it. In all these ways, experimental slips are demonstrably involuntary. People occasionally express surprise spontaneously, and, in the case of a truth-violating slip, they correct themselves spontaneously on 39% of all slips (Baars & Mattson, 1981); when GSR is monitored, increases are found immediately following slips, and even during correct responses if they can *potentially* turn into a rule-violating slip. Much lower GSR is found when the correct response can only turn into a rule-governed slip (Motley, Camden, & Baars, 1979).

Finally, there are strong indications that experimental slips resist attempts to control them volitionally. Slips researchers who have worked with these techniques for years continue to make slips in the tasks. Subjects who are fully informed about the nature of the task, and who are made to say rather embarassing slips, continue to make them (as we will see below).

Theoretically, the idea of "surprise at one's own utterance" can be viewed as a *mismatch* between two representations—the first being the intended utterance, the second being the perception of the slip. Intentions can be represented as complex and many-leveled goal structures (Baars & Mattson, 1981). Thus, it seems possible to make sense of the idea of an "involuntary slip" both operationally and theoretically. Now we can proceed to define several levels of "Freudian slips"—and see if they can, indeed, "reveal a state of mind."

Testing several Freudian hypotheses

Because Freud's writings on slips are occasionally contradictory, we have tested several levels of the Freudian hypothesis. From "weakest" to "strongest" theoretical constructs, these are:

1. *Linguistic priming hypothesis:* Are slips that express some idea made more often when that idea has been presented before in different words?
2. *Contextual priming hypothesis:* Are states of mind induced by nonlinguistic contextual information able to increase the number of slips that express that state of mind?
3. *Psychodynamic hypothesis:* Will the presence of an intention to *avoid* some

topic serve instead to increase the probability of slips that express the taboo topic? This is true psychodynamic hypothesis, since it assumes two opposing intentions, one suppressing the other; the suppressed intention can only be expressed involuntarily. It is noteworthy that Portia's slip in *The Merchant of Venice* is clearly a psychodynamic slip, as Shakespeare shows with such remarkable economy of expression. That is, Portia's slip reflects a conflict, expressing a thought which she was evidently trying to inhibit.

These hypotheses are surprisingly easy to test, given effective techniques for eliciting predictable slips. For hypothesis (1), we simply used the phonological biasing technique described above to induce slips like *rage weight–wage rate;* in addition to the phonological bias materials before the slip target, we added some "semantic bias." For instance, we might insert the words "salary scale" several exposures before the target *rage weight* to see if the rate of the slip *wage rate* would go up. The presence of semantic bias words almost tripled the rate of related slips, consistent with Freudian hypothesis (1) (Motley & Baars, 1976).

Testing hypothesis (2) was similarly straightforward. In order to induce a powerful state of mind, we made use of the psychologist's last resorts: sexual attraction and fear of shock. Only male subjects were used in this task, divided into three groups. The first was run by an attractive female experimenter, who volunteered to dress in a sexually spectacular fashion; the second group was told they might received an electric shock during the experiment, and shown some impressive-looking equipment (no shock was given); and the third group received neither of these treatments. All subjects were given the identical slip task, with six Sex-related slip targets (*lice legs–nice legs*) and six Shock-related targets (*shad bok–bad shock*).

The contextual manipulations more than doubled the rate of slips expressing sexual and shock-related ideas, but only in the appropriate context. In the wrong context, the rate of slips was not distinguishable from the rate in the neutral context. Thus, we may accept Freudian hypothesis (2.): that states of mind induced by context will indeed increase the likelihood of making a relevant, involuntary slip (Motley, Camden, & Baars, 1979).

What about Portia's "psychodynamic" slip? This is a bit more difficult to test. We need not only induce a slip expressing some state of mind, but we must also be sure that the state of mind is in conflict with a contrary state. Hypothesis (3) predicts that the rate of slips expressing the conflicted state of mind will actually exceed the rate that can be expected without conflict. Thus, Portia feels love (state 1) but must hide the fact from her suitor Bassanio (conflicting state 2). These contending forces keep her from expressing her love consciously and deliberately, but the resulting inner struggle somehow creates an involuntary expression of love.

We chose a widely used test of sexual inhibition, the Mosher Sex-Guilt Inventory (Mosher, 1966) in order to compare subjects who scored quite high, quite low, or medium on Sex-Guilt. The Mosher test has good reliability and appears to define a population that has some of the expected properties of sex guilt, suggesting that it has some theoretical validity as well. For instance, Galbraith (1968) reports that high-guilt subjects make very few sexual associations to sexual *double entendres* like "screw," compared to low-guilt subjects. This is consistent with the idea that high-guilt subjects avoid expressing sexual thoughts whenever they can. Similarly, Morokoff (1981) reports that high-guilt female subjects deny sexual arousal to erotic stories, even when a physiological measure of sexual arousal shows them to be *more* aroused than medium or low-guilt groups. Generally, it appears that high-guilt subjects will not express sexual thoughts, as long as they have voluntary control over their expression. But the evidence for physiological arousal also suggests that they may express *involuntarily* even more arousal than the comparison groups.

If this is true, we should find more sex-related slips in a high-guilt sample than in a low or medium-guilt sample (exactly the opposite of the Galbraith finding, which looked at *voluntary* free associations). This is exactly what was found. Using within-subject comparisons of sex-related vs. neutral slips in a sexually provocative context very much like the one used to test the previous hypothesis, we found that high-guilt males made an average of 2.7 more sex-related than neutral slips, while medium-guilt subjects made only 1.7 more sex-related slips, and low-guilt subjects 1.3 more. The difference between the high-guilt group and the two others is significant (Motley, Camden, & Baars, 1979). This is consistent with hypothesis (3.), the psychodynamic hypothesis, and further evidence for the idea that involuntary slips can express a state of mind, even a conflicted state of mind.

Much more needs to be done to replicate, extend, and model these findings. Nevertheless, we find them encouraging. It is more than eighty years since Freud published *The Psychopathology of Everyday Life* (1901/1938), and in this period very little progress has been made toward testing his provocative proposals. That they are indeed testable we can now be sure. Thus far, the evidence favors Freud's suggestions—whether this will continue to be true as we explore the implications more, we cannot know at this point. But we now have the theoretical and experimental tools for investigating these ideas properly for the first time.

Conclusions

In a larger context, we can see this paper as part of the stream of development that is currently called "Cognitive Science." That is, it is an attempt to use the fundamental insights derived from cognitive and computational theory to make sense of topics which human beings have talked about for many centuries—things like beliefs, emotions, motivation, and consciousness (viz. Norman, 1980). Many psychologists during the heyday of behaviorism expressed interest in "psychodynamic" phenomena (notably Watson, Hull, N. Miller, and even B.

F. Skinner), but they found it difficult to come to terms with such intuitively appealing ideas in a scientifically rigorous way. Viewed from the perspective of Cognitive Science, it now seems that two obstacles stood in their way: First, one needs compelling, reliable operational definitions of concepts like "emotional conflict." Secondly, and perhaps even more important, one needs a free hand in theory-construction. Only by letting the theoretical imagination range freely can we hope to model these ideas in an explicit and testable way. Because the behavioristic methatheory was reluctant to posit abstract theoretical constructs, it became impossible to use the theoretical imagination freely (see Baars, in press a). Today we are lucky that many of the barriers to creative theory and experiment have been lifted, and we can now try to really understand what people have known implicitly for so long.

A final, larger point that emerges here has to do with the relationship between the psychological laboratory and the real world. "Ecological validity" is one of our new slogans, and quite rightly. Too often in the past, psychologists have embarked on experiments that had no noticeable connection with real life. The solution, however, is not to give up experiments. In the case of slips, experimental work gives us an opportunity to elicit very precise, meaningful slips which we could never observe naturalistically. Spontaneous slips are far too rare and too variable to let us test the Freudian hypothesis naturalistically. The solution then is to do experiments that sample the real world, not crudely, but in its essence. And the only way to define the essence of a real phenomenon is to use appropriate theory. Thus, theory, experiment, and ecological validity compose a triad of interacting values, mutually supportive if we approach them properly. If one or two of the members of this triad are missing, our research will ultimately be sterile. But if we can respect natural phenomena, perform careful experiments, and develop imaginative theory, we stand a better chance today of gaining scientific insight into the human condition than ever before.

ADDENDUM: ON THE CONSCIOUS CONTROL OF ACTION

On finishing the above paper, I felt some dissatisfaction: certain issues were still left up in the air and others needed to be spelled out in more detail. I want to express my thanks to the editors and commentator for graciously allowing me to add some further considerations.

Our main concern in this paper is with "repression"—a concept that has been very problematic from a scientific point of view, partly because of theoretical difficulties, and partly because of difficulties in finding a plausible operational method for assessing it.

Some psychologists are apparently tempted to dismiss the issue of repression altogether. Against this militates the intuitive plausibility of the idea: who has not felt compelled to hide some feeling or thought from other people? And who has not suspected him- or herself of hiding a thought from oneself? A child of the

20th Century can hardly escape this consideration—indeed, no psychological idea has had more influence at large than the idea of repression. Too often in the past, psychologists have thrown out the baby of good ideas with the bathwater of sloppy theory and experiment. But instead of dismissing the idea of repression, we should devote considerable thought and effort to making it theoretically coherent and observable.

In general, we suggest that *repression may be inferred when there is a disjunction between the voluntary and involuntary expressions made by a subject.* If a subject is unwilling to make sexual associations to sexual *double entendres* (Galbraith, 1968), but makes an unusual number of sexual slips of the tongue, we may reasonably infer two conflicting tendencies, one which is "attempting to control" the other. This is by no means limited to sexual expressions—certainly the expression of anger, hostility, and violence tends to be socially inhibited. In universities, the expression of naive-sounding thoughts may be inhibited. We probably all inhibit words and actions that we fear may make us subject to ridicule. Among males in our culture, emotional expression of helplessness and grief may be inhibited. In political contexts, expressions of unpopular sentiments may be inhibited. And so on.

The operational definition of repression suggested above makes no distinction between repression and suppression, i.e., between unconscious and conscious inhibition of a thought or feeling. This is a real issue, and one that should be addressed eventually. But it is difficult at this point to think of a satisfactory way to assess the difference. (It may be that repression and suppression are at opposite ends of a continuum of automatization of the inhibitory process. When conscious suppression of some thought becomes habitual, it may tend to become unconscious and automatic, just like any other habit. Habitual conscious inhibition of a thought or a feeling may result in automatic and unconscious inhibition, i.e., "*repression.*")

Of all the theoretical terms in this discussion the most neglected one is the concept of consciousness. A detailed analysis of the theoretical implications of consciousness is presented in Baars (1983), and its application to the problem of control of action is discussed in Baars and Mattson (1981) and Baars and Kramer (1982). Here we will touch only on those aspects that are immediately relevant.

Baars (1983) suggests that conscious experience reflects the operation of a "global workspace" in the nervous system, a kind of central information exchange used by multiple specialized processors to communicate with each other. There is a great deal of evidence for this kind of organization, both psychological and neurophysiological. For instance, there is much evidence indicating that many areas of the cortex are locally specialized, although many of these specialized areas may participate in any complex function such as language comprehension or spatial analysis (Geschwind, 1979). Several neuroscientists have suggested that such specialized areas act as "distributed modules" (e.g., Arbib, 1980; Mountcastle, 1979), i.e., specialized processors which are extremely efficient in their particular tasks. Some cognitive psychologists have made similar suggestions.

Computer science models suggest that a collection of distributed specialized processors is very useful for handling routine tasks, but that this kind of system does not provide *flexibility* in the face of new conditions, a property that the nervous system has in abundance. A number of artificial intelligence models have therefore added a "global workspace"—a memory whose contents are broadcast globally to all distributed specialists (e.g., Reddy & Newell, 1974). This workspace permits specialized processors to interact with each other, so that together they can solve problems that cannot be handled by any single processor. This kind of system design seems to facilitate new, adaptive responses to new conditions. It also has a "family resemblance" to well-known psychological ideas about short-term memory, such as Baddeley's model of "working memory" (Baddeley, 1976).

Baars (1983) has presented a set of "contrastive analyses" comparing well-known conscious and unconscious phenomena, and suggests on the basis of this evidence that the nervous system is equipped with a similar global workspace that permits distributed specialized processes to interact with each other. All the contrastive facts regarding conscious and unconscious processes can be explained by assuming that conscious representations combine three necessary properties, as follows. Conscious representations are:

1. *broadcast globally* throughout the nervous system,
2. *internally coherent* because incoherent representations would trigger destructive competition, and
3. *informative,* in the sense that they trigger widespread adaptation among specialized processors.

These three necessary properties emerge naturally from the system architecture sketched above. Figure 1 presents a diagram of a simple first approximation of this model.

This is not the place to explore the evidence for this model in great detail (see Baars, 1983, in press b, in preparation; Baars & Kramer, 1982). Here we are primarily interested in two questions: (a) How does this model account for the conscious control of voluntary action? and (b) How do we tie all this into the issue of repression or suppression of a conscious feeling, thought, or image?

I. Conscious control of voluntary action

William James (1890) remarked on the fact that we do not usually have a detailed conscious experience of planning and executing an action. To illustrate this "executive ignorance," try moving a finger: what muscles control the finger? Were those muscles (actually located in the forearm) consciously accessed during this movement? James argues there is no conscious access at all: rather, he claims, there is a fleeting conscious *image of the goal,* which triggers

Globally Distributed Information:

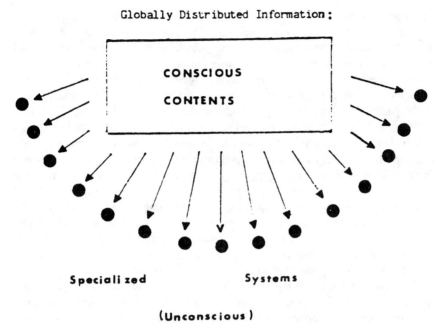

Figure I. A first approximation model of consciousness, viewed as the functioning of a *global workspace* in a distributed system consisting of many specialized unconscious processors. The global workspace is a central information exchange whose contents are broadcast to the distributed processors, which retain the processing initiative. Thus, the global workspace is not an executive, but it can be a medium for executive processors to use in communicating with subordinate systems.

off the appropriate unconscious effector systems that carry out the goal. This "ideo-motor theory" fits perfectly with a global workspace in a distributed system. This model suggests that a conscious goal image is broadcast globally, so that unconscious effector systems are recruited to carry out the goal. We have an image (visual, kinesthetic, or even verbal) of the movement of our finger—and our finger moves "automatically."

Actually, any conscious goal image exists in the context of a broader intentional goal structure which is largely unconscious, as shown in Figure 3 (Baars & Mattson, 1981). Suppose a graduate students wants to work toward a Ph.D. as an overall goal. Although he or she will do many things in pursuit of this ultimate goal, at any one time only intermediate *sub*goals are likely to be conscious. That is to say, one may be conscious of wanting to write a dissertation, but this conscious goal exists in a larger superordinate context of the goal of getting a Ph.D., which is not currently conscious, but presupposed; even though the goal of getting Ph.D. is not currently conscious, it continues to guide current conscious contents. Similarly, goals *subordinate* to the conscious goal may be unconscious at any one time, either because they are automatically executed, or because they can be filled in at a later time. Thus, the graduate student is unlikely to be conscious of controlling his or her feet in walking to the library, or of thinking ahead to the process of checking out books—the former is automatic, and the latter is not filled in, simply because it can be left until later. In sum, the consciously represented goal image is only a part of a larger goal structure, but it is the part that we can work on and alter at the present time (Figure 2).

Why doesn't every conscious goal image result in an action? William James (1890) suggests that most thoughts and images we have about goals are not executed because they run into competition from other conscious thoughts and images. That is, a conscious goal image must remain conscious for some time before the appropriate effector systems can be recruited to execute it. If the goal image encounters effective competition from other conscious events before this time, the goal image will disappear from consciousness and therefore will not be able to trigger the recruitment of the appropriate effectors. The global workspace of Figures 2 and 3 permits any specialized processor to compete with any other, thus allowing exactly the kind of competition postulated by James.

Here we have the makings for a theory of conscious control of voluntary action. Earlier in this paper, we proposed that the word "involuntary" is equivalent to "causing surprise in the actor at his or her own action." In contrast, voluntary action does not surprise us, because it already commands the tacit

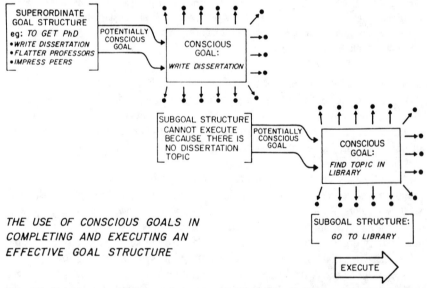

Figure 2. Conscious goals play a role in recruiting specialized effector system needed to carry out the goals. At any particular time many aspects of a large goal structure such as "Getting a Ph.D." may be unconscious—only goals currently at issue are conscious.

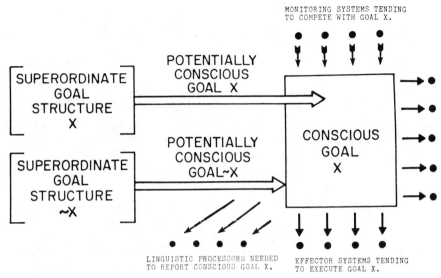

Figure 3. Competition can occur between different goal systems, possibly giving rise to the "psychodynamic" phenomena discussed in the text. This figure shows two goal structures attempting to place contradictory goals in the global workspace. Three groups of unconscious specialized processors are shown: (1) effectors prepared to execute some goal X; (2) effectors which monitor the global goal X and act to modify it, or interfere with its execution (labeled ~X); and (3) specialized linguistic processors which can monitor and report upon the conscious contents. The text describes a situation in which the competition between processor sets (1) and (2) will actually *reduce* the control one has over the probability of executing X, because the ~X processors reduce the global availability of goal X by competition, so that it cannot be acted upon by processors which could modify it. Yet goal X may still be available long enough to recruit highly automatic (and therefore fast-acting) effector systems, and thereby it may trigger undesirable actions. Such a model could account for the existence of persistent involuntary actions, such as stuttering, tics, and more serious forms of psychopathology, which all resist attempts at voluntary control. It can also account for the "psychodynamic" pattern of slips and autonomic activation described in the text.

consent of all systems that *could have* competed against the conscious goal. To illustrate this, let us go back to the example of the wiggling finger. Ordinarily we can wiggle our fingers with impunity, so that the conscious goal image for finger-wiggling encounters hardly any competition. But suppose the finger in question is resting near a button that will trigger off a painful electric shock? Or suppose someone tells us that finger-wiggling is the infallible sign exchanged by the members of a secret subversive society, or that only sick or silly people wiggle their fingers in just this way? Undoubtedly the conscious goal of moving the fingers would encounter competition from other conscious contents, which would prevent the goal image from remaining conscious long enough to trigger the appropriate movement. This situation is diagramed in Figure 3, where the conscious goal X encounters competition from systems that resist X in the current context (labeled ~X).

Note that Figure 3 shows *three* kinds of specialized distributed processors, able to receive information from the global workspace. First, there are effector systems able to carry out action X. Next, there are monitoring systems (~X), which can act to modify or compete with goal image X. And finally, there are the linguistic processors which can execute a verbal report of globally available events. All of these processors may have different response times, depending upon their complexity and novelty. (Complexity and novelty should increase response times, while simplicity and previous practice with the task should decrease response times in these processors.)

2. The breakdown of voluntary control: involuntary actions

Only one more step is required. How do we model he fact that there are indeed *involuntary* actions, actions which we regret having done the moment they occur? Some studies on the automatization of images and actions may provide an answer. First, Pani (1982) has presented a well-controlled study showing that the use of visual images in problem-solving drops very rapidly with practice—indeed, the correlations between the use of imagery and the practice trial number averaged $-.90$, indicating a consistent drop in consciousness of visual images over 18 trials. In terms of our model, we can suggest that images may either become completely automatic and unconscious, or that they become globally available for shorter and shorter periods of time, until finally they are globally available so briefly that they *can no longer be reported, even though they continue to trigger the appropriate effector systems.* In the remainder of this discussion, I will assume that the second case is true—that goal images are still broadcast globally, but more and more fleetingly with practice. (Naturally, this hypothesis must be tested.)

If goal images become more and more briefly available with practice, some clever studies by Langer and Imber (1979, 1980) begin to make sense. These authors found that more practiced subjects in a coding task were *more* willing to accept an incorrect assessment of their own performance than less practiced subjects. These authors argue that overlearning a task can reduce the knowledge the subject has about how the task is performed, and under these circumstances subjects should be more vulnerable to negative assessments of their own performance, because they cannot evaluate their performance anymore by themselves. This is exactly what we would expect, given the assumption above that the goal image becomes less and less available with practice. Automatic, highly prepared effector systems can continue to carry out the task (because they became more well-prepared and efficient with practice, and therefore needed less of a goal image to be triggered). But asking someone to do something novel, such as evaluating their own performance, should become more difficult, because the global goal image upon which this evaluation can operate is available only fleetingly.

Similarly, systems like ~X in Figure 3 can no longer edit and modify the goal image X. It is conceivable that an action can "slip out" in an uncontrolled way, because competing processors could not catch it in time. Goal image X can come and go very rapidly, because there are automatic systems able to execute it, and competing systems ~X are too slow to stop its execution. This is the view of involuntary action we will maintain in this discussion. It has strong implications not only for understanding slips of the tongue, but also for the "psychodynamic" results reported earlier, and even for understanding persistent, involuntary actions, such as stuttering, tics, and many kinds of psychopathology.

3. A modern version of psychodynamics: modeling competition between opposing intentions

A central concept in psychodynamic thought is the idea of competition between two different goals. This is hardly problematic: ever since the cybernetic models of the 1940s, the notion of a goal has been scientifically quite respectable. And it is hardly news that goals can sometimes be in conflict. But there is a subtler question which current psychological theory does not address very often, namely, what is the mechanism whereby one of two competing mechanisms comes to "take charge of" our actions? Or, to put it a different way, what are the competing goals competing *for?*

The modern ideo-motor theory described above suggests that goals compete for access to a global workspace which corresponds closely to consciousness. This is similar to suggestions by Norman and Shallice (1980), who claim that different motor schemata compete for access to a limited-capacity channel associated with conscious processes. However, the global workspace model suggests *why* different goal systems compete for access to consciousness: if conscious goals can be broadcast globally, then they can recruit effector systems able to carry out the goal.

Further, the above discussion suggests that the duration of such a global goal image may make a critical difference. Highly automatized actions may require only a momentary goal, and indeed these momentary goals may be executed before other systems have time to react to them.

The linguistic processors that generate verbal reports of conscious events are also distributed processors, just like the others (Figure 3). If these processors have a relatively long lag-time (as one might expect if they were generating a novel description of some conscious content), they might not be able to describe a global goal image that was very fleeting. But a very fleeting goal image may still be globally available long enough to trigger a highly automatic action. This presumably accounts for the difference Langer and Imber (above) found between new and automatic tasks: subjects could no longer monitor and comment accurately on their own performance of highly automatic tasks, because the linguistic processors needed to generate such a comment lagged behind the automatic processors needed to actually carry out the well-practiced task. By the time linguistic systems can generate a description of the fleeting goal image, it may already be gone.

Here is where a genuine breakdown of voluntary control may occur. Suppose that some systems ~X have tried to prevent the execution of goal X, and failed because goal X was executed very rapidly. At this point, the control systems may try harder to interfere with the global display of X. If goal X is slow enough, this may work; but if it is already automatized, the effect of competition should be to make the undesirable goal *less available* globally. According to the findings of Langer and Imber, this also means that there is less capacity to monitor, and presumably alter, the goal image. Thus the very attempt to compete with X for access to the global workspace may paradoxically *reduce* the capacity of monitoring systems to alter the undesirable goal.

This paradoxical result may in fact be the origin of persistent involuntary actions of the kind that we see in stuttering, nervous tics, and many kinds of psychopathology, which have the general property that *the more one attempts to control the undesirable action, the less control one has* (Baars & Kramer, 1982).

This line of thinking fits very well with some fascinating clinical reports. Recent research tends to confirm informal clinical experience indicating that, to gain voluntary control over stuttering and tics, it may be helpful to "practice the error." Thus, stutterers are asked to stutter *voluntarily* for 30 seconds every time they stutter involuntarily, and, as a result, the rate of stuttering often drops dramatically (Levine & Scheff, 1980; Levine, Ramirez, & Sandeen-Lee, 1982). This result makes perfect sense from our perspective: voluntary stuttering presumably causes a goal image to remain conscious for a longer time, without destructive competition to reduce its duration. And if it is available longer, other systems can act upon the goal image to modify it, so that it comes under the control of systems which failed to control it before. Paradoxical practice of the to-be-avoided action increases our ability to avoid the action.

Now we are finally ready to deal with the experimental results described above: for example, the fact that subjects who score High on a measure of Sex Guilt actually make more sexual slips of the tongue, in a sexual situation, than do people who score Low or Medium. Presumably, High Sex Guilt subjects are in conflict between approaching and avoiding sexually desirable people (X and ~X). This conflict can be modeled as competition for access to a global workspace between goal images for avoidance and goal images for approach. Goal images for avoidance do not encounter competition in these subjects, and are hence reportable by relatively slow linguistic processors. But goal images for approach do encounter competition from the avoidance goals, and are thus limited to very brief access to the global workspace. However, even such brief access may be long enough to trigger highly automatic or otherwise highly prepared responses expressive of the undesirable goal image. Our slip task presumably provides the kind of highly prepared response expressing the fleeting image of approaching the attractive person. The more these two intentions compete, the more the subject loses control over the unintentional expression of the prohibited goal, because the fleeting goal image cannot be modified as long as it is available for only a short time. Thus, the very effort to avoid thinking of the sexually attractive person in the situation paradoxically triggers the to-be-avoided thoughts. (Presumably the same sort of explanation applies to the finding that female High Sex Guilt subjects show more physiological sexual arousal to an erotic audio tape than do Low Sex Guilt subjects, even though their *voluntary* reports show the opposite tendency; Morokoff, 1981.)

This way of thinking about the issues allows us to explain a number of different phenomena, involving conscious control of action, in a very natural way. Many of the resulting ideas have a psychodynamic flavor, at least in the sense that they involve competition between contrary intentions. These are not quite the ideas proposed by Freud, because we make no claim that deep underlying conflicts cause these phenomena—rather, they may result from the normal functioning of the system that appears to control voluntary action by means of consciously available goals.

Some such theory is needed to answer the question we asked at the beginning of this paper about the likelihood of expressing a suppressed thought involuntarily. It is a fairly complicated theory to answer what may seem like a simple question. Fortunately there are numerous sources of evidence converging on the need for a theory of this sort (see above references). And, while simplicity is a virtue, it is worth remembering Einstein's remark that "a theory should be as simple as possible, *but not too simple.*"

REFERENCES

Abelson, R. P. (1981). The structure of belief systems. In R. Schank & R. P. Abelson (Eds.), *Computer models of thought and language*. San Francisco, CA: W. H. Freeman.

Anderson, J. R. (1983). *The architecture of cognition*. New York: Academic Press.

Arbib, M. A. (1980). Perceptual structures and distributed motor control. In V. B. Brooks (Ed.), *Handbook of physiology*. Bethesda, MD: American Physiological Society.

Baars, B. J. (in preparation). *A cognitive theory of consciousness*. New York: Cambridge University Press.

Baars, B. J. (in press a). *The cognitive revolution in psychology*. New York: Guilford Press.

Baars, B. J. (in press b). Psychobiological implications of a "globalist" theory of consciousness: Evidence, theory, and some phylogenetic speculations. In E. Tobach (Ed.), *Cognition: Language, consciousness, and thought. The T. C. Schneirla Conference Series* (Vol. 2). Hillsdale, NJ: Erlbaum.

Baars, B. J. (1982). Conscious contents provide the nervous system with coherent, global information. In R. Davidson, G. Schwartz, & D. Shapiro (Eds.), *Consciousness and self-regulation* (Vol. 3). New York: Plenum Press.

Baars, B. J. (1980a). On eliciting predictable speech errors in the laboratory: Methods and results. In V. A. Fromkin (Ed.), *Errors of speech and hearing*. New York: Academic Press.

Baars, B. J. (1980b). The competing plans hypothesis: An heuristic approach to the problem of speech errors. In H. W. Dechert & M. Raupach (Eds.), *Temporal variables in speech: Studies in honour of Frieda Goldman-Eisler.* Paris: Mouton, Janua Linguarum.

Baars, B. J., & Kramer, D. N. (1982). Conscious and unconscious components of the control of action. *Proceedings of the Fourth Cognitive Science Society Meeting.* Ann Arbor, MI: Cognitive Science Society.

Baars, B. J., & Mattson, M. E. (1981). Consciousness and intention: A framework and some evidence. *Cognition and Brain Theory, 4,* 247–263.

Baars, B. J., & Motley, M. T. (1976). Spoonerisms as sequencer conflicts: Evidence from artificially induced errors. *American Journal of Psychology, 89,* 467–484.

Baddeley, A. D. (1976). *Psychology of memory.* New York: Harper and Row.

Boden, M. (1977). *Artificial intelligence and natural man.* New York: Basic Books.

Bransford, J. D. (1979). *Human cognition: Learning, understanding, and remembering.* Belmont, CA: Wadsworth.

Bruner, J. S. (1957). On perceptual readiness. *Psychological Review, 64,* 123–152.

Ellis, A. W. (1980). On the Freudian theory of speech errors. In V. A. Fromkin (Ed.), *Errors of speech and hearing.* New York: Academic Press.

Erdelyi, M. (1974). A new look at the New Look: Perceptual defense and vigilance. *Psychological Review, 81,* 1–25.

Freud, S. (1938). The psychopathology of everyday life. In A. A. Brill (Trans. and Ed.), *The basic writings of Sigmund Freud.* New York: Modern Library (German original dated 1901).

Freud, S. (1966). *Introductory lectures on psychoanalysis.* (Trans. and Ed., J. Strachey). New York: W. W. Norton (German original dated 1920).

Galbraith, G. G. (1968). Effects of sexual arousal and guilt upon free associative sexual responses. *Journal of Consulting and Clinical Psychology, 32,* 701–711.

Geschwind, N. (1979). Specializations of the human brain. *Scientific American, 241,* 180–201.

James, W. (1890). *The principles of psychology.* New York: Holt.

Langer, E. J., & Imber, L. (1979). When practice makes imperfect: Debilitating effects of overlearning. *Journal of Personality and Social Psychology, 37,* 2014–2024.

Langer, E. J., & Imber, L. (1980). Role of mindlessness in the perception of deviance. *Journal of Personality and Social Psychology, 39,* 360–367.

Levine, F. M., Ramirez, R. R., & Sandeen-Lee, E. E. (1982). *Contingent negative practice as a treatment of stuttering.* Unpublished manuscript, SUNY at Stony Brook.

Levine, F. M., & Scheff, H. A. (1980, April). *Contingent negative practice as a treatment of tics.* Paper presented at the meeting of the Eastern Psychological Association.

Markus, H., & Sentis, K. (1980). The self in social information processing. In J. Suls (Ed.), *Social psychological perspectives on the self.* Hillsdale, NJ: Erlbaum.

McClelland, D. C., Davidson, R., Saron, C., & Floor, E. (1980). The need for power, brain norepinephrine turnover and learning. *Biological Psychology, 10,* 93–102.

Morokoff, P. (1981). *Female sexual arousal as a function of individual differences and exposure to erotic stimuli.* Unpublished doctoral dissertation, SUNY Stony Brook.

Mosher, D. L. (1966). The development and multitrait-multimethod matrix analysis of three aspects of guilt. *Journal of Consulting and Clinical Psychology, 30,* 25–29.

Motley, M. T. (1980). Verification of "Freudian slips" and semantic prearticulatory editing via laboratory induced spoonerisms. In V. A. Fromkin (Ed.), *Errors of speech and hearing.* New York: Academic Press.

Motley, M. T., & Baars, B. J. (1976). Semantic bias effects on the outcomes of verbal slips. *Cognition, 4,* 177–187.

Motley, M. T., & Baars, B. J. (1978). Laboratory verification of "Freudian" slips of the tongue as evidence of prearticulatory editing. In B. Ruken (Ed.), *Communication yearbook* (Vol. 2). New Brunswick, NJ: Transaction.

Motley, M. T., Camden, C. T., & Baars, B. J. (1979). Personality and situational influences upon verbal slips: A laboratory test of the Freudian and prearticulatory editing hypotheses. *Human Communication Research, 5,* 195–202.

Mountcastle, V. B. (1979). An organizing principle for cerebral function: The unit module and the distributed system. In F. O. Schmitt & F. G. Worden (Eds.), *The neurosciences: Fourth study program.* Cambridge, MA: MIT Press.

Neisser, U. (1976). *Cognition and reality: Principles and implications of cognitive psychology.* San Francisco, CA: W. H. Freeman.

Norman, D. A. (1980). Twelve issues for cognitive science. *Cognitive Science, 4,* 1–32.

Norman, D. A. & Shallice, T. (1985). Attention to action: Willed and automatic control of behavior. In R. J. Davidson, G. E. Schwartz, & D. Shapiro (Eds.), *Consciousness and self regulation: Advances in research, Vol. IV.* NY: Plenum.

Pani, J. R. (1982, November). *A functionalist approach to mental imagery.* Paper presented at the meeting of the Psychonomic Society, Minneapolis, MN.

Reddy, R., & Newell, A. (1974). Knowledge and its representation in a speech understanding system. In L. W. Gregg (Ed.), *Knowledge and cognition.* Potomac, MD: Erlbaum.

Reuter, J., Lorenz, P., & Davidson, R. J. (1981). Differential contributions of the two cerebral hemispheres to the perception of happy and sad faces. *Neuropsychologia, 19,* 609–613.

Schank, R. C., & Colby, K. M. (1973). *Computer models of thought and language.* San Francisco, CA: W. H. Freeman.

Sherwood, G. G. (1981). Self-serving biases in person perception: A reexamination of projection as a mechanism of defense. *Psychological Bulletin, 90,* 445–459.

Weinberger, D. A., Schwartz, G. E., & Davidson, R. J. (1979). Low-anxious high-anxious and repressive coping styles: Psychometric patterns and behavioral and physiological responses to stress. *Journal of Abnormal Psychology, 88,* 369–380.

Chapter 17

Remembering Past Experiences: Theoretical Perspectives Past and Present*

Douglas J. Herrmann

Hamilton College
Clinton, New York

The past, for each of us, is dear. It tells what we have been, explains what we have become, and foretells what we will be. Because the past is so important, both personally and practically, we spend a lot of time remembering the past.

Despite the importance of remembering the past, very little research has investigated the processes underlying this kind of remembering. This chapter addresses autobiographical remembering in three ways. First, it reviews the different ways we remember our past experiences; second, it discusses processes hypothesized to underlie such remembering; and third, it reports research by my students and myself concerning one of these ways of remembering.

At least three ways have been suggested for how people make contact with their memories of past experiences: recognition, recall, and recollection. Each way requires that an episode in memory be *accessed* and its contents *consulted*. The manner in which the memory is accessed and consulted is substantively different among the three kinds of remembering. Recognition and recall are well known to differ, so these types of remembering need not be discussed extensively here (Brown, 1976). However, the term "recollection" is sufficiently rare in recent memory literature that it deserves expansion. In recollection, a person remembers an experience by piecing together attributes of the experience after the attributes are found in memory (see Baddeley, 1983; Neisser, 1967). Recollection presumes a memory trace that is fragmented; recall and recognition

* I am indebted to Chris White for his work on the Trace Attribute Inventory and on Experiment 1. Thanks also go to Cheryl Neale for her work on Experiment 3, to Austin Briggs of Hamilton College's English Department for helpful advice on what attributes describe episodes, to David Burrows, Margaret Gentry, and Jonathan Schooler for their advice on this manuscript, and to Harold Gelfand for stimulating my thinking regarding the process of recollection. Requests for reprints should be sent to: Douglas J. Herrmann, Psychology Department, Hamilton College, Clinton, NY 13323.

presume a relatively integrated trace or a process that simply reads the remnants of a trace (James, 1890).

Since autobiographical memories may be remembered in any one of the three ways just mentioned, a full account of autobiographical remembering must ultimately address all three ways. It is beyond the scope of this chapter to provide such a full account. Nevertheless, some comments may be offered concerning the progress being made towards the full account. A great deal of research shows that recognition and recall of events may be explained in terms of the attributes of an event (e.g., when and where the event occurred) and feelings regarding the event (Baddeley, Lewis, & Nimmo-Smith, 1979; Bower, 1967; Underwood, 1969; White & Pillimer, 1979). In the case of recollection, much less is known about the remembering process (cf. Baddeley, 1983). Most of what is known pertains to the accessing of a memory. For example, three variables have been identified as central to the access of episodic memories. First, access may be intentional (as when one tries to remember a specific episode) or unintentional (as when the memory for an episode just pops into consciousness; Reiff & Scheerer, 1959; Salaman, 1970). Second, the attributes of cues influence the access of episodic memories. For example, affect terms tend to elicit recent memories more than object and activity terms (Robinson, 1976). Third, attributes of episodes affect access of episodes. For example, the probability of accessing an episode is inversely related to a person's age when an episode occurred (Crovitz & Schiffman, 1974; Rubin, 1982).

In the case of the attribute retrieval stage of recollection, however, essentially no relevant research has been done. Historically, two kinds of retrieval processes have been proposed for recollection (see Aristotle, circa 300 B.C.). For some memories, such as a well-memorized list, items on the list may be said to be *directly recalled* (Atkinson & Juola, 1974). For other memories, such as a prose passage, attributes of a story may, in addition to being directly recalled, be *inferred* or constructed (Bartlett, 1932; Neisser, 1967). Thus, recollection may occur primarily by direct recall of the episode or by inferring attributes of the episode from other attributes that are available for recall (see also Shoemaker, 1967, 1970). Of course, retrieval might involve both direct recall and inference. It may also be that certain attributes are directly recalled and other attributes are inferred.

The research reported in this chapter had the purpose of investigating the nature of attribute retrieval (direct recall, inference, or both) as a function of the kind of attribute that originally defined an episode. Four experiments were conducted using the same basic procedure. Before I describe the specific aims of each experiment, let me explain the common procedure.

PROCEDURES COMMON TO THE FOUR EXPERIMENTS

In each experiment, the subjects indicated what they would be able to recall, if asked, about past episodes of their lives. The particular episodes to which the subjects responded were recalled earlier either by the subjects themselves, their relatives, or the experimenters. Episodes generated by subjects were described by a two-word label, sufficient to remind them of the memory. Episodes generated by relatives or the experimenter were expressed by one or two sentences.

For each episode, the subject indicated whether he or she *could* remember each of many attributes of an episode and how this remembering occurred, i.e., directly or inferentially. Subjects were not asked to recall the precise nature of the attributes which they remembered; thus, a subject might indicate an ability to recall the location of a prior experience without telling the experimenter what the location was (e.g., Wilmington, Delaware). Reports of attribute recall were made on a response sheet called the Trace Attribute Inventory (constructed by myself and Chris White); the inventory is presented in Figure 1. The inventory has been so named to indicate its use as a guide to making an *inventory* of all pertinent *attributes* of a memory *trace* that a subject may remember. As the figure shows, the top of the form provides room for subject information, and the label or sentence describing the episode. In the left hand column are listed seven attribute categories (e.g., time) and varying numbers of attributes within each attribute category (e.g., for time: grade, year, season). These attribute categories and corresponding attributes were developed from the literature concerning the access of autobiographical memories (Robinson, 1976), the literature on prose memory (e.g., Schank & Abelson, 1979; Thorndyke, 1977), and the vocabulary of the description of episodes used in English literature. To the right of each attribute within an attribute category are four response blocks, identified at the top of the page as R, I, DNK, and NA. For each attribute of a particular episode, the subject checked one of the four blocks to indicate that he or she either directly (i.e., immediately) recalled the memory attribute (the R block), inferred the memory attribute (the I block), did not recall (the DNK block) the memory attributes, or that the attribute was not applicable (the NA block) for the memory. An example of an episode that calls for an NA response would be one that occurred completely indoors, making all outdoor attributes (exact location, general vicinity, appearance) totally irrelevant. The attributes required by the Trace Attribute Inventory sheet may be seen to be required also in recognition and recall, as well as in recollection. The differences in attribute retrieval among these three kinds of remembering lie in the number of attributes retrieved (recognition focuses on part of the episode) and the amount of added effort spent in attribute retrieval (recollection strives for attributes that recall fails to produce).

Analysis of responses on the Trace Attribute Inventory (TAI) involved data reduction at two levels. First, the analysis focused on the seven attribute categories, summing responses over specific attributes in a category. Thus, each attribute category was represented by a total for direct recalls, inferences, do-not-knows, and not applicables. These totals were converted into percentages in the following manner. For each attribute category, the percentage of direct recalls was computed out of the total chances to recall attributes ($R/(R+I+DNK)$);

The Trace Attribute Inventory

R = recalled;   I - inferred;   DNK = do not know;   NA = not applicable

Memory Label_____

	R	I	DNK	NA

I. Location of event — indoors
- exact place
- general vicinity
- appearance of room
outdoors
- exact place
- general vicinity
- weather

II. Time — age
- grade in school
- year
- season
- month
- day of week
- period of time (morning, afternoon evening)
- time of day (approximate hour)

III. Social Context — alone
- people present
- number of people
- characteristics of people (sex, age)
- relationship of people (family, friends, sweetheart, acquaintance)

IV. Feelings — kind of feeling (neg. - positive)
- strength of feeling (strong-weak)
- attentiveness (attentive-relaxed)

V. Nature of Behavior — activity level (active-passive)
- involvement (participant-observer)
- goal directed (goal-no-goal)

VI. Nature of Event — setting of event (accident, romantic, recreation, work, etc)
- unusualness of event (common-unusual)
- kind of event (physical-emotional)

VII. Related Events — prior events
- subsequent events
- consequent events

Figure I. Trace Attribute Inventory form used by subjects to indicate which attributes they could recall directly or infer, for an episodic memory.

likewise, the percentage of inferred attributes was computed in the same manner (I/(R+I+DNK)); the DNK percentages were not computed, since they follow from the R and I percentages. It should be noted that qualitative differences among attribute categories (e.g., abstract–concreteness of these categories) preclude comparison between them for either percent direct recall or inference.

Nevertheless, memory for a particular attribute category may be safely compared across kinds of episodes.

Prior research in our laboratory has found that the relative difficulty of recalling the seven attribute categories remained essentially the same over a test-retest interval of 2 weeks; hence, responding within at least a short period appears to be quite reliable. When subjects have been asked to recall the actual facts of an episode after completing the TAI, they have generally been able to recall or not recall in the way they indicated on the TAI. That subjects can overtly recall what they claim they can recall is not surprising (Morris, Gruneberg, Sykes, & Merrick, 1982). Nevertheless, the validity of estimates of amount recalled should not be confused with whether the recall accurately (or validly) represents the episode. Memory for autobiographical episodes is well known to be flawed (Field, 1981; Herrmann, 1983), so the same degree of inaccuracy can be expected in the memory traces sampled with the TAI. Inaccuracy in the memory trace should not be a barrier to the study of episodic memories, because, as far as the subjects are concerned, these memories provide the primary basis for the autobiographical knowledge of the subjects.

EXPERIMENT I

The first experiment used the Trace Attribute Inventory to investigate the retrieval modes by which people recollect memories from different periods of their lives (cf. Crovitz & Schiffman, 1974; Linton, 1975, 1978, 1979; Rubin, 1982). Sixty undergraduates from Hamilton College served in the experiment. Each subject began by recalling 10 experiences. For 20 subjects, it was required that these experiences occurred in their early childhood (defined as less than 8 years old). For another 20 subjects, the experiences were to have occurred in adolescence (defined as from 8 through 14 years of age), and, for the remaining 20 subjects, the experiences were to have occurred in adulthood (defined as 15 years of age through the present). When subjects recalled their experiences, they wrote a two-word label to represent the experience. Subsequent to episode recall, the subjects transferred the labels onto Trace Attribute Inventory sheets and then completed the inventories.

The results for the study are shown in Figure 2. A three-way ANOVA (attribute categories X retrieval mode X age at memory, with repeated measures across attributes and retrieval mode) found all possible main effects and interactions significant at the .05 level or better, except for the interaction between mode and age period. These effects may be seen in Figure 2 as follows. The direct recalls (in the left panel of the figure) occurred far more often than inferences (right panel), and the proportion of direct recall and inference varied over attribute categories. Finally, comparison of the function for the three age periods reveals that direct recall decreased with decreased age for two attributes (time, related events) and that inferred attributes increased for the related events

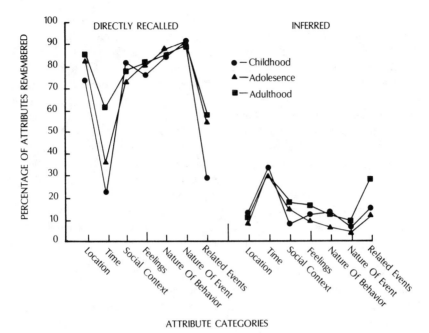

ATTRIBUTE CATEGORIES

Figure 2. Experiment 1: Mean percent of attributes directly recalled or inferred as a function of attribute category and the life period from which memories originated.

category. In a nutshell, Experiment 1 indicated that the retrieval stage of auto-biographical remembering primarily involved direct recall of the attributes of episodes.

It might be plausibly argued that the memories remembered in Experiment 1 are not *representative* of autobiographical memories, and, therefore, neither are its findings concerning mode of retrieval. According to this argument, spontaneous generation of past episodes elicits a person's most familiar auto-biographical memories (cf. Rubin, 1982), which, in turn, would be expected to require primarily direct recall. Thus, it may not be correct to conclude from Experiment 1 that episodic memories in general are retrieved mainly by direct recall.

EXPERIMENT 2

Experiment 2 tested the representativeness issue by asking subjects to complete Trace Attribute Inventory sheets for episodic memories that ranged in familiarity from high to low. If the hypothesis is correct that attribute retrieval is primarily inferential except for very familiar memories, then the percentage of direct recalls should decrease and the percentage of inferences should increase as the familiarity of episodes decreases. In Experiment 2, fifteen undergraduates from Hamilton College asked their parents or guardians to mail to me 12 brief descriptions (of approximately one or two sentences) of episodes from the subject's life, such that four episodes would be very familiar, four moderately familiar, and four vaguely familiar to their child. Parental descriptions were typically a sentence long and dealt with a wide range of topics, e.g., "The Christmas morning that Frank, who still believed in Santa Claus, got up too early and found us (mom and dad) putting presents under the tree"; "The time that Mary went to see her grandmother, who was very sick, at the hospital." On receipt of the episode descriptions, each description was written on Trace Attribute Inventory sheets, then randomly ordered, and given to the appropriate subject. The subjects then completed the sheets as described for Experiment 1.

The results of Experiment 2 were analyzed with a three-way ANOVA (familiarity level X attribute category X retrieval mode, with repeated measures across all three independent variables). The analysis found all possible main effects and interactions significant except the three-way interaction. The results of the analysis may be seen in Figure 3. Inspection of the figure, and comparison to Figure 2, reveals, first, data for the very familiar episodes of Experiment 2 agree very closely across mode and attribute categories with that obtained for spontaneously generated episodic memories in the first experiment. This pattern also held up

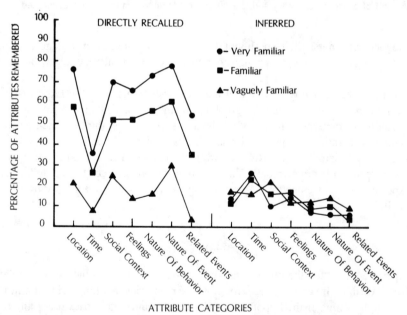

Figure 3. Experiment 2: Mean percent of attributes directly recalled or inferred as a function of attribute category and the familiarity level of childhood memories.

well for the moderately familiar memories. The breakup in this pattern in the direct recall for vaguely familiar episodes was apparently due to a floor effect in remembering the attributes of these memories. Of greatest importance to the results of Experiment 2 was the finding that inferential recall, shown in the right panel of Figure 3, remained constant as familiarity decreased, despite marked changes in direct recall with variations in familiarity.

EXPERIMENT 3

Experiment 2 indicated that the correct interpretation of Experiment 1 was that attribute retrieval in recollection generally involves direct recall. However, it still seemed reasonable that certain kinds of autobiographical memories might predispose people to infer attributes more often than the subjects did in the first two experiments. For example, it might be that people would infer more for *secondhand* memories (i.e., when a person forgets an episode but later learns about it from someone else, like a parent or friend) than for *firsthand* memories (i.e., when a person retains the original memory of the episode; Shoemaker, 1967, 1970).

Thus Experiment 3 solicited 12 more undergraduates to ask their parents or guardians to complete a brief questionnaire and to send the responses to the experimenter. The questionnaire defined firsthand and secondhand memories as above; then it asked the respondent to generate a one- or two-sentence description of episodes that they guessed would be remembered in a firsthand or secondhand way by their child. On receipt of the completed questionnaire, the information was put on Trace Attribute Inventory sheets, which were then completed by the subjects.

The results were analyzed with a three-way ANOVA (origin of memory X attribute category X retrieval mode, with repeated measures across all three independent variables). All possible main effects and interactions were found significant at the .05 level or better, except that memory origin (firsthand, secondhand) did not interact with attribute categories, and the three-way interaction was not significant. The nature of these effects can be seen by inspecting Figure 4. Comparison of this figure with Figure 3 of Experiment 2 and Figure 2 of Experiment 1 reveals again a remarkable consistency in the pattern of results across experiments. Contrary to the hypothesis, the proportion of inferences did not differ between firsthand and secondhand memories, although there was a tendency for certain attribute categories (feelings, nature of behavior, nature of event) to be inferred more for secondhand memories than for firsthand memories.

EXPERIMENT 4

Still in pursuit of conditions in which inferential recall would not be relatively uncommon, a fourth experiment was carried out. This experiment investigated

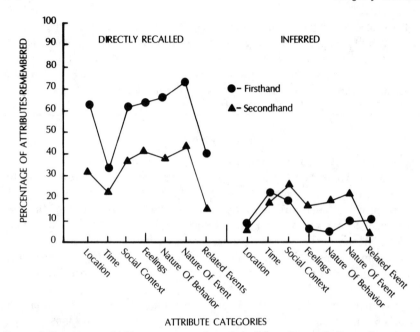

ATTRIBUTE CATEGORIES

Figure 4. Experiment 3: Mean percent of attributes directly recalled or inferred as a function of attribute category and the origin (firsthand or secondhand) of memories.

recollection as a function of another characteristic of episodes. Since everyone's past is unique, it may be that most episodes do not follow a script (Schank & Abelson, 1979), and, thereby, do not provide a basis for inference. Nevertheless, some episodes of our lives follow a script, e.g., birthdays, religious and national holidays. Inferential recall might be expected to be substantially higher for memories of events that occur on days that conform to a script than for events on days that do not. In Experiment 4, 18 more undergraduates were asked to *spontaneously* recall four episodes from their lives, and to also recall four episodes whose nature was *provided* by the experimenter, the episodes being the subjects' 6th and 7th birthdays; Christmas, or the first day of Hanukah; and the fourth of July when they were 7 years old. Trace Attribute Inventory sheets were completed for all eight episodes.

A three-way ANOVA with repeated measures in all three independent variables found all main effects and interactions were significant at the .05 level or better. The nature of these effects are shown in Figure 5. Inspection of the results for the spontaneous memories in the figure shows that they exhibited a pattern like the familiar-memory conditions of the previous three experiments. In addition, as predicted by the script hypothesis, inference was higher for script-like episodes than non-script-like episodes. Moreover, for script-like episodes, the overall level of inference was slightly higher than that for direct recall. It might

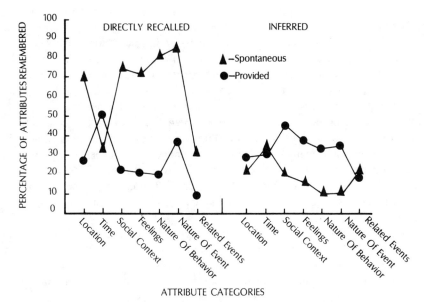

Figure 5. Experiment 4: Mean percent of attributes directly recalled or inferred as a function of attribute category and the nature of the memory (spontaneous and requested).

be argued that the difference observed here did not originate in the difference between unscripted episodes and scripted episodes; instead the difference may originate in whether memories occurred spontaneously or not. According to this rationale, memories recalled in a nonspontaneous fashion are less likely to be directly recalled and more likely to be recalled inferentially. However, the memories involved in Experiments 2 and 3 were also not spontaneous and they did yield minimal levels of inference. Thus, it appears that the presence or absence of a script was responsible for the difference in inference level of spontaneous and provided memories in Experiment 4.

DISCUSSION

The present experiments provide a coherent pattern of results. When recalling most episodic memories, subjects claimed that they retrieved attributes of the experience primarily by direct recall. Inferential recall was reportedly used infrequently except when the episode conformed to a script.

The conclusion that inferential processes are infrequent conflicts with the conclusions of investigators who claimed that these processes are prevalent in the paradigms they have studied. Constructive processes have been recognized as common in the retention of prose (Bartlett, 1932; Neisser, 1967; however, cf. Gould & Stephensen, 1967), in the acquisition and retention of emotionally charged episodic memories (Greenwald, 1980), and in the access of episodic memories (Williams & Hollan, 1981). However, there may be good reasons that constructive processes should occur frequently in these situations but occur infrequently in the present research. First, none of these precedents dealt with the retrieval of attributes; instead, they were concerned with the acquisition, retention and/or access of memories. Second, the content of material to be remembered in previous work was generally more scripted, and hence more amenable to constructive processes, than most of the memories recalled by subjects here. For example, the passages typically acquired in prose studies are more structured than most episodic memories. Third, the memories established in prose recall may be expected to be less vivid, less personally important, and less emotional than episodic memories (Rubin, 1984); such differences might be expected to foster greater use of inference in the remembering of prose than in the remembering of episodes.

Regardless of the findings in other paradigms, it might be argued that inferential recall in the present paradigm occurred more frequently than the subjects reported. Reports of inference may have been less than what actually occurred, because subjects might have inferred some attributes so quickly that they mistakenly judged the recall as direct. (Of course, the reverse is possible also, i.e., that some slow direct recalls might have been mistakenly identified as inferred.) However, there are no means currently for determining whether a recall is direct or inferred independent of a subject's self report. Until such a means is developed, it will not be possible to assess whether the percentages of recall reports are distorted by identification errors. In the meantime, the present results indicate that subjects report a small but not-negligible proportion of their recall of attributes occurs by a nondirect, inferential process.

The labelling of a response as ''inferential'' obviously does not explain the underlying process. Inferred recalls seem to be less spontaneously produced than direct recalls. That is, subjects' claim that inferred recalls reflect a collection of processes, while the same claim can not be made for direct recalls. Inferred recall may also occur, first, in the traditional sense of reasoning, wherein one or more attributes suggest the identity of another attribute, and then the suggested attributes help to gain access to the problematic attributes in memory. For example, a person initially may not remember that he or she met someone previously, but may later realize he or she knows the person after thinking about possible prior encounters with the person. Second, inferred recall in the traditional sense may not be possible, because too few attributes are available, leading a person to guess about attributes. For example, a person may ''remember'' that he or she knows another person because some information indicates this person was probably met previously. Third, inferred recall may occur in a Gestalt manner, wherein, after apprehending the problem (i.e., identifying what attributes are unknown), a period of incubation occurs, followed by a spontaneous realization of the desired attribute. For example, one may not remember that he or she knows a person initially, but later the memory of meeting this person pops into one's head. The present measure does not distinguish among the three kinds of inference (using reason to gain access to the true memory, using reason to make an educated guess, and unconscious problem solving that accesses the true memory). A clear appreciation of the bases of inferred recall necessitates research into these subvarieties of inference and the conditions that elicit them.

It should be pointed out that the proportions of direct and inferred recall analyzed here compare the amount of direct recall, or inferred recall, to the number of attributes presumably registered in memory during an episode. Proportions might have been developed also from the number of attributes retained since the experience, i.e., (D/(D+I)) and (I/(D+I)), with DNK attributes assumed to have been forgotten. When recall is adjusted for retention in this manner, the proportion of inferring increases with decreases in the amount remembered (D+I). This measure was not used in the present report for two reasons. First, the statistic of I/(D+I) or D/(D+I) presumes, as just mentioned, that all DNK attributes are totally forgotten by subjects. This assumption seems untenable; it is very plausible that additional thought or additional cues will elicit at least some of the DNK attributes. However, the idea of adjusting recall estimates for amount forgotten (such as by multiplying DNK by the proportion of attributes supposedly remaining in memory) is an excellent one which should be tried in future research. Second, the changes in I/(D+I) or D/(D+I) over memories obscures the fact that, except for scripted episodes, the amount of inferred attributes remained remarkably constant (around 16%). If efficiency of inferring does vary over memories differing in memorability, it would be expected that the amount of inferred attributes would vary along with the adjusted recall statistic (I/D+I). (See Gelfand's chapter for further insights into these measurement problems).

Thus, several arguments may be offered regarding why inferred recall might have been expected to be higher than obtained here. For example, precedents were cited for higher levels of inference in other paradigms; a rationale was noted for why subjects may have failed to detect all the inferring that occurred; a mathematical approach was mentioned which suggests higher inference levels than reported here. However, not all the arguments are in favor of greater amounts of inferring when recollecting episodic memories. On the contrary, there are good reasons why many memories should not afford much opportunity for inferred recall. When a memory is very familiar or salient, recollections may be so dominated by direct recall that few opportunities exist for inferred recall. When a memory is unfamiliar and obscure, the number of attributes recovered by direct recall may be too few to give clues to infer remaining attributes. Thus, except when an episode conforms to a script and possesses an intermediate amount of familiarity, inferred recall should be less than that for direct recall. The only mystery is why memories of intermediate familiarity, which might permit an inferring of attributes not recalled directly, are not subjected to more inferential processing than reported here.

Since people infer attributes infrequently when remembering nonscripted episodes, the question arises as to why? The data indicate that subjects limit the number of attributes that may be inferred, regardless of the number that may directly be recalled. For example, the level of inferred recall in nonscripted episodes remained relatively constant across all four experiments, while the level of direct recall varied widely. It is difficult at the present time to know why subjects might choose to limit inferential recall, especially for memories of intermediate familiarity. One reason may be to maintain the accuracy of episodic records. Since people tend to remember some of what they think about during recall, inferences have the potential, especially when inaccurate, for distorting the original memory (Loftus, 1979). While distortion may be tolerated in some ego-threatening situations (Greenwald, 1980), memory records must generally be stable and accurate for personal and practical adjustment. Thus, people may avoid inferring the attributes of past experiences to avoid contaminating their memory records and losing their principal link with their past. Another reason may be because inferential recall may require more cognitive effort than direct recalls, and that there are limits on the expenditure of this effort. It remains for future research to ascertain what is the best explanation of the constancy in inferred recall for nonscripted memories.

REFERENCES

Atkinson, R. C. & Juola, J. F. (1974). Search and decision processes in recognition memory. In D. H. Krantz, R. C. Atkinson, R. D. Luce, & P. Suppes (Eds.), *Contemporary developments in mathematical psychology.* San Francisco: Freeman.

Aristotle. (1905). De memoria et reminiscentia. In J. M. Robertson (Ed.), *The Works of Aristotle.* London: George Routledge and Sons.

Baddeley, A. D. (1983). Domains of recollection. *Psychological Review, 89,* 707–729.

Baddeley, A. D., Lewis, V., & Nimmo-Smith, I. (1979). When did you last . . . ? In M. M. Gruneberg, P. Morris, & R. N. Sykes (Eds.), *Practical Aspects of Memory.* London: Academic Press.

Bartlett, F. C. (1932). *Remembering.* Cambridge, England: Cambridge University Press.

Bower, G. H. (1967). A multicomponent theory of the memory trace. In K. W. Spence & J. T. Spence (Eds.), *The psychology of learning and motivation: Advances in research and theory* (Vol. 1) London: Academic Press.

Brown, J. (Ed.). (1976). *Recall and recognition.* New York: Wiley.

Crovitz, H. F., & Schiffman, H. (1974). Frequency of episodic memories as a function of their age. *Bulletin of Psychonomic Society, 4,* 517–518.

Field, D. (1981). Retrospective reports by healthy intelligent elderly people of personal events of their adult lives. *International Journal of Behavioral Development, 4,* 77–97.

Gould, A., & Stephenson, G. M. (1967). Some experiments relating to Bartlett's theory of remembering. *British Journal of Psychology, 58,* 39–49.

Greenwald, A. G. (1980). The totalitarian ego: Fabrication and revision of personal history. *American Psychologist, 35,* 603–618.

Herrmann, D. J. (1983). Questionnaires about memory. In J. Harris & P. Morris (Eds.). *Everyday memory, actions, and absentmindedness.* New York: Academic Press.

James, W. (1890). *The principles of psychology,* New York: Holt.

Linton, M. (1975). Memory for real-world events. In D. H. Norman & D. E. Rumelhart (Eds.), *Explorations in cognition*. San Francisco: Freeman.

Linton, M. (1978). Real-world memory after six years: An *in vivo* study of very long-term memory. In M. Gruneberg, P. Morris, & R. N. Sykes (Eds.), *Practical aspects of memory*. New York: Academic Press.

Linton, M. (1979). I remember it well. *Psychology Today, 13,* 81–86.

Loftus, E. F. (1979). The malleability of human memory. *American Scientist, 67,* 312–320.

Morris, P. E., Gruneberg, M., Sykes, R. N., & Merrick, A. (1982). Football knowledge and the acquisition of new results. *British Journal of Psychology, 72,* 479–484.

Neisser, U. (1967). *Cognitive psychology*. Englewood Cliffs, NJ: Prentice Hall.

Neisser, U. (1976). *Cognition and reality*. San Francisco: Freeman.

Reiff, R., & Scheerer, M. (1959). *Memory and hypnotic age regression*. New York: International Universities Press.

Robinson, J. (1976). Sampling autobiographical memory. *Cognitive Psychology, 8,* 578–595.

Rubin, D. C. (1982). On the retention function for autobiographical memory. *Journal of Verbal Learning and Verbal Behavior, 21,* 21–38.

Rubin, D. C. (in press) Vivid memories. *Cognition*.

Salaman, E. (1970). *A collection of moments*. London: Longman.

Schank, R., & Abelson, R. (1977). *Scripts, plans, goals, and understanding*. Hillsdale, NJ: Erlbaum.

Shoemaker, S. (1967). Memory. In P. Edwards (Ed.), *The Encyclopedia of philosophy*. New York: Macmillan.

Shoemaker, S. (1970). Persons and their pasts. *American Philosophical Quarterly, 7,* 269–285.

Thorndyke, P. W. (1977). Cognitive structures in comprehension and memory of narrative discourse. *Cognitive Psychology, 9,* 77–110.

Underwood, B. J. (1969). Attributes of memory. *Psychological Review, 76,* 559–573.

White, S. E., & Pillimer, D. B. (1979). Childhood amnesia and the development of a socially accessible memory system. In J. F. Kihlstrom & F. J. Evans (Eds.), *Functional disorders of memory,* Hillsdale, NJ: Erlbaum.

Williams, M. D., & Hollan, J. D. (1981). The process of retrieval from very long- term memory. *Cognitive Science, 5,* 87–119.

Chapter 18

The Interface between Laboratory and Naturalistic Cognition

Harold Gelfand

St. Bonaventure University, New York

OVERVIEW

In this chapter, I discuss the relationship between traditional laboratory and more recent naturalistic investigations of cognition. Some of the characteristics of naturalistic tasks are identified. The advantages and disadvantages of the laboratory and naturalistic approaches are considered, and the similarities and points of contact between the two approaches are emphasized. It is suggested that the two approaches to studying cognition can benefit, methodologically and conceptually, from encouraging a rapprochement between them, sharing methodologies and conceptualizations to their mutual advantages. The chapters by Baars and Herrmann in this volume are used to exemplify these possibilities. Methodological strengths and weaknesses of the two naturalistic research programs are identified. Theories from laboratory cognition that could provide alternative explanations of their naturalistic phenomena, especially the slips of the tongue investigated by Baars, are suggested. Finally, alternative analyses of Herrmann's autobiographical memory data suggest the existence of orderly relationships between direct and inferred memory. Other informative analyses, to exploit the richness and complexity of Herrmann's autobiographical data are suggested.

BASIC ISSUES

Scan the journals populated by the writings of cognitive psychologists in the early 1980s, and you will find reports of subjects remembering stories, faces, and crime scenes; identifying coins and the route from here to there; playing bridge, chess, and other games; and listening to musical pieces and compositions. These are the kinds of studies we have in mind when we speak of naturalistic memory or naturalistic cognition.

What we mean by "naturalistic" is easier to understand if we contrast it with laboratory research. Notwithstanding the terminology, it is not really the locale that differentiates the two types of investigations. Rather, it is the degree to which the tasks and materials given to the subjects correspond to those encountered in everyday life. Naturalistic cognition studies how people perform tasks that resemble those they encounter in their daily lives. Laboratory studies present tasks that are artificial or contrived for the purposes of the research being conducted, with little necessary resemblance to those we perform in our daily lives.

To convince yourself that the focus on naturalistic phenomena reflects a recent trend, compare the incidence of such reports in current journals to those in the 1970s or 1960s, in the same journals. Slips of the tongue and autobiographical memory both involve phenomena that are parts of our daily lives. As such, the research on these two natural phenomena reported by Baars and Herrmann in the preceding two chapters certainly merit inclusion in a volume devoted to consideration of recent trends in cognitive science.

Lest it seem too easy to resolve some issues implicit in the preceding paragraphs, let me elaborate on some aspects of this trend towards investigating naturalistic cognitive events, before proceeding to examine the work of Baars and Herrmann in greater detail. How do we decide what is or is not naturalistic, and which naturalistic events to investigate? Why should we study naturalistic cognition? Is such a focus really that recent a trend?

We may not all agree as to which tasks are naturalistic and which are not. Just as we have cultural ethologists, ethnographers, and naturalists, so too may we need cognitive ethologists, ethnographers, and naturalists. These new professionals would have to be keen observers of the human situation, whose job it would be to identify and catalog our naturalistic cognitive tasks or activities, and perhaps to specify the important ones. Neisser (1978) presented us with at least a partial list of ecological cognitive activities that he had culled from other investigators or identified on his own. Freud was also one such keen observer, and he brought slips of the tongue to our attention. I could challenge each reader to remember at least one, or your most embarrassing, slip of the tongue or pen, and feel confident that not one of you would be unable to do so. The fact that these slips are so prevalent, being part of all of our daily lives, is what makes it easy to categorize the research reported by Baars as naturalistic. Furthermore, the fact that we are all able to remember such episodes from our pasts, and that these remembrances include multidimensional detail (including what we were doing; with whom, when, and where we were doing it; and how we felt when we were doing it), validates the autobiographical memories studied by Herrmann as a form of naturalistic memory.

Although it seems easy to classify these two tasks as naturalistic, let me point out that there are artificial aspects to each of them as studied by Baars and Herrmann. Slips of the tongue occur naturally in our lives, but when Baars induces them artificially, are they the same phenomenon? The memories addressed by Herrmann were no doubt formed in the natural worlds of his subjects, but the remembrances of them, and the manner in which they are probed, are certainly artificial. The subjects are reporting about their memories in an artificial laboratory situation, instead of using their memories in the flow of daily life. The cues that arouse the memories of Herrmann's subjects may be different from the rich contextual cues that arouse our memories in the natural world. The subjects are asked to engage in remembering activity, something we are not usually asked to do directly in our daily lives. When we are asked to remember in natural situations, we are asked about a specific episode, whereas Herrmann's subjects could sometimes choose any episode to remember. Finally, even if our naturalistic memory probes focus on specific attributes, as Herrmann did, we rarely are asked whether we remember some aspect of an episode without being asked the specific content of the memory, either for information or as proof. Which, if any, of these artificialities would affect what we find out about memory, is an empirical question, just as it is an empirical question whether laboratory research in general gives us incomplete or biased information.

Identifying both naturalistic and artificial aspects of the tasks used by Baars and Herrmann forces us to recognize that naturalistic vs. laboratory is not a dichotomous variable. Like many of our tempting dichotomies, this one actually refers to a continuum of naturalness. The labels we use refer to ideal end-points, or ranges along the continuum, with no clear cut-off point or agreement amongst us as to where to differentiate between laboratory and naturalistic. Neisser (1978) may prefer investigations that are even more naturalistic, with the behaviors studied in their natural contexts, being affected by variables that occur in those contexts, not as tasks in themselves, but as functional elements of some humanly significant activity.

Before we invest too many resources in attempts to classify tasks as naturalistic or artificial, we should consider why it matters how a task is classified. The push to naturalistic approaches is predicated on assumptions about what cognitive psychologists are trying to accomplish and how best to achieve those goals.

The advantages and disadvantages ascribed to laboratory and naturalistic approaches are reminiscent of the distinction between (and sometimes incompatibility of) internal and external validity, introduced by Campbell and Stanley (1963) in their methodological treatise on applied social research. Internal validity fulfills our analytical or explanatory goal—isolating variables to enable us to identify causal relations. Internal validity is best achieved in controlled, laboratory experiments. But do laboratory experiments lead to powerful explanations of irrelevant phenomena? External validity focuses on establishing the appropriate correspondence between the people, tasks, and environments used in our research and those to which we wish to apply our research findings. Of course, external validity is best achieved in field or naturalistic settings. Given the trade-offs between internal and external validity, it was thought that the basic scientist might lean towards laboratory studies, while the applied scientist might prefer more naturalistic investigations.

What we are seeing now in cognitive psychology is that even basic researchers are employing more naturalistic tasks and materials, and they are being exhorted to do so (Neisser, 1978). Although basic cognitive researchers do not have an interest in a problem concerning a particular naturalistic task that requires immediate solutions, as an applied researcher might, they do want the psychology or theories they develop to have relevance to the cognitive functioning of human beings in their daily lives. The question is how to arrive at this goal. Proponents of naturalistic research assert that, if our ultimate goal is to understand cognition in everyday situations, we should study those situations directly. Granted that the concern with external validity developed from an interest in applied research, but in terms of ultimate goals as outlined earlier, even the most basic researcher has an applied focus. Thus, basic researchers can also benefit from greater ecological validity through naturalistic investigations.

Laboratory researchers counter that there are too many tasks in our natural worlds for us to investigate them all. Furthermore, to present any of the tasks in their naturalistic form would introduce too much complexity into our analysis and sacrifice too much control over relevant variables. Besides, the goal is to develop a general theory of human cognitive functioning, not a theory about a specific cognitive task. It is better for researchers to contrive a task, however artificial, that enables them to isolate and understand a basic cognitive process. One task may provide information about a number of processes, but a range of tasks may be necessary to get at all the major processes. If the processes identified are indeed fundamental ones, then those processes will have generality to a wide variety of naturalistic tasks.

Some contemporary critics argue that the laboratory approach has been a failure. Neisser (1978) can list few empirical generalizations about memory that we did not already know naturalistically, few successful theories, and no success at relating what is known from laboratory research to memory functioning in our daily lives. It is ironic that the laboratory approach is cited for the very deficiencies it saw as potential in the naturalistic approach. There has been a proliferation of laboratory tasks, which, rather than leading to general process theories, has resulted in theories that are task-specific, of paired-associate learning, serial recall, etc. (Tulving & Madigan, 1970). Furthermore, the tasks chosen for investigation have been so simplified and abstracted as to render them irrelevant to normal human functioning. Finally, even if laboratory investigations did provide information about individual cognitive processes, no progress has been made in working out the rules for combining the processes that are operative in complex, everyday cognitive tasks. These critics of laboratory research recognize that much laboratory research eventuates in task-specific models, just as naturalistic research does. If the specific tasks chosen for investigation by laboratory researchers have not led to the identification of general processes, then perhaps the researchers' goal of developing theories that are relevant to normal cognitive functioning can be achieved by investigating ecologically valid tasks. Even if we do not identify basic processes that will generalize to a variety of naturalistic tasks, we will at least come to an understanding of one such task.

Laboratory researchers may rejoin that their enterprise has not been the dismal failure characterized by some critics. My list of informative empirical generalizations and theories derived from laboratory research may be longer than Neisser's (1978), and somebody else's list may be still longer. Some of us may make more extensive claims about applying our laboratory based knowledge to an understanding of everyday memory phenomena than Neisser is willing to do. Laboratory researchers might even argue that the current surge in naturalistic investigations, rather than being an indictment of the laboratory record, is a tribute to its progress. The development of conceptualizations about memory, and of methods for studying it from laboratory research, has set the stage for naturalistic research, implicating tasks to investigate, questions to ask, variables to study, and methods for doing so. Finally, any failure of the laboratory approach to date does not imply that appropriate abstractions and conceptualizations will not be successful in the future, nor does it guarantee that the naturalistic alternative would be successful.

Comparing lists of the successes and failures of laboratory and naturalistic research is unlikely to provide us with a clear-cut winner in the quest for a best research approach. We have no clear criteria for the identification of successes, nor for comparing lists of assets and liabilities. Fortunately, we do not have to choose between the two approaches. The reality is that some researchers will continue to employ one approach, some will try the other, and some will straddle the invisible fence between them, or do both. Perhaps the message in their being along a continuum is that we should not try to choose between them. Indeed, the best strategy for achieving scientific progress may be to capitalize on the creative tension that exists between the two approaches. They can feed off one another, in a continually developing symbiotic relationship, to realize their common goal.

I have already alluded to how the laboratory researcher can benefit from the naturalistic approach. Our analytical drive may push us to simplify conditions, thereby obscuring important aspects of a task or what affects it. At this point, we might consider what it is that characterizes naturalistic tasks but is missing from the artificial tasks often used by laboratory researchers. I doubt that we have the complete answer, but a couple of things strike me about these naturalistic tasks in general, and about the examples with which Herrmann and Baars confront us in particular. First, the tasks are complex. The stimuli are multidimensional, the potential influencing variables are numerous, and the processes involved are many and diverse. Second, the events extend over a wider time range than is typical of the laboratory. The stimuli may continue to be processed or reflected on over time, the factors affecting them can extend over the same temporal range, and this extension over time allows for greater variability in the contextual, environmental, and personal characteristics operative during the processing of relevant stimuli.

If we want to make contact, ultimately, with naturalistic cognitive functioning, our laboratory research must address what we do with information in our cognitive worlds. We must also consider the naturalistic context and the variables operating that might affect how and what we do. Naturalistic investigations may be important in their own right, but consideration of such studies may also be the inspiration for laboratory experiments, helping to identify those memory phenomena and processes from everyday life that have to be abstracted, analyzed, captured, and perhaps even combined in the laboratory so that general process theories can be as comprehensive and ecologically relevant as possible.

I suspect that there are benefits for naturalistic researchers to derive from the laboratory tradition as well. As a cognitive psychologist with a commitment to laboratory research, I am not prepared to reject entirely the agenda of the basic researcher. Just as the laboratory researcher wants the results of laboratory research to be ecologically relevant, so I assume the naturalistic researcher wants to go beyond a loose-leaf folder or catalog full of descriptions of randomly chosen cognitive events. Consider what we have to do when we jump into the real cognitive world.

First, being people, we researchers could easily be overwhelmed by the complexity, or by a plethora of anecdotes about fascinating but unrelated cognitive occurrences. There is a certain ingenuity involved in finding questions to ask and systematic approaches to studying these complex phenomena. Just as in laboratory research, a level of abstraction is required to identify meaningful packages of naturalistic cognitive behavior. Both Herrmann and Baars are to be commended for carving coherent cognitive chunks out of the natural cognitive world. Whether the particular abstractions and findings of laboratory research will suggest meaningful naturalistic cognitive tasks whose investigation would be profitable, remains to be seen.

Second, we have to develop methodologies that will allow us to answer our questions. To what extent can we measure our phenomena objectively, and control extraneous variables, without sacrificing the richness of the naturalistic situation? Here is a place where progress in laboratory research can be applied to naturalistic research. Cognitive researchers have demonstrated creativity and ingenuity in the methodologies they have developed and the analyses they have devised to explore cognitive processes. I will have more to say about how Baars and Herrmann have met the methodological challenge when I deal with them in turn.

Third, and finally, we have to develop models and explanations for these complex phenomena. Just as our goal in the laboratory should not be a theory of paired-associate learning or of free recall, but rather a theory of memory processes, so should our goal in naturalistic cognition be a theory that is more comprehensive than a particular task. Theories developed in the laboratory may help us develop theories that span different naturalistic tasks. Indeed, it is reassuring to see the work on naturalistic cognition reported by Baars and Herrmann making contact with other theoretical developments and research programs in cognition.

That this kind of interplay is possible is suggested by the fact that the shift to naturalistic investigations, although fostering new journal outlets (e.g. *Human Learning*) has not been limited to those new journals, nor to new investigators. I take it as a healthy sign that the studies involving instances of naturalistic materials and tasks I mentioned at the beginning of this chapter shared space in journals with studies using free recall of lists of words, listening to pure tones, etc.

As I consider those journals, I wonder whether the shift to ecologically valid investigations, or the interplay between naturalistic and laboratory research, really reflects any recent trend in cognitive psychology. The shifts from studying nonsense syllables to words, from studying individual words to prose passages, from studying serial to free recall, and from measuring recall accuracy to measuring recall organization, all reflect attempts to introduce materials or tasks, or get at processes, that are more like everyday cognitive functioning. A recent example of the interplay between consideration of naturalistic phenomena and laboratory research is the work on updating memory (e.g. Bjork, 1978), but even that research was predated by a series of related studies using memory tasks developed by Yntema and Mueser (1960, 1962) 20 years ago to simulate the now salient task of an air-traffic controller. What may be new is the degree of naturalness which investigators are ready to undertake, and the number of investigators turning to such research.

Although I began by alluding to the work on slips of the tongue and autobiographical memory as naturalistic, I have also pointed out the laboratory influences on both research programs. It should be apparent now that I consider the work of Baars and Herrmann to stand at the interface of naturalistic and laboratory investigation. Their failures to choose one approach over the other, rather than reflecting nonproductive indecision, provide vivid examples of the salutory benefits to be derived from combining the best of both worlds. My discussion of their two research programs will focus on what they have achieved through this rapprochement, and how they could derive further benefit from the interplay between laboratory and naturalistic approaches.

BAARS: SLIPS OF THE TONGUE

Baars investigates one of those intriguing phenomena that capture our attention because we all produce examples of them and suffer the consequences, namely, slips of the tongue. Although usually on the lips of a speaker, on the couch of a therapist, or in the pen of a poet, Baars and his investigators have succeeded in bringing slips into the experimental laboratory. Not only can they induce subjects to produce slips reliably, but their method allows them to manipulate or observe other variables, to determine factors that bring about or are related to the occurrence of slips.

The evidence that phonological and lexical factors, as well as semantic, contextual, and even state-of-mind factors, influence the occurrence of slips, is impressive. I have no qualms about that evidence, and indeed, as a cognitive psychologist and frequent laboratory researcher, I am reassured by it. I am even more reassured by the continuities I see between this line of investigation of a naturalistic phenomenon and many other lines that cognitive psychologists pursue. At a methodological level, I see the use of error data to infer rules and regularities in cognitive processing, just as psycholinguists observe errors in language producers (*throwed* for *threw*) to infer their development of grammatical rules (e.g., Berko, 1958), or memory researchers observe errors in memory tasks (*hat* or *dog* for *cat*), to infer the nature of word encodings (e.g., Anisfield & Knapp, 1968; Conrad, 1964). At a conceptual level, I am pleased to see attempts by Baars and others to extend the conceptualizations they develop from observing slips to the full range of speech and language processing (see, for example, the volume by Fromkin, 1980).

While applauding the attempt to generate and test a theory of slips, it is with the particulars of the theoretical explanation that I have some concern. Actually, there are two aspects to my concern. One has to do with the specific theory Baars advances, and the other has to do with the choice of any theory that is specific to the slip-of-the-tongue phenomenon. Both aspects reflect the preference for parsimony and comprehensiveness that characterizes the theories generated in the traditional laboratory approach to cognition.

As to the choice of Freudian theory, it is not that I know the theory is wrong, but rather that I wonder whether all the constructs in it are necessary. Perhaps my hesitation is just the naturalistic activation of skepticism which is aroused in a cognitive or experimental psychologist by the terms "Freud" or "psychodynamic." That skepticism has no doubt been fueled by years of frustration at converting Freud's appealing concepts to testable hypotheses. Even Baars notes that Freud's ideas about slips were contradictory at times. Granted that Baars advances particular testable hypotheses about slips. But does confirmation of those hypotheses really require us to accept the entire package of Freudian concepts comprising the theory that spawned those hypotheses? Do we have to include psychodynamic forces, conflicts at an unconscious level, suppressors that prevent certain threatening information from reaching consciousness and that only allow certain intentions to be expressed involuntarily, and a central role for psychosexual development or drives, etc?

If slips are errors due to a conflict between the intended target utterance and the actual "slip" utterance, the implication is that both plans are *available* at some level, and the cognitive system must *choose* between them. This kind of conceptualization opens the door for many of the aforementioned concepts.

An alternative theory might be found by going beyond the bounds of the slip phenomenon. Findings and theories from the cognitive psychology literature may be sufficiently comprehensive to also account for these slips.

To get at what I mean by an alternative cognitive conceptualization, let me ask you to consider some slightly different experiments than those reported by

Baars. Suppose we gave subjects the exact task Baars used, using the same materials, with one exception. Each time Baars used a phrase like *bad-goof,* (which is amenable to the slip *gad-boof* in a phonological sense), or *rage-weight* (which is amenable to *wage-rate*), or *lice negs* (which could slip into *nice legs*), we will replace the vulnerable phrase with the likely slip phrase. Thus, the utterances which were slips by Baars's subjects will now be the actually present-ed and correct stimuli for my subjects. Now, we can manipulate or select the same variables as Baars did—phonological and semantic verbal context, wider context, and prevailing personality characteristics—and observe effects on ac-curacy or reaction time for what are now the *correct* responses.

My guess is that the accuracy and reaction times for these now correct re-sponses would be affected by the manipulations in the same orderly fashion as the slips were. Indeed, we already know about such effects under the heading of semantic priming, set effects, and so on (e.g., Meyer, Schvaneveldt & Ruddy, 1975; Tulving & Gold, 1963; Warren, 1972). We already have explanations for these phenomena that do not have to assume multiple plans and choices. Rather, in some top-down fashion (see Norman & Bobrow, 1976), the existing rules of language, the prior extra- and intra-experimental experiences, and/or the con-text, among other things, create expectations about upcoming stimuli. The sys-tem is biased towards perceiving stimuli compatible with those expectations, either because it looks for certain features first, or because certain features or stimuli in a conceptual network are already activated to some extent, therefore requiring less activation from the current stimulus to raise it above a criterion for passage to the response system. Indeed, the spreading activation notion (as in Anderson, 1976) mentioned by Baars is one way that experiences and expecta-tions can grease the rails for processing particular stimuli, or really, particular interpretations of a stimulus.

Note that experience, context, and the like in this kind of explanation operate without our alluding to active conflict. Indeed, while the stimulus may be ambig-uous for the *experimenter,* it is not necessarily so for the *subject.* The subject processes the stimulus until an interpretation is arrived at, and responds on the basis of that particular interpretation.

I hope you see my point. If this kind of model can account for reaction times when the slip responses are the correct ones, why can't it account for slips when they are errors? Concepts compatible with the slip are already activated, making it more likely that a stimulus will get processed and interpreted as a slip *before* it gets processed correctly. The incorrect interpretation is the only one, or the first one, to the response buffer, and it slips out. No choice, no conflict, no active suppression is needed—at least not yet.

Then you may ask, why is the speaker surprised or embarrassed? Stimulus processing may well continue *after* a response is selected for output, and indeed the chosen response may be monitored or fed back to compare to current stimulus states. This processing may result in recognition of a mismatch of one kind or another after it is too late to edit the response, producing a delay in the correct response. If anything, these ambiguities or competition for the subject come into play after the supposed conflicting interpretation has had its effect, and not before.

The results of the last experiment reported by Baars, to test his psychodynamic hypothesis, provide the strongest case that competing intentions to suppress actually induce the slips observed. Consideration of the order of events, and of alternative causal links, as a laboratory researcher is wont to do, suggests an alternative explanation I advanced earlier. The intention to avoid, rather than being the cause of the slip, may be the result of the same process that causes the slip. Sex-guilt may be (or involve or derive from) a supernormative concern with matters sexual. The concern translates into (conceptual or semantic) activation. That activation may be manifest in performances that are sensitive to such activation (e.g., slips of the tongue). The quality of the activation may lead to intentions to avoid in performances over which the individual has more control, thus leading to fewer sex-related free associations.

I will leave the reader to contemplate whether this conceptualization can account for slips, whether it is any different from the one Baars offers, and, if so, how to choose between them. But before I slip into another topic, let me remind you of another phenomenon from the cognitive laboratory. In the Stroop effect (Stroop, 1935), identification of an ink color, for example Red, is impeded when the ink is used to form the name of a competing color, for example "BLUE." That impedance often shows up as a delay in responding, and sometimes manifests itself in an error—responding "Blue" for the word ("oops!"), instead of "Red" for the ink color. It strikes me that these errors are speech errors, and indeed that they qualify as slips, and that even the correct but delayed responses are manifestations of the same processes as the ones that produce the errors. Models of the Stroop effect (e.g., see Dyer, 1973) do not suggest that the person must *choose* between the color and the word, that a conflict is actively confronted. Rather, one interpretation is arrived at faster than the other, namely reading before color identification, producing the effect. If we reverse the task, asking the person to read the word rather than name the color, we do not reverse the effect. There is no problem, because the correct interpretation is the one processed first. Slips and Stroop phenomena both involve effects of compelling competing stimuli. As such, they may share a cognitive explanation.

I began my comments on Baars's chapter by alluding to its continuity with cognitive psychology as explored by laboratory researchers. The methodological continuities should obviously be numerous, as Baars has used the tools and approaches of the laboratory researcher to validate his naturalistic phenomenon. I hope my treatment of the theoretical account of slips makes it apparent how we can capitalize on continuities between naturalistic and laboratory research even further. Slips may help us understand cognitive mechanisms, but the converse is also true. As I have indicated, our understanding of other cognitive phenomena

investigated through the laboratory approach may encompass slips or other naturalistic phenomena that we might otherwise compartmentalize in a task-specific
way for the purpose of theorizing. Identifying theories that are relevant may
require finding an appropriate abstraction, or identifying a common task-demand
or process that is engaged. And, of course, our continuing confidence in any of
the theories will depend on further tests of their predictions, along with consideration of other factors that guide our theoretical choices.

While exploiting the continuities, we should remain cognizant of the characteristics of naturalistic phenomena that attract their champions. Baars's findings,
that a variety of phonological and semantic sources can produce slips, and that
some sources have their effects because of the speaker's prior personal and social
history, demonstrate implicitly the multidimensionality of cognitive events and
their representations, as well as their extension through the temporal domain.
These themes will become explicit when I turn to Herrmann's work.

HERRMANN: AUTOBIOGRAPHICAL MEMORY

Herrmann chooses to investigate autobiographical memory because it is episodic. Yet laboratory list learning is also episodic, and autobiographical, because
it is about what *I* learned. Apparently we are to reserve autobiographical for
those memories which, though observed in the laboratory, were collected in
naturalistic settings.

What's so special about outside the laboratory? In a refrain of my general
comments about naturalistic cognition, Herrmann reminds us right away that the
episodes comprising autobiographical memory are rich and multidimensional.
Episodes consist of behaviors, feelings, goings-on, people, places, times, context, etc. Each of these attributes has many possible values, and the possible
values or states of one attribute, e.g., locations, are totally different from the
possible states of other attributes, e.g., feelings. Furthermore, episodes extend
over time and are reflected on over time before being left to memory. I am not
even certain of what unit from a laboratory task corresponds to a real-world
episode. Is the unit a word, or a list of words? Either way, the attributes are fewer
and less distinctive from one another than are Herrmann's. Yet, even in those
simplified laboratory situations, Wickens (1970) and others have noted the multidimensionality of stimulus encodings. If attributes of an episode interact to
influence memory, we can only find out by investigating a multidimensional
situation. We have done this in some of our laboratory investigations, the previously cited work by Yntema and Mueser (1960, 1962) being one example, but
perhaps more is needed.

Herrmann imposes some order on this complex situation by assuming that
remembering involves gaining access to an episode, followed by a process of
retrieving attributes from the accessed memory. He wants to study that retrieval
process to see how much of retrieval is direct and how much is inferred. Her-

rmann's direct and inferred recall remind me of FRAN'S ENTRYSET, or starter set, and associative search, for retrieval from a network (see, for example, Anderson & Bower, 1972). Here is another point of contact between theories developed in the laboratory and those in natural settings. Whether cross-fertilization between these two lines of investigation will lead to growth remains to be seen.

Of course, Herrmann must pay a price or two for the reward of tapping into these rich autobiographical memories. In laboratory memory research, we have objective ways of assessing whether subjects remember. Herrmann must accept the subjects' self-reports that they do remember an attribute, and whether they got to that memory directly or inferentially. Wanting to protect his subjects' confidentiality, and having no external standard of accuracy (e.g., Herrmann's own access to the episodes) available anyway, what choice does he have but to believe the subject? If we are at all suspicious of these self-reports, then we must question the levels of direct and inferred recall, and therefore their relative levels as well. At the least, we might want to examine the instructions given to the subjects about direct and inferred recall, but even that may not be sufficient to allay our concerns.

Elsewhere, Herrmann (Herrmann & Neisser, 1978) has argued for the believability of subjects' self-reports about memory. I would not dispute the particular causes for optimism cited by him. However, I also need not take the time or space to list the various reasons (based on intentions, ambiguity, ignorance, etc.) why subjects might misreport their memory or memory mode. To put Herrmann's procedure in perspective, imagine giving a student full credit on an exam for knowing a theory of memory, if the student said simply, "Yes, I know it." We have encountered this problem before, in psychophysics, perception, and cognitive psychology, and have been forced to find methodological solutions in the experimental laboratory. If we are unable to observe directly the accuracy of self-reports of autobiographical memory, we might at least demand that the self-reports show orderly relationships of the sort that would be predicted if the self-reports were valid.

Even if the assessments of direct and inferred memories are valid, I wonder about the meaning of the comparisons reported by Herrmann. There may be some purpose served by obtaining absolute levels of direct and inferred recall, and even comparing them. But we must exercise caution in any interpretations of underlying memory processes that we derive from these comparisons. The issue is posed as if we are trying to determine which type of remembering, direct or inferred, the subject chooses to use. Certain biases may operate that should lead direct recall to be higher than inferred memories, that give the individual no choice. Remember that Herrmann told us there are two stages, first, access to the episode, and then, retrieval of attributes. How do you get access to the episode except through one or more attributes, and thus, must not any accessed episode begin with an advantage for direct memory? Furthermore, inferred memories are presumably inferred from direct ones, so again we must have one or more direct ones before we can have any inferred ones. Finally, a low probability of inferred recall does not necessarily imply an inability to do so. Some, or many, of those attributes that were directly recalled may also have been inferable. It would not be unreasonable to suppose that, if the subject does both, he or she reports it as directly recalled, and that, if the subject can do both but only does one, direct recall is preferred or faster. Thus, the low incidence of inferred memories may simply be an indication of high levels of direct recall.

Extensive experience with the objective, analytical approach to laboratory memory research has sensitized us to the relationship between our choice of behavioral measures and types of analyses on the one hand, and theoretical formulations and interpretations on the other. These kinds of considerations, combined with my previous remarks about the potential interdependence of direct and inferred recall, stimulate my reservations concerning other inferences about inferred memory that Herrmann derived from the raw probabilities of inferred recall that he observed.

Perhaps in anticipation of skepticism about their validity, Herrmann resorts to another technique adopted in the field of perception to deal with self-reports of experience. If we cannot trust the absolute level of self-report, perhaps we can trust the relative levels under different stimulus conditions. It is this approach that leads Herrmann, and vicariously us also, to be amazed at the invariance of reports of inferred memory, despite large swings in direct recall produced by variations of different kinds in the episodes—their age, familiarity, etc. Indeed, the quest continues until a variable is found that affects inferred memory, leading Herrmann to speculate about the role of schema in inference.

A focus on inferred memory implies an interest in some process that is beyond the reach of direct recall. However, raw probabilities of inferred memory would seem an inappropriate measure of the relative rate of inference from memory under different conditions. Those differential raw probabilities might be by-products of differential opportunities to infer, produced by variations in direct memory (which might have priority over indirect memory, as asserted earlier). Instead, to get at inferred memory independent of direct recall requires the use of conditional probabilities, namely probabilities of inferred memory given no direct recall, P (I/$\overline{\text{D}}$).

Figures 1–4 show those conditional probabilities for Herrmann's Experiments 1–4, respectively (based on the means reported in Herrmann's Figures 2–5). Contrary to the raw probabilities, the conditional probabilities are not that low, nor are they that alike.

Figure 1 indicates that, given equal opportunity, we infer more from adult memories than from earlier ones. From Figure 2, it does seem that familiarity increases the likelihood of inference. Although the curves for first- and second-hand memories in Figure 3 seem noisy, let me suggest one ordering principle. If location, time, social context, and related events represent con*text*, and feelings,

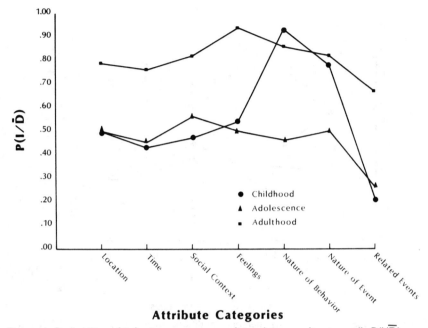

Attribute Categories

Figure 1. Probability of inferring memory conditional on no direct recall, P(I/D̄), as a function of attribute category and the life period from which memories originated (based on Herrmann's Experiment 1).

nature of behavior, and nature of event represent con*tent* of the episode, then do the data suggest that first-hand memories lead to more inferences about con*text*, while second-hand memories lead to more inferences about con*tent*? Finally, in the one case where Herrmann found a difference with raw probabilities, the conditional probabilities yield a difference in the opposite direction (see Figure 4). Those episodes provided because of their script character actually lead to fewer inferences than do spontaneous ones (except for inferences about time, but the provided episodes all referred to birthdays or holidays).

Is there a summarizing principle for all of these figures? I suggest that there is, and it's so simple as to be disconcerting. The stronger the memory, as reflected in direct recall (see Herrmann's figures), the more likely that inferences will be derived from it. Either the relationship between direct and inferred recall is an artifact because both types of recall are measuring the same thing—subjects cannot really tell which is which—or the message is that the more information in the memory trace, the greater is the basis for inference. As for the invariance in the raw probabilities of inferred recall reported by Herrmann, it seems to be the result of a tradeoff between opportunity to infer (greater when direct recall is low) and ability to infer (greater when direct recall is high).

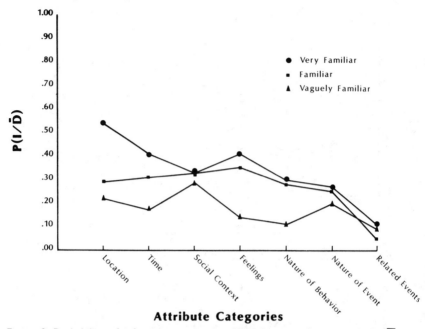

Attribute Categories

Figure 2. Probability of inferring memory conditional on no direct recall, P(I/$\overline{D}$), as a function of attribute category and familiarity level of childhood memories (based on Herrmann's Experiment 2).

If Herrmann has a model of inferred memory that warrants our focusing on his raw probabilities, he is going to have to clarify his formulation. And, if my reanalysis simplifies the situation too much, let me express some choices for further analyses to bring us back into contact with the supposed richness and multidimensional character of this naturalistic situation. Both Herrmann and I suggested that, when memory inferences are made, they are derived from available, or directly recalled, knowledge. It would be interesting to know whether inferences about a given attribute are systematically related to direct recall of other particular attributes. Theories of inferential memory may generate predictions about these kinds of contingencies.

There are other aspects of Herrmann's autobiographical memory data that could be examined without having to await a resolution of the nature of inference. As indicated earlier, one compelling aspect of autobiographical memory is its multifaceted nature. Despite Herrmann's caveats, I would want to know more about the attributes, or attribute categories. Herrmann was appropriately cautious about making such comparisons, but he did point out that comparisons involving the same attributes for different situations or episodes are not confounded by problems of attribute equivalence. Such comparisons got lost, perhaps because no differences were obtained, but they may merit further attention.

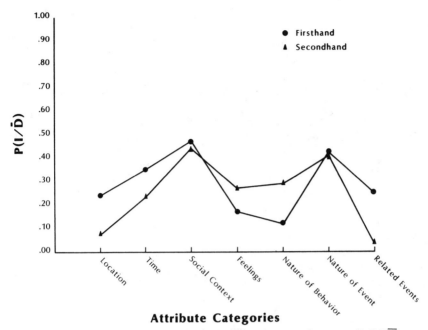

Attribute Categories

Figure 3. Probability of inferring memory conditional on no direct recall, P(I/D̄), as a function of attribute category and the origin of memory (based on Herrmann's Experiment 3).

There are other aspects of the data that could prove interesting, and would likely not be contaminated by the attribute factors that concerned Herrmann. What about the interdependencies among the attributes? Are episodes recalled in all-or-none fashion—retrieve all the attributes or none of them? Are there at least sets of attributes such that the attributes within a set are interdependent, but they are relatively independent of other attribute-sets? Similar analyses can be performed with the categories. Whether for individual attributes or categories, are the independent sets meaningful, like content and context?

At this point, it should be clear how the methods and analytical approaches derived from laboratory memory research can help mine the riches of the autobiographical situation. What is not yet clear is whether these explorations can lead to ideas for testing in the laboratory, or comprehensive theories to encompass both. The role of context, and the nature and organization of memory representations, might provide productive starting points.

CONCLUSIONS

To summarize, I thank Baars and Herrmann for stimulating me with some interesting cognitive performances, their subjects' and their own. Their research

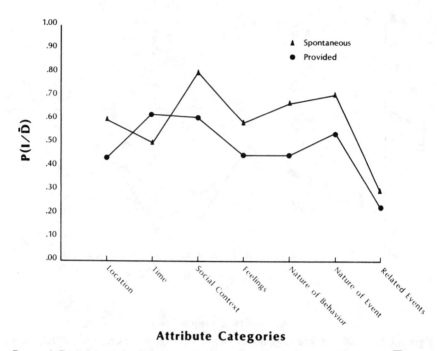

Attribute Categories

Figure 4. Probability of inferring memory conditional on no direct recall, $P(I/\overline{D})$, as a function of attribute category for spontaneous and provided childhood memories (based on Herrmann's Experiment 4).

programs make it clear that naturalistic phenomena can be explored by cognitive researchers, and that relating such investigations to the laboratory tradition can be mutually advantageous. Ecologically valid tasks, multidimensional stimuli, and multiple factors to affect them, can all be brought into the cognitive laboratory. On the other hand, laboratory research may already have provided objective, analytical methodologies and measurement techniques for those ecologically valid tasks. If these tools have not been developed yet, the laboratory approach may remind us of the need to develop the tools. Recognition of the commonality of tasks, or processes underlying them, may suggest common theoretical explanations for seemingly diverse phenomena.

Which of the particular relationships between the naturalistic research of Baars and Herrmann, and traditional laboratory research that I have pointed out, will prove to be relevant and informative, is a matter for future research and theorizing. There is no guarantee that an apparent relationship will prove to be important psychologically, nor is there a recipe available for relating these two approaches. However, as we move on to our own research programs, in the naturalistic or laboratory domain, I would urge that we not consider the availability of two approaches to require us to choose one and reject the other. Instead, integration of the two approaches, through a search for relationships and continuities, is likely to prove more productive for an understanding of human cognitive functioning.

REFERENCES

Anderson, J. A., & Bower, G. H. (1972). Recognition and retrieval processes in free recall. *Psychological Review, 79,* 97–123.

Anderson, J. R. (1976). *Language, memory, and thought.* Hillsdale, NJ: Erlbaum.

Anisfield, M., & Knapp, M. (1968). Association, synonymity, and directionality in false recognition. *Journal of Experimental Psychology, 77,* 171–179.

Berko, J. (1958). The child's learning of English morphology. *Word, 14,* 150–177.

Bjork, R. A. (1978). The updating of human memory. In G. H. Bower (Ed.), *The psychology of learning and motivation, Vol. 12.* New York: Academic Press.

Campbell, D. T., & Stanley, J. C. (1963). *Experimental and quasi-experimental designs for research.* Chicago: Rand McNally.

Conrad, R. (1964). Acoustic confusions in immediate memory. *British Journal of Psychology, 55,* 75–84.

Dyer, F. N. (1973). The Stroop phenomenon and its use in the study of perceptual, cognitive, and response processes. *Memory & Cognition, 1,* 106–120.

Fromkin, V. A. (1980). *Errors in linguistic performance: Slips of the tongue, ear, pen, and hand.* New York: Academic Press.

Herrmann, D. J., & Neisser, V. (1978). An inventory of everyday memory experiences. In M. M. Gruneberg, P. E. Morris, & R. N. Sykes (Eds.), *Practical aspects of memory.* London: Academic Press.

Meyer, D. E., Schvaneveldt, R. W., & Ruddy, M. G. (1975). Loci of contextual effects on visual word recognition. In P. M. A. Rabbitt & S. Dornic (Eds.), *Attention and performance V.* London: Academic Press.

Neisser, U. (1978). Memory: What are the important questions? In M. M. Gruneberg, P. E. Morris, & R. N. Sykes (Eds.), *Practical aspects of memory.* London: Academic Press.

Norman, D. A., & Bobrow, D. G. (1976). On the role of active memory processes in perception and cognition. In C. N. Cofer (Ed.), *The structure of human memory.* San Francisco: W. H. Freeman.

Stroop, J. R. (1935). Studies of interference in serial verbal reactions. *Journal of Experimental Psychology, 18,* 643–662.

Tulving, E., & Gold, C. (1963). Stimulus information and contextual information as determinants of tachistoscopic recognition of words. *Journal of Experimental Psychology, 66,* 319–327.

Tulving, E., & Madigan, S. A. (1970). Memory and verbal learning. *Annual Review of Psychology, 21,* 437–484.

Warren, R. E. (1972). Stimulus encoding and memory. *Journal of Experimental Psychology, 94,* 90–100.

Wickens, D. D. (1970). Encoding categories of words: An empirical approach to meaning. *Psychological Review, 77,* 1–15.

Yntema, D. B., & Mueser, G. E. (1960). Remembering the present state of a number of variables. *Journal of Experimental Psychology, 60,* 18–22.

Yntema, D. B., & Mueser, G. E. (1962). Keeping track of variables that have a few or many states. *Journal of Experimental Psychology, 63,* 391–395.

Author Index

Italics indicate bibliographic citations.

A

Abelson, R., 10, *15*, 48, *68*, 74, 75, 79, *87*, 95, *102*, 106, 111, *113*, 120, 121, *131*, *134*, 243, *259*, 264, 270, *275*
Acredolo, L.P., 39, *45*
Adams, C.C., 56, *66*
Aksu, A.A., *212*
Alba, J.W., 75, *82*
Allport, G., 97, 98, *102*
Amir, M., 201, *214*
Anders, T.R., 70, 72, *82*
Anderson, J.A., 287, *293*
Anderson, J.R., 76, 79, *86*, 122, *131*, 244, *259*, 284, *293*
Anderson, J.W., 72, *84*
Anderson, N.H., 74, *82*
Anderson, P.A., 75, *85*
Anderson, S.R., 196, *212*
Anisfield, M., 283, *293*
Anohkin, P.K., 37, *45*
Antinucci, F., 201, 202n, 206, *213*
Anzai, Y., 49, *66*, 77, *82*
Arbel, T., 201, *214*
Arbib, M.A., 251, *259*
Arena, L.A., 226, *238*
Aristotle, 263, *274*
Arlin, P.K., 77, *82*
Arnett, J.L., 70, 72, *83*
Aronson, E., 25, *31*, 94, *102*
Astin, H.S., 163, *170*
Athay, M., 116, *131*
Atkins, B.K., 226, *240*
Atkinson, R.C., 73, *82*, 263, *274*
Attig, M., 111, *113*
Atwood, M.E., 78, *85*
Auble, P.M., 77, *84*
Augustine, Saint, 217, *238*

B

Baars, B.J., 1, 13, *15*, 243, 245, 246, 247, 248, 249, 251, 252, 253, 258, *259*, *260*, 261

Baddeley, A.D., 73, *82*, 252, *260*, 262, 263, *274*
Bahrick, H.P., 27, 30, *30*, 105, *113*
Bahrick, P.O., 27, *30*, 105, *113*
Baltes, M.M., 92, 94, *103*
Baltes, P. B., 71, 79, 81, *83*, 89, 90, 92, 94, *102*, *103*, 122, *131*
Barker, R.G., 19, *30*, 88, *102*
Barsalou, L.W., 17, 23, *30*
Bartlett, F., 74, *83*, 120, *131*, 263, 271, *274*
Barto, A.G., 76, *87*
Bates, E., 201, *213*
Batterman, N., 23, *31*
Beaudichon, J., 54, *66*
Beck, P., 94, *103*
Beck, S.J., 97, *102*
Begg, I., *157*
Bellugi, U., 197, *213*
Belmont, L., 155, *156*
Bem, D., 169, *170*, 234, 235, *238*
Bem, S.L., 234, 235, *238*
Benbow, C.P., 163, 169, *170*
Benton, A.L., 148, 151, *156*
Berg, C., 71, *83*
Berko, J., 283, *293*
Berman, R.A., 211, *213*
Bernard, J., 167, 169, *170*
Berndt, T. J., 116, *131*
Berry, J.W., 177, *178*
Berti, F.B., 151, *157*
Berzonsky, M.D., 122, 123, *131*
Bever, T., 182, 183, *190*, 192, 198, 199, *213*, *215*
Bigi, L., 54, *67*
Birch, H.G., 155, *156*
Birren, J.E., 70, *83*
Bjork, R. A., 282, *293*
Black, J. B., 28, *30*
Blade, M.F., 164, 167, *170*
Blanchard-Fields, F., 90, *103*
Bleier, R., *170*

295

Bloom, L., 201, *213*
Bobrow, D.G., 284, *293*
Boden, M., 243, 244, *260*
Bonanno, M., 226, *238*
Bondareff, W., 127, *131*
Borgida, E., 120, 121, *131*
Bosk, C., 226, *240*
Boston, R., 211, *214*
Botwinick, J., 105, *113*, 127, 128, *131*
Bouissac, P., 185, *189*
Bower, G.H., 28, *30*, 77, *83*, 106, *114*, 263, 274, 287, *293*
Bower, T.G.R., 209, *213*, 221, *238*
Bowerman, M., 192, *213*
Boyer-Braem, P., 13, *16*, 22, 23, *32*, 118, *133*, 137, *146*
Boylin, W., 107, 111, *113*
Bradshaw, J.L., 152, 155, *156*
Braine, M.D.S., 198, 200, *213*, 219, *238*
Brainerd, C.J., 123, *131*
Bransford, J.D., 5, *15*, 77, *84*, 244, *260*
Breitmeyer, R.G., 72, *84*
Brekke, N., 120, 121, *131*
Brenner, J., 119, *133*
Brenner, M., 106, *113*
Briere, J., 235, *238*
Brinkmann, E. H., 165, 167, *170*
Broadbent, D.E., 17, *30*
Bronckart, J.P., 206, *213*
Bronfenbrenner, U., 19, *30*, 88, 89, *102*, 136, *146*
Brooks, L., 151, *156*
Brooks, V.R., 225, *238*
Brophy, J., 178, *179*
Broughton, J., 117, *131*
Broverman, D.M., 161, *170*
Brown, A.L., 53, *66*, 78, *83*
Brown, J., 262, *274*
Brown, R., 28, *30*, 183, *189*, 191, 193, 197, 211, *213*, 229, *238*
Bruner, J.S., 197, *213*, 244, *260*
Brunswik, E., 3, *15*, 19, *30*
Buczowska, E., 201, 206, *216*
Buffery, A.W.H., 161, *170*, 175, *179*
Bull, M.P., 27, 28, *32*
Bull, R., 27, *31*
Butler, R.M., 105, 107, *113*
Butler, S.R., *156*
Buzsaki, G., 118, *131*
Byrd, M., 74, *83*
Byrne, R., 49, *66*

C
Caharack, G., 72, *84*
Cairnie, J., 70, *87*
Callaway, E., 125, *131*
Camden, C.T., 13, *15*, 247, 248, 249, *261*
Campbell, A., 111, *114*
Campbell, B.A., 37, 38, 39, *45, 46*
Campbell, D.T., 89, *102*, 278, *293*
Canestrati, R.E., 94, *102*
Cantor, N., 107, *114*, 120, 121, *131*
Cantril, H., 98, *103*
Card, S.K., 71, 72, 79, *83*
Carlsmith, J.M., 94, *102*
Carmichael, L., 231, *238*
Carter, B., 150, *157*
Caselli, C., 201, *213*
Cazden, C.B., 197, *213*
Ceely, S.G., 111, *114*
Cerella, J., 70, 71, 72, *83*
Cermak, L.S., 44, *45*
Chafe, W.L., 201, *213*
Chalkley, M., 194*n*, *215*
Chance, J.E., 165, 167, *171*
Chandler, M.J., 90, *103*, 117, 122, 123, *131, 132*
Chapman, R.S., 201, *213*
Charness, N., 72, *83*
Chase, W.G., 79, *83*
Chi, M.T.H., 23, *30*, 76, 79, *83*
Chiesi, H.L., 6, *15, 16*
Childs, B., 148, *156*
Cioffi, J., 155, *156*
Clancy, P.M., 212, *213*
Clark, E.V., 207, *213*
Clark, R.D., 118, *133*
Clifford, B.R., 27, *31*
Coates, S., 177, *179*
Cohen, L.J., 122, *132*
Cohen, N.J., 11, *15*, 43, *45, 46*
Colby, K.M., 244, *261*
Cole, C.M., 236, *238*
Cole, M., 51, *66*
Cole, S., 78, *83*
Comrie, B., 192, 194, 196, 205, 209, *213*
Connor, J.M., 164, 165, 166, 167, *170*
Connor, S., 177, *179*
Conrad, R., 283, *293*
Converse, P.E., 111, *114*
Cook, T.D., 89, *102*
Corrigan, R., 209, *213*

Costa, P.T., Jr., 108, *114*
Craik, F.I.M., 35, *45*, 72, 73, 74, *83*, 105,
    114, 120, 124, *132*
Crawford, M., *239*
Cromer, R.F., 192, 193, 207, *214*, 220, *239*
Crovitz, H.F., 263, 266, *274*
Csapo, K., 124, *133*
Cunningham, W.R., 71, *83*
Cutting, J., *156*

D
Dafoe, J., 106, *114*
Damon, W.J., 117, *132*
Danks, J.H., 229, 230, *239*
Darley, J.M., 116, *131*
Dasen, P.R., 191, *214*
Davidson, R.J., 243, *261*
Day, J.D., 78, *83*
Day, R.H., 221, *239*
Dayhoff, S.A., 233, *239*
Dayley, L.J., 236, *238*
de Villiers, J.G., 54, *66*, 201, *214*
de Villiers, P.A., 54, *66*, 201, *214*
Dember, W., 130, *132*
Demming, J.A., 70, 79, *83*, 94, *102*
Dempster, F.N., 79, *83*
Denney, N.W., 92, *102*
Deutscher, M., 91, *102*
Devescovi, A., 201, *213*
DiLollo, V., 70, 72, *83*
Dinneen, F.P., 227, *239*
DiPietro, R.J., 226, *239*
Dittman-Kohli, F., 71, *83*
Donlon, T.F., 175, *179*
Dulit, E., 122, *132*
Dwyer, C.A., 178, *179*
Dyer, F.N., 285, *293*
Dyk, R.B., 152, *157*

E
Egeth, H.E., 27, *31*
Eimas, P.D., *156*
Eisdorfer, C., 94, *102*
Ekstrom, R.B., 109, *114*, 175, *179*
Elias, C., 232, 235, *240*
Ellis, A.W., 243, *260*
Ellsworth, P., 94, *102*
English, L., *239*

Enright, M.K., 7, *16*, 41, *46*
Epstein, J.J., 226, *239*
Erbaugh, M.S., 201, 207, *214*
Erber, J.T., 105, *114*
Erdelyi, M., 243, *260*
Ericsson, K.A., 79, *83*
Eriksen, C.W., 72, *84*
Erikson, E.H., 105, 107, *114*
Ernst, G.W., 76, *84*
Evans, D.A., 48, *67*
Eysenck, H.J., 98, *102*

F
Fagan, J., 7, *16*, 41, *46*
Falk, J.L., 98, *103*
Faloon, S., 79, *83*
Familant, M.E., 72, *84*
Faterson, H.F., 152, *157*
Fee, E., 177, *179*
Feltovich, P.J., 23, *30*, 80, *85*
Fennema, E., 163, *171*, 177, *179*
Feshback, N.D., 177, *179*
Field, D., 266, *274*
Finegan, E., 226, *239*
Finucci, J.M., 148, *156*
Fischer, F.W., 150, *157*
Fisher, S., 226, *239*
Fiske, S.T., 9, *16*, 95, *104*, 116, 120, 122,
    132
Fitzgerald, J.M., 116, *132*
Flavell, E.R., 119, *133*
Flavell, J.H., 50, 51, 53, 54, *67*, 116, 119,
    125, *132*, *133*
Fletcher, P., *214*
Floor, E., 243, *260*
Fodor, J.A., 81, *84*
Follett, K., 137, *146*
Forbes, D., 116, *132*
Foss, M.A., 99, *103*
Fox, L.H., 162, 163, *171*
Fozard, J.L., 70, 72, *83*, 112, *115*
Frader, J., 226, *240*
Frankel, D.G., 201, *214*
Franklin, J.C., 105, *114*
Franks, J.J., 5, *15*, 77, *84*
Freeman, M., 166, 167, *170*
French, J.W., 109, *114*
French, L.A., 53, *66*
Frenkel, E., 201, *214*
Freud, S., 242, 249, *260*

Friedman, W.J., 204, 208, 209, 211, *214*, 220, *239*
Frieze, I.H., 154, *156*, 169, *171*
Frisse, P., 208, *214*
Fromkin, V.A., 283, *293*
Furth, H., 228, 229, *239*

G

Galang, R.G., 201, *215*
Galanter, E., 7, *31*, 47, *67*
Galbraith, G.G., 249, 251, *260*
Gallup, G., 118, *132*
Gardner, B., 183, *189*
Gardner, E.F., 109, *114*
Gardner, H., 137, *146*
Gardner, R., 183, *189*
Gary, J.A., 175, *179*
Gelman, R., 118, 119, *132, 134*
Gentner, D., 75, 81, *84*
Gerbert, L., 202*n*, *213*
Geschwind, N., 251, *260*
Ghiselin, B., 229, *239*
Giambra, L.M., 72, *84*
Gibson, E.J., 26, *31, 156*
Gibson, J.J., 19, 25, *31*
Glaser, R., 23, *30*, 76, 79, 80, *83, 85*
Gleitman, L.R., 151, *156, 157*
Glucksberg, S., 229, 230, *239*
Gold, C., 284, *293*
Goldin, S.E., 49, *67*
Goldstein, A.G., 165, 167, *171*
Goldstein, M.D., *86*
Golinkoff, R.M., 200, *214*
Gonda, J., 79, *85*, 92, *103*
Good, T., 178, *179*
Goodenough, D.R., 152, *157*
Goodman, S., 53, 54, *67*
Gordon, S.K., 107, *113*
Gottfredson, G.D., 234, *239*
Gould, A., 271, *274*
Grady, K., 169, *171*
Gray, J.A., 161, *170*
Gray, W.D., 13, *16*, 22, 23, *32*, 118, *133*, 137, *146*
Greenberg, J.H., 196, *214*
Greeno, J.G., 78, *84*
Greenwald, A.G., 106, 110, 111, *114*, 272, 274, *274*
Gregory, R.L., 75, *84*
Grossman, J.L., 106, *114*
Grudin, J., 75, *84*

Gruneberg, M., 3, *15*, 266, *275*
Grzanna, R., 125, *133*

H

Hacker, S.L., 233, *240*
Haggerty, L.C.G., 225, *239*
Hahn, M., 70, *86*
Hakuta, K., 201, *214*
Hallion, K., 124, *134*
Hamilton, D.A., 107, *114*
Hamlin, R.M., 72, *84*
Hannigan, J.H., 118, *131*
Hardy, J.A., 200, *213*
Harker, J.O., 89, *103*
Harner, L., 211, *214*
Harris, D.B., 81, *84*
Harris, J., 3, *15*
Harris, K.S., 151, *157*
Harrison, L., 233, *239*
Harshman, R.A., 175, *179*
Hart, H.L.A., 135, *146*
Hartley, A.A., 72, *84*
Hartley, J.T., 89, *103*
Hasher, L., 43, *45*, 75, *84*, 111, 112, *113, 114*
Hayes-Roth, B., 47, 48, 49, 54, 55, *67*
Hayes-Roth, F., 47, 48, 49, 54, 55, *67*, 78, *84*
Hediger, H., 185, *189*
Heider, E.R., 22, *31*, 229, *239*
Heider, F., 136, *146*
Heilman, A.W., 177, *179*
Hempel, A.M., 99, *103*
Herrmann, D.J., 12, *15*, 266, 274, 287, *293*
Hertzog, C.K., 71, *83*
Hick, W.E., 72, *84*
Hickey, T., 89, *103*
Hier, D.B., 175, *179*
Higgins, E.T., 116, *132*
Hilgard, E.R., 42, *45*
Hill, F.A., 236, *238*
Hirst, W., 72, *84*
Hirtle, S.C., 78, *85*
Hjertholm, E., 54, *67*
Hobbs, J.R., 48, *67*
Hockett, C., 183, *189*, 224, *239*
Hofer, M.A., 39, *45*
Hoffman, M.L., 117, 124, *132*, 140, *146*
Hofstadter, D.R., 76, 77, *84*
Hogan, H.P., 231, *238*
Holding, D.H., 79, *84*, 105, *114*

Hollan, J.D., 27, *32,* 272, *275*
Hollingworth, L., 160, *171*
Hood, L., 201, *213*
Hopper, P.J., 196, *214*
Howard, D.V., 71, 73, *84,* 106, *114*
Hoyer, W., 70, 72, 73, 75, *84, 86,* 92, 94,
    99, 100, *103,* 105, 112, *114*
Hulicka, I., 93, *103,* 106, *114*
Hull, C.L., 20, *31*
Hultsch, D.F., 89, 94, *103*
Hunt, E., 71, *83, 84*
Hunter, I.M.L., 79, *84*
Hyde, J.S., 161, *171*
Hyman, L.M., 209, *214*

I

Imber, L., 256, *260*
Inhelder, B., 51, *67*
Isaacson, R.L., 42, *46*
Itoh, M., 155, *157*
Iverman, I.Y., *157*

J

Jacklin, C., 154, *157,* 164, *171,* 174, 175,
    176, *179*
Jackson, L., 153, 155, *156,* 176, *179*
Jacoby, L.L., 43, *45,* 75, *84,* 120, *132*
Jakobovics, E., 177, *179*
James, W., 252, 254, *260, 274*
Jeffries, R., 78, *85*
Jenkins, J.J., 5, *15*
Jenkins, J.S., 120, *132*
John-Steiner, V., 52, *67*
Johnson, D.D., 176, *179*
Johnson, D.L., 177, *180*
Johnson, D.M., 13, *16,* 22, 23, *32,* 118, *133,*
    137, *146*
Johnson, N.S., 28, *31*
Johnson, P.B., 154, *156,* 169, *171*
Juola, J.F., 273, *274*

K

Kagan, J., 40, 42, *45,* 123, 129, *132*
Kahneman, D., 120, 122, *134,* 144, *146*
Kail, R., 38, *45*
Kandel, G., 148, 155, *156*
Kaplan, G.A., 25, *31*
Karp, S.A., 152, *157*
Karuza, J., Jr., 91, *102*
Kausler, D.H., 106, *114*
Kaye, D., 70, *86*
Kazdin, A.E., 101, *103*

Kearsley, R.B., 40, *45*
Keasey, C.B., 127, *132*
Keenan, E.L., 194, *214*
Keil, F.C., 23, *31,* 74, *85*
Keller, H., 186, *189*
Kennedy, M., 105, *114*
Kihlstrom, J.F., 120, *132*
Killinger, W.A., Jr., 28, *32*
Kilpatrick, F.P., 98, *103*
Kinder, D.R., 116, *132*
Kirker, W.S., 126, *133*
Klahr, D., 49, *67,* 75, *85*
Klaiber, E.L., 161, *170*
Klapp, S.T., 79, *85*
Kline, D.W., 70, *85*
Klonoff, H., 105, *114*
Knapp, M., 283, *293*
Kobayashi, Y., 155, *157,* 161, *170*
Koch, S., 183, 187, *189*
Kohlberg, L., 54, *67,* 136, *146*
Kohn, L., 201, *213*
Kohn, M.L., 79, *85*
Kolers, P.A., 43, *45, 46*
Koniecznae, E., 201, 206, *216*
Kosierowski, N., 91, *102*
Kosslyn, S.M., 123, 129, *132,* 229, *239*
Kozin, M., 28, *32*
Kramer, D.A., 70, 77, *85*
Kramer, D.N., 251, 252, 258, *260*
Krauss, I.K., 70, *85*
Kriss, M., 106, *115*
Kruk, R.V., 70, 72, *83*
Kubinski, W., 202*n, 214*
Kucharski, D., 40, *46*
Kuczaj, S.A., 211, *214*
Kuhn, T., 183, 187, *189*
Kuiper, N., 126, *133*
Kulik, J., 28, *30*

L

LaBerge, D., 80, *85*
Labouvie, E.W., 91, *103*
Labouvie-Vief, G., 56, *67,* 79, *85,* 90, 91,
    92, 94, *103*
Lachman, J.L., 93, *103*
Lachman, R., 93, *103*
Lakoff, R., 233, *239*
Lamiell, J.T., 99, *103*
Lander, E.M., 105, *114*
Langer, E., 75, *85,* 94, 95, *103, 104,* 124,
    125, *132,* 256, *260*

Langley, P., 76, 77, *85*
Lanktree, C., 235, *238*
Larkin, J.H., 78, 81, *85*
Larsen, R.J., 99, *103*
Lasaga, M.I., 71, 73, *84*, 106, *114*
Lash, L., 186, *189*
Lawick-Goodall, J., 118, *133*
Leaffer, T., 226, *239*
Lee, D.N., 25, *31*
Lehman, H.C., 78, *85*
Lehrke, R., 160, *171*
Lempers, J.D., 119, *133*
Lenat, D.B., 78, *84*
Lenneberg, E.H., 229, *238*
Lesgold, A.M., 79, 80, 81, *85*
Lester, P.T., 79, *85*
Levin, I., *156*, 204, 208, *214*
Levine, F.M., 258, *260*
Levy, J., 152, 153, 155, *157*, 175, *179*
Lewin, K., 97, *103*
Lewis, V., 263, *274*
Liberman, A.M., 150, 151, *157*
Liberman, I.Y., 176, *179*
Light, L.L., 75, *85*
Lightbown, P., 201, *213*
Limber, J., *239*
Lindeman, M.L., 226, *240*
Linden, E., 183, *189*
Linton, M., 266, *275*
Linville, P.W., 120, 122, *132*
Lishman, J.R., 25, *31*
Lisman, S.A., 35, 36, *46*
Lockhart, R.S., 73, *83*, 124, *132*
Lockheed, M., 175, *179*
Locksley, A., 120, 121, *131*
Loftus, E.F., 27, *31*, 73, *83*, 231, *239*, 274, *275*
Lonky, E., 127, *134*
Lord, M., 177, *179*
Lorenz, K.Z., 20, *31*
Lorenz, P., 243, *261*
Lowenthal, M.F., 128, *133*
Lucas, D., 7, *16*, 41, *46*
Lucas, T.A., 119, *133*
Luria, A.R., 53, *67*, 79, *85*, 90, *103*
Lyons, J., 194, 195, *214*

M

Maccoby, E., 154, *157*, 164, *171*, 174, 175, 176, *179*
Macfarlane, A., 221, *239*

Mackay, D.G., 235, *239*
Maclay, H., 226, *239*
Macnamara, J., 219, *239*
MacWhinney, B., *194n*, 201, *213*, *215*
Madigan, S.A., 279, *293*
Makita, K., 148, *157*
Malmi, W.A., 225, *240*
Maltzman, I., 55, *66*
Mancuso, J.C., 111, *114*
Mandler, G., 73, 75, *85*
Mandler, J.M., 28, *31*
Mann, V.A., 151, *157*, 176, *179*
Maratsos, M., *194n*, *215*
Markman, E., 54, *67*
Markus, H., 107, *114*, 243, *260*
Marshburn, E.A., 79, *85*
Martin, G.B., 118, *133*
Martyna, W., 231, 234, *240*
Marx, J.L., 221, *240*
Masland, R.L., 155, *157*
Matlin, M.W., *240*
Mattson, M.E., 246, 247, 251, 253, *260*
Mawer, R.F., 78, *87*
Mazurkiewicz, A.J., 178, 180
McAndrews, M.P., 71, 73, *84*, 106, *114*
McArthur, D.J., 75, *85*
McArthur, R., 177, *179*
McCauley, C., 121, *132*
McClelland, D.C., 243, *260*
McCloskey, M., 27, *31*
McCrae, R.R., 108, *114*
McDermott, D., 48, *67*
McFarland, R.A., 70, *85*
McFeely, W.S., 144, *146*
McGee, M.G., 176, *179*
McGuinness, D., *157*
McKeever, W.F., 175, *179*
McKeithen, K.B., 78, *85*
McKenzie, B.E., 221, *239*
McLeod, P., 71, 72, *86*
McNeill, D., 218, *240*
McVey, K.A., 55, *67*
Meacham, J., 55, *67*, 90, *103*, 106, *114*, 128, *132*
Mebane, D., 177, *180*
Meddin, J., 118, *132*
Meehl, P.E., 99, *103*
Meichenbaum, D., 53, 54, *67*, 116, *132*
Mergler, N.L., *86*
Merriam, S., 113, *114*
Merrick, A., 266, *275*

Mervis, C., 13, *16*, 22, 23, *32*, 118, *133*, 137, *146*
Metzger, R., 112, *115*
Meyer, D.E., 284, *293*
Meyers, K.A., 234, *241*
Miller, G.A., 17, *31*, 47, *67*, 198, *215*
Miller, J., 74, *86*
Miller, K., 112, *115*
Miller, P.H., 54, *67*
Miller, R., 201, 206, *213*
Miller, S.A., 53, *67*
Minsky, M.L., 111, *114*
Mischel, W., 107, *114*, 116, 117, 120, 129, 130, *131, 132*, 141, *146*
Molliver, M.E., 125, *133*
Monge, R.H., 109, *114*
Moore, B., 130, *133*
Moran, T.P., 71, 72, 79, *83*
Mori, K., 155, *157*
Morokoff, P., 249, 259, *260*
Morris, C.D., 5, *15*
Morris, P., 3, *15*, 266, *275*
Morrison, J.H., 124, *133*
Moscovitch, M., 42, *46*
Mosher, D.L., 248, *260*
Motley, M.T., 13, *15*, 246, 247, 248, 249, *260, 261*
Moulton, J., 232, 235, *240*
Mountcastle, V.B., 251, *261*
Muellar, E., 119, *133*
Mueller, C.W., 35, 36, *46*
Mueser, G.E., 282, 286, *293*
Munsterburg, H., 27, *31*
Myers, C.T., 164, 167, *171*

N

Naditch, S.F., 177, *180*
Nash, J., 168, *171*
Nash, S.C., 177, *180*
Natale, F., 201, *213*
Neely, J.H., 73, *86*
Nehrke, M.F., 107, 111, *113, 115*
Neisser, U., 3, 8, 9, 14, *15*, 27, 28, 29, 30, *31*, 72, *84*, 120, 125, *133*, 136, *146*, 222, *240*, 245, *261*, 262, 263, 271, *275*, 277, 278, 279, 280, 287, *293*
Nelson, K., 120, *133*
Nerzworski, T., 112, *115*
Nessel, J., 181, *189*
Nesselroade, J., 81, *82*, 89, *102*
Neugarten, B.L., 128, *133*

Neves, D.M., 76, 79, *86*
Newell, A., 48, 49, *67*, 71, 72, 76, 79, *83*, 252, *261*
Newman, R.S., 55, *67*
Newport, E.L., 192, *215*
Nickerson, R.S., 105, *114*
Nilsen, D.L.F., 194, *215*
Nimmo-Smith, I., 263, *274*
Nisbett, R.E., 81, *86*, 93, *103*
Norman, D.A., 1, 2, 5, *15*, 249, 257, *261*, 284, *293*
Nowlin, J., 94, *102*

O

O'Barr, W.M., 226, *240*
O'Doherty, B.M., 70, *85*
Olivier, D.C., 229, *239*
Orlando, C., 151, *157*
Ortony, A., 120, *133*
Osgood, C.E., 197, *215*, 226, *239*
Overton, W.F., 75, *86*
Owens, J., 106, *114*

P

Paivio, A., 124, *133, 157*
Pani, J.R., 256, *261*
Paris, S.G., 55, *67*
Parlee, M.B., 161, *171*
Parsons, J.E., 154, *156*, 169, *171*
Patterson, F., 183, *189*
Pea, R.D., 49, *67*
Perkins, D.N., 76, *86*
Perlmutter, M., 72, *86*, 105, 112, *115*
Perry, W.G., 130, *133*
Petersen, A.C., 161, *172*
Pettito, L., 182, 183, 184, *190*, 223, *240*
Phoenix, V.G., 226, *240*
Piaget, J., 51, 52, *67, 68*, 74, *86*, 119, 204, 208, *215*, 219, *240*
Pillimer, D.B., 263, *275*
Plude, D.J., 70, 72, 73, 75, *84, 86*, 112, *114*
Polson, P.G., 78, *85*
Poon, L.W., 70, 71, 72, *83*, 112, *115*
Pople, H., 80, 81, *86*
Posner, M.I., 72, *86*
Post, T., 70, *86*
Potter, M.C., 30, *32*
Pressey, S.L., 70, 71, 79, *83*, 94, *102*
Preston, R.C., 176, *180*
Pribram, K., 17, *31*, 47, *67*, 125, 126, *133*
Price, L.A., 109, *114*

Prince, E.F., 226, *240*
Pryor, J.B., 106, *115*
Puckett, J.M., 106, *114*
Pylyshyn, Z.W., 78, *86*

R

Rabbitt, P.M.A., 70, 72, 73, *86*
Radulovic, L., 199, 200*n*, 203, *215*
Ramirez, R.R., 258, *260*
Randi, J., 185, *189*
Rapoport, M.D., 151, *157*
Reaves, C.C., 72, *84*
Rebok, G., 56, *66*, 72, *84*, 94, *103*
Reddy, R., 252, *261*
Rees, E., 76, 79, *83*
Reese, H., 75, *86*, 89, *102*
Reichenbach, H., *215*
Reid, H., 91, *102*
Reiff, R., 263, *275*
Reinert, G., 79, *86*
Reitman, J.S., 78, *85*
Remington, R., 175, *179*
Resnick, L.B., 23, *32*
Reuter, J., 243, *261*
Reynolds, H.N., Jr., 25, *31*
Richards, B.S., 136, *146*
Riegel, K.F., 75, *86*, 117, *133*
Robinson, G.M., 232, 235, *240*
Robinson, J., 109, *115*, 263, 264, *275*
Robinson, T.E., *134*
Rodgers, W.L., 111, *114*
Rodin, J., 94, *103*, *104*
Roediger, H.L., 34, *46*
Rogers, T., 126, *133*
Roodin, P.A., 124, 127, *134*
Rosch, E., 13, *15*, *16*, 22, 23, *32*, 118, *133*, 137, *146*, 212, *215*, 224, *240*
Rosenberg, B.G., 161, *171*
Rosenberg, R., 159, 160, 162, *171*, 182, *190*
Ross, M., 106, *115*
Rovee-Collier, C.K., 7, *16*, 41, *46*
Rozin, P., 151, *156*, *157*
Rubin, D., 3, *16*, 28, *32*, 263, 266, 267, 272, *275*
Ruble, D.N., 154, *156*, 169, *171*
Ruddy, M.G., 284, *293*
Rueter, H.H., 78, *85*
Rumbaugh, D., 189, *190*, 222, 223, 224, 225, *240*
Rumelhart, D.E., 120, *133*
Russell, M.J., 221, *240*
Rybash, J.M., 124, 127, *134*

S

Sacerdoti, E.D., 48, *68*
Salaman, E., 263, *275*
Salthouse, T.A., 71, 72, *86*, *87*
Samuels, S.J., 80, *85*
Sandeen-Lee, E.E., 258, *260*
Sanders, H.I., 105, *115*
Sanders, R., 182, 183, *190*
Sapir, E., 192, *215*, 229, *240*
Saron, C., 243, *260*
Sasanuma, S., 155, *157*
Savage, E.S., 222, 224, 225, *240*
Savage-Rumbaugh, E.S., 223, *240*
Saynisch, M., 70, *86*
Schackman, M., 165, 166, 167, *170*, 177, *179*
Schacter, D.L., 42, *46*
Schaie, K.W., 71, 79, *86*, *87*, 89, 90, 91, 93, *102*, *103*, *104*
Schank, R.C., 48, *68*, *87*, 120, *134*, 244, 261, 264, 270, *275*
Scheerer, M., 263, *275*
Scheff, H.A., 258, *260*
Scheiber, F., 70, *85*
Scheidt, R.J., 71, 79, *87*, 93, *104*
Schenker, A.M., 195*n*, *215*
Schiffman, H., 263, 266, *274*
Schneider, J.W., 233, *240*
Schneider, W., 74, *87*, 95, *104*, 112, *115*, 124, *134*
Schooler, C., 79, *85*
Schvaneveldt, R.W., 284, *293*
Schwartz, G.E., 243, *261*
Sebeok, J., 182, 186, 189, *190*
Sebeok, T., 182, 186, 189, *190*
Segalowitz, N.S., 201, *215*
Seidenberg, M., 184, *190*, 223, *240*
Sells, L.W., *171*
Selman, R.L., 116, *134*
Sentis, K., 243, *260*
Serbin, L.A., 164, 165, 166, 167, *170*, 177, *179*
Shallice, T., 257, *261*
Shatz, M., 119, *134*
Shaukweiler, D., 150, 151, *157*
Shaw, M.L., 74, *87*
Shelton, J., 53, *67*
Sherif, C.W., 161, *171*
Sherman, J., 161, 162, 163, 164, *171*, 173, 174, 175, 177, 178, *179*, *180*
Sherwood, G.G., 245, *261*
Shields, S.A., 159, 162, 168, *171*

Shiffrin, R.M., 73, 74, 87, 95, 104, 115, 124, 134
Shlechter, T.M., 9, 16
Shoemaker, S., 263, 269, 275
Shortliffe, E.H., 80, 81, 87
Sicoly, P., 106, 115
Siegler, R.S., 49, 68, 74, 75, 85, 87
Silveira, J., 234, 240
Simon, D.P., 76, 77, 87
Simon, E., 72, 73, 83, 87
Simon, H.A., 48, 49, 66, 67, 76, 77, 80, 85, 87
Sinclair, H., 206, 213
Sinclair-de Zwart, H., 192, 204, 215
Singer, J., 128, 132
Sinnott, J.D., 77, 87
Skinner, B.F., 1, 16, 20, 32
Slater, P.C., 28, 32
Slobin, D.I., 191, 193, 198, 199, 201, 202, 203, 212, 215, 229, 240
Smith, C.S., 205, 206, 215
Smith, F., 198, 215
Smith, I.M., 164, 171
Smith, M.O., 148, 153, 155, 156, 157, 176, 179
Smithells, J., 178, 180
Smoczynska, M., 199, 203, 215
Snyder, M., 231, 240
Somberg, B.L., 70, 71, 72, 86, 87
Souberman, E., 52, 67
Spear, N.E., 35, 36, 37, 39, 40, 41, 42, 45, 46
Spelke, E., 26, 30, 32, 72, 84, 118, 132
Sperling, G., 17, 32
Sperry, R.W., 153, 155, 157
Spilich, G., 6, 15, 16
Spitzer, L., 94, 103
Squire, L.R., 11, 15, 16, 28, 32, 43, 45, 46
Stafford, R.E., 161, 171
Stahlke, H.F.W., 224, 240
Stam, J.H., 227, 240
Stanley, J.C., 163, 169, 170, 278, 293
Stefik, M., 48, 68
Stein, A.H., 178, 180
Stein, B.S., 5, 15
Steinberg, D.D., 228, 229, 230, 240
Stephany, U., 201, 205n, 215, 216
Stephenson, G.M., 271, 274
Stericker, A., 234, 235, 240
Sternberg, R.J., 72, 87
Sternglanz, S., 166, 172

Stevens, A.L., 81, 84
Stitt, C.L., 121, 132
Storandt, M., 105, 113
Stroop, J.R., 293
Sullivan, M.W., 7, 16, 41, 46
Sutton, R.S., 76, 87
Sved, S.M., 72, 84
Swacker, M., 226, 240
Sweller, J., 78, 87
Sykes, R.N., 3, 15, 266, 275
Symmes, J.S., 151, 157
Szwedek, A., 216

T
Talland, G.A., 70, 87
Tannen, D., 226, 241
Tanz, C., 197, 215
Taylor, S.E., 9, 16, 95, 104
Tellegen, A., 99, 104
Terman, L.M., 160, 172
Terrace, H., 182, 183, 184, 190, 222, 241
Thomae, H., 128, 134
Thomas, J.C., 112, 115
Thompson, S.A., 196, 214
Thomson, J.A., 25, 31
Thorndyke, P.W., 264, 275
Tobias, S., 163, 172
Todd-Mancillas, W.R., 234, 241
Toglia, M.P., 9, 16
Toivainen, J., 207, 216
Tooney, N., 163, 172
Trevarthen, C., 118, 134, 153, 155, 157
Tsao, Y.C., 148, 156
Tulving, E., 35, 42, 45, 46, 279, 284, 293
Turiel, E., 116, 134
Turner, A.A., 78, 85
Turner, T.J., 28, 30
Tversky, A., 120, 122, 134, 144, 146

U
Underhill, R., 195n, 216
Underwood, B.J., 43, 46, 263, 275
Uranowitz, S.W., 231, 240

V
Vanderwold, C.H., 134
Vellutino, F.R., 151, 157
Venza, V., 201, 213
Vesonder, G.T., 6, 16

Vogel, W., 161, *170*
Voss, J.F., 6, *15, 16*
Vygotsky, L.S., 53, *68*

W

Waber, D.P., 154, *157,* 175, *180*
Wade, N., 181, 188, *190*
Walaskay, M., 107, 111, *115*
Walker, A.G., 231, *241*
Walker, A.S., 26, *30*
Walker, L.J., 136, *146*
Wallat, C., 226, *241*
Walsh, D.A., 89, *103*
Walter, A.A., 231, *238*
Wang, Y., 80, *85*
Ward, M.R., 78, *87*
Warren, R.E., 284, *293*
Warrington, E.K., 41, *46,* 105, *115*
Waterman, D.A., 78, *84*
Watson, J.B., 228, *241*
Watson, W.C., 125, *134*
Watson, W.S., 164, 167, *170*
Waugh, N.C., 112, *115*
Weinberger, D.A., 243, *261*
Weinman, C., 94, *103*
Weinstock, C.S., 107, 108, *115*
Weiskrantz, L., 41, *46*
Weist, R.M., 194, 199, 201, 205, 206, 207, *216*
Welford, A.T., 72, 79, *87*
Wellman, H.M., 54, *67*
Wells, G., 201, 207, *216*
Wertsch, J.V., 54, *68*
West, C., 225, *241*
Wheeler, K., 25, *31*
Whitbourne, S.K., 107, 108, 111, *115*
White, S.E., 263, *275*
Whorf, B., 192, *216,* 228, *241*

Wickens, D.D., 286, *293*
Wilensky, R., 48, *68*
Wilkening, F., 209, *216*
Wilkie, F., 94, *102*
Willems, E.P., 88, *104,* 136, *146*
Williams, D.M., 70, 71, *83*
Williams, M.D., 27, *32,* 272, *275*
Williams, M.V., 70, *83*
Willis, S.L., 79, *83,* 122, *131*
Willsdon, J.A., 154, *157*
Wilson, T.D., 81, *86,* 93, *103*
Windelband, W., 97, *104*
Winograd, E., 28, *32*
Witherspoon, D., 42, 43, *45*
Witkin, H.A., 152, *157*
Wittig, M.A., 161, *172*
Wittlinger, R.P., 27, *30,* 105, *113*
Wood, P.K., 75, *87*
Woods, A.M., 70, *83*
Woodward, J., 184, *190*
Wright, H.F., 88, *102*
Wysocka, H., 201, 206, *216*

Y

Yarmey, A.D., 28, *32*
Yeager, J., 54, *67*
Yntema, D.B., 282, 286, *293*

Z

Zacks, R. T., 75, *84,* 111, 112, *114*
Zaidel, E., 155, *157*
Zajonc, R.B., 124, 125, 127, *134*
Zarebina, M., 199, *216*
Zelazo, R.R., 40, *45*
Zellman, G.L., 154, *156,* 169, *171*
Zevon, M.A., 99, *104*
Zimmerman, D.H., 225, *241*

Subject Index

A

Adaptive aspects of cognition, 14, 21, 118
Affect, 9, 123–126, 129, 135, 140
  affective commitment, 9
  affective evaluations, 124
  affective processing, 124–126
  affective stimuli, 124
  Wundt's tripartite theory of feeling, 124
Aging, 56, 65–66, 69–82, 105–108, 111–
    113, 122, 127–128, *see also* Develop-
    mental aspects of cognition *and* Life-
    span perspectives
  age deficiencies, 70–74, 80–82, 96, 111–
    112, 127–128
  cognitive, 69–82
    computational representations, 76–77
  expert system of, 70, 78–82
Alcohol and cognition, 4, 33–36
Ancient theories of memory, 34, 263
Animal communication, 182–186, 189, 221–
    225, 237, *see also* Language
  ape language, 182–186, 189, 217, 221–225
    Nim, 183–184, 222–224
    Washoe, 183–186, 223–224
  Clever Hans, 182, 185, 189
Applied cognition, 116–117
Applied psychology and cognition, 4, 27
Artificial intelligence, 18, 19, 48–49, 76, 81,
    135, 136–139
  intelligent tutoring, 76, 80
Associative capacities, 37–38
Attentional processes, 72, 78, 89, 92
Attribute retrieval, 263–274
  stage, 263–264, 266–267
Autobiographical memory, 5, 9, 12, 105,
    108–113, 135, 140–146, 262–274,
    276–277, 280–281, 286–291
  childhood memories, 109, 265–273
  memory task, 109, *see also* Self-report
    memory tasks
  reminiscing behavior, 105–108, 110–113
  research procedures, 110–113, 266–271

Automatic processing, 9–10, 43, 55, 73–74,
    80, 95, 111–112, 140, 142–143, 252–
    258

B

Behavior modification on cognitive activities,
    53, 92
Biological aspects of cognition, 7–8, 11, 21,
    33, 45, 125–127, 129, 153–155, 159,
    161–162, 168, 175–176, 178, 243,
    251, 255, 257, *see also* Memory
    disorders
  brain lateralization, 7, 11, 125, 153–155,
    175, 178
  holographic model of the brain, 125–127
Brunswik's ecological model, 3, 4, 14, 19
  macro-environmental situations, 3–4

C

Categorizations, 12, 22–33, 118, 121, 136,
    212, 224–225
Cognitive biases on memory, 106–108, 110,
    113
  beneffectance, 106, 108, 113
  cognitive conservation, 106, 108, 113
  egocentrism, 106, 108, 113
Cognitive control processes, 69, 73–74, 76–
    79, 81–82
Component information processing, 69–71,
    78–79, 82
Concept formation, 21–23, 137
Conscious control of action, 250–259
  control of voluntary action, 252–257, 258–
    259
  global workspace, 251–253, 255–258
  ideo-motor theory, 253, 257
  involuntary actions, 256–259
  research evidence, 258–259
  specialized brain areas, 251–253, 255–258
Consciousness, 11, 14, 243–244, 250–259,
    263, 283–284
  repression, 250–251
  suppression, 251, 283–284

Constraints on cognitive behaviors, 5, 6, 106–
    108, 110, 113
Construct validity, 89, 91
Constructivist theory of memory, 9, 76, 119,
    263, 271
Cross-cultural perspective, 12, 149, 191

D

Developmental aspects of cognition, 33, 37–
    41, 45, 51–66, 69–74, 89–96, 101–
    102, 107, 113, 117, 119–123, 129–
    131, 135–136, 139–140, 141, 153–
    155, 174, 192–200, 204–212,
    218–222, 238, *see also* Aging *and*
    Lifespan perspectives
development research strategies, 56–57, 89–
    96, 101–102
developmental differences in control pro-
    cesses, 73–74
developmental differences in elementary
    mental operations, 71–73
infancy, 37–41, 119, 221–222

E

Ecological approach to perception, 24–26, 130
    see also Ecological validity *and* Natu-
    ralistic aspects of cognition
affordances, 24
ecological optics, 24
Ecological aspects of cognition, 2–3, 6, 8,
    11–14, 18–21, 24–27, 29–30, 37–39,
    55, 88–91, 95–96, 100–102, 129, 135,
    136–139, 243, 247–250, 272–280,
    288, 292, *see also* Naturalistic aspects
    of cognition
contextual factors, 2–3, 18–21, 28, 30, 39,
    55, 88–91, 93, 95–96, 101–102, 237,
    243, 247–250, 278, 280, 288
ecological validity, 2, 12, 19, 88–91, 100,
    129, 135, 136–139, 141, 250, 279,
    290, 292, *see also* Naturalistic aspects
    of cognition
definitions of, 2, 3, 19, 88–89
Ecological research methods, 12–14, 100–
    102, 250, 278–293, *see also* Laborato-
    ry investigations of everyday behaviors
    and Naturalistic research methods
interface between laboratory and naturalistic
    methods, 13, 278–282, 291–293
Effortful processing, 9, 24, 26, 74, 78, 111–
    112, 142–143, 274

Episodic memories, 263–274
Ethology, 12, 19, 117, 185
Expert cognition, 5, 69–82, 91, 96
    medical expert knowledge, 79–80
External validity, 89, 91, 178, 179
Eyewitness testimony, 5, 26–27, 29, 226
    John Dean's testimony, 8–9, 28, 226

F

Flashbulb memories, 28

H

Heuristics, 18, 53, 78, 81–82, 122, 144–145

I

Iconic memory, 18
Idiographic research methods, 12, 14, 97–102
Information-processing approach to cognition,
    2, 3, 5, 18–19, 47–50, 65–66, 70–72,
    106, 204
Inter-individual differences in cognition, 5, 8,
    10, 50, 69, 72–74, 79, 81–82, 96–
    101, 112–113, 169, 178, 229–230, *see
    also* Personality factors *and* Sex-related
    issues
multilinguals, 229–230
Internal validity, 89, 91, 278

J

Jamesian theory of psychology, 14, 252, 254

K

Knowledge structures, 74–75, 79, 81–82, 120
    mental representations, 81

L

Laboratory investigations of everyday cog-
    nitive behaviors, 13, 21, 23, 56–65,
    108–110, 247–250, 278–282, 290,
    292, see also Ecological research meth-
    ods *and* Naturalistic research methods
mis-en-scenè created by the experimentor,
    13, 93, 94
Language, 4, 12, 54, 183–184, 191, 193–200,
    206, 210, 218–220, 223, 227–238,
    251, *see also* Animal communication
    and Linguistics
acquisition, 191–204, 206–212, 217–223
American Sign Language, 183–184, 221–
    225

comprehension, 151, 198, 238
and the deaf, 183, 186, 221–225, 228–229
Helen Keller, 186, 221
definition of, 188
design features, 182, 224–225
pidgin signs, 183–184
research, 181–183, 187–189, 225–227
Kuhnian notions on science, 183, 187
maturity of the field, 187–188
naturalistic methods, 225–227
structure, 196–204, 212–221
case markings, 196–197, 199
inflectional morphology, 198, 200, 219–220
transitivity, 196, 201–203
verb concepts, 200–204, 220
word order, 196–197, 199–204, 212, 219–221
and thought, 54, 191, 218–220, 227–237, see also Linguistic determinism
typology, 194–204, 219–220
analytic-synthetic dimension, 194, 196, 198–200
agent–patient relationships, 194, 198, 219–220
agglutinating-fusional dimension, 194–197
Learning, 1, 12–13, 20–21, 30, 33, 35–42, 49, 101, 115, 164, 249
and remembering, 40–42, 45
research methods, 12, 20–21, 30, 39–42, 101
theories, 1, 12–13, 20–21, 30, 249
Level of cognitive processing, 105–106, 110–113, 140–141
Lifespan perspectives, 47–49, 56, 65–66, 105–108, 111–113, 122, 128–131, 139, see also Aging and Developmental aspects of cognition
adulthood, 105, 110, 111, 113, 122–123, 128–131, 139
Linguistics, 6, 183, 191–205, 211–212, 225–232, 255, 257, see also Language and Sex-related issues
cross-linguistic perspectives, 191–205, 211–212
linguistic determinism (Whorfian hypotheses), 6, 183, 192, 227–237
linguistic relativity, 227–231
neurophysiological aspects, 251, 255, 257
real-life settings, 225–227, 232

M
Mechanistic view of cognition, 75–76, 119
Memory disorders, 7, 37, 41–45, 125, 127
dissociation of memory, 41–44
global amnesia, 7, 41–44, 125
memory load, 42
source amnesia, 42
Memory trace, 262–264
Mental imagery, 233–237
Metacognition, 54, 62–65
Model human processor, 71–72
Multidimensional aspects of cognition, 123, 130, 277, 280, 286, 290, 292
Multiple memory systems, 8, 11, 33–36, 39, 41, 45

N
Naturalistic aspects of cognition, 3–5, 12–13, 27–30, 129, 225–227, 237, 245–250, 263–274, 276–282, 285–292, see also Ecological aspects of cognition
definition of, 276–277
naturalistic research strategies, 12–13, 27–28, 129, 225–227, 278–279, 281–282, 285
Nature–nurture controversy, 174–178

P
Perception, 21, 24–26, 38, 41, 144, 153–156, 175, 251, 285, see also Sex-related issues
biological factors, 251
form identification, 152–155, 175
perceptual difficulties, 38, 41
Stroop effect, 285
Personality and cognition, 7, 108–113, 116, 128, 140–143
experiential openness/closeness dimension, 7, 108–113, 128, 141–143
Piagetian theories, 7, 47, 49, 50–52, 54, 66, 117, 136, 139, 192, 204, 208, 211
logical-mathematical reasoning, 139
neo-Piagetian positions, 7, 49, 192
cognitive determinism, 192, 211
reflexive abstraction, 51–52
Planning behaviors, 4, 5, 10, 47–66, 100
developmental models of planning, 49–52
neo-Piagetian approach, 49–50
Piagetian approach, 51–52
opportunistic model of planning, 48–49, 55
"planning-in-action," 5, 10, 56, 63–66

Planning behaviors *cont'd*
  rule-assessment approach, 49–50
  Soviet approach to planning, 52–53
  transactional approaches to planning, 50–55,
    64–66
    coordination of means and ends, 54–55
    transactional opportunities in planning, 55–
      56, 64–66, 100
Production systems, 69, 78–80, 82
Prospective memory, 128
Prototypes, 21–22, 120–121, 224–225
Psychodynamic theories, 14, 29, 107–108,
    111, 113, 128, 130, 242–243, 247–
    256, 283, 285, 286
  Freudian notions, 29, 242–243, 247–259,
    283, 285, 286
Psycho-social crises, 106, 107–108, 110–113,
    128, 130, 143–145
  ego integrity, 107, 111, 113
  identity, 107–108, 143–145
    a real life example of identity formation,
      144–145
Psychopathology, 249, 257

R
Remembering behaviors, 35, 36, 40–45, 55,
    110–113, 262–274, 286–292
  direct recalls of attributes, 263–273
  inferential recalls, 263, 265–274, 286–290
    Gestalt qualities, 272–273
  interdependence of direct and inferential re-
    calls, 288–291
  raw probabilities of direct recalls, 288–291
  recognition memory, 44
  recollections, 262–263
  state dependent retention, 35
Remote memories, 27–28, 105–113
  very long term memories, 27–28
Repisodic memories, 8, 9, 12, 29

S
Schemata, 10, 14, 28, 74, 120–123, 126,
    140–141, 243, 257
  affective schemata, 120–123, 129–130, 140
  self schemata, 129, 141, 243
Scripts, 10, 28, 69, 74–75, 86, 111, 120–121,
    270–271, 273–274, 289
  action scripts, 10, 74, 80
  knowledge scripts, 74–75, 80, 120–121
  nonscripted episodes, 270–271, 273

Self factors in cognition, 116, 118, 127–129,
    141, 143–146, 243
  self-appraisal, 128–129
  self-concept, 128–129, 141, 143–146, 243
Self-report questionnaires, 9, 12, 14, 108–
    110, 220–249, 264–267, 269, 287–
    288
  Experiential Inventory Questionnaire, 108–
    110
  Mosher's Sex-Guilt Questionnaire, 248–249
  Trace Attribute Inventory, 9, 12, 264–267,
    269, 287–288
Semantic memory, 18
Sex-related issues, 2, 7–8, 147–149, 151–
    155, 158–170, 173–178, 225–226,
    231–238
  biological factors, 7, 8, 153–155, 159,
    161–162, 168, 175–176, 178
  cultural aspects, 149, 176–178
  generic-masculine pronouns, 231–238
  historical and political aspects, 8, 147, 158–
    162, 168–170, 173–175
  Hollingsworth's works, 159–160
  intellectual abilities, 159–160, 173, 175
  linguistic development, 7, 154–155, 176
  mathematical abilities, 8, 161–164
  nonsexist language, 231–238
  reading problems, 7, 148–156, 175
  research studies, 152–154, 165–167, 174–
    175
  sex-biased language, 231–238
  sexist nature of U.S. schools, 169, 177–178
  Sherman's bent-twig hypothesis, 173, 178
  trainability of visual spatial skills, 164–167,
    177
  visual-spatial differences, 7, 8, 151–156,
    162, 164–168, 175, 177–178
Short-term memory, 18, 252
Slips of the tongue, 13, 242–250, 255, 257,
    259, 277, 282–286
  experimental research methods, 243, 248–
    250
  Freudian hypotheses, 243, 247–250
  involuntary action, 247–250
  speech production, 245–247
Social cognition, 4, 116–121, 123–131, 135–
    140, 245
  in children, 117–120, 129–130, 136, 139
  definition, 116
  morality, 117, 126, 136
  neurological aspects, 125–127, 129

personal commitment, 127, 129–130
process-oriented approach, 128–130
real-life examples, 137–138
social competence, 122, 126–127
states of mind, 245
Socialization, 8, 55, 128, 158, 169, 176–178, 237
Speech, 4, 52–54, 205–207, 227, 245–247
  ambiguities in speech production, 245–247
  errors, 227
  regulating function of, 52–54
  time, 205–207
States of mind, 243–249
  conflicted states of mind, 244–246, 248–249
  definition of, 243–244
Stereotypes, 120, 211
Structuralism, 51, 119

T
Temporal understanding, 204–212, 220
  cyclic time, 209–210
  evolution of temporal systems, 205–212
  helical model, 209–210
  Piagetian linear time problem, 208–209
  time and language, 205–212, 220
  verb tenses and time, 205–207, 210–212

U
Updating memory, 282

W
Working memory, 252
Writing systems, 148–151, 176
  logographic, 145–151
  phonographic, 148–151